I hope this letter finds you well...

by Rev. Dr. Clanton C.W. Dawson, Jr.

Forward: Rev. Dr. Molly Housh Gordon

Editor: Steven Zweig

Cover photograph: Valérie Berta

Cover design: Benjamin Zweig

With thanks to Laura Johnston, Opinion Editor, *Columbia Missourian* who enabled the editing and reprinting of these articles.

ISBN 979-8-234-04790-8

Library of Congress Control Number 2026908748

About Rev. Dr. Clanton C.W. Dawson, Jr.

“Clanton Dawson is my former pastor and one of my most formative mentors in ministry. Long before he ever wrote a column, he taught me what it looks like to hold faith and public life together with integrity. His writing reflects that same pastoral grounding: a deep love for people, an uncompromising commitment to truth, and a refusal to let faith be reduced to rigid dogma detached from lived experience.

“Across these columns, Dawson elevates conversations committed to the liberation of all people -across race, sexual and gender identity, economic status and religious affiliation. He writes from faith, but never narrowly. He communicates a faith practice accountable to the real conditions of people’s lives, attentive to suffering and open to transformation. His words consistently push readers beyond what is comfortable and familiar, insisting that justice and dignity require both courage and imagination.

“These essays forced conversations many would prefer to avoid. They imagine the formation of an enlightened beloved community transcendent of a distant ideal. They reflect a moral obligation we must actively choose. As a journalist, a minister, and someone shaped by Dawson’s witness, I am grateful that these columns now live together in one place, continuing the prophetic work of a man destined to impact lives beyond this moment in history.”

Carl W. Kenney II, Assistant Professor,
University of North Carolina at Chapel Hill

“Clanton had the mind of a teacher and the soul of a preacher. That made him smarter than most preachers and more eloquent than most teachers."

David L. Weddle, Professor Emeritus of Religion, Colorado College

Acknowledgement/Dedication

I want to first thank God for allowing my husband, the Rev. Dr. C.W. Dawson, for being a very important part of my life!

This book of his personal articles is dedicated to all of our beloved children, our precious grandchildren and our beautiful great-grandchildren.

His legacy will live forever through them.

I also dedicate this book to everyone who played an important part in life through the years. Thank you and I love you!

Heaven is truly beautiful, just you wait and see.

So live your life, laugh again, enjoy yourself, be free.

Then I know with every breath you take you'll be taking one for me.

Author unknown

Maria Dawson
March 2026

Clanton and Maria Dawson,
February 13, 2000

Forward

CW Dawson was a prodigious scholar, a wise pastor, a brilliant philosopher and a firebrand for justice. And he was all that from a place of true and faithful humility. He lived his commitments to justice by being just, by seeing the good in those around him, and by treating each person with the utmost dignity across every spectrum of human experience.

His theological commitments pushed boundaries. Where many of his colleagues were concerned with who was in and who was out, for CW everybody was in, and he preached and taught with the commitment to make it so. He spoke often of care for LGBTQ individuals in the church. He rebuked the sins of classism, racism, colorism, and every other -ism. He reminded us that God in Her wisdom loved us all alike with a love that transcends our paltry human limits. He spoke prophetically of our human mandate to dismantle systems that oppress in the service of a God that frees.

CW's research investigated where many Black church folk feared to tread - the bias around skin color that made its way into their own communities. And wasn't that just like him; never afraid to go straight to the taboo subject and ask the hardest questions right there at the heart of the matter. We see him do it over and over in the writings that follow - asking us the questions that matter and gently pushing us to do better and be better - to live up to who God made us to be.

I think CW enjoyed being a rabble-rouser. I can still picture his eyes sparkling as he challenged someone who needed a particular kick in the rear. He had a mischievous streak in the service of justice. He backed it up with fierce commitment to the common good and proven success in social change. When Mid-Missouri faith organizers fought predatory payday lending practices, got confederate statues removed from the county courthouse, and won Medicaid expansion in Missouri, CW was there leading the way.

There were few religious contexts where CW could not be at home - from the evangelical megachurch to the Black Baptist pulpit to the small UU congregation full of agnostic progressives - he could speak the language of faith and justice that we all understood. This is an incredible and rare gift — the capacity to be fully yourself, clear in your faith commitments, and to successfully carry those commitments into such a wide variety of places. He was a powerful ambassador for his faith precisely because he held it without fear of difference, because he did not insist on it - he simply lived his faith joyfully in front of us in a way that was spacious and hopeful and full of love.

CW's mentorship of many sons and daughters in ministry is a living legacy that will continue on far into the future. But CW's influence extended far beyond the Church. His column, his scholarship, and his deep leadership in the wider Columbia community made a lasting influence in Mid-Missouri and far beyond.

The spirit moves in a special way when folks stop trying to get a seat at the tables Jesus would have flipped and make themselves instead a big, wide Welcome Table, in His name. That's what CW did. So many ministries and faith communities and projects for justice are thriving now because CW Dawson made a place for them at the table... Because he lived his faith powerfully and humbly and joyfully... Because he shared his brilliance with us so generously.

The world echoes now of his presence, magnified in each of our lives. We miss him powerfully. We remember him lovingly. We are sustained, now, by the deep wisdom he left for us in the writings of this volume.

Rev. Dr. Molly Housh Gordon
Minister, Unitarian Universalist Church of Columbia
Columbia, Missouri

TABLE OF CONTENTS

YEAR	PAGE
2016	6
2017	24
2018	68
2019	105
2020	145
2021	184
2022	215
2023	244
2024	274
Dawson CV	292

2016

To discuss racism, we must cast aside our fears

August 30, 2016

This article is the first of a series of three columns about race and racism.

It is clear that all of us need to engage in a serious conversation about race and racism. Our lack of attention to the phenomenon has created problems that we no longer can ignore. It has affected our universities and colleges, our churches and places of worship, our work environments, our city, state, and national government, law enforcement, and the judicial system, just to name a few arenas of our socio-political life.

Regardless of education, economic status, or labor expertise, all of us feel the effects of race and racism. It is time to confront the issue. As a starting point, I share with you a story from my own life.

This summer, I took two of my grandsons (8 and 10 years old) to a unity march and gathering at the Boone County Courthouse courtyard. The event was sponsored by the Rev. Melvin Stapleton and the Restoration Church of Columbia. As you will remember, Restoration Church was a center of conversation regarding race and violence because the church is in one of the central Columbia neighborhoods that had experienced numerous shootings in its vicinity. Several community groups and individuals participated: Christians, non-Christians, Anglo-Americans, African Americans, males, females, gay, straight, older and younger. It was a microcosm of how we like to think of ourselves as Columbians. All who gathered voiced a commitment to unity and dismantling racism in its various forms. I knew it would be a peaceful march and gathering. As the grandparent of grandsons and granddaughters of color, I wanted them to experience an event of social consciousness. It was what I had hoped.

At the end of the event, my 8-year-old grandson asked me an interesting and provocative series of questions: "Pa-Pa, what is race, and what is a racist?"

Because I do not believe in giving children more information than they are emotionally and intellectually able to handle, I talked about racism as a way of thinking that makes some people think a certain group of people are superior or inferior to another group of people, generally based on color. With a curious, confused look on his face, he shook his head, and replied, "Pa Pa, that's just silly!" He was satisfied, but I realized, again, that the questions of race and racism plague our society in powerful ways.

There is a hesitancy, however, to have an in-depth conversation about race and racism. As an African-American who has lived in this society long enough to have both experienced and witnessed segregation, the promise and failures of integration, and the seduction of diversity programs that in the end are "sound and fury signifying nothing," I know how difficult it is to talk about race and racism in an honest and meaningful way.

I have participated (or been asked to participate) in a number of formal conversations about race and racism lately. Two weeks ago, the predominately white and very vocal social activist group Race Matters, Friends, invited me to lead a discussion on Bryan Stevenson's book "Just Mercy." Last Saturday, I was a participant in a discussion of Ben Watson's book "Under Our

Skin" with conservative, evangelical white and African-American pastors and ministers who represent some of our largest and most prominent conservative congregations in this city. On Sept. 13, I will be a panelist for a discussion on "The Church and Race" at Calvary Episcopal Church.

At the Saturday meeting, I stated that I think it is harder for white people to engage in racial dialogues than it is for people of color. Some white people worry about being labeled as "race-baiters" or "race–traitors." Some are terrified that they will use the wrong terminology or express themselves awkwardly and be called a racist. Others are trapped in wishful thinking: they believe the illusion that if we do not talk about race and racism, the problem associated with these concepts will just disappear.

While I understand fear, we cannot let our fears prevent our conversation about race and racism. The problem of race and racism will not disappear, but I believe race can be understood, and that racism can be dismantled so that we — all the people — can experience the great American ideal: to live together in a society where life, liberty, and the pursuit of happiness is a reality for all Americans and not just a few.

Unpacking four theories of race — and two undeniable facts

September 6, 2016

This article is the second of a series of three columns about race and racism.

"And with all thy getting, get understanding."

This week I seek for us to engage in a discussion about race per se. For the sake of clarity, please note that I am operating with two rudimentary presuppositions.

The first is that there is a distinct and an important difference between a conversation regarding the nature of race, and a conversation engaging racism. While race, as a concept, is intricately intertwined with racism as a social phenomenon, race and racism are two separate entities. This column will address race, the next will ponder racism.

My second presupposition is that it is possible to have a conversation about race and racism without being divisive. To assume that all conversations regarding race and racism will only further divide us is categorically ridiculous. Rational people can participate in a complex and difficult conversation, both agreeing and disagreeing, without the demonization of the other.

What is needed is a commitment to both thinking and feeling. Thought without an emotional commitment results in cold, callous theorizing, void of compassion, and absent of power to address the lived experiences of people. Emotionalism without serious thought only produces unwarranted accusations and meaningless, unconstructive rhetoric. We must, however, engage in this dialogue: to avoid it threatens the very stability of this great democratic experiment.

Given these presuppositions, I posit that part of the problem of discussing race is that we operate with multiple concepts about race that prevents coherent dialogue.

There are four concepts that vie for dominance when we discuss race. Forgive me having to use large brush strokes in presenting these ideas, but because of the need for brevity, I cannot give full articulation to each concept. I hope, however, that my limited unfolding of these concepts will at least demonstrate that people operate with different ideas of what race is, and that many times we assume that we are in agreement about the nature of race when, in fact, we are not.

The first belief is that race is tied to physiological and genetic make-up. Many people think that the physio-genetic markings of certain populations determines the race of the group and thus the race of the individual members of the group. Accordingly there exist different races: blacks, whites, Asians, Latinos, etc. Each racial group possesses certain racial characteristics (positive and negative) that each member of the group possesses. Characteristics such as: all black people have rhythm and are good at sports, all Asians are good at math, all Latinos are hard workers, and all whites are intellectually gifted. We are all aware of exceptions to this idea and yet it continues to be pervasive in racial conversations.

The second idea is that race is a social construct. This idea is the most dominant idea among academics particularly in the social sciences. According to social constructionism, race, like money and religion, is constructed by a society and the idea is fortified by the institutions a society erects. Of course the problem is that within this society there exist social constructs that are real, like money; and social constructs that are not real, like the tooth fairy. The question for those that believe race is a social construct is whether race is real, or is it not real?

The third idea regarding race is that race is an individual, existential choice. Every person decides for themselves what it means to be black, white, Asian, etc. Bi-racial people have been very helpful in this area. They refuse to allow physiological race theorists and social constructionists to box them into a racial group. Instead, they adamantly affirm both sides of their racial heritage and determine for themselves what it means to be "X."

The fourth concept of race is that it is the result of class conflict and is grounded in economic disparity and socio-political oppression. The belief here is that the racialization of groups is absolutely tied to privilege and power. Therefore, race is a way of exercising dominance over the "other."

Given the different conceptual ideas, one can see why race discussions are so chaotic. While each of the above concepts contribute meaningfully to a discussion, each of them are incomplete. I maintain that there are two facts that we need to uphold in all our discussions regarding race:

1. There is one race and it is the human race. While we may be of different hues and tones, we are all human. We may identify with a particular group, and indeed the presence of struggle and oppression are real, but we are one race, not different races.

2. All Americans are African Americans. Humans first evolved (or were created) in Africa. Much of what we hold as essential to being human occurred on the continent of Africa. I may be a black African American, and you may be blond, blue-eyed, and "white," or have strong Asian female features, but all of us are African Americans.

In understanding these facts about race I believe we can get pass the "one-trick" ponies, as one of the critics of my last column stated. He is correct that our discussions of race have to move beyond the "black-white" binary and talk about the effects of race and racism across the board. But we have to start with the recognition that we are all human, and that we are all African American.

An end to racism will come with embracing multiculturalism

September 13, 2016

"It is not our differences that divide us. It is our inability to recognize, accept, and celebrate those differences." — Audre Lorde

In my previous column, I suggested that there is a clear and distinct difference between race and racism. One way of positively engaging in a constructive dialogue about race and racism is in affirming two facts about race. The first is that we are all human beings with the power to both act and think; and, second, that all people born in America are African Americans.

Some may object to this line of reasoning because they state that, "I am promoting scientific theory as fact." However, all "facts" are grounded in theory. It is impossible to advance a "fact" that is not theory-laden (epistemologically, historically, mathematically, scientifically, metaphysically, theologically, etc.) unless one wishes to wallow in the dark pit of total skepticism, which I refuse to do. The anthropological evidence is clear: All human beings originated in Africa. The ontological argument is equally compelling: We are more than complex neuro-physical organisms. We are human beings with consciousness and intentionality.

Given these notions as umbrellas for our discussion, I define racism as a body of knowledge concerning the nature of race. Racism can be both positive or negative. Positive in affirming our unique developments and characteristics as racialized members of the society; negative when we use our racial thinking in a manner that purports superiority of one population over another.

By logical deduction, all of us are "racist" per se, in that all of us operate within an idea or concept of race: a concept of what it means to be Black, Anglo, Latino, Asian, etc. Because of the negative connotations attached to the word "racism" many people prefer to use the term "racialism" instead. I am not convinced that a change in terminology settles the problem, but at least it is constructive attempt to move us forward.

When confronting negative racism, most people talk about it in two ways. Many people suggest that overcoming racism demands a transformation of thinking on the personal level. Advocates of this position believe that we can eliminate racism if all Americans have a change of heart: a transformation that causes us to see every person as "a person." If we can begin to see people as individuals, and stop employing stereotypes we have inherited from families of origin, social prejudices, or the media, we can get past the negative effects racism is having on our society. "Let's just all be Americans," they exclaim, "and forget this race stuff, and this country (and city) will be fine." At least, this is the claim.

The second mode of discussing racism is that racism is systemic. The claim here is that racism has polluted every structure within the socio-political and economic sphere of America. The justification of the claim pivots on the examples of discrimination and disenfranchisement experienced by people of color in the U.S. Systemic racism, they assert, determines who is considered the proper immigrant, who goes to prison and who does not, who is employed or under-employed, where certain people are forced to live, who is stopped by the police, how people of color are portrayed in the media, who receives proper education, and who are the beneficiaries of privilege and power. In this view, it is the presence of systemic racism that is destructive to people of color. It is systemic racism that needs to be dismantled and dismantling systemic racism demands more than singing "Kum Bah Yah" and "We Shall Overcome."

The problem is that racism consists of both negative attitudes on the personal level and systemic racism on the socio-political and economic level. Both are destructive to people of color and to the society as a whole. It is a vicious circle: attitudes fuel the systems, and the systems enhance the attitudes. To address systemic racism without demanding a change of heart is an exercise in futility. Institutional change aimed at systemic racism without a change in character will only produce laws that negative racists will find ways to circumvent. We have been creating legislation to prohibit racial discrimination since the Civil Rights Movement, and yet our racial problems still persist.

I am neither an integrationist nor a separatist. I have no desire to lose my uniqueness as a black African American through a process of assimilation. Neither am I an advocate of Black Nationhood. I believe that a sincere commitment to multiculturalism is the way to go.

First, it addresses the need for racism to be overcome on the personal level, but it also acknowledges the necessity of addressing the need for dismantling systemic racism as well. Second, it acknowledges from the start that all of us have something important and significant to contribute to the advancement of this country. Third, it rejects both "melting pot" fantasies and "separatist" ideas while embracing the need for all groups to be both included and allowed to be active participants at the decision-making table.

If we are going to overcome negative racism in America, we must commit to a posture of multiculturalism. Without it, we will never learn to accept each other as mutual and necessary participants in making American society a better America. With it we will move toward a nation indivisible with liberty and justice for all. I believe, with hope, that we can overcome negative racism, but there must be a change in character, and in the systems that deny the potential of full development and progress of people of color. Multiculturalism can pave the way.

Patriots live out their values in service to creating a nation for all

September 20, 2016

"I love America more than any other country in the world, and, exactly for this reason, I insist on the right to criticize her perpetually." — James Baldwin

What is the mark of true patriotism? Is it standing with one hand over my heart and singing the "The Star-Spangled Banner"? Does repeating the Pledge of Allegiance several times a day demonstrate how much I love this country? Does the practiced oration of overpaid athletes and entertainers who call for social equity and racial equality but practice gross materialism prove deep commitment and undying loyalty? What is the true mark of a patriot?

I am a proud, black, African-American man. My ancestors mixed tears in the mortar and placed prayers in the bricks of this country. I love this home of James Brown, Mahalia Jackson, Langston Hughes, Miles Davis, Frederick Douglass, W.E.B. Du Bois, Mary McLeod Bethune and Leontyne Price.

My father served in the United States Army's 9th Cavalry during World War II. He served during the time of segregation. For his participation in the Burma Campaign, he received a Purple Heart and a Bronze Star. He left America a soldier in a segregated military, served and bled for his country. Upon his return he was called a nigger by the very society he fought to defend. He was refused access to public transportation, to "white" eating establishments, and to white churches. Yet he loved this country while hating her ways. The Rev. Clanton "Gabe" Dawson Sr. was a patriot.

My mother was born in Oklahoma near what is now known as Vinita. She was born on Native American territory, before Oklahoma became a state. As a young girl, she worked in my great uncle's barbecue place on 12th and Vine in Kansas City, Missouri. There she met Count Basie, Ella Fitzgerald, Charley "Yardbird" Parker and many more famous Black American musicians and entertainers.

My mother later worked as an occupational therapist until she was injured on the job. Afterwards, she cleaned houses for people who called her "girl," cooked in restaurants where she could not order food, and cared for people who thought she was "less than." But "Sister Dawson" was a proud black woman who maintained an unyielding faith in God and America. Gladys Dawson was a patriot.

My mother and father were products of the Black Church: a church that believed in authentic black faith that hated racism but forgave and loved the racist. They taught all of us to love America even when America was cruel and barbaric. When my mother died, the Social Security Administration did not want to pay her death benefit because she was not (in its estimation) an American citizen. She was the victim of "birther" foolishness before President Obama. Former Gov. Mel Carnahan interceded stating that if my mother "wasn't an American citizen, none of us are!" The Social Security Administration acquiesced and made the payment. In the midst of our sorrow, we still loved America.

I understand protest. It is a necessary tool in a democracy for calling attention to the injustices that occur. Yet protest without progress is hallow and shallow. Protest must be grounded in a sincere love of the nation. I have watched too many "protesters" become nothing more than photo-op seekers, and too many demonstrators be vocal when the camera is running, but absent when the real work of building a nation has begun. I have also observed lots of flag-waving hypocrites who "pledge allegiance" when their privilege and access to power is maintained, but revolt when room is made for the disenfranchised, the oppressed, and the poor. What does it mean to be an authentic patriot?

Real patriotism is constituted by a willingness to serve in order to make this democratic dream a reality. It is not sensationalized Islamophobia, systemic racism, institutionalized sexism, or persistent homophobia. Sincere patriotism is an act of love when situations are unlovable, fortitude in the midst trying social conditions, and a resolve that demands resolution and not emotional rhetoric.

It is evidenced by police and community activists alike, who live their lives to protect and serve the whole community and not just the affluent or acceptable. It is manifested by firefighters, emergency personnel and soldiers who put their lives on the line to benefit all Americans, by teachers who teach not to fulfill standardized tests, but to build character and a sense of compassion in their students, and by clergy of all faiths who attempt to love the people like God loves the people, and by everyday people who in hope that one day we, as a nation, will truly be one nation with liberty and justice for all. These are the real patriots.

With underpaid, overworked police, minority communities pay the price

October 4, 2016

I initially intended to write about black self-hatred and how anti-black racism contributes substantively to the phenomenon. Instead, I find myself reflecting on the subject of policing and the black community.

Once again, we are in shock and disgust at the recent killings of black men by the police in Charlotte, North Carolina, and in Tulsa, Oklahoma. Two hundred black people, an alarming number, have been killed by the police in 2016 as of Oct. 1, according to the Guardian's "The Counted" project. The Washington Post reports that unarmed black males are five times more likely than whites to be shot by police.

These numbers turn our attention to policing here in Columbia.

Much has been said about the Columbia Police Department. Recent data suggests that the CPD has an implicit or explicit bias toward black and brown drivers. Specifically, drivers of color have been more likely than white drivers to be stopped. The chief of police denies that racial profiling is occurring, but the testimonies of black and brown citizens say something very different.

Many black citizens, from prominent pastors and educators to common working folk, tell tales of being stopped for "DWB" — Driving While Black. Race Matters, Friends and the Minority Men's Network have been diligent in bringing this issue to the attention of Columbia and demanding that the Columbia Police Department be better trained in community policing and vigorously address its implicit bias.

To deny that implicit bias exists is foolish. Implicit bias exists in every segment of American society. That said, I have a different idea about addressing community policing that I have heard no one articulate.

First, the minimum pay for police officers and firefighters should start at $65,000 a year. Police officers are grossly underpaid. If we raised the salaries of the police from the $40,000 to $50,000 range to $65,000, we could attract the cream of the crop from police academies, and not just those who are willing to take the job. With better pay, we can have and demand better trained, racially sensitive police officers.

Second, we need to cut shift lengths to eight hours from 12. I do not want armed, exhausted police officers in stressful situations; this is a recipe for another killing. We have seen what happens after a black person is killed by the police. One way of being proactive is to make sure police officers are neither underpaid nor overworked.

Third, we need police officers to spend time with the people they have been hired to protect and serve. When the police do not spend time with the community, they operate by stereotypes, and not knowledge. Police need to know both the individual and cultural identities of people. The level of trust between the black community of Columbia and the police is not good.

It is a perverted situation when individuals fear the police more than criminals in the community. This can be corrected if officers spend more time getting to know the citizenry, and the citizens have an opportunity to know police officers as people.

I realize my critics will argue that this is liberal balderdash, and what we need is for police to be tougher and citizens to be more law-abiding.

All of us want good policing. No one wants a wimpy police force that cannot do its job. But I am tired of seeing black men and women killed by the police, and communities at odds with law enforcement. We need a change before another tragedy occurs.

Voter ID amendment doesn't pass the smell test

October 18, 2016

"I'm against voter fraud in any form, and I have long supported a national voter ID card. But ID cards need not — and must not — restrict voting rights in any way, shape or form." — Andrew Young

Like most people in America, I have been engaged in lots of political conversations. Trump vs. Clinton has been the main focus of attention, but it is not the only one. Many conversations have arisen regarding local candidates and amendments that Missourians will be asked to vote upon this November.

One amendment that is particularly interesting is Amendment 6. It reads: Shall the Constitution of Missouri be amended to state that voters may be required by law, which may be subject to exception, to verify one's identity, citizenship, and residence by presenting identification that may include valid government-issued photo identification?

Opponents to Amendment 6 suggest that if the amendment is enacted, the overall cost to taxpayers would be in the neighborhood of $17 million. More conservative estimates given by resources such as "Ballotpedia: The Encyclopedia of American Politics" state that the cost to Missouri taxpayers could be more than $2.1 million. Whatever the cost, it will be paid for by taxpayers, and to my knowledge, the Missouri legislature has not figured out how it will pay for the measure if it passes. I am sure most Missourians do not want a tax hike for something like this amendment.

I asked many people if they found it problematic that the amendment will require unnecessary new voting restrictions and make it harder for perhaps thousands of people to vote, particularly the elderly and people of color. The responses I received were surprising to me. Some wondered why the measure is generating so much opposition when everyone should have some form of ID.

Others offered a more historical perspective, hearkening back to past attempts by politicians to prevent one segment of society from voting. One elderly woman told me the amendment will affect many voters in the big cities the same way that poll tests put up barriers to black voters. She put it this way: "This amendment has the same smell to it, and generally if a thing doesn't smell right, it's not right!"

I agree with this voice of wisdom. Something about the amendment just doesn't smell quite right.

As difficult as it is to get people to vote, why would we pass an amendment to make it harder, unless there is a hidden political agenda at play? To my knowledge there is no documented case of voter fraud recorded in Missouri. So what else is at stake, and why are we trying to change the rules?

Too many people fought and died for the right to vote. Regardless of your political stance, do not let tricky politicians interfere with the right of Missouri citizens to vote. Everyone deserves an opportunity to voice his or her concerns and cast a ballot. Do not let those with a hidden agenda shut your mouth and steal your constitutional right to vote. Vote no on Amendment 6.

Conflicted about the election? Whatever you do, don't sit this one out

October 25, 2016

"Democracy is not just the right to vote, it is the right to live in dignity." — Naomi Klein

The upcoming election has all of us caught in the throes of conversation and reflection. Indeed, the presidential campaign will be hotly contested: accusations on both sides, with some facts as filler.

Whatever happened to elections based on a candidate's platform, and not who can sling the most mud? Alas, that is a conversation for another day.

Three days ago, I was discussing the presidential election with two of my ethics students. A very astute woman of color said her conservative religious convictions will not allow her to vote for Hillary Clinton. The hate-filled rhetoric from Donald Trump frightens her in regard to the direction he would possibly take the country. Therefore, she has decided she will not vote.

It always bothers me when Americans, particularly blacks, tell me they are not going to vote. I think about the tremendous sacrifice that blacks, as well as whites, Hispanics, and Native Americans, have made so all can cast a vote. I wonder how we can be so self-absorbed or self-righteous to proclaim that we will not vote, but complain about the outcomes.

Whoever becomes president will affect this country for the next 25 years. The next president will have the opportunity to name three to five Supreme Court justices who will remain in office for 20 to 25 years. Quite frankly, that is more important, in many ways, than who is president for the next four to eight years.

Not voting is problematic for me on another level, as well. Not voting affects quality of life on the local level. Seats in the U.S. Senate, House of Representatives and state legislature are open, as are those of the governor and Boone County commissioners. Whom we elect to those positions directly influences what kind of Missouri, Boone County and Columbia we will be.

And let us not forget amendments such as Amendment 6, which attempt to suppress the voting power of many across this state.

I am tired of insensitive officials who do not care about the welfare of our children and senior citizens, nor about the lack of affordable housing for low to medium-income people in Missouri and Columbia. For example, will anyone make predatory payday loan companies stop robbing the "least of these" and make all lending institutions loan money to all people at reasonable interest rates? Who we vote into office can make a difference in our everyday lives by taking action on these issues.

I appeal to all of you, regardless of your political affiliation, to get out and vote. Take someone to the polls with you. Speak about the necessity to vote everywhere you go: your church, beauty parlor, neighborhood stand and barber shop. This may be one of the most important ever elections for the fate of this country!

Let us not miss our opportunity to be part of a solution instead of the problem

President alone can't make change — only we can do that

November 1, 2016

"Whom shall we send, and who shall go for us?" — Isaiah 6:8

On Nov. 8, America will send someone to the White House to be the next President of the United States of America. On that Tuesday we will determine, by voting or not voting, whether Hillary Clinton or Donald Trump will be president. But more than that, we will be stating who shall represent our hopes, dreams and aspirations for this democratic society.

Our current situation is reminiscent of the sentiment of the above quote. While Isaiah understood it as a call to be a prophet of Israel, I think it is an equally profound question for all contemporary Americans: Whom shall we send, and who shall go for us?

I have matured as an American political thinker. I no longer am prey to the hype and rhetoric politicians throw our way. I watched stubborn, racist Congress members try to stop a great man named Barack Obama from becoming a great president purely out of anti-black racism and self-serving politics.

These last 8 years have taught me much about where we are in America. Social experience has taught me that a president can only do so much. Change takes a Congress that is willing to work and not posture like peacocks. Change will demand a Congress that is willing to move beyond biases and political agendas for the good of the whole society. I know Trump cannot "make America great (or is it white?) again," nor can Clinton make us "better together."

Whatever we are going to "be," the power for self-determination and transformation is in our hands. If we are to be greater, it is on our shoulders to drop our pettiness. If we are to be a united society, we must make it happen.

Many people call this year's presidential campaign one of the most divisive in American history. Perhaps. I do know that the divide between us has widened. We live in at least two Americas: one white, and one non-white; one rich and one not rich. The socio-political realities for the two Americas is very different.

The person we send must keep the dream of one America before us and must be committed to bridging the racial, economic and social gaps. There is enough hatred and mistrust among us. We need someone who will go and work for us and not the multinational corporations or lobbyists.

I asked my ethics students how many were going to vote this election. I was surprised and disheartened when only half of the students in all sections raised their hands to state they would be voting. If you have read my columns, you know I vehemently urged them to vote. But, what was most hurtful to me is that they did not want to vote because they did not believe it would matter. Their hope is almost gone, and their skepticism regarding change is at its zenith.

Our hope must be grounded in three things: the idea of that we can create a society that visibly demonstrates equality and justice; the goodness of the human spirit, and the power of an ultimate reality that is for us and with us.

Hope without the material conditions to make it a reality is mere wishful thinking. We can create the conditions that can make the hope and dream of who we are at our best come true. Hope can never be placed in a politician alone. It must be placed in something greater than ourselves. The first task in accomplishing that is being clear about who we shall send and who will go for us.

Keeping the faith after taking an electoral beatin'

November 15, 2016

"Hold fast to dreams, for if dreams die, life is a broken-winged bird that cannot fly." — Langston Hughes

Last week, I took, in the vernacular of my people, an old-fashioned "whippin'."

I am not talking about a physical beating. Instead I took a socio-political beating. Not one candidate or amendment I voted for or against won. I know

I am not the only one that feels bruised and battered.

Many people have expressed to me their fears and disappointment over the results of the elections. A colleague who is Muslim received an anonymous death threat the day after the election. One African-American child told me he was afraid that President-elect Trump was going to send all Black people back to Africa. One of my Latino colleagues told me that his 9-year-old niece asked him if Trump will deport her back to Mexico. Children should not live in fear of the President of the United States of America.

I assured the African-American child that no president has the power to send Black Americans to Africa, but I understand his and other citizens' fears, particularly seeing some of the statements made by Trump supporters across this country.

Meanwhile, civil protests around the country confirm that many Americans are angry and frustrated with the way election resulted. Clearly we live in a divided nation, and the election has only widened the divide. The prevailing question is, after a beating, what do we do now?

One thing to do is look at the facts. Trump won the electoral vote but not the popular vote. Many ardent conservatives stress that Trump concentrated on key states, and if he would have expanded his campaign he would have won the popular vote as well. Perhaps this is the case, but I suggest that such a sentiment is enthusiastic afterglow.

It's also clear that the Electoral College needs to be abandoned. There was a time when it was a necessity, when most white males who were eligible to vote were ignorant and not privy to sophisticated information. Those days have long gone. The voting population now consists of educated white males, women and people of color who have access to information and are well-informed. The bottom line is that the Electoral College needs to be dismantled or greatly reformed.

I have taken many beatings in my time and have given a few as well. One of the things I have learned from a beating is this: If you can take a beating, you learn how to give one. This is not the time to give up hope and be caught in the throes of malaise and dismay.

There is an old song from the authentic black church that all of us who support progress and an America that will move forward should make our anthem. It goes like this: "I'm going to watch, fight, and pray ..."

This is a time to watch what develops in the next few months. I admit my faith in the President-elect wanes when I hear that he wants Rudy Giuliani, Stephen Bannon, and Reince Priebus in positions of power. We must be more vigilant than ever before. Let us be attentive to what happens. Perhaps Trump will be better than we think. The universe has the unique ability to surprise. At any rate, our duty is to watch.

We must also fight for justice and equity more now than ever before. Most wars are not won or lost in a single battle. We lost the battle, but the war for an America that demonstrates liberty and justice for all wages on. We must fight the good fight so that all of us may enjoy life, liberty and the pursuit of happiness and not just those who have access to privilege and power.

Finally, we must pray. We all need to reconnect with the God that we know and speak with at the altar of our hearts. It is in our prayers that we find the energy and strength to fight on another day. The fact is we may have lost last Tuesday, but one day will be our day.

Congratulations to Trump's supporters. Enjoy your day. But please know that our day is coming and until then, we will watch, fight and pray.

Predatory lending has no place in our community

November 22, 2016

"There is no more neutrality in the world. You either have to be part of the solution, or you're going to be part of the problem." — Eldridge Cleaver

"Every successful individual knows that his or her achievement depends on a community of persons working together." — Rep. Paul Ryan

The question Martin Luther King Jr. posed to us in the title of his pivotal work in 1967 addresses us now. King asked: Where do we go from here: chaos or community?

The question haunts all of us who recognize that we live in a divided country, and that the hope for unity is grounded in our finding a way to standtogether. It is unquestionably true that a house divided against itself cannot stand.

The social and political problems of our country threaten our very existence as a democratic society. The problems are not merely white problems or black problems, nor conservative versus progressive. They are people problems that set us at odds: Christian, non-Christian; wealthy and poor; black, white, brown and red; older and younger; gay and straight; male and female.

Despite the rancor of critics, I am steadfast in my pursuit of ways we can join together and solve problems instead of engaging in the demonization of each other and questioning one another's motives.

I have not spent my time listening to echoes of hatred, nor have I been hypnotized by neo-liberal or conservative ideology. Experience has painfully taught me that both liberals and conservatives, white people and non-white people, will abandon a cause if they feel the cost is too great of a personal burden. But I have also witnessed people of all shapes and sizes, hues and tones, and various backgrounds work together for the good of this society. I admit it does not happen often, but it can happen because it has happened.

My life's calling is trying to make this place called America a better place for all citizens. Given this statement of purpose, there is a problem before us that threatens chaos, but by a united effort we can reap the fruits of true community.

The problem? Predatory lending agencies that lend money to the poor and economically disadvantaged with lenient lending policies but also with incredible interest rates, holding recipients in economic bondage with little to no chance of recovery.

There are payday and title loan centers in Columbia that have interest rates up to 350 percent and higher. Given that the borrowers are in financial trouble before they receive the loans, at 350 percent interest their problems are multiplied in a manner that makes their economic situation quickly go from bad to worse.

All Americans find themselves in situations where they need to borrow money. From the wealthy business mogul to a guy on the street corner, emergencies arise that force one to borrow. I am not against the practice of institutions lending money to the underclass. I object to institutions that loan money at such high interest rates that make it impossible for the loans to be repaid. Christians call such a practice "usury." Others simply call it robbing the poor.

Whatever one calls it, it is wrong and creates chaos, not community.

I suggest two actions to address the problem of predatory lending. First, we need the religious social justice community and the evangelical Christian community to unite in action to stop the devastation of predatory lending that is severely affecting our community.

It is time for evangelical churches like The Crossing, Christian Chapel, Woodcrest, Friendship and Second Progressive Baptist Church to join hands with the Unitarian Universalist Church, the Roman Catholic parishes, Rock Bridge Christian, Missouri United Methodist, Broadway Christian, Bethel Baptist, the Baha'i, the Islamic Center, Congregation Beth Shalom and all other local faith communities to call for the immediate cessation of predatory lending. All of them have the attention of the movers and shakers of this community. Each faith community has the resources and populations to create effective change. I, for one, am tired of talking about the problems and bickering over who is one type of creed or another. It is time to do something.

As president of the African American Clergy Coalition of Mid-Missouri, I have issued this challenge to the evangelical Christian churches that I meet with on a regular basis. Social justice churches connected with Faith Voices Columbia have already wrestled with this issue. Now is the time to stop acting as though the "other" side has leprosy and sit down and "reason together." If these religious groups will address this issue with one voice, things will change.

Second, I propose that all citizens and groups in Columbia who are opposed to predatory lending join to call on the Columbia City Council to ban predatory lending and establish fair lending regulations. The city can do this without permission from the state because the city has a home charter. If enough people band together to call for a change, a change will happen. The time to unite is now.

Stopping predatory lending in Columbia could be a step toward unity.

Banning books, changing words won't end racism

December 6, 2016

"The evil that is in the world almost always comes of ignorance, and good intentions may do as much harm as malevolence if they lack understanding." — Albert Camus

"It is easier to take back a rock once it is thrown than to take back a word once it is spoken." — Scottish Proverb

What is the power of words? Two interesting articles I read in the past two weeks caused me to reflect on this question.

The first is an interesting post in NPR's Code Switch blog by Gene Demby, who asks, "Is it racist to call someone racist?" The context of the article is that a group of white nationalists gathered in New York for a rally. Journalist Adrian Florido asked one of the leaders if the use of the label "alt-right" was simply camouflage to cover views many would call racist. The leader went on to say that the term "racist" is derogatory, and that if we can sanitize the word, perhaps new meaning could arise from its use. While the subject matter of the article is interesting, it is the title that is arresting. Is it truly racist to call someone a racist?

The second article, which I found in the Christian Science Monitor, discusses how the Accomack County Public School Board in Virginia is considering pulling two American novels from its libraries and classrooms. The books are "The

Adventures of Huckleberry Finn" and "To Kill A Mockingbird." According to the report, a parent is calling for their removal because of the negative racial stereotypes and repeated use of the "n" word in the literature.

When are words harmful and destructive to the society and when are they necessary for our social and intellectual development? And who decides which is which?

The case of calling someone racist is not a difficult proposition. The philosopher Kwame Anthony Appiah is quite helpful is this area. In his article, "Racialism," he suggests that because of the pejorative nature of the term "racist," we should instead use the term "racialism" since what we are talking about when referring to people of color are merely "socially racialized" segments of the population.

He says there are two types of racialists: Intrinsic racialists, who despite education and experience hold negative stereotypes and refuse to release their negative beliefs, and extrinsic racialists, who may at first hold negative beliefs about racialized members of the population, but after education and experience, banish from their thinking negative beliefs and stereotypes.

White nationalists can claim that they are not negative racists, but old-fashioned common sense says the opposite is true. The use of negative stereotypes and words by the "alt-right" is negative racism in its ugliest form. It really is a no-brainer.

The banning of "To Kill A Mockingbird" and "The Adventures of Huckleberry Finn" is wrong. The books do not promote racism, and teaching the literature can instead help undo it. If they are taught the right way, students will realize how hurtful words can lead to harmful actions. They also will understand that while America can be mean and cruel, we must never see one another in that kind of negative light again.

Only by boldly and honestly seeing how we once behaved and spoke can we rise to a new level of excellence.

C.W. DAWSON: Reclaiming our joy 12 days before the holidays

December 13, 2016

So many people seem to have the bah-humbugs this holiday season. It appears to be, in part, a result of the contentious presidential election we all experienced. Some of it is due to a lack of finance in the face of a crass materialism during the holiday season, or we just do not "feel it!" Whatever the reason, many just do not seem to be experiencing holiday joy.

While the traditional twelve days of Christmas begin December 25th, I suggest a modern twelve days before Christmas to help regain our joy. Like the traditional Christmastide, this "pre-holiday-tide" (my word creation for lack of a better term) advances that each day we are to engage in an action of a certain type — for someone else or for ourselves — in the hope that it will rekindle the joy of the holidays. Here is my suggested list of activities for both you and me:

Day 1 — Treat yourself to an international coffee or tea (or non-alcoholic drink of some kind) that you have never experienced before. There are many coffee spots in Columbia or where you live that would love to help you find a coffee or tea that will thrill your palate. I am going to try some Ethiopian Yirgacheffe coffee and some Gyokuro Genmaicha tea.

Day 2 — Call an old acquaintance. I have recently reconnected with a man I have not spoken with for 44 years. We were high school classmates at Joplin Memorial High School. Time, change in geography and experiences separated us. Finally, we have reconnected. We have a lot of catching up to do. When was the last time you spoke to an old military friend, a fellow college classmate or an old community friend? Don't you think it is time to reacquaint?

Day 3 — Start reading an old book and a new one. Reading in our society is a lost art. We know how to text, tweet and Snapchat, but when was the last time you read a book? I am going to read two and two: "Invisible Man" by Ralph Ellison and "Their Eyes Were Watching God" by Zora Neale Hurston, and "A Christian Justice for the Common Good" by Tex Sample and "Ten Seconds to Peace: An Every Day Approach to Mindful Living" by Jeffery Beach. Whatever your taste, turn off the television and read something.

Day 4 — Forgive someone or something that hurt you. Forgiveness restores peace and joy. To carry a grudge weighs one down. Forgive someone, some institution or some event that caused you pain. Remember, forgiveness is not about the other person, it is about you.

Day 5 — Do something sensually pleasing. Before you take me to only be talking about sex (although that can be quite sensuously pleasing) I am talking about your other senses. Go get a massage, experience an acupuncture treatment, workout with Ken Greene's tai chi group or take a quiet bubble bath with scented candles. Too many of us live in our head so much, or are so stuck in the grind of survival, that we forget to please our bodies. Do something sensuous. Don't just survive — live!

Day 6 — Get to know an intellectual/cultural "other." Are there folks that you have stereotypes about? Too often our xenophobia controls our understanding of others that do not look , act or think like us. Get to know someone from whom you differ. Years ago I saw George Will in an airport. I knew from his writings that we disagreed about most things. I went up to him, introduced myself and asked if we could share a cup of coffee and talk while we waited on our respective planes. To my surprise I learned that we shared similar experiences, and agreed on more things than I ever imagined! Yes, we are political opposites, but he became human and not just an "other." Get to know an "other." In fact, I am going to call Hank Waters of the Columbia Tribune and invite him for coffee — I want to try and get to know him, even if we disagree about most things.

Day 7 — Perform a random act of kindness. Pay someone's layaway bill at Walmart, buy the meal of the person in front of you at the fast food restaurant or pay for someone's groceries at the store. Don't do it because they meet your standard of worth or importance, but do it just because. An act of love works wonders for you and someone else.

Day 8 — Spend five separate five-minute periods in silence and meditation/prayer. Get to know you again. Connect with the energy and person within. Notice that moments of silent prayer or meditation are good for you physically as well: they help lower your blood pressure and ward off heart attacks and strokes. You may not be able to do much about the storms of life around you, but you can quiet the inner storm for a moment

Day 9 — Laugh out loud. Find some comedy or think of a past event that made you laugh to tears. Laugh, laugh and then laugh again.

Day 10 — Write a letter or a note. Send a thank you note to someone that was gracious to you. Let someone know you are thinking of them. Compose a love letter to your lover. Write a letter to one of your children or grandchildren, niece or nephew. Whatever you do, write, don't text. People keep letters and notes — forever.

Day 11 — Compliment a hater. We all have people who do not like us. They do not have a reason, they just do not like us. The best way to beat a hater is to: 1) be successful; and, 2) compliment them when they speak badly of you. Value your haters; they remind you that you are doing something important.

Day 12 — Turn off all social media for the day. That's right, no Facebook, Snapchat, Twitter, Instagram and the like for one whole day. What will you do all day? Talk to real people, play games (remember spades?), drive your automobile without being on the cellphone or look someone in the eye at the mall. Be a human again and not a technobot.

Celebrate with me a modern twelve days of Christmas or whatever you celebrate. But let us celebrate one another and take back our holiday joy

Kwanzaa is a celebration for all of us

December 20, 2016

"Where justice is denied, where poverty is enforced, where ignorance prevails, and where any one class is made to feel that society is an organized conspiracy to oppress, rob and degrade them, neither persons nor property will be safe." — Frederick Douglass

"The moment we break faith with one another, the sea engulfs us and the light goes out." — James Baldwin

From Dec. 26 to Jan. 1, millions of people throughout the United States and Canada will celebrate Kwanzaa. This authentic African-American celebration (the other authentic African-American celebration being Juneteenth) attempts to reunite African-Americans with their African cultural and philosophical foundations. Grounded in communitarianism and created by Mualana Karenga in the 1960s, Kwanzaa is a celebration of the African in African-Americanism. At one time, Kwanzaa was offered as an alternative to Christmas. However, over the years, it is celebrated by not only Christians, but by members of religious traditions throughout the African Diaspora. Kwanzaa asserts seven principles in Swahili, called Nguzo Saba, as guides to a rightful observance of African heritage and correct living. These principles are omoja, which means unity; kujichagulia, or self-determination; ujima, collective work and responsibility; ujamaa, cooperative economics; nia, purpose; kuumba, creativity, and imani, which means faith.

Although the celebration of Kwanzaa has risen in popularity over the years, many people question why it should be celebrated.

It is clear to me that the African-American community is a fractured microcosm of the larger Anglo-American culture in which we are submerged. African-Americans not only have to confront racism daily but also the insidious phenomenon of black self-hatred.

Many argue it is the residue from slavery, while others blame living in an environment of crass materialism, militarism and xenophobia as the cause. Whatever the reason, the fact is that black self-hatred has devastated our community.

It is evidenced by not only black-on-black crime, but also and more prominently in the distrust and negative attitudes displayed on a daily basis to one another.

Gone are the days of the Last Poets who sang, "We wore our sunglasses at night, and called our women 'Baby.'" Now we call each other "dog," "gangster" or worse, rather than "brother" or "sister." Publicly and privately, far too many black people demean the mothers of our babies, the fathers of our brothers, and the leaders of our community worse than the oppressors.

The principles point us back to the right direction. It is not by accident that "unity" is the first principle.

Far too many African-Americans have forgotten the wonderful challenge of being, what W.E.B. Dubois called, "two souls in one black body." Assimilation may be pleasing to conservative white Americans, but for African-Americans it should be anathema. It is our right and responsibility to determine for ourselves what we shall be, what we call ourselves, and what is the correct course and action for the African American community. And let us be clear: Being pro-Black does not necessitate being anti-white, Latino, or Asian. Being pro-African American is simply a reaffirmation of a West African saying, "I am because we are."

That said, Kwanzaa is not just for African-Americans. It is for all people who wish to see a segment of this nation rise to a place of equity and equality in this country. When other racial groups celebrate Kwanzaa with African-Americans, it is a clear demonstration of support for the economic and cultural development of a people born of struggle.

One does not have to be African American to believe we all need to find our purpose again or embrace an idea of creativity that brings prosperity to all of us. After all, while Kwanzaa is an authentic African-American holiday, it is also American. Therefore, all Americans are invited to celebrate Kwanzaa. I personally suggest the citywide Kwanzaa celebration at Joshua House in Jefferson City on Dec. 30. I recommend it, not because I will be the keynote speaker, but because Joshua House and Pastor Adrian Hendricks will make you feel welcome.

I hope you will take the time to celebrate Kwanzaa this year. It will refresh and refocus you for the coming new year.

Be resolute in the new year

December 27, 2016

"How few there are who have courage enough to own their faults, or resolution enough to mend them." — Benjamin Franklin

As 2016 ends, many people will take this time to reflect and make resolutions for the coming year. It is a time of making promises to improve and regain what Aristotle calls arête, or excellence of character.

If you are like me, you have made many resolutions in the past, and, alas, failed to keep or fulfill them. This year will be different. I share with you 10 resolutions for the coming year, and I hope they inspire you. Here is my list:

1. Perform more random acts of kindness. Christmas is one of those times when we all exercise a sense of benevolence to others. However, this year I want to make being kind and showing kindness a more essential part of my life.

I will buy a cup of coffee or pay the grocery bill for the person behind me in line. I will be a secret Santa in July or have a conversation with a homeless person and not just give loose change and keep moving. I am resolved to spend more time at Loaves and Fishes. I am convinced that the way to make the world a better place is not by talking, but by taking action.

2. Spend more time with family and friends. We all are so captured by work schedules that spending time with family and friends is difficult indeed. And yet, when it is all said and done, only family and friends will be with you in the good and bad times.

I am going to play with my grandchildren and tell family history so the next generation know who their ancestors were and what they accomplished. Reconnecting with the people who love us — not because of what we do, but because of who we are — is more precious than wealth. Solid relationships demand time, and time is what we can find.

3. Construct a more intimate relationship with Ultimate Reality. I am a person of faith, but please believe that I am not talking about just going to church (or the mosque or synagogue). Instead I am talking about getting to know the God of the altar of my heart.

What do I know about the wellspring of life that I did not receive from a catechism or book of creeds? I want to get to know the God of my history so that I can state unequivocally like my fore parents, "She (He) walks with me and talks with me, and tell me I am Her (His) own."

4. Be more socially and politically active. I am embarrassed to say that I did not attend a City Council meeting or School Board meeting in 2016. That is going to change. I have marched and demonstrated, but I need to know my city, county, and school representatives. This year we will get to know one another.

5. Be a more courteous driver. I hate being cut off in traffic. I confess that many expletives have poured from my lips when people are discourteous in traffic. I am RESOLVED TO BE THE EXAMPLE I WANT TO SEE! I will extend courteous behavior while driving, and maybe it will be contagious.

6. Be a good tipper. The people who serve us are poorly paid. I can make a financial difference if I am consistently a good tipper. Let us tip our servers well — 'nuff said!

7. Make fitness a part of my daily routine. I hate running! I really do not like to walk either. However, this is the only body I am going to have, so I might as well take care of it. Let's watch our diet and exercise. It makes sense, so let's get on with it.

8. Stop smoking. Need I say anymore?

9. Mentor a young person. I am tired of hearing about the problems of our youth. It is time to mentor a young person. Whatever our respective gifts may be, someone needs our coaching and support.

There are only approximately 100 African-American philosophers in this country. I am one of them, and it is time for me to take a young man and woman under my wing. The point is we need to mentor and not put down our youth. Who will join me in this task?

10. Be kind to myself. It has taken me a long time to love me. Finally, I like me. I think in 2017 we need to be kind to ourselves and say positive things about who we are.

We need to forgive ourselves for past failures and affirm our victories. Love you — and be kind to yourself because you are somebody!

These are my resolutions for 2017. Maybe they will encourage you to put together some for yourself.

2017

A call for social and political vigilance

January 3, 2017

"There is a significant Latin proverb; to wit: Who will guard the guards?" — Josh Billings

2017 promises to be a very interesting year. On every level of our political experience, change has come. A new president of the United States will take office. A new governor will lead the state of Missouri. With the coming transition of political power all of us will be affected in both small and great ways. There are some things we must watch very carefully as we move into 2017.

We must watch how the racial climate will be affected by the policies of both the president-elect and the new governor. Will both the president and the governor work toward racial equity which is sorely lacking in this country, or will white separatists like the "alt-right" have the greatest influence on the leadership of this country? President-elect Donald Trump and Gov.-elect Eric Greitens both promised to bring people together. For unity to exist, the president and the governor must both acknowledge that there is a mammoth gulf in trust that exists between conscious people of color and conservative whites in America. How will they regain and restore trust for not only those who have access to privilege and power, but for those who have been the historical and recent victims of systematic and personal racism?

Second, we must be observant as to how the vast economic disparity that exists in America and Missouri will be constructively addressed. Both Trump and Greitens promise that jobs will be brought to America and Missouri. Yet what type of jobs? Will we have a host of minimum-wage jobs that keep the working poor in the economic condition they already experience? If that is the strategy, it will not work. At the same time, increasing the wealth of the wealthy is a vacuous notion. Adam Smith's "invisible hand" is invisible because it is non-existent. The fact is the rich are getting richer and the poor are getting poorer. We need policies that will overcome the economic gap for so many in America and Missouri.

Third, we must be seriously cognizant of the problems of the educational system in this country. "No child left behind" was an absolute failure. The drop-out rate of secondary students is ridiculously high for a sophisticated society like ours. Too often the educational system is not preparing our children to be successful, but rather sets them up for the prison industrial complex. We need Trump and Greitens to stop the school-to-prison pipeline.

These are not the only three issues that need our attention. Clearly, we have environmental concerns that need addressing. Too many Americans are still without proper health care. The overwhelming cost of child care in this country holds many young families in the grip of near poverty. We need real leadership and not ranting tweets on Twitter nor macho pretentiousness.

Our country and state are in a critical state of affairs. We shall see if a serious populist movement is underway or nothing more than "white black-lash." Either way, let us be vigilant as we watch the social and political policies unfold.

A tribute to Huston Cummings Smith

January 10, 2017

"God has to speak to each person in their own language, in their own idioms. Take Spanish,

Chinese. You can express the same thought, but to different people you have to use a different language. It's the same in religion." — Huston Smith

On December 30, the world lost a great scholar, teacher and friend to humanity. The eminent Huston C. Smith died in his home in Berkley, California, after a long illness. Huston Smith was born in 1919 to Methodist missionary parents in Suzhou, China. He became one of the most respected teachers of world religions we have ever known.

Most people who took an "Introduction to World Religions" course are acquainted with this great mind. He wrote over 12 books, the most well-known being "The Religions of Man" in 1958, later reissued as "The World's Religions" in 1991. The book is still being used on many college campuses today and has sold over 2 million copies.

Smith was known for not only being an articulate communicator of the major religions of the world, he also was a practitioner of some of the world's major religious traditions. He studied Vedanta Hinduism in India, Zen Buddhism in Japan, kept the month-long fast of Ramadan and was a frequent participant of Jewish Passover. He did not just talk about religions; he immersed himself in the religious traditions because he understood that one cannot truly understand another until you pray with, break bread with and worship with a community of faith that is not your own. He did not participate to criticize; he participated to learn and experience something greater than himself.

While teaching at the then-segregated Washington University in St. Louis in the mid-1950s, Smith brought in the Rev. Dr. Martin Luther King Jr. to be a guest lecturer — a bold undertaking to say the least. He did it because he perceived that King needed to be heard, and that faith without acts of justice is meaningless.

In 1996, he published with Bill Moyers a five-part series on world religions for PBS. Many believe that Smith acquainted and introduced eastern religions to America. He unashamedly believed in the veracity of faith even to the point of assisting in the official recognition of Native American religious practices and authentic religious expressions.

I believe Smith never received the recognition he deserved as a transformative thinker, astute scholar and masterful lecturer. He taught us that one can appreciate the faith of another and still be true to one's own religion.

He was born and reared a Methodist Christian, but understood that no one religion, sacred text or doctrine contains all the truth about an Ultimate Reality. The ability to acknowledge and affirm the faith of someone who is Buddhist, Muslim, Jewish or Hindu does not make one less Christian.

It is simply, but powerfully, apprehending that the truth of an ultimate reality is bigger and richer than Hinduism, Buddhism, Judaism, Christianity, Islam or any religious position.

Huston Smith reminded all of us that an Ultimate Reality is greater than any of our human constructs. Perhaps that is why we are urged in Exodus 20 to have no graven image of God.

Huston Smith taught us that religion at its best unites people, and at its worst, divides us. We now live a world where people will deny others fresh water because of the God of profit and refuse to recognize another's humanity who happens to be black, white, latino, native American, gay, transgender, etc., because their Bible or other sacred texts states that such people are unworthy.

Part of the problem is because we have too many ignorant, self-righteous navel-gazers leading churches, mosques and synagogues in our world.

The other part of the problem is a dangerous pervasive misunderstanding prevalent within far too many communities of faith. Too many faith communities are under the delusion that faith is an "us against them" enterprise. The true purpose of religion is to teach us how we are one. The purpose of the great religions is to create inclusive conclaves of sanctuary, not exclusive monoliths of prejudice and division. Huston Smith reminded us that when we lose our purpose, we lose our focus. And when religious communities lose their focus, anyone that is not like them is the enemy.

I thank God for Huston Smith. He will be greatly missed. However, his lessons of truth will resonate in the minds of those who seek truth, justice and unity forever. I hope this column finds you well.

How shall we remember?

January 17, 2017

Across the country, people have gathered and are gathering to celebrate the life and message of the Rev. Dr. Martin Luther King Jr. The "I Have a Dream" speech will echo out in churches and other places of assembly, calling attention to Dr. King's commitment to non-violent direct action and social-political and economic transformation. It is odd, is it not, that we celebrate the idea of 'a beloved community' on the precipice of the inauguration of the most divisive and unpopular president in the modern history of this country. What a contrast.

I do not know about you, but I am tired of gathering and singing "We Shall Overcome." I want to yell — WHEN?? If I attend one more MLK Celebration that attempts to sing "Lift Every Voice and Sing" and no one around me knows more than the first verse, I may scream. It is the Negro National Anthem and black people do not know the words? I want to overcome, not sing about it. Freedom is like grace; it is free but not cheap. It is available only through hard work, fearless protest and focused endeavor.

Some people are suggesting that the best way to remember Dr. King this year is to employ one of the non-violent strategies that he supported during the Civil Rights Era. The suggested strategy is to engage in a one-day economic boycott on Jan. 20, the day of Trump's inauguration. Clearly if black, brown and socially conscious individuals of all colors and persuasion would engage in an economic boycott, it would arrest the attention of the financial community in this country. Since many of the myopic "Trumpeteers" think we are simply being noisy, one-trick ponies, make them listen to the sound of silence as we refuse to spend our money. People pay attention to a lack of money even before they hear the voice of justice.

While I understand the power of a boycott, the problem is that it is unsustainable given the mindset of this materialistic society. Sacrifice has become a bad word: look at how many of our youth walk around with $200 sneakers on their feet, nothing in their heads and the audacity to have their chests puffed out expecting to receive more! It would be different if it was only young people, but it is not. People of all ages have been seduced by "the money-trap." To engage in a successful boycott requires large numbers of people to be willing to say "NO!" for one day. I think it is a great idea but more is needed. A revolution in thinking as advocated by Carter G. Woodson and Pablo Freire respectively needs to take place so our economic power is felt for more than one day if the goal is systemic change and not mere sounding brass and tinkling cymbal.

The question before us is how we shall remember Dr. Martin Luther King, Jr., in a way that is not trite and meaningless. One way is that we need to find a way to seriously harness wealth and make it work for the people. Succinctly, we must stay out of predatory payday offices and rent-to-own rip-off stores, and center our money. For example, if the black churches in Columbia would pool their money together — we could cause serious economic change to take place for the people who come to us for prayer. One thing is for sure, the conservatives and evangelicals in this country will make sure that their money will work for them and not against them. In honor of Dr. King, we need to learn how to make money work for us, and stop saying "The Lord will provide" when the Lord is providing right now.

Whatever strategy we use, let us work for the social, political and economic freedom we have sung about for so long.

Finding the solutions to our problems

January 24, 2017

"Democracy must be built through open societies that share information. When there is information, there is enlightenment. When there is debate, there are solutions. When there is no sharing of power, no rule of law, no accountability, there is abuse, corruption, subjugation and indignation." -Atifete Jahjaga

"Rarely do we find men [people] who willingly engage in hard, solid thinking. There is an almost universal quest for easy answers and half-baked solutions. Nothing pains some people more than having to think." -Martin Luther King, Jr.

Last week I attended the Columbia Martin Luther King Jr. celebration at Progressive Missionary Baptist Church. It was a well-attended event with a good mix of people and cultures. Indeed, it was inspiring and meaningful. Mayor Brian Treece was in attendance, as well as other members of the City Council. What captured my attention most profoundly were the eloquent and profound remarks of the mayor. He stated that Columbia was large enough to be a microcosm of all the problems that confront the nation but small enough to find solutions to our problems.

I agree with the mayor that Columbia is a mirror of what confronts us as a nation. We look idyllic when we compare ourselves to St. Louis, Chicago, New York and other large metropolitan areas. But the fact is we too face the problems of drugs and crime, a disturbing school drop-out rate, underemployment and unemployment, racial profiling of the police department, inadequate housing and apathy.

But we also have groups of people who are committed to finding real solutions to the problems. Race Matters, Friends continues to raise the issue of community policing and how important training is for the Columbia Police Department . Faith Voices of Columbia is committed to fighting for social and racial justice. I am hugely impressed by the women's marches (in Columbia, nationally and internationally). Their agenda to accomplish "ten actions in one hundred days" warrant attention and support. I am even encouraged by the large evangelical community in Columbia. While they tend to lean toward gradualism, I believe they want to correct the systemic and personal wrongs that happen in Columbia. We just must be vigilant in reminding them that "nothing ventured — nothing gained."

Three things must happen to find solutions to what ills us in Columbia. First, we must engage in open and honest conversation across racial, socio-political and religious lines. Too often we speak out of our emotions, which in turn assassinates meaningful dialogue. While we have come out of a divisive political campaign, we need to find a way to rise above the negative rhetoric and create meaningful discussions regarding what it means for all citizens of Columbia to have a good quality of life. Our future generations demand no less.

Second, we must find a way to include those who have been historically marginalized in the conversation. They may not have PhDs or impressive corporate resumes, but they understand struggle and have something to say that we need to hear. Seniors, farmers, factory workers, social service recipients and the lot have something to contribute. Too often we speak for people but not listen to them.

Third, we must commit ourselves to an idea of a common good and not just having our way. We all understand our rights. But what are we willing to sacrifice for the common good of Columbia? If we are not willing to seek the common good above and beyond our own individual agendas, we will never be the community we ought to be. Again, we look good, but now it is time for us to be as good as we look.

I hope that we work diligently to find the solutions to our problems. How wonderful it would be if the religious, academic, political and business sectors would call a summit to find a way to address our problems that also includes ordinary citizens of Columbia. It would be a step in the right direction.

The destructive power of fear

January 31, 2017

"Courage is knowing what not to fear." - Plato

I awoke this morning to the devastating news of the attack on a mosque in Quebec City, Canada. Reuters News Agency reported that six people were killed with eight people wounded. While the violence in Canada may have little or nothing to do with Mr. Trump's ban on Muslim immigrants, it takes very little imagination to connect his executive order with fanning the flames of Islamophobia here and around the world. The tragedy happened after the ban and the announcement from Canada's Prime Minister Trudeau stating that refugees were welcome in Canada. We Americans used to have the same mindset until fear overtook our common sense.

I define Islamophobia as the irrational fear of Islam. While specific to Muslims, it is grounded in a general fear of the other. Most people are not knowledgeable of Islam. Many see it simply as a strange religion where people dress differently or the author of terrorism against the against the U.S. and Europe. I know allegedly well-educated people who irrationally hate Muslims simply because they are Muslims. When asked what are the essential principles of Islam, these people do not know, and frighteningly, they do not care. They just hate Islam and all Muslims.

Fear can make normally coherent and rational people act in very destructive and divisive ways. Clearly, there are some violent and terroristic elements in Islam: ISIL and Boko Haram to name two. But there are some frightening elements in Christianity also. Have we forgotten that the people who waged violence against abortion clinics, lynched African-Americans, slaughtered Native Americans and perpetuated horrible acts of violence against the LGBT community all claimed they were acting on their Christian beliefs? And before someone wants to take this statement as evidence of the evils of religion, remember that some of the worst acts of genocide in human history were committed by Stalin, Mao and Pol Pot, all non-Christian, non-Muslim, non-religious people. Religion does not make people fear-crazed; people controlled by fear act in crazy, outrageous ways — religious and non-religious.

We are a country of immigrants. The majority of us came to this country from somewhere else: some by force, and some by choice. If this democratic experiment known as the United States of America is to last, we cannot continue to divide people by religion, color, gender and preference/orientation. President Trump may be solidifying his base with his executive ban, but he is dividing the nation and breeding fear senselessly. I call for all of us to stand with our Muslim brothers and sisters and call for an end to Islamophobia. The judgment of people must be determined by demonstrations of character, not nationalistic fear. I call for rational people to speak out against this injustice of prejudiced division based on religion and color and demand that we be the people of our ideals and not a people ruled by fear. Once we upheld a vital ethical principle of law, "All people are innocent until proven guilty." This principle is not only for the judicial process, it ought to be a fundamental principle of life in America. Let us return to those principles and stop the madness that is being fostered.

Black History Month a time for remembering

February 7, 2017

"If there is no struggle, there is no progress." — Frederick Douglass.

"One day our descendants will think it incredible that we paid so much attention to things like the amount of melanin in our skin or the shape of our eyes or our gender instead of the unique identities of each of us as complex human beings." — Franklin Thomas, activist, philanthropist, and former president of the Ford Foundation.

African Americans throughout the nation are celebrating February as Black History Month. It is appropriate to do given that African American history is American history. I posit that to know our history is to protect ourselves from making the mistakes of the past and to prepare ourselves for the possibilities of the future. It is impossible to recount the story of this country without retelling the deeds, accomplishments and contributions of African Americans in the United States.

Sadly, most celebrations of the history of black people in America is confined to stories about the Rev. Dr. Martin Luther King, Jr., Rosa Parks, Harriet Tubman and Booker T. Washington. Often overlooked is the fiery oratory of Frederick Douglass, the challenge of Mary McLeod Bethune or the call to economic freedom of Malcolm X, just to name a few. Perhaps we neglect to remember many within the scope and depth of the history of black people in America because it makes us uncomfortable. To engage black history with depth is to acknowledge the good and the bad in this society. We enjoy films like Hidden Figures, but we cringe at the story of Marcus Garvey.

Black history is a story of a people born of struggle. It is a story of a people caught in the tension of assimilation and resistance. Thus, it is the story of the power of the human spirit to overcome epistemic, socio-political and economic obstacles. A key element in good storytelling is to begin the story correctly. Too often we begin the story by stating that black people came to this country as slaves. False! When the first 20 black people came to this country in 1619, they came as Africans and were made slaves. Second, when Africans came to America and were enslaved, not all of them were Muslim. Some were Christian via as members of the first Church, the Coptic Christian Church. Many came with adherence to their tribal traditions of worship. Starting the story correctly is paramount to telling the story truthfully.

I hope you will take the time to learn more about our common history during Black History Month. Attend events that portray the struggle of black people in America. Educate yourself because knowledge is power. Perhaps the retelling of this story will help us unify and not be the divided country we are presently.

The question of immigration looms

February 14, 2017

The last week has caused many of us great consternation as we watch another issue tear the nation apart. We have watched the President's attempt to ban immigrants from seven countries. Fortunately, the judiciary has frozen the ban — at least temporarily.

While the courts were busy, so was the U.S. Immigration and Customs Enforcement Agency. KTLA News Agency reported that over one hundred Latinos were detained and deported in the Los Angeles area alone. Reports of detainment and deportation rang out across the nation with the epitome of buffoonery culminating in the deportation of Garcia De Rayos.

The President is traveling down a very dangerous road. The anti-Latino, anti-Muslim movement masked as "a concern about national security" is ripping the country apart. This is no longer a democrat versus republican issue; it is an issue that reflects who we are as a people and what we stand for as a republic. Is Garcia De Rayos truly a threat to our country? Are we so frightened that we need to ban citizens of Muslim countries carte blanche?

We are watching families who have contributed to this nation being torn asunder. My Muslim and Latino colleagues, friends and students live in fear everyday now because they do not know who of them will be next to experience a visit from ICE. As the Trump terror continues, the country I love is becoming more and more unrecognizable. We are watching a democratic experiment being transformed into a fascist state.

It is time to stop the lunacy before it becomes more than we can control. Our children and future generations demand better of us. It is time to be the land of the free and the home of the brave and reject the xenophobia that is now upon us. The universe will not hold us guiltless if we do not stop what we are doing.

We need people to call lawmakers and oppose the ban and the acts of terror perpetrated by ICE. We need to raise our voices and call for the common good. We need faith communities of every kind to resist the movement of division and dehumanization. We need Christian Evangelicals to quit hiding behind their claims of neutrality and live faithfully to the good-news. It is a fact undeniable: one is either part of the solution, or part of the problem. There is no middle ground.

There is hope. I am watching people protest with fervor across the country. I am encouraged that the judiciary has stood firmly in opposition to the ban. I am even hearing Trump supporters (some, not many) say that Trump is going in the wrong direction on this matter. And so, I am encouraged. But more is needed by citizens who believe in the American ideals that formed this republic.

For the real security of this nation, stand in opposition to the ban on Muslim immigrants and the deportation of Latinos. We are better in our diversity, but weaker when we act by fear.

Community policing needs total buy-in from residents

February 21, 2017

"To know the good is to do it." — Socrates

On Monday night, I attended the Columbia City Council meeting to support the resolution offered by Fourth Ward Councilman Ian Thomas calling for a proactive community engagement process about policing.

Many members of the Columbia community attended and spoke in support of the resolution, including Traci Wilson-Kleekamp and T.R Griggs of Race Matters, Friends, the Revs. Molly Housch-Gordon and Brad Bryan, and sociologist Andrew Twaddle. After an interesting debate among council members, the resolution passed.

We need to applaud Thomas for bringing the issue of community policing to a resolution. Race Matters Friends has been ardent in its call for "community-oriented policing" in Columbia, as has the Mayor's Task Force on Violence. Now we have a resolution that can provide the opportunity to move forward in a constructive and serious manner to address the lack of trust between the Columbia Police Department and citizens of the city.

We must also applaud Mayor Brian Treece and the members of the City Council for passing the resolution. It would have been easy for the council to allow pusillanimity to rule the night. Instead the council boldly stepped out on faith and passed the resolution.

Conceptually, we understand the need for community-oriented policing. No one wants a Ferguson in Columbia. But what does community-policing look like?

We must construct a process that is theoretically sound and pragmatically implementable. How do we programmatically build bridges that benefit the community and the police? I want police officers to be able to do their jobs and for the community to regain a sense of trust in law enforcement.

There is a long history of racial bias and profiling in Columbia that cannot be denied. Admitting it is necessary for us to move forward in community policing. Acknowledgment of error is always the most necessary step for creating a fundamentally new approach.

We must make sure that as many stakeholders as possible are included in the progress of implementing a community-oriented policing plan. Too often, certain members of the community are excluded from the strategy creation process. Obviously, we want members of the City Council, the city manager, the police chief, and the business and faith communities to be part of the strategy process.

It would be great if Barbara Harrell, Julie Middleton or Mary Ratliff were included. But we also need plain, ordinary folks like Paula Hayes and others who live in the tension of police-community relations every day to be part of the discussion. We need more than the black or white bourgeoisie involved in this project. We need as many stakeholders as possible.

We also must address the shortage of police officers and the subsequent problems of low morale among the rank and file. I have said this before, but it is worth repeating: We need to pay officers better, improve their facilities and technology, and provide training/continued education opportunities for them to improve their skills. In doing so, we can attract more good officers to Columbia. (I also think this true for firefighters, but that is a conversation for another day.) It is a dangerous situation for the citizenry at large to have stressed out, overworked police officers in Columbia. Such is the formula for tragedy.

We have a lot of work to do. I, for one, stand ready to assist the city and the community in the implementation of a community-oriented policing program that increases unity in Columbia.

In doing so we can move toward being one of the great cities in this country. Join with me in making this possibility a reality.

After the celebration, what now?

February 28, 2017

"If we accept and acquiesce in the face of discrimination, we accept the responsibility ourselves and allow those responsible to salve their conscience by believing that they have our acceptance and concurrence. We should, therefore, protest openly everything ... that smacks of discrimination or slander." — Mary McLeod Bethune

Now at the close of celebrating February as Black History Month, we turn our attention to addressing the issues that confront the black community. The issues that challenge the black community challenge society. I love celebrating the accomplishments of black people: a people born of struggle. But celebration without commitment to advancement of the contemporary black community is worthless hoopla. Those who have accomplished much since 1619 did so with a directed vision. We must have the same if the liberation of black people is to be a reality. We can list for days the problems, but liberation is not mere problem-solving. Something deeper must take place.

While white negative racism cannot be denied and everyone admits it must be discontinued, the fact is that white people must deal with their own racism. Black people cannot do the work for them. While as a black man I can and must speak out against both personal and systemic racism, white people need to engage in sagacious reflection on how they individually and collectively perpetuate negative racism in this society. White people must confront their own demons if we are ever to be one nation and one people.

Black people have demons of their own to wrestle within this society. To fulfill the hopes and dreams of our fore parents we must conquer our demons. The first demon to overcome is black self-hatred. For far too long we have seen each other as the enemy. Instead of encouraging one another, too many of us are the first to criticize and demean another black person. What happened to black pride and black unity? If we do not learn to be our own best cheerleaders, how can we expect other people to celebrate us? We can no longer blame black self-hatred on slavery. We must be responsible to each other and lift each other up.

Second, we must commit to educating ourselves. I am not talking about having a degree. I know lots of people with degrees that are ignorant to the causes of oppression. We must begin to understand the material conditions that contribute to our oppression. In the era of Donald Trump, the "alt-right" and growing hate groups, it is past time to free our minds from reality T.V.; hip-hop that promotes drugs, sex and money; prosperity religiosity that masquerades as Christianity; and the continued dependence on systems, people and programs that keep us in bondage. We must educate our children if the school system will not. We need to educate each other as to how to create an alternative economy where we spend money among ourselves and not make those who have access to privilege and power richer. The goal of freedom is not training our children to be athletes, entertainers or hustlers. If Frederick Douglass is correct that education makes a child unfit for slavery, then it is true for adults. The world we live in is complex, but not so complex that we cannot figure out the games played against us. We just need to commit to being victors and not victims. Education — not a degree — is the key.

Lastly, we need a spiritual revival. Notice I said spiritual and not religious. We have allowed white, Western, European thinking to rob us of the spiritual power that once caused our fore parents to have hope in the context of hopelessness. A spiritual revival will re-focus our direction and fortify our resolve to "run on to see what the end will be." Most of what we are experiencing with black-on-black crime, massive depression and low or lack of self-esteem is grounded in spiritual emptiness. As James Weldon Johnson stated, we must return to the "God of our weary years and the God of our silent tears who has brought us thus far along the way." Without a spiritual revival, we will continue a downward spiral that leads to destruction.

We have much to do. We have celebrated. Now let's go to work.

Honoring the women of our lives

March 7, 2017

"You gain strength, courage and confidence by every experience in which you really stop to look fear in the face." — Eleanor Roosevelt

"A bird doesn't sing because it has an answer, it sings because it has a song." — Joan Walsh Anglund

For the month of March, we turn our attention to celebrating the accomplishments of women who have made society, the world and our lives better.

Throughout the history of humanity, women have provided exceptional contributions to science, technology, religion, the humanities and the social sciences. Despite formidable obstacles, blatant prejudice and horrific violence, women have stood and overcome.

It is important to remember the great women of history, but it is also important to remember the millions of unsung women who shaped our character and molded our integrity. The countless mothers, sisters, cousins, nieces and fictive kin who wiped our tears (and our bottoms), encouraged us in our failures and exclaimed as our greatest cheerleaders in life.

I believe that it takes a man to make a boy a man, but it takes a woman to make a man a good man.

I have been fortunate to have had strong women in my life. From my mother, who was always there to encourage and pray for me, to my wife, who has learned to love a man of passion and faith who sometimes lives in his head too much.

I think of the women of excellence in the black church and in the black intellectual tradition who taught me that it is more important to "sing" than to look for compliments, and more precious to give the best of oneself than to receive. I am still surrounded by great women, for which I am blessed and grateful.

Take time this month to learn about and reflect on the great women of our lives. Without women, we, as men, would be lost.

I learned that if you want something discussed, ask men, but if you want a task completed, give it to women. Celebrate women this month, they are worthy of acclaim and our highest esteem.

Rumination on the anniversary of my birth

March 14, 2017

As of March 12, 2017, I have inhabited the earth for six decades and three years. Within my lifetime, I have experienced numerous moments of exhilarating joys and debilitating sorrow.

I have watched a human land on the moon and an African-American become President of the United States. I have been horrified by seeing a young, lynched, black, male, body hang from a light pole and have experienced as an adolescent the Ku Klux Klan burning a cross on my mother and father's lawn.

In my lifetime, I have gone from "colored" water fountains, black and white televisions and segregated buses and restaurants, to sipping champagne in the mayor of Paris' mansion, eating couscous in Morocco and drinking sherry with my professors at Princeton. I have encountered both the hope and failure of the integration movement and have watched drugs almost kill Black progress in the post-Civil Rights Era.

I have lived at the zenith of American society, and I have also lived at the bottom. I have observed a people move from shanty houses to public housing known as the "projects" and have wondered "whose project is it?" I have worked with Opportunities Industrialization Centers and Leon Sullivan. I survived the rebellions of Watts, Detroit, and Newark and Ferguson.

I have talked shop with Cornel West, Cain Hope Felder, James Cone, J. Alfred Smith Sr., Maulana Karenga and the Dalai Lama. I have also listened to the frightening pronouncements of the "alt right" and white supremacist groups growing in this country. I have been graced to have sit at the feet of Angela Davis, Rudy Dee, Maya Angelou, and have heard the fiery oratory for justice and freedom from Malcolm X, Bobby Seal, Eldridge Cleaver, Martin L. King, and Wyatt T. Walker.

Indeed, I have experienced much in these 63 years.

Experience is a good thing, but the most important question is, what have I learned? After all, even a rock has experiences. These things I have learned along life's way.

Never let people put you in a box. Always walk your own path and create your own style. It is more important to be true to one's own authenticity than to be accepted by the fickle crowd.

If you feed your gift, your gift will make room for you. I believe every person has a gift within them. I have learned that we give either feed our gift, or let it die within us. If we nurture it, the gift will open world of possibility for us.

True success is determined by how many people one helps and mentors, not by material acquisition. It is an old saying, but it is still true. The rich live well, but they who serve and mentor others sleep well. True success ought to allow us to sleep well.

- All people are of worth and respect.
- Be a peacemaker, not a peace-seeker.
- There is a difference between knowledge and wisdom. The goal is to garner both.
- READ! Even dogs play with toys, but humans ought to be able to read.
- Be quick to complement and slow to criticize.
- Every person makes mistakes, but only a fool makes the same mistake twice.
- Love justice, seek mercy, and walk humbly before God.
- Never lose your passion.

I hope these thoughts aid you in your life journey.

What do we mean by 'community'?

March 21, 2017

"We must become bigger than we have been: more courageous, greater in spirit, larger in outlook. We must become members of a new race, overcoming petty prejudice, owing our ultimate allegiance not to nations but to our fellow men [persons] within the human community." — Haile Selassie

On Thursday, March 23 at 6 p.m., Faith Voices of Columbia and Turning Point will host a forum on poverty and homelessness at the Wilkes Boulevard United Methodist Church. Residents of the First Ward are invited to attend this event and voice their concerns about the needs of the First Ward to the City Council candidates Pat Kelley*, Clyde Ruffin and Andrew Hutchinson (I removed titles not to be disrespectful but to maintain equality of persons).

This event has prompted me to reflect on "community." What do we mean when we say "community"? Is it merely a term to refer to a geographical area, or is something else implied in the word? Community must mean more than geography. Community comprises a sense of relationship and shared vision.

I realize that I am operating from an experiential prospective in that as a child I grew up with a healthy sense of community. In the black community of my youth, neighbors knew each other and watched over us with concern and responsible action. Community members supported us in academics and athletics. Our teachers were also our fellow churchgoers. Gay people were always part of the black church of my youth, and white people were always welcome in our institutions even though we were not welcome in their institutions. The community encouraged us and told us that we could be anything we wanted to be. They formed "fictive kinships," such that community was family. Segregation did not stifle communal resiliency; instead it heightened our sense of hope and change. We shared a common vision: No matter who you were or what the larger dominant society asserted, we were somebody.

Somewhere along the way we have lost such a sense of community. The quest for material acquisition, status, power and wealth has wreaked havoc on the idea of a connected community. We no longer know our neighbors. Our desire to be "fictive kin" has been replaced by inflexible and callous individualism. Too often the locks on our doors are secondary to the locks on our hearts. Selassie is correct that we must be bigger than we have ever been before if we are to develop community in the true sense of the word. We are called to invest in our children, protect our seniors, benefit the homeless and create meaningful employment for those who are systemically rejected.

I live in the First Ward. I hope this event will help us rekindle a sense of community and cooperation. Too many people see the First Ward as "the troubled community of Columbia." People fear coming to Douglass Park because, in their minds, it is a place of violence, alcohol and drugs. They forget that the First Ward consists of people who, like them, love their children and families and want the best for us and the entire city. The First Ward is the home of Blind Boone and historic institutions like Second Missionary Baptist Church, Fifth Street Christian Church (Disciples of Christ) and St. Paul A.M.E. Church. It is the place of Columbia College, Hickman High School and Jefferson Middle School where minds are being equipped and transformed. I am proud to live in the First Ward, and every day I and others are trying to make the First Ward a "community" and not just an aggregate of people sharing the same geographical location.

Despite the divisions and disparity that exist in America and Columbia, let us recommit to building community.

Society lacking civility

March 28, 2017

I just finished reading Steve Calechman's article in Men's Health and found it very interesting. The column is titled, "I Said Hello to 10 People for 10

Days. Here's What Happened." In it, he talks about how as a writer he lives mostly in his head and over time has built a sort of isolationist behavior spending most of his time thinking and arguing with himself instead of interacting with other people. He went on to share how simply saying "hello" to 10 people a day for 10 days gave him a happier disposition and revealed some interesting people along the way.

Calechman's column caused me to ponder on how civility has been lost in our society and how simple gestures that good home training instilled in us when we were young has become a thing of the past. Little things such as opening a door for someone or saying 'thank you' when someone opens a door for you can make all the difference in the world. Remember how a sign of good manners was to say, "Good morning" or "Good afternoon?" Now the vogue thing is to look "hard," make no eye contact, and keep it moving.

We are all aware that intentional civility has positive health effects on the human body. The more we greet one another, laugh, engage in conversation and just be plain nice to one another, the more it decreases our stress levels, increases endorphins and creates positive, productive environments for work and play.

Have you ever wondered how civil society would be transformed if we began to practice being 'civil?' How many acts of violence and events of hatred would be curbed with a simple, "Hi, how are you?" Of course, pleasantry will not solve the institutional and systemic problems that plague contemporary society, but it may create an atmosphere where we can commit to finding solutions to our problems instead of automatically characterizing others as the enemy.

A great African-American preacher by the name of Narcisse used to say, "It's nice, to be nice!" I think he is correct. Civility can transform us into healthier people, physically and emotionally, and it can make the world we live in gentler and kinder. The bottom line is that it costs us nothing but a little time, minor effort and courage.

Palm Sunday is a symbol of defiance

April 12, 2017

Generally, I do not use this column as a platform to discuss theological issues, but this week I am making an exception.

I am doing so because what I have to say is not just for Christians but for all of us who yearn for something different and humane.

For the Christian community, this is the high time for the church. It began Sunday with Palm Sunday and concludes with Easter, or, as some prefer, Resurrection Sunday. When I first read the Palm Sunday sermon given by Kurt Vonnegut at St. Clements Episcopal Church in New York City in 1980, it prompted me to look at the event of Palm Sunday in a new way. Vonnegut, a Christ-believing agnostic, is once again urging us to look at Palm Sunday, Good Friday and Easter differently.

Reflecting on this week, I have come to agree with Vonnegut that we have been looking at the wrong end of a miracle. Since 325 A.D., when the Europeans stole the Church by the power of Constantine, most Christians have celebrated Palm Sunday but have forgotten the purpose of the Nazarene's entrance into Jerusalem. Palm Sunday was an act of defiance against the religious, socio-political and economic status quo of his time.

The "triumphant entry" (in the vernacular of what philosopher Soren Kierkegaard calls Christendom) is not a time of paltry sentimentality. It is a time of protest and defiance against the systems and powers that hold the poor, disenfranchised, bruised and broken in hope-shaking oppression.

The Christian saga states that Jesus of Nazareth came into Jerusalem riding on a donkey. On the other side of town, Herod was parading into Jerusalem draped in the symbols of power and regality. The rich and powerful constituted Herod's crowd, but Jesus' motley group was made of the poor, rejected and the downtrodden.

The fact that those who had been divided by the systems of oppression and dehumanization came together in shouts of hope is the first part of the miracle. Imagine the miracle that would manifest itself if the poor, the homeless, the victims of the judicial system, those marginalized by religious rigidity and narrow thinking, blacks, Latino/as, gays, transgender people and heterosexuals came together to voice a united cry of hope amid a divided and fractured America. It happened on Palm Sunday.

The second part of the miracle of Palm Sunday was that people tore down palm leaves to cover the road for the entry of the man from Nazareth. It was a criminal offense to damage a palm tree in Jesus' day. One could be fined or imprisoned for such an act. Yet the crowd defiantly stood against the law to state in a powerful way that human affirmation and the preservation of dignity is more important to God and humanity than obedience to rules that benefit the rich and powerful.

If the church and other religious communities are to have a meaningful place with people, they must shake off the shackles of complacency and lead in the movement of defiance against unjust law and practices.

That is why I am so very proud of the Unitarian Universalist Church of Columbia. Under the leadership of the Rev. Molly Housh Gordon, the congregation unanimously and defiantly voted to become a "sanctuary church" in this time of senseless deportation and Herod-like edicts coming from President Trump.

Notice that the congregation's vote was held on Palm Sunday. To become a sanctuary city or church is a bold and courageous move. They understand that courage and defiance is needed if we are going to be the people of God and not the lapdogs of the powerful.

You will notice if you read Matthew's account of Palm Sunday that the first thing Jesus does after the entry into Jerusalem is to go into the Temple of Jerusalem and turn over the tables of the money-changers. I suggest that is what caused him to be executed on Friday.

We all know that when bold people disrupt the economic process, those in power will attempt to kill you. Ask Malcolm, Martin, the Kennedys and countless others who questioned and threatened business as usual. Yet defiantly Yeshua (Jesus' Hebrew name) demands that a house of prayer is to treat people rightly, stand on the side of the poor and oppressed and create the possibility for the fundamentally new in the lives of everyday people. Forgive me, but I suggest both religious and secular institutions need to disrupt the economic flow of things. We need to put people first — not maintain the status quo.

Palm Sunday is a symbol of defiance. Whether Christian or not, we need to stand defiantly. We can change things if we stand together. If we do so, we shall not only look at the right end of a miracle but also become miracle-workers.

A reflection on the threat of war

April 18, 2017

"I'm goin' to lay down my sword and shield, / Down by the river- side, / Down by the riverside. / Down by the riverside, / I 'm goin' to lay down my

sword and shield, / Down by the riverside, / And study war no more!" -Negro Spiritual

Thomas Paine once wrote, "These are times that try men's [human] souls." Indeed, Paine's words echo in our consciences as we stand on the precipice of war. Every day we are confronted with rumors of war. Most people I speak with wonder whether we are going to engage in a conflict with North Korea, Russia or both. Saber rattling by all parties is intensifying and rational people are curiously reflecting on one simple question: Are we really going to war?

What sits at the root of our concern is a two-fold problem. First, we know that combined the three countries have enough nuclear fire power to blow the entire world up 16 times. Second, we are also painfully aware that the leaders of each of the three countries are irrational actors. We have a man elected President not by the popular vote, but by the electoral college, who wants to be king and not POTUS. The leader of North Korea is a man who will kill his own family members with no sense of remorse. What do you think he will do in an armed conflict? And, we all know Putin is a gangster. Each of these men have access to nuclear weapons and that, ladies and gentlemen, should frighten us greatly.

One would think that at this point of human development that we would have figured out two simple truths. The first is that no one wins at war. The devastation and death that results from war provides no winners, only survivors in the least, and, total annihilation at the most. The second is that war accomplishes nothing. War only increases hatred and division within the human experience. The cost of lives and resources can never be justified. In the 21st Century we need to use our combined technology, creative imagination and limited natural resources to improve the human condition, not destroy it.

It is time to lay down our swords and shields and find a better way to settle our differences. I am reminded of an 'old school' song that goes, "war (huh), what is it go for? Absolutely nothing!" I pray that we do not engage in war with Russia or North Korea or anyone else. If we want to engage in an activity, why not try to concentrate on fixing the problems of America like meaningful employment, correcting broken educational and judicial systems or insuring decent housing? Only the foolish and morally bankrupt want to engage in war. Let's stop the madness and return to some semblance of rationality.

Our judicial system is essentially unjust

April 25, 2017

"Where justice is denied, where poverty is enforced, where ignorance prevails, and where any one class is made to feel that society is an organized conspiracy to oppress, rob and degrade them, neither persons nor property will be safe." - Frederick Douglass

Last week, I spent a considerable time in the Boone County Courthouse. I was testifying at a sentence hearing on behalf of a local man whose family I have known for over 30 years. Fortunately, the young man did receive probation, for which I and the family are quite happy.

While the case I was involved in went well, my heart was continuously broken as I watched case after case come before the seated judge. Two things were apparent quickly.

First, most people in the courtroom to stand before the judge were black, and the executors of justice were white — defense lawyers, judges, prosecutors and the representatives of probation and parole.

The racial disparity and what racialized group was in power was starkly evident. No wonder many people say that when you are black and/or brown, and you go to court looking for justice, all you find is "just us!"

The second thing that was perceptible was that many people there were of a lower economic class and ignorant of the charges they faced. They knew they were facing trouble, but the ramifications of the charges they faced was beyond their comprehension.

In the Nicomachean Ethics, Book Five, Aristotle states that for a society to be just it must have the capacity and willingness to exercise both distributive and rectifying justice. It must guarantee a system that will reward resources to those who work fairly, and it must be able to rectify wrongdoing.

What Aristotle never imagined is a system as broken as the American judicial system. The fact is that if one is poor, black and/or brown you go to prison, and the wealthy get away with almost anything they wish. Due to the privatization of prisons in America, Jane Alexander is correct when she states that prisons are the new slavery in America.

Public defenders are so overworked they only get to meet their clients the day of court just to know who the client is they are defending. The prosecuting attorney has stacks of cases that would boggle the average mind. And let us not forget — we will kill people in this state. We need to overhaul the entire judicial process from top to bottom.

The question that comes is how? Where do we begin to correct such a dilapidated system of "just us." Clearly, we need public outcry for change and renewal. We need people of authority to streamline the system and provide education for both defendants and their families. We must find humane ways to prosecute offenders and care for victims. For instance, making rape victims relive their horror in court over and over again is ridiculous. There must be a better way.

We all must be committed to finding a better way to execute justice in America. It is of no comfort to realize the judicial systems in other countries are worse than our system.

I do not live there. I live in America, in Missouri, in Columbia, and I want a change for us.

Kudos to the churches of Columbia

May 9, 2017

"What you have done to the least one of these, you have done it unto me." - Matthew 25:40, paraphrased

An amazing event took place in our city on the weekend of April 29 that is worthy of celebrations. Over 40 churches participated in what was entitled "For Columbia," a work event to repair and remodel homes for low- income and senior citizens in Columbia's center city community.

The churches involved ranged from conservative evangelical churches such as The Crossing to more liberal social justice churches such as Wilkes Boulevard United Methodist Church. Congregants of various churches joined together to cut down dead trees, repair porches and provide remodeling for many residents who could not afford to have the work done.

In pouring down rain, I watched crews work tirelessly on houses that needed serious repair. They charged nothing to residents, but performed the work as an expression of Christian love to folks who may or may not be Christian, and likely not members of their congregations. It was awe-inspiring to witness.

Churches often frustrate me. I understand why many people have given up on the church. Too frequently churches are havens of self-righteous navel gazing, fixated on going to heaven instead of creating a better society. Many argue that the role of churches is only spiritual, and that to engage in social justice or acts of benevolence is to be too political. Those who take such a position have forgotten that the Nazarene instructed his disciples to pray and work under the concept that they were to create a society that was to be "on earth as it is in heaven."

To not participate in addressing injustice and need is a violation of Christian principle. An elder preacher once said to me, "If we are not going to be about the work (Christian), then we ought to take down the sign." I agree. Investing in just building impressive campuses and edifices and not people at every level of the human predicament is nothing more that pseudo-religious egoism. It is not Christianity.

But on the weekend of April 29, churches acted with a sense of koinonia (community). They acted like who Christians ought to be. They joined together to assist a community in need. They labored out of a concept love with tangible results. Today some residents are living in a better house, and again, it was all repaired and remodeled at no cost. That weekend the church made me proud.

It is easy to criticize. It is much harder for some people to say, "Nice job!" The work of last weekend by Columbia churches was honorable and noble. Attempting to be Christian does not make one better than anyone else, but it does (or should!) create a greater sense of responsibility to the least of these among us.

When you think about it, there are several religious groups that serve residents of Columbia on a regular basis. Think about St. Vincent's, Love INC, Turning Point, Loaves and Fishes, St. Francis House, Shiloh Christian Center's community dinners and Room at the Inn, just to name a few. These organizations are committed to making Columbia a better place for all its citizens. That is what Columbia Christians ought to do. We, whether Christian or not, should applaud and contribute to their efforts.

Socrates once stated that, "to know the good is to do the good." So, kudos churches for a job well done. You recognized need, and "did the good." Please keep it up. We need your tangible witness.

Shooting of Clarence Coats raises specter of racial bias

May 16, 2017

This weekend, an African-American man by the name of Clarence Coats was killed by the police in central Columbia.

The Columbia Police Department told the Missourian that a gunfight occurred between police officers and Coats, which resulted in his death. Many rumors and allegations are in motion in the Columbia community. Some say Coats was firing a weapon in the community but aiming at no one. Others state that Coats was a clear and present danger to residents and the police, and that the police responded with reasonable force after assessing the situation.

The one fact beyond question is that Coats, a member of a multi-generational family of Columbia's African-American community, is dead. He was killed by the Columbia Police Department.

Our hearts go out to the Coats family. For a parent to bury a child is both unnatural and painful beyond words. The natural order of things is for the children to bury their parents. When the process is in reverse, the sorrow is overwhelming, regardless of reasons. My sincere condolences to the family.

In the wake of this tragedy, questions regarding police methods of de-escalation and implicit bias are aflame once again. Was there an alternative available to the police that could have produced a result other than death? This is not a new question nor one without contemporary and historical impact. We are all aware of incidents of police using excessive force in volatile situations.

The deaths of black men across this country make all of us ask what else could have been done to prevent such a tragedy. To ask this question does not make you anti-police. I, for one, am a supporter of good community policing and of good police officers. In fact, I needed the help of police at my residence a few weeks ago. A CPD officer by the name of Chris Williams arrived at my residence promptly. He investigated the situation professionally and discussed the situation with me with a sense of compassion, courtesy and respect. I do not think this was a unique experience. I think rather that Officer Williams exemplifies what is good about the Police Department and what community policing can be. The problem is that there are too many police officers that either think that all black people are violent lawbreakers who must be confronted with force or that we are ignorant sub-humans who cannot think and speak with knowledge, rationality and passion.

Of course, the issue of racial bias will arise while discussing the death of Coats. Was racial bias at play? All rational people know that race always plays a part of the intersectionality of American life. To deny it is to live in the absurd. The problem for me is that there are no objective criteria by which we may judge how much negative racial thinking plays a part in this and other similar situations. This is compounded by the fact that we live in very different, racially shaped worlds, and that historically race has been denied as a factor in interpersonal affairs when we all know it has been a major factor. I do not know how to resolve these problems.

I realize that the Missouri Highway Patrol is investigating the incident, and I have profound respect for the department as they tend to be better trained and more racially sensitive than most city police officers. But are they free of all racial bias? Who can come to an investigation of this magnitude without prejudice, a sense of white privilege, historical pain, etc. and access the situation with a clear, rational judgment that is not — some way — racially biased? The problem is overwhelming.

The more poignant question is: How can we arrest our negative racial thinking to rightly judge incidents that result between the police and people of color in a way that benefits the common good?

The tragedy of the death of Coats stirs up all these questions and many more. My belief is that we can find a way to improve the relations between police and people of color in such a way that no parent will have to bury their child because of a police shooting.

My hope is that we find it soon.

Despite turmoil around us, we can find peace within

May 23, 2017

"I am not saying this because I am in need, for I have learned to be content whatever the circumstances." —Philippians 4:11

"When you are discontent, you always want more, more, more. Your desire can never be satisfied. But when you practice contentment, you can say to yourself, 'Oh yes – I already have everything that I really need.'" — The 14th Dalai Lama

One of the true signs of spiritual development is the acquisition of contentment. To have a sense of contentment is not the same thing as being satisfied. Indeed, with the amount of division, pain, and suffering we observe in the world, no one can be satisfied with current state of affairs. Given the reality of the contemporary human experience, contentment seems to be an almost impossible dream. Far too many people we know are angry, stressed, disenchanted and disconsolate. We all need a greater sense of contentment, but where can we find it?

We have all been taught that materialism and wealth are ways to become content with life, however, the facts belie the assertion. Things alone do not make us happy. Things can give us momentary joy, but things get old and their luster vanishes quickly. Wealth is insatiable and reminds us of the truth of the Notorious B.I.G.'s song, "mo' money, mo' problems." Physical beauty fades, and fame is fickle and fleeting. Even pie-in-the-sky religiosity leaves us empty, and cool rationality makes us barren. None of these quench our thirst for contentment.

All of us strive to find something that will give us a genuine sense of contentment and well-being. I suggest that the garnering of contentment is a process, an act of which Aristotle would call "energia," a constant practice aimed at happiness, absent of frustration or despair with one's circumstance. One does not possess contentment overnight. It comes with time. Contentment understands two important truths: trouble will not last always, and, one's circumstance needs not be one's conclusion. In the sentiment of Heraclitus, the one thing that is permanent is change itself.

Perhaps the starting point for acquiring contentment begins with an internal activity. I suggest the following.

• Learn to accept, forgive, and love oneself. What we are is what we are. Sure, improvements can be made, but they are never to be made to be like someone else. Who we are is precious and special. There is nothing we can do about the past, except learn from it. Forgive yourself, move on, and love yourself.

• Never argue with a fool. Do not engage in senseless conversations with irrational people. This will only exhaust you and fill your mind with foolishness that disturbs one's contentment.

• Avoid envy and jealousy. They poison the mind and the spirit.

• Love freely without hidden agendas, and love will come back to you—freely.

• When people show you who they are, believe them. How many times have we tried to make people what we want them to be. We are not God, so stop trying to make people in our image and likeness.

• Commit to something greater than yourself. At the end of the day, you will sleep well knowing that you helped someone along life's way.

• What is for you is for you. Never worry about someone taking something or someone from you. If it is yours, it will remain. If it is material, it can be replaced. If it is a person, love will always persevere. Even death cannot rob you of the love you share. Therefore, stop fretting about things and people.

• Mature to a point that you do not need other people's permission to think your own thoughts or speak your own words.

• Magnify the greatness of life. Read a classic book, quiet yourself to reflect on great poetry or prose. Listen to great music. You are surrounded by greatness. Too often we are consumed with mediocrity and forget the great accomplishments of people-past and present. Think on things that are great; it will inspire greatness in you.

In practicing the discipline of contentment, contentment will grow within. My prayer is that we all learn to be content. My hope is that contentment will come to you soon.

LeBron James is right — being black in America is tough

June 6, 2017

Last week, the Los Angeles residence of LeBron James was vandalized with the "N-word" spray-painted on the front gate of his home.

The event prompted James to once again speak about racism in America: "No matter how much money you have, no matter how famous you are, no matter how many people admire you, being black in America is tough. We got a long way to go for us as a society and for us as African Americans until we feel equal in America."

What has happened in recent times that would make a person of James' wealth, star-power and status suggest that African-Americans do not feel equal in the country they helped build?

One reason is that there has been an increase of acts of racial intimidation against people of color over the past few years. The Southern Poverty Law Center counted 867 cases of hateful harassment or intimidation in the United States in the 10 days after the Nov. 8 election. Many people believe the rhetoric of Donald Trump has emboldened hate groups.

Even here in Missouri blacks do not feel equal. The new Vehicle Stops Report from the Missouri Attorney General's Office is quite alarming. The report shows that the racial disparity index for black drivers in Columbia has jumped to its highest level since the attorney general began collecting data in 2000.

In 2016, black drivers made up 10 percent of Columbia's driving population, yet they accounted for more than 30 percent of traffic stops by Columbia police. In other words, black drivers in Columbia were pulled over three times more often than should be expected, and four times the rate of white drivers. Either African-Americans are the victims of police stereotyping or they are Columbia's worst drivers.

Many of us know that in most cases it is the former and not the latter. The question is whether the Columbia Police Department and the Columbia City Council will take this report seriously and start to profoundly support a program of community policing that will address citizens' concerns, or will the report be filed away and dismissed?

It is puzzling to me that, while the documented statistical evidence overwhelmingly points to the fact that we as Americans have a continuing racial problem in America, so many remain aloof.

The problem is demonstrated by the countless acts of racial intimidation, the death of African-Americans by the police, the constant racial profiling by every institution in this society, the undeniable disparities in education, unequal economic opportunities for people of color, the blatant social inequity and inequality that African-Americans experience daily, and yet few people seem to be alarmed. Far too many white people believe that the reports are false, irrelevant, exaggerated or unimportant.

Intrinsic racists, regardless of the evidence, believe that racism is a projected fantasy by black people who are too lazy to assimilate into the dominate culture; or, they think that blacks are simply wallowing in self-pity, using the "race card" for sympathy and enjoying being, in the words of W.E.B Du Bois, "America's Problem." Is it not interesting that White America has played the "race card" without guilt or shame since 1619, and yet will cry foul when a black person utters dissent?

Some things in America have improved, but we still have a long way to go. If Lebron James can feel it, imagine what black and brown folk in poverty perpetually experience. It is time for a change. Dr. Martin Luther King Jr. was right: "injustice anywhere is injustice everywhere."

While it is tough to be black in America, we must not lose hope that we can become a just society. Let the enemies of freedom and justice hate — that's what haters do.

We who believe that character, expertise and moral resolve are more important than color must be vigilant in our pursuit for equity and equality. We cannot stop demanding justice even if the president of the United States, or anyone else, tries to shut our mouth. We need to actively engage in affirming the beauty, wealth and strength of being black.

The prevailing question is, do we as contemporary black people have the fortitude to rise to the occasion? We must not only overcome anti-black white racism, but we must confront and subdue anti-black self-hatred. I can testify that some of the most asinine and vehement rhetoric, as well as constructed obstacles to impede progress, have come not just from intrinsic white racists, but also from blacks who love to see the demise and destruction of their people.

We must re-educate ourselves to love the blackness within us and reject anti-black symbols of beauty, intellect, personhood and success. Once I met a man in Detroit who, by shining shoes, sent eight children to college and a black woman who, as a single parent, earned her doctorate degree in library science from the University of Michigan. Both are successful and are worthy of honor. Character determines our worth, not the European hierarchy based on color, materialism, greed and domination.

We cannot be thin-skinned. We must prepare our hearts and minds for the battle that is upon us. We need people dedicated to justice and liberation of every race to join the fight for the common good. United we shall stand, divided we shall all fall.

A call for better fathers

June 13, 2017

On Sunday, Americans will celebrate Father's Day. The celebration of the role of fathers in the life of the family is attributed by many to Sonora Louise Smart Dodd of Spokane, Washington, who organized the first American celebration on June 19, 1910.

Many scholars, however, suggest that the celebration of fathers may be over 4,000 years old, going back to the Babylonians. Historical accounts allege that a young boy by the name of Elmesu carved a "Father's Day" message on a clay tablet wishing his father good health and long life. The phenomenon of celebrating Father's Day continued through the middle ages under the Roman Catholic Church and is practiced in many countries around the world.

These days, fatherhood is a tradition under siege. In many families, fathers are "absent and unaccounted for." In many homes, mothers play the role of both parents. Children grow up without ever knowing a father's love. There are various socio-psychological theories as to the cause of this problem. However, whatever the cause of absentee fatherhood, the result is still the same: We are producing children who have no fathers in their lives.

Despite the absence of many men willing to take up the role of being fathers, it is still important to celebrate Father's Day. It is the conceptual reality of fatherhood that makes the day important. My hope is the conceptual reality will become an actual reality. Let me be clear.

We must understand that there is a difference between being a father and being a sperm donor. Fathers understand that the role is a lifetime commitment. No matter how old the child becomes, children always need the nurture and support of their fathers. It is a wonderful thing to push the swing of your baby girl or teach her how to throw a baseball. It is a priceless experience to instruct your son on how to ride a bike or shoot a jumpshot, but it is of greater importance to teach our daughters and sons how to people of character in a time where the lack of character permeates the culture. Baby-makers are only around for the thrill of sexuality. Fathers and mothers teach children how to stand when the odds are against them and that moral strength and integrity is of greater worth than money and material gain.

Fathers extend to their children unconditional love.

I had a conversation with a man after the Orlando Pulse massacre who told me that if his son brought his boyfriend to his home, he would try to kill them both. On another occasion, a professor of philosophy once told me that if his daughter married a Christian, he would disown her. How ridiculous! A father loves regardless of sexual orientation, religious difference and racial choice. If one's son or daughter becomes a Muslim, Buddhist or even an atheist, true fathers love them anyway. Fathers love despite their children's choices. As a father, one may not may not agree with what their children value, but once again, the love shared is paramount to anything else. By the way, there are no "step children." If you love their mother, they are your children as well: not by biology, but by love.

Our children need men who are willing to step up their game and be the fathers that our children need so desperately. In the African-American community, it is without question that the absence of fathers has caused tremendous damage to the social, cultural, intellectual, moral and spiritual base of the community.

Yes, other groups suffer the same problem, but I suggest they do not suffer to the extent of the black community. The oppressor broke up families during slavery to dominate and control black life. Brethren, let us stop practicing slave methodologies and return to our rightful place with our children. They need us. They yearn for our love and support. Let us commit to being the best fathers we can be on this Father's Day and every day.

Churches have moral obligation to confront racial inequity

June 20, 2017

"How dare we come before God with our prayers when we commit atrocities against the one image we have of the divine: human beings?" — Elisabeth T. Vasko

Allow me to begin by stating unequivocally that I am a theist, and I am trying to be Christian. While I do not practice a traditional theism or mainstream Christian theology, I am nonetheless committed to the teachings of Jesus, and I try to be a faithful disciple. I am not perfect. I make mistakes, yet I am trying to "walk the walk" and not just "talk the talk." Because I have a big God, I can affirm Islam, Judaism, Hinduism, Buddhism, Daoism and other faith expressions as legitimate forms of connection with an "ultimate reality." While this column will concentrate on

Christianity, it may address other faith communities as well. However, I leave their representatives to give voice to their own social condition.

The Christian church has, in many areas, lost its purpose and vision. One area is racial justice in America. While some churches have engaged in the project of making racial justice a reality instead of merely a concept, the majority of churches have refused to be part of the solution.

It amazes me that Sunday mornings are still perhaps the most segregated times of the week in most communities across the country, and Columbia is no exception. While each church may pontificate on the need for diversity and inclusion, American Christianity most often practices archaic methodologies of integration: Non-whites and whites may join our congregations if they look like, act like, speak like and practice the faith like the majority. Otherwise, one is not welcome. As long as most Christian churches continue in this vein, they will never understand the issues of racial injustice that plague the black and brown community, nor will the historic black church understand the struggle of white people to overcome their attachment to individual, institutional and systemic racism. One group desperately needs the other if churches, and society at large, are to achieve the common good.

There are three main inhibitors to the need to address racial justice. The first is using tokenism to address the problem of racial injustice. Too often, majority-white or majority-black churches will recruit "model persons" of a different racial group to as mode of addressing the problem. White churches will seek non-confrontational blacks and Hispanics and say, "See? We are doing something about racial justice because we are an integrated church."

What is not stated is that underneath this evangelistic effort is the mindset that we do not want too many of "them" because they will change our comfortable way of worship and challenge our theological and doctrinal assumptions. That is why white churches may be "disturbed" when black members are angry about the killings of Trayvon Martin, Michael Brown, Clarence Coates or Philando Castile. In the same regard, some black churches shrug off the killing of white police officers in Dallas or the sacrilege committed on Native American sacred ground by an oil pipeline. In many ways, tokenism is more dangerous than segregation, for it assumes that there are acceptable and unacceptable people within racial groups, and members of the majority have the authority to declare which is which. Tokenism only perpetuates a sense of racial superiority.

The second is this idea of gradualism, an approach that assumes that racial equity and equality will happen if we just take our time and move slowly. Gradualism asserts that the church and American society must not make people "uncomfortable" but allow the natural course of history to work out the problems of racial injustice. "Just be patient and pray about it," a gradualist might say. In the meantime, racial injustice remains or worsens. Poor whites, blacks and Hispanics are dehumanized and victimized every day. How can we move slowly if we are "being killed all the day long?"

The third inhibitor to racial justice is the proclivity to maintain the status quo. There are some who'd argue that the status quo is established by God, thus to protest the status quo is to question God. Of course, this is the same argument purported by Nazi Germany, South Africa under apartheid and the United States during slavery and segregation. To end racial injustice, the church, black and white, must loudly protest the killing of black men and women, the unjust deportation of immigrants and acts of atrocity against Native Americans. When the church stands up, things change. I once heard theologian James Cone say that the church must decide if it is going to stand on the side of injustice or on God's side. Standing against racial injustice and challenging the status quo is standing on God's side. The call of Joshua confronts the Church mightily: "Choose ye this day whom you will serve."

There was a time when the historic black church refused to participate in tokenism, gradualism and maintaining the status quo. But since the emergence of "prosperity gospel and ministry," the black church has taken on the characteristics of the oppressor. It opiates its congregation with entertainment and flights of fancy about heaven instead of remembering that the Nazarene commanded that the purpose of the church was to build community and make things "on earth as it is in heaven." Instead a pseudo-theology has become the vogue: To hell with the world, I just want to get to heaven.

There is hope. There are still churches who have not lost sight. They realize that if you want to see God, God can be found in the faces of humanity. When racial injustice exists, the will of God is ignored, and the result is a dead faith, vacuous worship, and the erosion of the human condition.

Sexism needs to be purged from church

June 27, 2017

There is a long and pervasive history of sexism within the Christian church. Christianity, birthed in a patriarchal society, carried this view as the dominant interpretive method of scripture and practice for centuries. Beginning with the early church fathers Augustine and Jerome, particularly, sexism continues. I posit that sexism is one of the greatest challenges to the contemporary church.

The notion that women are inferior to men and, therefore, incapable of leadership in the Church and society defies reason and scripture. Women have proven their capacity for leadership in every vector of society — not that we needed any proof to accept them as equals.

Can anyone in good conscience truly believe that women lack the intellectual and moral ability to be leaders? Apparently so: All too many congregations and church leaders hold fast to an archaic concept of female inferiority.

Some cling to an ancient notion that women are the seed of evil planted in the human predicament by Eve's rebellion in the Garden of Eden. Biblical fundamentalists point to the second creation narrative as proof of the inferiority of women. But if one takes Genesis literally, you have to acknowledge that Adam was present and equally guilty in the Eden incident and that the first creation narrative asserts that God created both women and men in God's image and they both were to be stewards of the earth.

The disturbing question that we refuse to ask is why have we chosen the second narrative and rejected the first? Perhaps the answer lies in sexism and not with God.

A far more sinister concept held by many in the Christian Church is that God intended men to "rule" over women and that to allow women fair and equal opportunities in the leadership of the Church is to be disobedient to the will of God. After all, they say, God is a man and Jesus was a man, so God intended men to rule. The fuzzy logic of this kind of reasoning is obvious but nonetheless dangerous. I suggest that such thinking is theologically bankrupt, demeans the image and likeness of God contained in womanhood, and is used to legitimize physical, psychological and social violence against women. It is even more disturbing to note that some women in churches succumb to this type of thinking and are the most avid and vocal supporters of male dominance in the Christian community.

Carter G. Woodson insisted in his pivotal work, "The Re-Education of the Negro," that there needed to be a re-educational process launched by and for African Americans. Likewise, a re-education of the Church must take place regarding sexism.

Fortunately, some Christian communities have started to address the problem. The United Methodists Church, the African Methodist Episcopal Church, United Church of Christ, the American Baptist Church, the Episcopal Church, the Christian Methodist Episcopal Church, Unitarian Universals, the Disciples of Christ, some Pentecostal sects, and many non-denominational churches are placing women in the role of leadership.

But more needs to be done. Some of the Christian communities I have mentioned will support and employ women as pastors and denominational leaders, but then will send women to tiny congregations where they must lead multiple congregations just to have enough to survive or place them in impossible situations and compel them to be a "superwoman." All the while they give the large, well-staffed congregations to males.

If Christianity is to take its rightful place in the world, churches must grow up, overcome the seduction to patriarchy and confront sexism at every level. We must reject ancient and antiquated ideas about women and their role in the life of the church, and hear what the spirit is saying to the church. Our job as Christians is to tear down every barrier and stronghold that enslaves women or men in the Christian community. Sexism is an evil in our midst and it is our calling to confront and overcome it.

Celebrate American ideals this July 4th

July 4, 2017

It is difficult for many Americans to celebrate Independence Day this year with any patriotic gusto.

Given the increase of divisive rhetoric and action from the Trump Administration, the travel ban, the continued assault on transgendered people, increasing economic disparity, the onslaught against social programs that affect the most vulnerable, and the persistent violence on blacks and other people of color, few people feel like celebrating America's birthday. We all appreciate the holiday, but the lusty expressions of nationalism is absent in many sectors of our society.

And yet I suggest that a celebration of America is exactly what needs to happen. I am not talking about the perverse celebration of "Make America great again." Instead, I am talking about celebrating the great ideas of this democratic experiment.

What ideals should we celebrate? Freedom, for starters. While freedom is not necessarily applied equally throughout society, we are freer than many places in the world. No one can stop my praise or protest of American policy. I am free to worship or not worship, to dream the impossible or hope for the future. The vicissitudes of life do not conquer the ideal of freedom that Independence Day reminds us of.

Freedom comes with a price. Freedom must allow for the senseless oratory of the racist and the malcontent as well as the sensible and the enlightened. Despite the pain such freedom constitutes, I would rather have freedom extended to the irrational than to have freedom suppressed at any level.

One of my fundamental beliefs is that though we must endure foolish tweets, mean-spirited pronouncements of the "alt-right" and other hate groups of every tenor and hue, the universe bends toward truth and justice, and in the end truth will have the last say. On this Independence Day, I celebrate an ideal that unequivocally promises freedom for all.

Independence Day inspires my belief in justice. I am not talking about the justice system or what we understand as justice being administered in most institutions in this country. The type of justice experienced by most Americans is dictated by race, money and status, which, by definition, is a travesty.

I am talking about real justice, where every person is treated with respect and dignity. One of my ethics students recently told me, "Dr. Dawson, with America's history of discrimination and greed, the idealistic society you envision will never happen!" How sad to hear this from the young generation.

The realization of a just society demands two things: a conceptual vision of justice and the commitment to work toward it. I believe the American ideal of a just society can become a reality.

Spare me the discourse about how the framers of the Constitution were racist and sexist. An idea is bigger the writers of the Constitution, political parties and self-interested groups. I believe that most Americans want an America that lives up to its ideals and does not sink to the lowest common denominator.

All of us want our children to be treated fairly, our work to be honored and our elders to live in dignity. The ideal of justice is a bedrock of what is best in us and most hoped. When I celebrate Independence Day, I celebrate a vision of a just society where there truly is "liberty and justice for all."

Men and women from every part of society and every racial group fought and died for the ideals I'm talking about. It is easy to be bitter and discouraged to the point that Independence Day becomes just another day off of work. But I affirm that we should cling to the ideals despite the pain of the past and present.

No society is perfect, but democratic venture called America can be perfected. By holding fast to these ideals, believing enough to envision a new way, and possessing a willingness to work toward that which we hold most dear, we can create a free and just America. Because I believe it, I celebrate Independence Day.

Will you join me?

Violence and the community

July 18, 2017

"And they shall beat their swords into plowshares, and their spears into pruning hooks: neither shall they study war anymore." Isaiah 2:4

Once again senseless violence has stricken the Columbia community. According to the Columbia Missourian, Jamar Lamont Hicks, 26 years old, was shot early Sunday morning near the Break Time convenience store, 2709 E. Broadway. He was pronounced dead shortly after the arrival of medical personnel. Two other persons were also shot, but they are in good condition according to recent reports.

Another young man, who happens to be black, is dead. By report he was a victim of senseless violence. The fact that he was black is of interest to me as a black man in America. However, even more importantly, he was young. My sources report he had children and had recently celebrated the birthday of his mother. Violence turned a time of celebration into mourning and left children without a father.

The stories of violence in America are not new. Every day we hear stories of death and violence in places like St. Louis, Kansas City, Chicago, Detroit, New York and Los Angeles. We Columbians, until now, have thought of these events as something that happens "in other places" but not in Columbia, Missouri. As a resident the First Ward, I hear stories of shootings and violence almost every day. Some are reported, many are not. My ward is one of the wards that gets the most attention regarding violence and shootings, but no area of Columbia is immune from this growing crisis. Whether we recognize it or not, episodes of shootings, violence and death have risen in idyllic Columbia.

Why these happenings should capture our attention is because it is not a black, Anglo, Hispanic or Asian problem. It is not a liberal, moderate or conservative phenomenon. It is a Columbia problem that potentially affects every member of the community. Bullets are equal opportunity entities: They kill people equally, regardless of race, religion or creed. Any of us, at any time, can become the victim of a stray bullet.

We no longer can blame the problem on "outsiders." The fact of the matter is we have home-grown youth of every color and hue aspiring to be gangsters. Too many young people believe shooting someone makes you a "man or a real woman" and going to prison acquires one "street cred." While I do not think there is a causal connection between violence and movies, music and videos, there is at least a strong influential link between violence and what our children and youth listen to and see.

What is also on the rise is a spirit of vigilantism. Most of my neighbors, college students, members of the various churches I speak in are carrying firearms and have weapons in their homes. They have decided that the police cannot stop the rise of violence in Columbia, so they are armed to fight fire with fire. One Anglo senior citizen told me that every member of her reading club carries a firearm. She stated, "Pastor Dawson, Columbia has changed, and we are going to have to change with it. I will not be a victim."

The Mayor's Task Force on Violence wrestled with this problem for two years. They made recommendations to the city manager and city council on how to address the problem. To date, the city manager has failed to implement the recommendations given by the task force. Perhaps this last incident will prompt the city manager and council to place the recommendations at the top of the list of things the council needs to address.

Local government cannot solve the problem alone. Columbia citizens must be proactive if we wish for Columbia to be a safe place to live and rear our children. We must work together for the common good. Neighborhood associations must be strengthened. Churches, mosques, synagogues and communities of faith of all kinds need to form a union of commitment against violence. We must not just care about our individual children but care for all our children, our seniors, our fellow Columbians. Politics reminds us of our differences, but the threat of violence must inspire a united effort to protect our loved ones.

Today a mother mourns for her son, and some children grieve because of the death of their father. One victim lost to violence is a loss for all of us. We, together, can stop the violence that plagues us and we must: Our corporate futures demand that we stop the violence.

Community policing discussion should be driven by grassroots approach

July 25, 2017

Last week, the Columbia City Council voted to table the community policing proposal presented by Fourth Ward Councilman Ian Thomas. While the idea of a community-oriented initiative is a good thing for the whole of Columbia, the proposal demonstrated several flaws as it was presented.

The proposal was top-heavy in its construction. "Expert consultants" were employed to craft the document. Great. But to have outside consultants construct a document for Columbians, at $130 an hour, and not glean knowledge from individuals within Columbia who, too, are experts regarding community policing seems odd to me.

There are several qualified people who not only have the theoretical and educational knowledge to fashion a substantial proposal but also know the history of police-community relations in Columbia. To have a document of this magnitude, we should turn to the people who know Columbia. Experts and theorists have their place, but let us enlist the people in our community who have their lives invested in Columbia.

More people who have been the victims of bad policing need to be heard in the construction of a community policing policy. I am not just referring to people of color but also poor whites who, because they do not "look right," are subjected to abuse and harassment as well.

There is a real distrust of the police in the identified wards in Columbia. Blacks, Hispanics and poor white residents need to be heard about how to construct a productive policing policy for Columbia. I appreciate Thomas' desire to include as many stakeholders as possible, such as the Chamber of Commerce, Columbia Public Schools personnel and the Columbia Police Association.

However, it seems that "the least of these" have been excluded from the conversation, and that is a tragic mistake. The poor, the disenfranchised and the victimized need to be heard as well if the proposal for community-oriented policing is to be more than sounding brass and a tinkling cymbal.

I support a community policing initiative. The Mayor's Task Force on Community Violence called for it, and I agree with them. Mary Ratliff of the Columbia NAACP has called for a community meeting to discuss community policing at the end of August. I hope people from every sector of the Columbia community will show up and voice their concerns and ideas. I also hope someone will show up to say something good about the Columbia Police Department as well. There are many good police men and women on the force. The good things they have done need to be articulated as well. We need to encourage good cops to be even better as well as talk about episodes of bad policing.

My fear is that individuals who need to be heard most will not speak out. Many of my neighbors are intimidated by the powers to be and fear negative reprisal. Some are just disillusioned. Some are so angry about events of the past that they do not believe the historical problem between the police and certain segments the Columbia community will ever be resolved.

Only when we commit to speaking truth to power and working toward the fundamentally new can a better community-police relationship come to fruition. Thank you, Councilman Thomas, for moving on this issue. All of us support the idea of community-oriented policing, we just objected to the initial proposal. We have time to revisit it and make it better.

Let us unite and work toward a better Columbia.

Rediscovering the joy of friendship

August 1, 2017

'A person that hath friends must shew oneself friendly." —Proverbs 18:24a

"One of the most beautiful qualities of true friendship is to understand and to be understood." — Lucius Annaeus Seneca

What is friendship? Last Saturday it was my honor to preach the "homegoing celebration" of my niece's stepmother. At the time of remarks and in conversations with people after the funeral, I heard many talk about how they loved the deceased and what a dear friend she was to them.

In the last five years of her life that she spent in a nursing home, I wondered, how many of them had called her or gone to visit her. Isn't that what a friend would do? It seems that the art of friendship has been muddled and may be lost in our world of social media "friends" and followers. It is sad to think that intelligent men and women would think that most folks on our social media sites are really our friends. Again, what is friendship?

Taking a cue from Aristotle's "Nicomachean Ethics," true friendship requires three components. First, true friendship is grounded in utility: the person is useful to you, and you are useful to the friend. Friends are people you can count on in good times and in bad times. The relationship is reciprocal: you can depend on them, and they can depend on you. Far too many relationships posing as friendship are one directional and parasitic: if you can give them what they want, they claim to be a friend. But when the storms of life are raging, status is lost, or, money and material things are gone, the alleged friendship disappears. Such "good time" friends are not friends at all. They are merely acquaintances.

Second, friendship asserts a mutual affirmation of talents or gifts in the other. True friends find and enthusiastically celebrate the talent of the other. They do not participate in jealousy, nor do they envy the other's gifts. They are each other's cheerleaders and seek ways to help the other develop and prosper. All of us have enough haters and mindless critics. Friends discover ways to encourage, and critique, when necessary, but in love. Friends know how to disagree without being disagreeable.

Third, friends simply enjoy each other's company. Spending time with one another solidifies a friendship. In a consumer society, wealth and power are held in high esteem. But friendship holds one another's presence in the highest regard. They realize that the conversations they share create memories that endure long after death. Friends seek to understand and to be understood.

If I am correct in this portrayal of true friendship, it is not a wonder why most of us have many acquaintances but few friends. Friendship takes work and a commitment of time. Friendship requires risk. If one must show friendliness to have friends, that in turns means we must risk rejection, sorrow, and the willingness to overcome fear. Perhaps that is the reason many people are comfortable with many superficial relationship and avoid creating meaningful friendships. After all, rejection is painful, and it takes time to recover from a broken heart.

I am reminded of a song by the group Whodini that asks, "Friends, how many of us have them, the ones we can depend on?" Perhaps it time for all of us to take stock of who are our real friends and who of our acquaintances are merely perpetrating a fraud.

Hold fast to your real friends. Cultivate those relationships for they will bring forth some of the greatest joys in life. Be friend and you will garner a true friend.

Events of Charlottesville are proof that racism remains

August 15, 2017

"When a person shows you who they really are, believe them." — *Maya Angelou*

Once again one of the ugliest parts of American society has displayed itself again. Last weekend white supremacy groups gathered in Charlottesville, Virginia, to remind us of what is worst in us. Their gathering called "Unite the Right" gave them national coverage to spout their racist, anti-Semitic and homophobic sentiments. While the putrid rhetoric they espoused was bad enough, the senseless death of one of the counter-protestors, Heather Heyer, exacerbated the situation.

We all know that racism abounds in our society. Yet the events of Charlottesville still amaze us. One of my colleagues, who is white, told me that he just didn't want to believe that the rise of white supremacy was "this bad." I guess he thought that people of color who have been trying to call the country to attention to the increase of violence and hate in our society have been making up their outrage or have been making a mountain out of a molehill. The fact is that many Americans believe that racism will go away if we just ignore it, or do not talk about it. Charlottesville reminds us that racism of the worst kind is alive and growing.

I was intrigued by the fact that most of the counter-protesters shown by the media were also white. In some ways the presence of the counter-demonstrators, the immediate denouncement of hate groups by President Trumps' daughter, the outrage voiced by Republicans and Democrats, faith leaders, and others increased my hope that more white Americans are realizing that the Neo-Nazis, alt-right, Ku Klux Klan and other white supremacist groups are not just a threat to Americans of color, non-Christians and the LGBT community. They are a threat to the very fabric and ideals of all Americans. I am encouraged.

However, isn't it interesting that the media and spokespeople from every sector still talk in terms of the demonstration and counter-demonstration as a "protest." I wonder, if most of the counter-demonstrators had been black and brown, would they still have called it a "protest" or would they call it a "riot"? The choice of words is important. Something to think about.

Why are we shocked that President Trump did not denounce the white hate groups by name until Monday? Those groups are part of his base, evidenced by he influence of Steve Bannon. If he denounces the groups, he cuts a deep part of his constituency. At least President Trump did speak on Monday, though it was too late for my taste. He should have been the first person to denounce hate groups, not the fourth. Such is the state of politics in America. We should also not be surprised that Gov. Eric Greitens has not spoken about the NAACP's Travel Advisory regarding Missouri and drivers of color. No politician is going to drive away their supporters unless, under political pressure, one has too.

The most frightening thing regarding what happened in Charlottesville is that the hate groups that showed up in Virginia are also in every state in America. What shall we do about the potential threat they pose to all of us? First, we can pray those who do not support the vehement hatred they articulate will speak out against racism with a greater sense of love and commitment to justice for all.

In the meantime, let us not wait for this evil to take shape. We can work harder for racial justice for the greater good of this society. We can teach our children and grandchildren that racial hatred is wrong, and stop cowardly saying, "Well, that is just the way they are."

We can educate ourselves that we are aware the acts of racial violence in American history and commit ourselves to never allowing them to happen again. The truth of the matter is that if we do not learn how to live together, we shall all die together. And that, ladies and gentlemen, would be the saddest commentary of all: that our prejudices resulted in our destruction.

A tribute to Dick Gregory, who put justice over comedy

August 22, 2017

On Saturday, satirist and social justice warrior Richard Claxton Gregory died in Washington, D.C. He was 84.

I first heard Gregory in the early 1970s as an undergraduate student at Cornell College. I watched and listened to this 95-pound man mesh humor and serious social critique together in a way that made all of us look at America with both reflective criticism and hope. Slowly drawing on his cigarette, he brilliantly forced us to look at ourselves, our failures, our strengths and our potential to transform America. He told the story of how the mayor of St. Louis, his hometown, had given him the key to the city, but later as he attempted to check in at one of the prominent hotels in St. Louis, the hotel refused him lodging because he was black. He quipped, "They gave me the key to the City, but then they changed all the locks." His humor was piercing.

Gregory dedicated his life to social change. He marched with Martin Luther King Jr. in Selma, was arrested and brutally beaten in Birmingham, was a prominent voice in protesting the war in Vietnam. He was one of the first people to say we should protest the war, but love the Vietnam veterans for their courage and sacrifice. Unfortunately, we did not listen.

In 1999, he was diagnosed with lymphoma cancer. He rejected chemotherapy and centered himself in holistic medicine. He treated himself with vitamins, an herb-filled diet and exercise. His cancer was arrested. His commitment to plant-based foods and exercise served as the birthing ground for what was later called "the Bahamian Diet." Health and nutrition was a center point of his work.

His dedication to social justice came with a price. His earlier days as a comedian was confined to African American clubs. But eventually, Gregory broke the color line and performed in the white clubs in San Francisco, New York and Chicago. Gregory writes in his autobiography, "I've got to go up there as an individual first, a Negro second. I've got to be a colored funny man, not a funny colored man."

His accomplishment in being "a colored funny man" brought him a lucrative income. His commitment to protest and social activism meant white club owners avoided booking him as regularly as other comedians. If there was a conflict between a performance and an opportunity to support a just cause, standing for the right was more important to him than doing a stand-up comedy show. The choices he made, however, resulted in a loss of income. He was forced to sell his 400-acre Plymouth, Massachusetts, home and move into an apartment with his wife and 10 children. It was a painful transition, but one he was willing to endure for the cause of social justice. For Gregory, some things were more important than money.

Socrates once said that an unexamined life is not worth living. Gregory forced us to examine our corporate and individual lives. With humor and poignancy, he compelled us to examine who we have been, who we are now, and envision who we can be in the future. There are many people who make me proud to be a Missourian and Dick Gregory is one of them.

Rest in peace, Mr. Gregory, and thank you for your lessons on living the examined life.

Community meeting misses voices of the underprivileged

Aug 29, 2017

Last week, I attended, along with about 200 other people, the community policing meeting at Second Baptist Church, sponsored by the Columbia Branch of the NAACP. Not only were the mayor, city manager, chief of police, and members of the City Council present, but there was also a wide variety of interested citizens in attendance. I encourage you to read George Kennedy's account of the event for a more detailed perspective.

I was very happy with this meeting being called. I was glad that the Second Baptist Church opened its doors to host the crowd. I was inspired that Mary Ratliff and members of the Columbia NAACP, along with Traci Wilson-Kleekamp and members of Race Matters, Friends, worked collaboratively on the meeting agenda. I was encouraged by the presence of city leaders. I applauded City Council members for coming out and listening. It was good that representatives of the faith community were in place.

Some very good things happened at the meeting.

I was disappointed, however, that a significant population of Columbia was absent: The people most affected by police profiling and who greatly need to be heard in regards of creating a community policing philosophy.

am talking about the people in public housing, on or near Greensboro Drive, Demaret Drive, and Garth Avenue, or those in the neighborhoods of Sexton and Wilkes. The professional and intellectual elite greeted the attendees, facilitated the meetings, articulated their plans, concerns, and ideas very well. I appreciate the gifts of the middle and upper-class. But those voices that needed to be heard most were not present.

To compound matters, people who are most in tune with the plight of the poor and disenfranchised in Columbia were not placed as central voices. People like the Rev. Brad Bryant from Wilkes Boulevard United Methodist Church, Glen Cobbins, or, the Rev. Marcus Reynolds, the Director of Turning Point — they all could have leny their perspective more prominently.

I respect those who facilitated, opened the meeting and made it happen. I have ultimate respect for Mary Ratliff. She has stood as a soldier for justice when some of the very people who benefited most from her work and sacrifice wouldn't and didn't even say "thank you." At her personal, financial, and emotional expense, she has stood against injustice when many were saying to her, "sit down and shut up."

Justice can no longer be the private mission of any one group, whether it is NAACP, Race Matters, Friends, the Mayor's Task Force on Violence. To overcome the problem within our community, "the least of these among us" need to be heard and acknowledged.

If a meaningful philosophy of community policing is to be enacted, intersectionality must be at the center of the work. I thank the middle-class blacks and whites at the meeting for their voices. They need to be heard. But the rest need to be heard also.

If we ignore the validity of their lived experiences, we are only engaging in self-righteous navel-gazing.

9/11 a milestone moment, as a person and as a people

September 12, 2017

On Monday, I celebrated 40 years of being an ordained minister. My ordination was a day of great joy. Surrounded by friends and family, I took on the challenge of being a proclaimer and practitioner of hope, love and justice with awe and a heightened sense of responsibility. I have experienced much in 40 years.

Ministry for me has been a composite of success and failure, victory and defeat, potency and weakness. Forty years later, I still count it a privilege to have been a pastor to thousands, and I consider it an honor that so many people have allowed me to "meet them where they are along life's way."

This Monday, however, I wept as I remembered the horror of 16 years ago when the World Trade Center and the Pentagon were attacked. The date is of personal significance to me, as two of my Princeton classmates were killed that day.

This horror was not new to me; I have experienced terrorism many times in my life. My great uncle was lynched by the White Citizens Council. I witnessed my mother have feces and urine poured on her at a march in Skokie, Illinois. The KKK burned a cross on our front yard while I was in high school.

I have endured a homemade bomb explosion at my home, watched the police try to intimidate citizens of my community, been shot at twice and have had to survive the indignities all people of color must endure daily. I know terrorism.

Yet, 9/11 was a day different from anything I had experienced. I believed that I was safe and secure from foreign enemies in America.

We were all awakened from that illusion. During my remembrance, I mourned for my classmates and their families. Now, I realized that all of us could be attacked by enemies both domestic and foreign at any time and at any place.

Combining these two events on the same day makes for strange bedfellows and mixed emotions.

Since I believe that all we experience in life prepares us to rise to the next level of personal development, I asked myself, "What have I learned from these experiences? What can make me and us better?"

I learned that no person or country is immune from suffering. We all must experience it. The question is not whether we will experience tragedy, but how will we handle it?

When it comes to how we treat others, will we see all who do not look like, act like, pray like or speak like us as the enemy?

While tragedy struck on 9/11, I watched Americans of every color, race and creed come together. While that has not lasted, it does demonstrate how we are capable of unity. The choice is ours.

The same is true within Christianity. We can be the most supportive, encouraging people in the world; or we can be the most hateful, judgmental folk who have walked the planet. We have the option to be bridge-builders or stone-throwers.

We have not looked or acted very well lately. Perhaps remembering 9/11 will cause us to commit to being the best we can be, instead of sinking to the lowest common denominator. I hope we choose to be the best. That is my choice.

Fierce conversations are long overdue on police and racism

September 19, 2017

Here we go again. After the acquittal of St. Louis police officer Jason Stockley, who shot to death 24-year-old Lamar Smith, they city has erupted in protest.

Someone asked me, "Why are people so upset?" After all, the police have a right to protect themselves when they feel threatened. Police officers do indeed have the right to defend themselves when they are in danger.

The problem is that defense is not an excuse for excessive force. Isn't interesting that not one officer has been convicted of killing a black or brown youth? One person speaking with me with passionate clarity stated that the reason so many black youths have been killed by the police is that these youths are combatant and fail to respond to the police rightly. In order words, it is their fault they were killed.

I remember a story about a lynching in Mississippi. The perpetrator stated that the man would not have been hanged if he hadn't been standing by the tree. The story sounds disgustingly familiar.

The most blind among us can see that all the police officers charged with criminal violence against black youths were not justified, and the case of Stockley and Smith case is supremely suspicious. When I asked the man, what should people of color do when they feel threatened particularly by the police, he was thunderously mute. When caught in false clarity, the result is often silence.

This brings me to Columbia Police Chief Ken Burton's interview in the Columbia Missourian. Many critics of Burton want to label him as a racist. Perhaps. I try to be cautious about calling someone racist. Most whites from his generation who have not done the hard work of understanding race and racism are negatively racist. This is not an excuse, just a fact of American life.

In opposition to some of my fellow blacks here, I do not think all Columbia police officers are racist. I do think that all of them, including Burton, need serious training and education. As the chief of police and as a fellow Columbian, Burton needs to do the work. He needs to understand what the data is saying and embrace it. He must stop having his feelings hurt because of the hard conversations that need to be heard. Having a conversation with Mary Ratliff is not good enough to understand the problem.

All of us must not only address the problem of racial injustice and racial profiling, we must also be about understanding and dismantling the material conditions that create the problem in the first place. Racism is not merely of the heart and one's feelings, it is also systemic and institutional. If the leadership does not begin to understand this, what hope do we have that the rank and file will understand it?

I hope at the next community meeting called by the NAACP that we will not be seduced into being gentle speaking blacks and modest white sophisticates, but truly enter tough, hard conversations about what is needed to be a better community. Sometimes these conversations are painful, but — pardon the chiché — no pain, no gain. It is time to move beyond the boundaries of false clarity and build a beloved community.

Acts of evil put value of life in focus

October 3, 2017

I awoke this morning to tragedy. Once again, we are exposed to senseless violence. The latest report coming out of Las Vegas is that 59 or more people have been killed with hundreds wounded while attending a concert on the Las Vegas Strip.

The alleged assailant, Stephen Paddock, 64, killed himself before police could apprehend him. The Las Vegas shooting surpassed the attack in Miami as the largest mass killing in modern U.S. history. President Trump called this tragedy, "an act of pure evil." There seems to be a lot of acts of pure evil every day.

Last week, we were consumed with worry and concern about our fellow citizens in Puerto Rico. Will they have enough food and water to survive? Can the military help so many that need so much? Why has the assistance to Puerto Rico been so slow? The questions go on seemingly without answers. Many people wonder if the population of Puerto Rico was majority white instead of black and brown would the response been so slow. But before any of these questions can be answered, another crisis emerges.

There are lots of acts of pure evil all around us. The mayhem in Charlottesville, Virginia, the beating of an African-American clergyman in St. Louis, the killings of black youth by the police across the country, the growing violence against transgendered people, and the plain old ugliness perpetrated in American society daily.

I heard a preacher say that we are reaping God's wrath because of our sinful ways. That is an easy — but fallacious — response to these events.

These events remind us that evil can be equal opportunity destroyer. What affects one of us, affects all of us. We can no longer pretend that our wealth, status, race, creed, intellect or sexuality make us immune from the manifestation of evil in the world.

Maybe something else is happening with us as human beings. What is unquestionable is that these events are forcing us to acknowledge that we need each other.

Isn't it interesting that when tragedy happens, we forget our differences and rally to one another's assistance? It is sad that it takes chaos and destruction to shake us from our self-centeredness and into fulfilling our fundamental character as human beings.

We need each other for comfort, empowerment and completeness. German philosopher Edmund Husserl suggested that death has a way of making us place our priorities in order. One of our first priorities is each other. After all, no individual is complete without a community.

Our government should learn from that truth and put people first. Instead of tax cuts for the rich, or using tax money for private jets, how about placing funding more mental health treatment? Better mental health care may have saved lives in Las Vegas, Miami, Colorado and other places we now remember because of the acts of evil that occurred there.

Perhaps, if we stop being obsessed with former President Barack Obama and Obamacare, stop trying to prevent NFL athletes from exercising their constitutional right to protest, and quit acting like a 4-year-old with North Korea, we can be about the real business of caring for people regardless of race, creed or color.

My frustration with the black church

October 10, 2017

I begin my mornings with meditation, reflection, and prayer. During my routine, I watch Bishop T.D. Jakes at 6:30 a.m.

I do not agree with many of his ideological and theological assumptions, but recently he preached about frustration, and it caused me to reflect deeply.

Like so many in this country, I am frustrated. I am frustrated by the socio-political division that is so obvious to many and oblivious to others. Even before Swedish researcher Gunnar Myrdal articulated the connection between race and American life, we have been painfully aware that America is a country of at least two nations: one black and one white.

I had hoped that unity between the two would become a reality in my lifetime. I am no longer sure. The racial disparity between whites and blacks has worsened. Part of the reason is that we refuse to recognize that racism cannot be dismantled by the infamous "getting to know you" mindset.

Racism is a three-tiered phenomenon: It is personal, systemic and institutional. Unless our attempts to dismantle racism address each level, we will continue to live with what Gunnar Myrdal called the "American dilemma."

I am frustrated with the lack of vision and commitment to liberation found in too many African-American churches, which were not only established to be places of worship, but also to be part of Christ's call "to set the captive free."

It was to be a vehicle for liberation from oppression and bondage within the human condition: spiritual, social, economic, psychological and political.

It was within this institution that the history of black people was to be rehearsed and remembered, an inclusive theology to be constantly expanded and placed at the forefront, and a sense of hope was to be proclaimed.

Nowadays, the contemporary African-American church, in too many cases, has sold its birthright as a liberator, to an insensitive, inauthentic, evangelicalism which is crushing the historic church, and producing an exclusive, elitist, navel-gazing church in "blackface."

We have become the oppressor's child, copying his theology, worshipping his agenda, and substituting our God-given mandate and mission to become an entertainment center rather than an empowering bulwark. Subsequently, we have focused on going to Heaven while our people are living in hell.

I am frustrated with the senseless violence that has gripped every community in this country. It is violence that saps our internal strength, whether in Las Vegas or Columbia.

The question remains: Do we as Americans hate ourselves so much that we would rather kill one another than help one another achieve the potential for individual good and corporate well-being? I hate hearing my grandchildren and their friends talk more about their fears of being shot or killed more than their aspirations for the future.

The violence we are experiencing in American society is killing not just fellow citizens, it is wreaking havoc on our children's and grandchildren's dreams. For that reality, history will not hold us blameless.

What I have learned is that frustration starts with investment. I am invested in trying to help create a beloved community that is black, white, Latino, LGBT, old, young, male and female.

Because we have invested the best that we are in this enterprise, frustration arises. Frustration comes from having an expectation. I expect people to be human and compassionate; to seek how to be one instead of more ways to be fractured.

I expect my government to put people first. I expect the president to give real aid to Puerto

Rico and not throw hand-towels. I expect churches to lead and not make excuses. My frustration stems from the fact that people can be better than the ways we act.

Yet, amid my frustration, I have hope. I choose to hope for the fundamentally new within this society. I hope for a day that violence will cease and mutual care will prevail. I hope that one day in America, racism will be truly dismantled and sexism and homophobia will be a sad chapter of our past instead of our present. I hope one day I will experience the black church taking its rightful place in the African-American community and society. I hope.

One presidential choice is clearly dangerous

October 11, 2017

The past weeks have produced both awe and disgust as we observe the presidential race. Republican candidate Donald Trump has caused us to speak like Alice in Lewis Carrol's novel as things just get "curiouser and curiouser!"

We now know that Donald Trump has avoided paying taxes by taking advantage of loopholes in the tax system and brags about being a genius, has repeatedly spoken about women in the most pejorative ways and calls it simply "locker room talk," and will leave his running mate Mike Pence "hanging" in a public debate when Syria is discussed. While the second presidential debate may have solidified Trump's base, it did little to bring thinking Americans closer to him in this race.

According to the latest CNN polls, Hillary Clinton has won both debates, but she has been less than dazzling. Her bone-headed mistake regarding the infamous emails still causes great concern for many Americans. Clinton is not the orator her husband was and that has in many ways hurt her in the eyes of the public. Many consider her "stiff" and "robotic," though obviously knowledgeable.

When Trump first announced his candidacy for president, I thought it was a joke. The joke is not funny. It is baffling that so many support him in the race. I will not make the mistake of calling his supporters "deplorable," but they really worry me. Is the motto "Make America Great Again" so compelling for some Americans that they would be willing to trust the country to a racist, sexist, Islamophobic, irrational man who thinks about himself more than anyone else? Clearly the answer is yes.

It is crystal clear that Clinton is more knowledgeable of both international and domestic affairs than Trump. His claim to "bring companies back to America" is simply foolish wishful thinking. No one tells multinational corporations what to do, and the only incentive for them to return to America is money.

Unless American workers are willing to work at the salaries of fellow workers in Mexico, Indonesia and Honduras (just to name three), these large companies are not bringing jobs back to America. American workers are not going to work for such low wages — nor should they. Such is the plight of capitalism — the rich get richer, the poor continue to get poorer, and Americans get left behind for the almighty dollar.

Underneath the Trump-mania, I wonder if the real cause of support is the resentment of the fact that President Barack Obama was elected twice. Without question, anti-black racism has risen in this country in direct proportion to the rise of Trump. President Obama took this country from one of its lowest socio-economic levels in its history to a qualitatively superior level in spite of a stubbornly resistant and disrespectful Republican Congress. Yet he and Michelle are constantly the butt of cruel racist cartoons and statements. What ever happened to giving someone credit for a job well done?

As the presidential campaign continues, I hope that America does not choose Trump. I think we will all regret him as president of this country. Clinton may make major gaffes of judgment, but she is not dangerous.

Donald Trump, I believe, is dangerous. We must not be seduced by the emotionalism of his rhetoric.

A principle of compassion should guide our lives, politics

October 17, 2017

Everyone I speak with is concerned about the racial, economic, and spiritual divide that continues to worsen every day.

These people come from various racial groups, economic levels, educational backgrounds and different communities of faith. All acknowledge we are a divided society, and yet all of us are in a quandary about what we should do about the problem. Should we protest more, pray more, seek better economic programs? Is the root of the problem eradicated by either Adam Smith or Karl Marx? Will being more religious or nonreligious make things better? One person suggested to me that investing in more complex technology will settle the issue. I doubt that very seriously.

Public intellectual and social critic bell hooks suggested in the essay "Love as the Practice of Freedom" that what is necessary for us to overcome our divisions is for members of this society to "adopt an ethic of love."

She is right. She is not talking about some mushy sentimentality or a embarking on the quest to reach Utopia. Instead, she is pointing to a commitment to embrace an ethical norm which asserts that the mutual care and concern about another's well-being is worthy to practice and affirm. It is the acclamation that we ought to help Puerto Rico, the homeless, our neighbor next door and the ex-felon because they are fellow human beings!

The struggles we all endure daily can harden our spirits, causing us to distance ourselves from each other. The daily hardening comes in many forms: the rude young person or senior at the store, the insensitive teacher who gets perturbed because you asked a question, the arrogant minister who wants you to "love the sermon" but will not shake your hand, the driver on the cell phone who cuts you off in traffic and makes you speak in "tongues" that are not holy, and the ungrateful child or spouse that always wants but is slow to give. Consequently, we start to question one another's motives, we engage in character assassination or dismantling another's legacy. Without compassion, we threaten, bully and coerce others, perhaps on social media these days, to get our way. All these things and more become common occurrences, from the national level to our communities, when we do not adopt a principle of love and compassion.

I understand that what hooks, Gautama Buddha, Jesus, and other moral leaders preach is easier said than done. We all have feelings and memory. We are aware of the ways we have been cruel to each other. We know it on a personal and universal level. Once a person has been truly hurt, it is difficult to incorporate an idea of compassion for others. It is easy to become bitter and not want to be bothered with anyone's predicament or situation. It is hard to be passionate when you are being treated dispassionately on many sides.

Yet, adopting a principle of compassion is possible and necessary if we are ever going to be more than a divided and contentious democracy. A shift must take place among us, else we shall crumble and fall as a nation. Our greatest threat is not the enemies outside our borders, but the growing hostilities that are within this society. The possibility lies in forgiving as we want to be forgiven, and accepting as we want acceptance. The necessity is obvious if we desire the common good.

Adopt a principle of compassion so that all of us may live well and live better.

Behind inequality, greed is the real enemy

October 31, 2017

"Take some more tea," the March Hare said to Alice, very earnestly.

"I've had nothing yet," Alice replied in an offended tone, "so I can't take more."

"You mean you can't take less," said the Hatter: "it's very easy to take more than nothing." - Lewis Carroll, Alice in Wonderland

Most people would agree that greed is one of the most pernicious forces we face in American society and the world community.

I am defining greed as an inordinate desire for the possession of something. We generally recognize it as an excessive eagerness to accumulate wealth and obtain money. Aristotle was correct in saying that greed, as an activity, has no real aim except acquisition itself.

One of the problems with greed is that it is insatiable. When seduced by greed, one can never buy enough things or ever have enough money. Have you noticed that all of us are constantly battling with the temptation of "the more the better?" Modern society judges people by how much they have, or by a person's power to obtain material things.

Think about the last time you attended a gathering of people and someone asked you, "What do you do for a living?" It is a question that assesses your ability to consume. The assumption is the more you can consume, the more important you are.

Greed leads to the devaluing of people. Clearly, greed drives the economic gap between the rich and the poor in this country.

Writing for Huffington Post, Gary Reber, founder of For Economic Justice, explains how the quest for profit means taking people out of the equation: "The real problem, which is the cause of the accelerated growth of economic inequality, is that the system, as presently structured, empowers a narrow group of Americans to concentrate ownership of wealth-creating, income-producing capital assets — the non-human factor of production (primarily productive structures, machines, tools, super-automation, robotics, digital computerized operations, etc.). Productive capital is non-human and is the result of technological progress, which never ceases to march forward as it makes jobs in every sector of the economy more scarce."

Conservatives insist that the economy is better under the current administration. They point to the unemployment rate as proof that we are on an upswing. What many forget is the unemployment percentage does not account for the number of people who are still unemployed who have exhausted their benefits, nor does the report show the vast numbers of people who are woefully underemployed. These people and their experiences of poverty are not represented, but are rather a forgotten piece of statistical data. Their humanity is devalued.

Greed lies at the heart of the problem: the greed of the wealthy is eradicating the middle class and dooming the underclass to a generational curse of repeated poverty. The greed of employers causes employees to work more for less, and the seductive power of greed has created staggering credit card debt as well as making "rent to own" piracy a growing and lucrative business.

The evil of greed is not only being felt in this generation but among our youth as well. One of my grandchildren wanted a pair of $200 sneakers. His father almost bought them for him until he realized his son cannot shoot, pass or dribble! We are rearing a generation of youth that also want more and more and feel entitled to such.

What can we do about this? Maybe the answer is simpler than we think.

My conservative religious friends say we need a spiritual transformation to be liberated from the power of greed. That will take care of the problem on the personal level, but it does not address the systemic and institutional perpetuation of greed. We need to challenge the structures that create the material conditions that makes greed monstrous.

Unless we find a way to curb insatiable greed, we shall experience a hideous and barren future. There was a great saying — often attributed to Mahatma Gandhi — "Live simply that others may simply live."

Adopting this in every level of society would be a start.

Safety, civility are also casualties in Sutherland Springs

November 7, 2017

The horrific massacre in Sutherland Springs, Texas, leaves us all stunned and saddened. The current report states 26 people were killed and at least 20 people have been wounded. It is reportedly the largest mass killing in modern Texas history. More and more we are being shaken by senseless acts of violence. It seems even more frightening that such violence would happen at a church.

Potential motives and explanations have been presented. They run the gamut: psychological, interpersonal, spiritual. The problem is that none of these help us reconcile the fact that people in a place of worship would experience that kind of tragedy.

After all, the place where Christians worship is called "the sanctuary" — by definition, it is a safe place. But for the nine members of the African Methodist Episcopal Church in Charleston, South Carolina, or for the 26 worshippers killed in Texas, the sanctuary was not safe.

Once at a church in Detroit, we were robbed at gunpoint after collecting the offering. Fortunately, no one was killed. For years, the psychological effect of that event haunted me. I would dream about it. I started carrying a 9 mm with me to church. I would pray the blessing over the collection with my eyes open.

Fear held me captive for years. I cannot imagine the horror one would feel after watching fellow church attendees shot and killed in front of their eyes.

There used to be a time that people had a respect for the church. Congregants could feel free of molestation, theft or murder. The people I grew up with would say,"If I can just get to the house of prayer, everything will be alright."

But now going to church can be as dangerous as going to a concert, school or a club. For far too many in our society, they are the same: entities not worthy of respect.

Also lost is a respect for life. In my youth and in my community, if a person killed another person, there was at least a reason: breaking in my house, trying to steal my property, or protecting myself and family from the KKK and other unjustified acts of aggression, and the like. Now we are experiencing random killing and mayhem. We have become insensitive to the right of life.

I am not talking about the confused rhetoric of the anti-abortionists. I am talking about the callous manner that we as human beings think about the lives of others who do not look like us, worship like us, speak or dress like us. Sometimes it is racially or religiously centered, and sometimes it is economically and class-driven. But always it is a total disregard for life.

What is wrong with us? What happened to the common thinking that every life is precious? This is not about gun control — bad people who want guns will find them. This is about a lack of self-control within us: from road rage, to the death of the 26 in Texas, to the killings of young black men by the police, to the heartless deportation of Latinos.

We must restore a sense of common civility. We are living, acting and speaking at one of the lowest levels possible in this society. We cannot blame President Trump. He only has opened the door to being divisive and hateful. No, the problem that creates the events like those in South Carolina or Texas or Las Vegas is within us all.

My prayers go out for the victims, families and friends of the Sutherland Springs massacre. My prayers go out for the victims of senseless violence everywhere. I pray for you and for me.

Put complaints aside and find your reasons to be thankful

November 21, 2017

It is so easy to complain. We complain about what we don't have and envy what others possess. We worry about the future and curse ourselves and others about the past.

Honed and nurtured in a consumer society, we are always looking for whatever corporate America models as the newest and most stylish. The more we have, the more we want, and the more we want, the more we complain. It is time to step out of the rat race, reflect and give thanks.

I was sharing this sentiment to several people on Sunday. They tepidly agreed that we should be grateful, and in the next breath, they went on a 20-minute tirade about what was wrong with America, with themselves, with how the youth do not have respect for traditions, with the judicial system, with racism, and on and on.

I quietly asked what they were doing to address these problems, and to my alarm they said, "Nothing." After all, the problems are too big, and the people in power do not care.

They were content to just complain.

All of us are aware of the problems in this society and the troubles in life. None are immune from things that create weal and woe. Sometimes it seems we experience more woe than weal. And yet, there are many things for which we ought to give thanks.

First, we are alive. Many philosophers have argued it is better to exist than not to exist, and it is better to live at a higher form than a lesser form. I agree with this, because in existence we have choices. To have choices is autonomy. In life, I hear the birds sing and experience the chill of fall turning to winter. I may not have all the choices I want, but it is better than no choices. Life gives me the opportunity to experience friends and foe. I welcome both. My friends bring me joy, and my haters keep me praying. I am thankful for life's experiences.

I am thankful for family. I have a wife who loves me and children and grandchildren who love and respect me. Watching my grandchildren discover the world makes me see it with a new sense of wonder and awe. Watching my children develop and grow as adults gives me hope for the future. Hope is precious, and beyond value. I am thankful for awe, hope and wonder.

I am thankful for a living faith. My ultimate reality helps me make sense out of nonsense, see people as part of the human family, and frees me from the quagmire of difference and otherness. Faith reminds me that if I stand on the side of justice, though deterred, justice will win in the end. My faith says the universe bends toward justice.

I am grateful that I can do what I love: write, teach and preach. I watch people go to jobs they cannot stand, and yet every day I have the rare privilege to create and produce something of meaning. I have a new book on race forthcoming. I get to challenge young and older minds to think outside the box and commit to excellence. I can see peoples' lives transformed by "the foolishness of preaching." For this I give thanks.

If we take the time to reflect, each of us have much to be thankful for this Thanksgiving. Take a moment, breathe deeply and give thanks.

Effective youth program deserves community support

December 12, 2017

There are several programs in Columbia that demonstrate the best of who we are. One such program is Fun City Youth Academy of Columbia. For more than 40 years, it has engaged area youth and their parents in academic, cultural and recreational programs that promote academic achievement, self-respect and social responsibility.

Fun City offers year-round programming with Saturday Academy during the school year and Summer Academy for eight weeks during the summer break.

Next year will be the sixth consecutive summer that Fun City and Columbia Public Schools have partnered to offer the Summer Academy, a program which combats "summer fade" by helping students retain the skill levels they attained during the school year.

Literacy is the focus and is taught by CPS Sensation staff in the morning and FCYA staff in the afternoon.

In the past, Fun City has not required afternoon staff to be certified teachers. This year, however, three out of the five teachers hired by FCYA were certified to teach in Missouri. Next summer, Fun City intends to hire only certified teachers. FCYA staff provide hands-on, minds-on activities in science, art, African-American heritage, money management and more. Additionally, students receive free breakfast, lunch, snack and have a safe, individualized, structured, fun and affirming place to go on weekdays.

Many working parents use the Summer Academy as reliable childcare service.

This summer, we served 89 students and their families; 71 percent percent of our students were members of single-parent families and nearly 87 percent of students qualified for free or reduced lunch.

The Summer Academy serves a very diverse group of students.

This year's demographics show that the students were 65 percent African American, 26 percent multiracial, 4 percent white, 3 percent Latino, 2 percent Asian.

Many Columbians have benefited from the programs Fun City provides.

My children and grandchildren have participated in Fun City and the results were outstanding.

Fun City reports that 67 percent of their students increase their reading skills with 68 percent improve their math skills.

I know that my children improved academically, and I bet others can claim the same. Fun City's Program Director Bonnie Yantzi has done a tremendous job, and she deserves our support.

This is the month for giving. I am asking individuals, civic organizations, and churches to financially support the program of Fun City.

Fun City does not receive United Way support, so all our gifts are important. Individual gifts are tax-deductible.

In the spirit of giving, please support Fun City. It is an investment in our children.

To donate, go to funcityyouthacademy.org and look for the "Contribute" page.

Christmas: a reminder to practice peace, goodwill

December 19, 2017

It is difficult sometimes to possess a correct spirit during this holiday time. I am not talking about a religiosity that is exclusively unique to Christianity. While I affirm African-American Christianity as my personal practice, the spirit of this time is greater than any individual religion.

All the main religions of the world share a similar spirit when observing their "holy days." What is the universal spirit to which I am referring? It is the spirit of peace and goodwill toward all. That is the real message of Christmas. Somewhere along the way, the message has been lost.

Nowadays, Christmas is about crass materialism, in the words of Ice Cube, "simple and plain." We are obsessed with how big the Christmas tree is, how many lights we can show off, and of course, how many expensive presents are under the tree on Christmas morning. I love sharing gifts — I like receiving and giving. But when that becomes the focus of the holidays, the spirit of the season is lost. In the end, we are left with a sense of emptiness, indebtedness and despair.

I suggest that if we look at the story of Christmas without religious hostility, doctrinal explanations and all the traditional stuff that clouds our reflection, we see something quite different from what we experience these days.

The story is about a poor family, caught in the throes of suspicion and ridicule, and in the worst possible circumstances, that gives life to a child whose very presence says to the world that the ultimate reality is with us: Jewish, Gentile, Christian, non-Christian, black, white, male and female. And, given that fact, we can hope for "peace on earth and goodwill among all."

The spirit of the season is a lived hope. Hope is not wishful thinking. Hope demands that the conditions of the hope have a chance to be materialized. Wishful thinking is just that — wishing without the possibility of it ever becoming a reality. When one watches the news for one day, it is easy to think that the hope for peace and goodwill among us is just wishful thinking. There is so much violence, pain, division, and devastation all around us. The fires in California remind us that you can be on the top of the world one day and sleeping in a shelter the next. In every corner of the earth there is conflict — at home and abroad. So, can we really hope in the spirit of peace and goodwill among us all?

One of the things I have learned over the years is that the spiritual must be grounded in the social, or it makes no sense. If "spiritual truths" are only about going to heaven, they are useless. All spiritual truths have a practical aspect. Advocating for peace and goodwill is in our hands. When we stop being "peace-seekers" and become "peace-makers," the peace of this season will become a reality. If we want goodwill, we must practice goodwill. It seems so simple, yet it also seems to be so difficult for us to do.

This season, let us think more about how we can be the conduits for peace and goodwill. Let us rise above political bickering and pseudo-intellectual pretentiousness and be about the business of transforming hope into reality.

To you and yours: Peace on earth, and goodwill among us all.

2018

Suggestions for improving ourselves and our world

January 9, 2018

It is the time of year that we make resolutions. January always causes us to ponder areas in our lives that need improvement. We resolve to eat better, work out more, save more than we spend, etc. Indeed, these are noble and worthy goals. Like last year, I present to you some things that you might want to add to your list. My hope is that these suggestions will improve who we are, and the world around us.

1. Reconnect with a friend or family member you have not communicated with lately. When was the last time you talked to your old high school classmate, or spoke to your aunt? In reconnecting, two things usually happen: you find out how life has presented all of us with some strange events, good and bad; and, how we have survived no matter our lot. Reconnecting has a way of reminding us that we are products of our personal history. Reconnecting has a way of blessing you and giving you the opportunity to be a blessing to someone else.

2. Forgive someone. Life is so short. Why hold on to hatred and bitterness when joy can be acquired simply by saying (and meaning it!), "I forgive you."

3. Encourage someone. All of us have ugly, negative people around us. It is easy to fall into negativity when constantly bombarded by it. Do not be a hater. Strive to encourage someone every day. Lift up others, even when it seems that others are slow to encourage you. And, when others do not encourage you, encourage yourself.

4. Read something that inspires greatness in you. Great books are great for a reason. They have inspired women and men from every walk of life. If you do not like the classics, read contemporary literature. But whatever you do, avoid garbage. If we are what we eat, we also become what we read.

5. Pray/meditate more, curse and complain less. The physical benefits of prayer and meditation are without question. A routine of prayer/meditation lowers blood pressure, strengthens heart functions and aids brain activity. Cursing and complaining do the opposite and accomplish nothing. The choice is obvious.

6. Engage in acts of random kindness. I said this last year, but it is worth repeating. It really is nice to be nice. Somewhere along the line we have lost the importance of kindness. Somehow, we must reclaim the idea that kindness is a necessary part of being human. Kindness must be extended not only to family and friends, but to the stranger and particularly the "aliens in our midst!"

7. For 30 days in a row, tell your beloved that you love them. We ought to tell our beloved "I love you" every day. But life can immerse us in routine and we forget. So, for 30 days, tell your beloved you love them by voice, card, text, crayon, something. Watch what happens!

8. Recommit to non-violence. If nothing else, the death of young Mr. Anthony Warren is a grim reminder that we must commit to non-violence. Mr. Warren was a bystander who loss his life by a stray bullet. Bullets have no names on them. They just kill. Guns are not the only weapons we use to commit violence. The most lethal are our tongues. Here's a non-violent pledge that's adaptable: "I won't harm you with words from my mouth, nor weapons of my hands, I love you, I need you to survive."

9. Create something. When was the last time you wrote a poem, or a song, created something with your hands, baked your special cake, or enrolled in a calligraphy class? One of the ways, as humans, we are in the image and likeness of God is that we are creators. Be like God, go create.

10. Play more. A couple of weeks ago I noticed that my grandsons did not know how to wrestle. Well, I got down on the floor and we had a free-for-all wrestling session. We laughed, talked stuff and played. I realized that I had not played for a long time. I play chess daily online. But I do not play chess for fun — it is serious with me! When was the last time you played something just for fun? If it takes you more than a moment to remember, it has been too long. This year let the child in you come out and play.

It's time to move beyond dreaming and do the work before us

January 16, 2018

Once again all over America we will reflect on Martin Luther King Jr.'s "I Have a Dream" speech. It is the most remembered speech of this great orator and visionary. I asked my class last week, "Can someone tell another speech Dr. King gave during his time?" No one knew any of his other speeches. One student did mention the Letter from the Birmingham Jail, which pleased me.

I doubt that my class is different from most Americans: everyone knows The Dream speech, few remember the Letter from the Birmingham Jail, a small contingent is aware of "Drum Major Instinct," "The American Dream," "Give Us the Ballot'" or any other of King's speeches.

I think it is because The Dream speech gives us warm feelings, is easy to articulate, and is fun to superficially contemplate. It is easy to attend a diversity breakfast, or a MLK Day Celebration, hold hands at the end, sing "We Shall Overcome" and believe we have fundamentally addressed the "race problem" of America. We have not.

The fact of the matter is that America is divided and becoming more so every day. We are more fractured now than we were in the Civil Rights Era. At least during the time of King, we had a sense of consciousness and community. Anglo-Americans and African-Americans realized that the ways things were was wrong.

Nowadays, we don't say X or Y is wrong. Grounded in our pseudo-sophistication we say, Joe or Jane may act wrongly, but objective wrong and evil doesn't exist. But in the days of the "movement," we unequally stated that racism is evil and those who willfully perpetuate racism are also evil.

There was no middle ground: one was either part of the solution or part of the problem. We have transformed Dr. Martin Luther King Jr. into a black "Casper Milktoast," and diminished The Dream speech into "let's just have warm, fuzzy feelings about each other."

The Dream speech is about dismantling the institutions and structures of oppression: racial, economic, social, political, and spiritual.

The children of former slaveholders must acknowledge that their parents were slaveholders or else holding hands with the children of slaves is meaningless.

We must realize that the social structures that grant privilege and power to the rich are still at play and must be confronted and dismantled, or singing "We Shall Overcome" is nothing more than sound and fury signifying nothing.

Race and economics go hand in hand. The system is keeping all of us in bondage and is pitting us against each other. The rich and powerful understand that the Nazarene was correct, "A house divided against itself cannot stand."

The root of the problem is this: If we are ever to become a nation where The Dream will be realized, we need to move beyond dreaming and become actors. Racial disparity is tied to economic disparity.

To address racism, we must confront the economic gulf between the rich and the poor. Dr. King knew this.

Remember the March on Washington was The Poor People's March on Washington. Dream speech and the Civil Rights Movement was grounded in the black/white binary of the times.

But, I posit that The Dream was larger than just Anglo- and African-Americans. The Dream includes all people of color and all Americans who are trapped in the systemic evil that is destroying our country.

It is time to move beyond dreaming and do the work that is before us. Only then shall dreams become reality. And if God be for us, nothing can stand against us.

A Tribute to the Rev. Dr. Wyatt T. Walker, 1928-2018

January 30, 2018

On Tuesday, Jan. 23, 2018, a great man of equality, justice, and freedom died. His name was Wyatt T. Walker. Dr. Walker was chief of staff for the Rev. Dr. Martin Luther King, the third leader of the Southern Christian Leadership Conference and pastor of Canaan Baptist Church, Harlem, New York. He was also my friend and one of my mentors.

The History Makers website states: This "Harlem Preacher" was born on Aug. 16, 1928, in Brockton, Massachusetts, to John Wise and Maude Pinn Walker. He attended primary and elementary schools in Merchantville, New Jersey, and went on to attend Virginia Union University in Richmond, Virginia, where in 1950 he earned his B.S. degree in chemistry and physics and graduated magna cum laude. He remained at Virginia Union and attended the Graduate School of Divinity, where he received his M.A. degree in 1953. He met Dr. Martin Luther King, Jr. at an interseminary meeting, forging a connection that continued until Dr. King's assassination in 1968.

Walker, together with Dr. King, founded the Southern Christian Leadership Conference (SCLC) in 1957; he served as the organization's third executive director in 1960 and helped Dr. King organize the March on Washington for Jobs and Freedom. In 1964, Walker left the SCLC and worked as a marketing specialist for the Negro Heritage Library, which aimed to make African-American history a more integral part of the revisionist school curricula. Three years later, Walker became the Senior Pastor of Canaan Baptist Church in Harlem, New York City, where he would serve for 37 years.

At Canaan Baptist, Walker re-energized the music program, leading it down a new path to several choral albums. In 1975, he earned his D.Min. degree from the Colgate-Rochester Divinity School, where he wrote his dissertation on the music of the black religious tradition. The urban affairs liaison for New York Gov. Nelson A. Rockefeller, Walker served on the national committee on the American Committee on Africa, which brought many African leaders to the Canaan Baptist Church, including Nelson Mandela. He concerned himself deeply with the apartheid struggle in South Africa as founder of the Religious Action Network of the American Committee on Africa in 1988.

I first met Dr. Walker as my teacher at Princeton. His passionate oratory captured our attention. He was a master at weaving together theoretical concepts, practical experience and robust humor. Walker made his students re-examine assumptions with penetrating questions: What is God like from the Western European perspective and from the African-American perspective, what should America be, and how should Christian faith influence change in the areas of racial and economic inequality? Walker, along with Dr. James Cone, Gustavo Gutierrez, the Rev. Leon Sullivan, Dr. William Augustus Jones and Dr. Cain Hope Felder made me deeply analyze my thinking about being African-American and Christian. They planted the seeds social justice in my mind and spirit. He caused those seeds to grow.

I will never forget Wyatt T. Walker. America should not forget Dr. Walker either. It seems each Black History Month we talk about the same African-Americans over and over ad nauseum and forget about other soldiers of hope, male and female, who worked diligently to make the dream of this democratic experiment a reality. It is a dream not yet realized, though still possible. We who took time to know you shall miss you, Dr. Walker. Rest in peace, my friend.

Black history is a history worth learning

February 6, 2018

Throughout this country, Americans will celebrate February as Black History Month. It is an annual observance not only in the U.S., but also in Canada, Great Britain and the Netherlands. It began in the U.S. in 1926 with educator and author Carter G. Woodson who first named it Negro History Week. Woodson wanted the celebration to be in the month of February because February held the birthday of President Abraham Lincoln, whom many African-Americans, at that time, believed had freed the slaves.

The purpose of celebrating Black History Month is twofold.

First, the organizers of the formal celebration of African-American History wanted generations of African-Americans to always remember their heritage and the champions of the struggle for freedom and dignity.

Proponents of African-American History desired "a collective consciousness" to reside prominently in the African-American psyche. The narrative is a collection of creators, educators, inventors, warriors and healers.

The first purpose was to eradicate African-American ignorance about our ancestors, our struggles and our victories.

We are more than slaves; we are a gift to the world. The thinking is that if African-Americans knew who they are, they will not succumb to seductive attempts of the slave owners (then and now) to enslave our bodies or our minds. It was to provide a pedagogy that would free the oppressed and to form them into victors and not victims.

Black History Month was created to remind us that because the "we" exists, the Individual is of importance and not the reverse.

The second purpose of Black History Month is to educate Anglo-Americans that African-Americans are Americans, too.

We are more than entertainers. We have tears in the bricks and blood in the mortar of this country.

It saddens me that most Anglo-Americans only know about five African-Americans of history: Harriet Tubman, Frederick Douglass, Martin Luther King, Jr., Malcolm X and Rosa Parks. Our public school system is woefully poor at teaching African-American history.

What happened to Mary McLeod Bethune, Benjamin E. Mays, Zora Neale Hurston, James Baldwin and Marcus Gravey?

Some of the ignorance is because the recollection of African American history is too painful for many Anglo-Americans.

Some of the neglect is an arrogant anti-black racism that believes the only history worth knowing is white, Western European, Anglo-American, male history.

African-American history opens a path for this country to move beyond people being "colors," to people being people with a legacy that is part and parcel of this democratic society.

We need to drop the melting pot mindset and think of ourselves as a mosaic: each of us unique and important to making the picture vivid and beautiful.

If we are to be one in purpose, then we must learn to celebrate African-American History Month. It is a story both learning and retelling.

The Economic Imperative for the Future-Investing in Ourselves

February 13, 2018

"God and nature first made us what we are, and then out of our own creative genius, we make ourselves what we want to be. Follow always that great law. Let the sky and God be our limit and Eternity our measurement." –Marcus Garvey

One of the saddest commentaries on African-American life is the lack of economic investment in African-American enterprises.

While there is great economic disparity between black and white communities, there is also a lack of cooperation within the African-American community regarding where and how we spend our money.

We neither support nor encourage black entrepreneurship as we ought to. Instead, black dollars are spent with white institutions.

There are some attempts to change this economic situation in places like Atlanta, Chicago, Kansas City and Baltimore. Indeed, such efforts should be applauded. But, overall, African Americans spend tremendously more money outside the black community than within it.

It is time (past time) for the African-American community to address this issue in a serious manner. For some African Americans, the problem exists because there is a residue mentality from slavery that states, "If it is white, it is better: better in quality, service, and production." For others, it is an expression of black self-hatred: the lack of trust and respect for black people and what they create and produce.

Even black Christians do not spend black dollars with black churches, they spend black dollars in and with Anglo churches.

According to a Nielsen Company study in 2016, African Americans had a collective buying power of $1.1 trillion. The same study estimated that this collective buying power would rise to $1.3 trillion in 2017 (Britini Danille, Clutch Magonline).

In the same article, it was stated that the top Anglo manufacturers only spend 3 percent of their advertising budget on commercials to attract African-American consumers. Why? Because they know they have a significant consumer block in their back pocket: the African-American community.

This Black History Month we must not only reflect on the past, we must also think about the future, especially our collective economic future.

We must strategize how we can circulate black dollars 10 times before it leaves the African-American community. When a black businessperson does a good job, we must celebrate him or her, not hate on each other. If a black businessperson takes advantage of the community by providing poor service and outrageous prices, we organize and collectively put them out of business and find another black person who will do the job correctly.

The internet has opened the world for all of us. If American businesses refuse to hire our people, open economic doors for the community and recognize African Americans as consumers with tremendous collective buying power, we must spend our money with those who will respect our money, including international markets.

The present economic situation for black people in America has forced us to invest in ourselves if we are to move from being victims to becoming victors.

We deserve more than mere survival, we need to thrive. We have an economic imperative to fulfill. The power to do so is in our hands and in our pockets.

The black community needs to create political change

February 20, 2018

This year the African-American community has a golden opportunity to greatly affect the local, state and national political composition. We have seen a couple of things that are undeniable.

First, it is clear the current national and state legislatures do not care about the overall plight of people of color, nor those who are the most in need.

One must only remember how Puerto Rico was treated during its recent natural disaster or watch how the current legislature in Jefferson City fails the issues that are most pressing: adequate medical care for all Missourians (particularly rural citizens) and predatory payday lending.

Instead, legislators continue to foster an atmosphere of division and distrust.

Given the truth of the first observation, second, we must find a way to mobilize our collective power if a change is going to happen. We no longer merely can pray for it or wish something would change. We must make it happen.

The primary order of business is to form a political bloc led by the African-American community.

The block must consist of labor, other groups of color, Christian and non-Christian faith communities, the LGBT community and the poor white community. African-American history has taught us that when the oppressed rid themselves of their personal agendas and biases, they are a force to be reckoned with.

United, we can change the course of history.

Traditionally, the rich and the powerful have been very successful in keeping all of us divided.

Everyone knows united we stand, divided we fall prey to all the tricks and propaganda issued by those who profit most. But if African Americans would hold hands with others who have been victimized by a callous conservative agenda, we can move what seems to be an unmovable mountain.

First, we need to call a mass meeting to determine what five (a random number) issues we want addressed.

We all have myriad issues we want to solve, but if a coalition can agree on five issues and be victorious, imagine what will happen with the next five?

Second, we must place our personal prejudices aside and work for the common good. The squabbles over religious doctrine, secular ideology and personal desires for retaliation must come second to determining the common good that needs to be achieved so that America may live up to its ideals.

The common good must be the goal, not getting my way.

Third, we must learn how to confess our wrongs, forgive and trust each other. We have all sold each other out along the way: African Americans sold out Native Americans who allowed us to live free on Native American reservations when, everywhere else in America, segregation was the rule of the day.

The white church needs to admit the majority supported and perpetrated racism and has benefited from it.

Straight people have treated the LGBT community horribly, and some LGBT people have been racist.

Some secularists have used their intellect to overlook the social and political realities that have oppressed far too many.

We have all made mistake. Now we must move forward, but we cannot do so without forgiveness and trust.

Fourth, we must organize a coalition thrust to vote in November. Mobilizing the vote provides a platform for radical change. Many were disappointed about the national election for president in 2016.

But one battle need not determine the war, unless we allow it to be the conclusion. We need to get folks out to the polls and vote on the issues that we collectively support. And if representatives have refused to vote in a way that promotes the collective good, we vote them out of office: Democrat or Republican.

It is no longer about the political party. It must be about who cares for the common good.

Black history is American history. If we do not pay attention to our collective past, we will repeat past mistakes.

We have a golden opportunity to make change real. We need the African-American community to lead the way. The time of excuses is over. We shall either be part of the solution or continue to be part of the problem.

I hope we learned something from Black History Month

February 27, 2018

As we have come to the end of Black History Month, I believe there are some things we need to cherish. If the month was nothing more than thinking about some American heroes and heroines of African descent, then the month was for naught. The month should have motivated all Americans to see our failures as a republic and to pledge not to allow the sins of the past to be our sins of the present and future.

The last few weeks, I have been teaching a course on the African-American church in the American context at the Calvary Episcopal Church in Columbia. This is the third such opportunity granted me.

The first was this summer with The Crossing in Columbia, and the second was with the Unitarian Universalist Church of Columbia.

You quickly will notice no historically African-American church or organization is listed because not one has asked me! One African Methodist Episcopal community member said to me, "if black Christians in Columbia aren't careful, white Christians in Columbia will know more about the history and development of the black church than African-American Christians."

Sad, but true.

During the discussion the question was asked, do I believe that one day America will be a fully integrated and equable society? I stated my hope is such visions will become a reality, but I do not see it happening in my lifetime. Several things impair the fruition of such hope:

There is a lack of commitment to a multicultural society where equity and inclusion rule. Too often we are focused on diversity instead of inclusion. The result is that we settle for tokenism, which is the antithesis of a multicultural society.

There is a pervasive and hideous lack of trust among us: black, white, Latino, Asian, Native American, LGBTQ, disabled, seniors, rural, urban, male, female, Christian, non-Christian, etc. I asked one of my ethic classes if they would be willing to give up one right for the good of American society, the majority said resoundingly, "NO! Why?" Because to give up a right is to give someone else an advantage, and "people cannot be trusted!" The distrust resides also within groups, so it is a double whammy: We don't trust folks that are like us, and we do not trust folks who are different than us.

We have lost a sense of kindness. We have become arrogant and rude. Social grace is almost obsolete. This phenomenon has fostered a mindset that the world and the country owe us something. The only thing owed to any of us is opportunity. James Brown said it best, "I don't want nobody to give me nothing, open up the door, I'll get it myself."

African Americans who were brought here to be slaves tried to teach us something of paramount importance: If we work together, all things are possible. I hope we learned something from Black History Month that kindles the flames of the fundamentally new. I hope.

Celebrate Women's History Month through the women who shaped us

March 6, 2018

March is Women's History Month. Celebrating the story of women in this country always has been quite natural for me given the way I was reared. History was never just "his-story," it was also "her-story." My family of origin took great pride in recognizing the accomplishments of women in history. Sojourner Truth was talked about in our home more than George Washington, and Eleanor Roosevelt was more popular than Franklin D.

Two ideas were present throughout my formative years. First, it took a man to teach a boy how to be a man, but it took a woman to teach a man how to be a good man. The second prominent idea was that no black man in America would have survived slavery and Jim Crow segregation without the work of black women. More times than can be recorded black women gave their bodies, endured beatings and experienced humiliations beyond our understanding to literally keep black men alive! Many a black man possessed a job or avoided a lynching all because a black woman or black women persuaded a cruel power merchant to "leave him alone!"

There was an expectation that black women were to be strong. No mealy-mouthed cream puffs were honored in my home or the community that reared me. Even in the black church where the official leadership was male, everyone knew the real power was in the hands of black church women. The saying was, "If you want something discussed, give it to the men; but, if you wanted a task accomplished, give it to the women." Black women organized the "benevolence" to make sure families survived economic hard times. The women counseled the emotionally exhausted by reminding the youngest to the oldest — "We are here, and ain't going nowhere!" They acted as midwives, led spiritual revivals, ran their homes with incredible tenacity and love. I was surrounded by industrious, creative, strong, black women.

Womanism was the mode of action for the black women of my past. Before I knew of Bella Abzug, I was well acquainted with womanist methodology. They walked beside a man not behind him. They understood victory over oppression was a joint effort. Yes, there were sexists among us black men who had been fooled by white, Euro-American ideology. But they soon found out painfully and quickly that overcoming racism only happened when men and woman worked together as equals. Patriarchy would cause black women to let a black man fall flat on his face and see that sexism is the bastard kin of racism. You cannot uphold one and claim to reject the other.

It seems to me that to authentically celebrate Women's History Month we must celebrate the women who have shaped our lives. How about Wynna Faye Albert, Sarah Belle Jackson, Almeta Creighton and Odelia Buckner and the countless others who attempted to teach us to be women and men of integrity and black pride. Join me in celebrating March as Women's History Month.

We must seriously tackle the problem of violence in Columbia

March 20, 2018

Monday night, the Columbia City Council discussed the issue of violence in our city and how we might dismantle this disturbing phenomenon. I am praying they have vision, wisdom and a meaningful dialogue. Clearly, we are a microcosm of the growing violence in our society. Yet, for Columbians, we have somehow viewed ourselves as above the threat of violence. After all, we have a legacy of being one of the best small towns in America. We have a growing business district, several good academic institutions, prominent research and advanced medical facilities, and the look of an integrated community. How could violence be a problem in educated, talented, prosperous Columbia, Missouri?

Part of the problem is that we have not told the truth about who we are. We have always blamed violence on "those other people" who have moved into the community. We have blamed violence on folks from St. Louis, Kansas City, New Orleans, etc., who have moved to Columbia. The fact is Columbia has a recorded history of violence. One needs only to tell the reason why many know our area as "Little Dixie," or the other truth regarding the Sharp End or the history of violence inflicted on communities of color, LGBT and individuals who have spoken up against wrongs committed in Columbia. There has been an anger brewing beneath the surface for many years.

The situation has worsened by the growing economic disparity between the wealthy and the poorer members of Columbia. There are lots of people who are very financially secure in Columbia, but there are many more citizens who can barely make ends meet. The conservatives may feel proud they have cut social services that poor people need, but the rest of us just feel a growing anger. When we watch our seniors have their food stamps cut and our children grow hungry, the result is anger and violence. And when we watch people who have unlimited access to privilege and power speak as if they understand the plight of the working poor, the result is anger and violence.

Drugs and guns have ravaged our community. Anywhere in Columbia, at any time of day or night, anyone can purchase their drug of choice and an automatic weapon, if they have the money or some tradable commodity. I am so glad wealthy people have realized opioids are a problem. They have been a problem in black, brown and white poor communities for generations. The same is true about guns. The Wild West mentality must cease because we are killing each other. Was it that we did not know, or that we did not care?

While we hate the phrase, it is none the less true: By our arrogance, unconcern and failure to address the real problem, 'The chickens have come home to roost.' What we failed to address before now haunts us.

Ignorance, under- and unemployment, drugs and guns feed the phenomenon of violence. If we allow our racism, sexism, and/or homophobia to prevent us from addressing the problem in a serious way, the violence will become worse. I am a man of faith, but we cannot pray the problem away. I am an educated man, but we cannot theorize the problem away either. We need the civic, business, faith, labor, and education leaders to stop posturing, come together and stop telling a false narrative of who we are. We must seriously tackle the problem of violence in Columbia. The lack of doing so is too horrifying to fathom.

Trump's moral character may cause his downfall

March 27, 2018

I read an interesting op-ed column the other day asking if the alleged affair between President Trump and porn star Stormy Daniels will hurt the president with voters. I think the answer is both yes and no.

I do not think Mr. Trump's base cares anything about his moral character. This is not the first time Mr. Trump has been accused of questionable sexual conduct. It did not prevent him from being elected president and there is not enough support for impeachment. His supporters are simply interested in securing privilege and power for the wealthiest Americans and dismantling Barrack Obama's progressive agenda for America. They are locked into his rhetoric, enjoy his reckless behavior and could care less about his lack of what Aristotle calls arête, or excellence of character. For those who support Mr. Trump the scandal regarding Ms. Daniels is merely an expensive blushing moment that will soon pass. A supporter I spoke with stated at least Trump did not commit a crime like Gov. Eric Greitens. Interesting distinction.

I think Trump supporters see Stormy Daniels as an opportunist looking to make fast money. Clearly, she is popular now on the TV talk show circuit. She will make lots of money for a little while. When her story becomes "old news," she will fade away like most of her former films.

The Trump/Daniels story however is causing a problem with conservative evangelical Christians. Conservative evangelicals always have asserted that character is essentially important to the worthiness of a candidate, particularly one who wishes to hold the highest office in the land. The continued stories and allegations regarding Mr. Trump's sexual misconduct is not taken lightly by conservative evangelical Christians, especially by women. We could see a major rejection of endorsement and support for Mr. Trump by evangelical women who will forgive one mistake but not repeated sexual impropriety. Isn't it interesting that the group that may cause Mr. Trump's downfall will not be Black Lives Matter, social justice warriors or liberal Democrats, but white conservative evangelical Christians who insist that good character is paramount to be the President of the United States? If Mr. Trump continues to demonstrate a lack good moral character... they will remove him. Now that would be a twist.

In the coming days we will see if the allegations of sexual misconduct by Mr. Trump are true or false. We also will see if the conservative evangelicals will stand on their principles or succumb to the political rights agenda. Either way it shall be interesting to see.

It's been 50 years since King's death and not much has changed

April 3, 2018

"Here was a man who believed with all his might that the pursuit of violence at any time is ethically and morally wrong; that God and the moral weight of the universe are against it; that violence is self-defeating; and that only love and forgiveness can break the vicious circle of revenge."- Dr. Benjamin E. Mays, President, Morehouse College, 1968

Fifty years ago, America paused in horror as one of the prophets of justice and peace was killed on the balcony of the Lorraine Motel in Memphis, Tennessee.

A nation grieved as we learned an assassin's bullet had ended the life of the Rev. Martin Luther King, Jr. It was one of the dark moments in our history because again we were reminded how we love to kill our prophets. His words and actions not only spoke to the deep problems of our nation, but also they captured the conscience of the world. He told us that love can overcome violence and hatred, and that justice would roll like an ever-flowing stream, yet, violence ended his life.

Across this country and around the world we will gather to think about the message of MLK. The question that looms large is this: Are we better as a nation 50 years later?

Sadly, the answer seems to be no. The racial disparity in America is worse than it was at the time of MLK's death. Then, we believed (or at least hoped) it was possible to be a united democratic republic. We held fast to a belief that while America would conquer the evils of racism, crass materialism and militarism. Today, the increase of racial division and hatred can be witnessed on every level. White nationalism is growing, not waning. Coupled with the huge economic gap between white and black Americans, one wonders: Will we (all of us) ever overcome?

And yet, I am encouraged because I see groups of Americans banding together to stand for justice. I see women standing against sexism and sexual harassment, students standing against violence and demanding stronger gun control, assemblies of African Americans strategizing about economic self-reliance, and parents and communities calling for better police action grounded in community policing. These small but powerful actions move us toward the dream of a united society in the face of huge obstacles. But nothing worth having comes easy.

One thing I have learned in these 50 years: Death may close the mouth of the messenger, but it cannot silence the message. God and the universe stand on the side of justice over and against the greedy, the unjust and the immoral. Fifty years later, I still have hope. Do you?

Trump should be judged on his leadership, not on his relationship with a porn star

April 17, 2018

Recent reports alleging sexual relations between President Trump and former adult actress Stormy Daniels have vaulted issues of moral integrity into the mainstream of public discourse. All of us, Christians, non-Christians, conservatives, moderates and liberals, are pondering the relationship between moral integrity and one's ability to lead. While the crux of the conversations center around President Trump, the issue is broader than that. Does a society have the socio-political right to hold its leaders to a high moral standard? It is a question for all people in positions of leadership and not just for the president of the U.S. Wherever leadership is in play, the question of moral integrity is at the forefront.

The recent interview with James Comey has brought the issue to a head. His statement that Mr. Trump is morally unfit to be president has us in an interesting situation. There is a social expectation that our leaders should be of good moral character, but who or what should set the criteria as to what constitutes the necessary and/or sufficient conditions for moral character in leadership? Should it be religious leaders or moral theorists? How about supposed business ethicists, behavioral psychologists or sociological theorists? Should it be the ordinary Jane or Joe working person? Clearly none of these groups agree on 1) what is moral; and 2) what is good leadership.

When Comey states that Mr. Trump is morally unfit to be president, it assumes a consensus on morality that does not exist in contemporary American society. The Comey comment begs the question: Who is morally fit to be president, and, given the degrees of compromise and deception necessary to be a world leader, can one maintain high moral integrity and remain president of the U.S.? The job demands moral compromise on a myriad of levels.

Let me be crystal clear. I am not a Trump supporter. I believe that we elected an egomaniac to be president who in turn wants to be king. Between 60 and 70 percent of Americans disapprove of his practice and policy as president. He continues to perpetuate division and hatred in this society, and his lack of concern for the most vulnerable is despicable.

Yet, I believe it is wrong to question his ability to be president based purely on whether or not he had a consensual sexual relationship with a porn star, a playboy bunny or anyone else. That is a matter between Trump and his wife, not us. Our rampant voyeuristic mentality has caused us to invade the private, personal arenas of people that should remain private. None of us are so morally perfect that we can cast stones at Trump for a sexual indiscretion. All of us have made mistakes, and all sexually healthy persons are capable of a similar mistake.

There are far too many important issues to wrestle with these days: school systems that are failing to properly educate our children, but they are preparing them for the penitentiary, seniors and veterans that lack basic resources to survive, predatory lending institutions that keep our people in poverty, sexual harassment in the workplace, ageism that treats some of our most gifted citizens as throwaways, community policing, gun violence, and on and on. For these things, we should hold Mr. Trump accountable. The handling of domestic and foreign issues reveals the character (or lack of character) of a good leader. But digging into his sex life is beneath us, not our business, and it's not worthy of our attention.

We must all learn how to forgive

April 24, 2018

"I am no better or worse/ Than any other soul/ I cannot judge that any individual is in full control of its/ Thoughts or actions/ At any particular time." – Dick Dalton, PhD

One of the greatest tests of the human spirit is learning how to forgive. No matter when an offensive act occurs in our lives, memory keeps the event fresh. The anger, pain and shame can be overwhelming to the human psyche. We are experts at "faking it," we cleverly create masks to hide what is going on the inside. Yet negative emotions have a way of finding avenues of escape. No matter how good our masks are, sooner or latter we explode. I suggest that learning to forgive is paramount to personal health as well as to becoming the community and society we can be.

Generally, forgiveness needs to be employed on two levels: forgiveness of others, and forgiveness of ourselves. Embracing the idea that no human being is in full control of their actions and thoughts, always helps us to forgive others. To expect perfect moral/social action from other people but wanting others to forgive us because of our intentions is unjust. Nevertheless, far too many people operate by such a paradigm. Alas, to err is human, to forgive divine.

My grandmother watched the KKK lynch her brother, on their property, in front of the rest of the family. Though the group was robed and hooded, she knew who the perpetrators were by their boots. She and her siblings often went into town to shine shoes. Anyone who has ever worked with a shoe knows the shoe, and she knew who they were by their shoes. Afterward, when people asked her, "Did she hate them for what they did?" she vehemently stated, "No! I don't trust their word, nor believe in their religion (they were all deacons and officers at the white church in town). But, I do not hate them because I refuse to let them control my life and interfere with my relationship with my Lord." Forgiving others is an act of freedom. It is the defiant and passionate refusal to let someone's actions make you a slave!

The hardest act of forgiveness may be the forgiving of one's self. All of us have made mistakes large and small. Some mistakes occurred out of ignorance, some out of arrogance. In the still place of reflection we know we did it. We may blame others, difficult circumstances, or insensitive systems and states of affairs... but the truth reminds us that we are responsible for our bone-headed actions. However, understanding we are no better or worse than anyone else opens the way to forgiving ourselves. We must accept the fact that all of us can only do whatever we can do at any given situation. Sometimes we act with excellence and nobility, sometimes like slugs and vermin, and everything in between. What is key is asking ourselves, what have we learned about ourselves? For example, from my mistakes I realize I am capable of being hot-tempered. Audacious, arrogant, small-minded people who say and do mean and hurtful things can get under my skin and make me blow up. Since I know this about myself, there are three things I do: I work diligently on being at peace with myself and others through prayer, meditation, and what Buddhists call "right action"; I refuse to carry a gun; and, I refuse to let my ego rule. Thus I will walk away from an irrational confrontation. Forgiving ourselves demands learning from the past and making the necessary changes so not to repeat the mistakes of the past.

I urge all of us to forgive. By forgiving, you shall be forgiven.

Fun City is vital to Columbia

May 1, 2018

Last Saturday evening, Fun City Youth Academy presented its seventh community champions dinner and silent auction. The event was hosted at the Progressive Missionary Baptist Church, 702 Banks Ave., where the Rev. Roderick Williams is the pastor. A nice crowd of supporters, alumni and guests gathered to show their support for Fun City. Several were honored for their work in Columbia: Melita Walker and Ms. Chrystal Graves as founders of BOLD Academy; CPD Officer Tony Parker; Mrs. Stella Johnson for her work as a longtime educator; and the Lifetime Achievement Award was presented to Mr. Rod Kelly. Under the leadership of Board President George W. Norman, Jr. and Director Bonnie Yantzi, Fun City has continued to make a positive impact on the lives of youth in our community.

I was pleased to see the list of donors and sponsorships Fun City Youth Academy received. Both conservative churches, like The Crossing church, and liberal churches, like The Unitarian Universalist Church of Columbia, financially support Fun City. Perhaps next year, churches like First Baptist Church, Missouri United Methodist Church, Broadway Christian Church, First Christian Church, C2, Woodcrest and other large majority Anglo churches will put Fun City in their budgets. After all, it would be another positive act of huge impact to demonstrate their commitment to confronting their historic racism and contributing to the development of Columbia's most needy youth.

My knowledge of Fun City stems back to days of Wynna Faye Albert, Sarah Belle Jackson, William Thompson and Beulah Ralph, just to name a few. Many of Columbia's African-American adults participated in the activities of Fun City in their youth. Many of those same adults now send their children to Fun City. Fun City has helped produce some of our best and most successful citizens. It still is attempting to do the same in the present.

Fun City Youth Academy needs all of us to participate in helping to develop Columbia's youth. We are aware of Columbia's Boys and Girls Club's tremendous work, but the need is larger than one organization. There are three main ways you can help: 1) Volunteer your time. Help with trips, volunteer to help in the math and reading program, or just be present as a role model. 2) Volunteer your talent. There are so many gifted people, particularly seniors, in Columbia that can significantly help Columbia's youth develop and grow. How about volunteering to teach a money management course or gardening? What about teaching a simple course in bike repair or astronomy? We are a talented community. If we pool our resources, imagine how much more of a powerful influence Fun City could be in the life of our children. 3) Donate to Fun City Youth Academy. Its good work is obvious. Let's support those who are doing a great job.

Kudos to Fun City Youth Academy. Keep up the good work. You make us better and proud to be in Columbia.

A Tribute to James H. Cone

May 8, 2018

"In a racist society, God is never color blind. To say God is color blind is to say God is blind to justice and injustice, to right and wrong, to good and evil. Certainly, this is not the picture of God revealed in the Old and New Testaments."

"Blackness is an ontological symbol of what oppression means in America." – James H. Cone

On April 28, America lost one of its greatest theologians, and I lost a mentor and friend. The Rev. Dr. James H. Cone was one of the premier thinkers of black theology and black religion in the 20th century. While he never served as pastor of a church or headed a social action committee, his voice and thought influenced thousands of Christians who take the struggle for social justice seriously.

I met Dr. Cone in 1977. I was a graduate seminarian at Princeton, and he was a visiting professor of theology. When I met Dr. Cone, I thought to myself, "What a kind, short man. His Afro is bigger than he is!"

During his time at Princeton, we had many talks about what constitutes a liberation theology centered in the Black experience, what the role of the Black Church must be, how Black Christianity was and is fundamentally different than White, Western European, Anglo-American Christianity. He would often say to me and other students that in the life of the Church — and in life in general — we had to decide if we wanted to be popular or be correct. Those words ring true today.

We stayed in touch over the years. He came to lecture for me at the Second Baptist Church in Columbia when I was the minister there. While in the graduate Philosophy Department, I served on a committee that brought James to MU for a public lecture. He had just finished his book "Martin & Malcolm & America," and his lecture was grounded in that research. He demonstrated once again his brilliance and astute understanding of life and faith in America.

Cone should be ranked with the Church's best theologians. Unfortunately, he probably will not be. His penetrating analysis frightened many Anglo-theologians and parish ministers. His call for justice and a stance against oppression caused many black pastors to be slow to receive his ideas. Cone made all of us in the Church realize that we either had to stand on the side of privilege and power, thus be popular; or we had to stand on the side of the poor and oppressed and correct. In the final analysis, Cone was convinced that God always stands on the side of the poor and oppressed. Cone's life demonstrates that he stood with God on the side of the oppressed.

I urge you to read a book by Cone and to let it challenge your mind and spirit. Check out Bill Moyer's interview with Cone called "Reconciling Histories." You may find it on YouTube and Films on Demand. It will give you a good sense of James H. Cone.

And so, I say to Dr. Cone, my brother, rest from your labor, I shall truly miss you. Thank you for your teaching and example. I will simply say: See you later. I know you standing by the tree where the leaves from which are good for the healing of a nation. Rest in Peace.

Tragedy and triumph in the wake of Santa Fe school shooting

May 22, 2018

Last weekend our hearts were made to grieve again by the senseless violence at the Santa Fe High School in Santa Fe, Texas. 10 people were allegedly killed by 17-year-old Dimitrios Pagourtzis. The facts are still being reviewed by law officials as to the cause of the incident. My most sincere condolences go out to the families of the victims. If the truth be told, we may never know the true cause of this incident. Can we ever really know another's internal state?

I doubt it.

We all realize, however, that something must be done about how easy it is to acquire and possess a weapon in this society, as well as, the absolute necessity for more mental health care in this country.

These tragedies are increasing in frequency, they are occurring everywhere. No community seems to be exempt. Once upon a time, parents sent their children to school with the utmost confidence that they would be safe. Now parents and grandparents are in fear that something horrible will happen at school.

The question is no longer will such a horrific act happen again, now the question is only where. Politicians, social scientists, clergy, law enforcement, school administrators, and psychologists ponder how to resolve these matters of school and church violence, as well as the presence of violence in American society.

We have a myriad of questions, a plethora of theoretical possibilities, but no one seems to have an answer.

One clue to triumphing over the violence that plagues us, however, is grounded in a question: whatever happened to our sense of honoring human life? The sacredness of life is almost non-existent. We are quick to articulate how we as individuals are important and unique. But it seems we have a problem in articulating how we as a common humanity are special and worth saving. In the old days we called that compassion. Now we are quick to arm ourselves with distrust of others. No wonder the concept of community is foreign.

Our children see it. They watch and listen how we disparage each other. If we do not honor one another as adults, how can we effectively teach our children to hold all people of value and worthy of respect? James C. Livingston suggests in Anatomy of the Sacred that we are both complex human animals, and part of the divine. Nowadays it appears that our animalistic character is overtaking our divinity. Thomas Hobbes, in Leviathan, Chapter 13, states that the human condition is "a war of every man against every man."

Respectfully, I proport that there is an alternative.

When we all make a conscious and intentional commitment to love one another instead of killing one another, the state of war we experience will be transformed into a beloved community. Once we commit to a principle of love, and not sickening sentimentality, our children will also seek a love ethic. Will such a commitment to love eradicate all problems? Yes and No.

Some people have become so hardened by the ebbs and flow of life that committing to such a principle seems impractical if not impossible. What a love principle can do is start us valuing each other. It can create an atmosphere where we work with one another and not against one another. It also can triumph over the hardest heart.

Together, in love, we can solve all problems.

I still believe that love can find a way to turn violence into mutual compassion and respect. Does anyone else still believe this with me?

The questions is no longer will such a horrific act happen again, now the question is only where.

Report shows CPD four times more likely to stop African American drivers

June 5, 2018

Again, the issue of community policing in Columbia is before us.

The 2017 Vehicle Stops Report published by the Missouri Attorney General's Office points to the fact that African-American drivers are four times more likely to be stopped by the CPD than Anglo drivers.

Columbia City Councilperson Ian Thomas writes, "While African- American drivers were stopped at a rate 3.28 times higher than their proportion in the population, White drivers were stopped at a rate of just 0.76 of their population, yielding an overall disproportion of 4.30. If you are African-American in Columbia, you are more than four times more likely to be stopped by a CPD officer than if you are white."

The report is disappointing, but not surprising to the people of color in this community. We talk about the problem in every place of meeting for black and brown people: church, the clubs, barber shops, beauty parlors, and even on our college campuses. Race Matters, Friends has been speaking out about this issue for a while. Perhaps we will take what they, and others, have to say seriously.

Instead of calling them "a group of angry women," maybe we need to get past our patriarchy and realize that they are attempting to make us be a better community.

Last semester I conducted an eight-week course on the Black Church in America at Calvary Episcopal Church in downtown Columbia. I invited my students from both Columbia College and Moberly Arear Community College-Columbia to attend at their pleasure. My students of color were quick to ask me if they would be safe downtown since the meetings would be in the evenings. They were worried about being stopped by the CPD.

There are several ways to think about the pervasive fear of being stopped in Columbia. Some people believe that black and brown people in Columbia are the criminals in our community. They commit the most offenses and therefore are stopped justifiably.

One person said to me, "If you people would stop breaking the law, you would not be stopped." The problem for me is that such stereo-typical thinking is damaging to the common good of our city, and dangerous if held by any members of law enforcement. Most black people I know in Columbia are not law-breakers. They are too busy trying to survive, care for their families, and make sense out of the nonsense we confront daily.

Some people believe the whole issue of community policing is being blown out of proportion. These people believe there may be a couple of incidents of racial profiling now and then, but for the majority cases it is just the irrational rhetoric of racial separatists.

One woman stated, "Columbia is a wonderfully diverse community where all people are treated fairly. If we would stop trying to exacerbate minor occurrences, the problems will disappear. Racism is dead particularly in Columbia."

I agree that we do look wonderful. On any given day you can walk around Columbia and see all kinds of people. The problem is that we do not act like we look.

Racism is not dead particularly in its systemic and institutional manifestations.

My personal experience with the Columbia Police Department has been mostly positive. People like Lieutenant. Jill Schlude, SWAT Captain. Lance Bolinger, Sgt. Robert Fox and others always have been professional and courteous. Once I encountered an officer that was stupid and unprofessional, but that encounter was an exception not the rule in my experience with the CPD.

Even when my wife and I were stopped for DWB (driving while black), afterward they were apologetic and professional (they explained that we were stopped because we had a "weak headlight!"). However, the sheer stopping of people of color based on a racial profile is unacceptable on every level regardless of how courteous an officer may be.

The fact that Chief Burton does not acknowledge this phenomenon is perplexing. Perhaps with the new data we can correct a correctable social problem and be the community we look like.

The lessons of fatherhood never end

June 12, 2018

On Sunday, we take time to honor fathers, and those strong women who have had to be both father and mother in their homes. To those women, we salute you and hold you in the highest esteem.

One of the things that is apparent about fatherhood is that the ability to make babies does not make one a father. Such men are merely sperm donors. Fatherhood takes work, time and steadfastness. Simply trying to "do it like my ole man did it" is ahistorical and fallacious.

It is a different time with different dynamics. As men we must learn how to be fathers to our children. The lessons of fatherhood never end. No book can teach a man how to be a father. Fatherhood is trial and error, listening and speaking, and acting responsibly. Some lessons I have learned I share with you.

1. No two children are the same. Each child has a unique personality. If you treat them the same, you can kill their individuality and prevent them from possessing a good sense of self. Treat each child rightly, but not the same.

2. Might does not make right. Bullying a child never works. Because you are bigger they may obey you, but they will not respect you. Take the time to explain why you demand X. If the reasons don't make sense to you, then maybe you should reconsider what you are asking. Children are smarter now. Saying to a child, "Do X because I said so" will not cut it anymore.

Remember, as fathers we are trying to rear rational human beings not thoughtless robots who merely take orders.

3. Do not be afraid to set limits. It is our job to set limits, and it is the work of a child to test limits. That's life. But not setting limits creates weak adults who become susceptible to "every wind and doctrine." "No" is not a bad word.

4. If you give respect, you will receive respect. We have forgotten the importance of respect in this society: respect for ourselves, and for other people in the world. We must recapture respect if we are to be good parents. That means we must respect our children as potential adults if we want respect as actual adults.

That does not mean to train a child to be a mealy-mouthed Casper Milktoast. I have learned you can express any sentiment if it is grounded in respect. Too many of our children, and even adults, think it is right and cool to be disrespectful.

Dads, we must nurture a spirit of respect in our children. After all, as a parent we are the first role models. What we do, our children will copy. It goes without saying, but I will anyway—NEVER, EVER, EVER, DISRESPECT YOUR CHILD'S MOTHER, or Father, if you are a woman who must serve double duty. Do not speak badly about her or him, never lay your hands on her or him, and never curse her or him.

Bad things happen to fathers that forget this rule!

5. Teach by example that the best things of life have nothing to do with money. We have become so materialistic that we have children who claim moral bankruptcy due to affluenza.

Really? We all must "grind." Some of us work several jobs to make ends meet. As a member of the working poor, I understand how easy it is to fall into the temptation of making everything about money. But stop and remember that the birds do sing, laughter is a great medicine and the love of family and good friends is more precious than gold. As fathers, teach our children the joy of play for play's sake, and not to go to the NBA, NFL, etc.

Life is short but there are some marvelous things in life. Encourage our children to rediscover wonder.

Happy Father's Day to all the fathers.

This Juneteenth we turn our attention to the southern border

June 19, 2018

Today, June 19, African Americans across this country are celebrating what is called Juneteenth, Emancipation Day or Freedom Day.

It is the day we commemorate the end of institutional slavery in the United States. On June 19, 1865, Maj. Gen. Gordon Granger came to Galveston, Texas, to inform a reluctant community that President Abraham Lincoln two years earlier had freed the slaves and to press locals to comply with his directive.

Why did it take two years to get the news out?

Your guess is as good as mine. However, since that historic day in Texas, Juneteenth has provided an opportunity for black people to reflect on the past and hope for the future.

Today the commemoration is painful as we watch how the current administration is treating our Latin brothers, sisters and children on our southern borders. The separation of families reminds us of how the slave-masters would separate black families and sell them to other slave owners.

While the selling of human beings at any time is morally blameworthy, at least the slave owners made sense: they separated families to make a profit. The current action of separating families at the detainment centers makes no sense. It is simply unquestionable cruelty.

President Trump (I call him President Trump out of respect for the office, not the person), in defense of his immigration policy and the subsequent treatment of the people at the centers, said that "America will not become an immigrant camp."

Really? America is already "an immigrant camp"! All of us, other than Native Americans, came here from other places. We are all immigrants. The difference is that the people at the border are people of color, and thus, in the mind of the President, they are not worthy of humane treatment or moral consideration.

Only a fool does not see that race is a major component in Mr. Trump's policy on immigration. Ask yourself, would Mr. Trump treat Swedes and Norwegians this way? No. And heck no! Most egomaniac intrinsic racists are ahistorical. Mr. Trump is no different.

Sadly, according to some recent polls, 27 percent of Americans think the president is doing the right thing on this issue. Encouragingly, 73 percent of Americans realize his treatment of immigrants and his policies regarding immigration are ridiculous and wrong.

I think our treatment of immigrants, especially the children, will come back to haunt us for decades down the road. The emotional and psychological trauma that these children have experienced, they will never forget. They will tell their children and their children's children about the horrendous mistreatment they endured at the hands of our government. The story of the victims will not be forgotten, and the anger the story provokes will not subside. America will have to deal with the anger in her future.

We of faith know that one of the things that raises God's ire is the mistreatment of children. God is not pleased with how we are handling the issue of immigration. Separating the families is no less than child abuse. People who abuse children displease God. There are consequences for abusing those God loves, and believe me, in the words of Henry "Box" Brown, "your arms are too short to box with God!" We do not want to have to answer to God for what we are allowing to be done to immigrant children. But as the universe bends toward justice, we will have to answer to an "ultimate reality" if we keep silent.

I hope the bipartisan Congress will stop the president's madness. I hope you will write and call your representative and encourage them to stand on the side of justice and stop this attack on immigrants and their children. I hope you will speak out and say enough is enough.

That would be a great way to celebrate Juneteenth as Freedom Day.

Two wrongs don't make a right

June 26, 2018

Last week White House Press Secretary Sarah Huckabee Sanders decided to have a meal with some of her friends at the Red Hen Restaurant in Lexington, Virginia.

Stephanie Wilkerson, the restaurant's owner, recognized Sanders and asked her to leave her establishment because she worked for President Donald Trump. According to The Washington Post, Wilkerson offered as justification the following: "I explained that the restaurant has certain standards that I feel it has to uphold such as honesty, and compassion, and cooperation."

What?

Everyone who reads my column knows that I am not a Trump supporter. My critics unfortunately think that because I do not support the policies and actions of Mr. Trump, I must be a liberal Democrat. Such is the narrow-minded thinking of two-dimensional people.

To set the record straight, I am a moderate and an independent. I believe in the right person for the job.

Such a person is one who displays an excellence of character and, is unshakably committed to the common good. Political party should not matter.

I am a student of history. History reveals that Democrats are as guilty of two-faced political action as Republicans. For example, Abraham Lincoln, a Republican, did not want to sign the Emancipation Proclamation but was forced to do so by Northern industrialists who saw the slaves as potential workers for the factories.

Lyndon Johnson, a Democratic president, did not want to sign the 1964 Civil Rights Act but realized that if he did not work with Dr. King he would have to deal with Minister Malcolm X, which would have crippled his war-machine efforts in Vietnam. Both parties have betrayed people of color. For me, it's about the person, not the political ideology.

My mother taught me that two wrongs don't make a right.

I believe she was correct. In the case of Sarah Huckabee Sanders, Wilkerson's actions were discriminatory.

It was wrong, as Ice Cube would say, "simple and plain." Denying Sanders service because she works for Trump is as bigoted and wrong-headed as the Cuba Libre Restaurant and Rum Bar of Washington, D.C. asking a transgendered woman, Charlotte Clymer, to leave because she wanted to use the women's restroom.

African-Americans can remember the time we were not allowed to enter restaurants (even in Columbia) because of the color of our skin and the nap of our hair. Native Americans painfully remember what it is like to be denied access to churches, restaurants and schools. Discrimination is not only illegal, it is immoral. It exhibits the worst of who we are. Wilkerson's claim that her action "upholds standards of honesty, compassion, and cooperation" is ridiculous, even if my friend Democratic Congresswoman Maxine Waters thinks it was the right thing to do.

Sorry sis, I love and respect you, but, you are wrong, too.

Whatever happened to reasonable and rational dialogue? I would love to sit down for a cup of coffee or iced tea, and have a conversation with one of my conservative critics. I did it once with conservative thinker George Will. I found him to be articulate, brilliant and a good person. I just think he is wrong. Why didn't Wilkerson seize the moment to have a conversation with Sanders? That would have been the rational thing to do.

Wilkerson employed her feelings instead of her mind. Too often people get caught-up in their feelings, instead of using the sense God gave a goose. If we thought more and felt less, we might find a way to settle our divisions and create the democratic dream we all share, "with liberty and justice for all."

Why I do not support Proposition A

July 10, 2018

Several people in Columbia have asked me to comment on whether I support Proposition A, otherwise known as the "right-to-work" initiative that will be on the August ballot.

While I am aware that many states have voted in favor of right to work, the statistical data suggests that right to work is detrimental to workers.

According to the Economic Policy Institute as of May 2018, workers in right to work states make significantly lower wages than their counterparts in non-right-to-work states.

This is supported by the Current Population Survey, from the U.S. Bureau of Labor Statistics.

According to the data, white workers make 3.7 percent less than white workers in non-RTW states. Black workers make 4.4 percent less than black workers in non-RTW states, and Latino workers make an astonishing 7.4 percent less than Latino workers in non-RTW states.

Women too are disadvantaged by the right-to-work proposition. Statistically, it is estimated that all hourly workers will make around $1,500 less per year with the passage of the RTW proposition.

Women will see a decrease in wages of approximately $2,000 per year, with African American wages reduced by $2,500 to $3,000, and Latinos experiencing a reduction in wages nearing $6,000.

The economic disparity that exists nationally and locally is a serious problem. If the statistical data (via the U.S. Bureau of Labor) is correct about the economic consequences that result from the adoption of right-to-work laws, adopting Proposition A will hurt all Missourians significantly. It will be particularly detrimental for women and people of color.

The goal of a just community should be to create the common good. Right to work increases the economic disparity we all experience. A decrease in wages for the hourly worker who is trying to feed a family, pay utilities and/or just try to exist is wrong. Workers need more money, not less. With the rising prices of groceries, utilities and gasoline, decreasing wages construct an unjust and untenable living situation.

Advocates of Proposition A state that right to work is intended to protect and aid nonunion workers.

But the fact is that U.S. labor laws already protect nonunion members in the work force. Right to work simply does not provide enough common good for workers (union or nonunion) to make it worth the economic hardships that it produces.

If we truly want to help the working population in this country, we need to increase the minimum wage. All of us know the price of everything has gone up tremendously. Every time I go to the store there are four or five people in the aisle who want to have a short prayer meeting before we look at the prices of meat and produce, in hopes that prayer will keep us from cursing.

Since the prices are increasing, the minimum wage should be increased as well.

Of course, capitalists will in turn increase prices, but with a wage increase at least the working poor will have a chance to survive with dignity.

I cannot support Proposition A. I hope you will think about the pros and cons of Proposition A and afterward vote with me against right to work. I sincerely believe it is bad for Missouri.

The narratives we employ determine our reality, actions

July 31, 2018

For the last few weeks I have been facilitating a course at the Crossing Church entitled, "That We May Be One: Overcoming the Racial Divide." This is one of several discussions on race that I have facilitated with churches in Columbia over the last year: The Crossing Church (now twice), The Unitarian Universalist Church of Columbia and The Calvary Episcopal Church of Columbia.

I will be facilitating a course with Missouri United Methodist Church in the fall, and possibly one with St. Andrews Lutheran and/or First Baptist Church, Columbia in the spring. During these conversations on "The Black Church in America" and "Overcoming the Racial Divide," I have been acquainted with several narratives about Columbia, America and race.

The reason I want to share some of these narratives with you is that I am convinced that narratives determine the thinking and actions of the people that advocate them. What we hold as "the" narrative among other narratives constitutes what we think about reality: economic, personal, social, political, spiritual and ontological.

Narratives, more than paradigms, determine how we think about things, what we say, and how we act and interact with one another.

The second reason I think we should examine the narratives we employ is because if we are ever going to be a society aimed toward the common good, we need to be acutely familiar with the other narratives that are around us. If understanding is the best thing in the world, understanding, without necessarily acquiescing, is vital to the quest.

By narrative I mean the prevailing story we use to derive meaning and purpose in the midst of the daily chaos we experience.

It is the story we tell ourselves, our families and our companions. When the issue of race arises, the narratives used are particularly pertinent. They affect whether we shall obtain unity or remain in discord and division. Race is not the only issue, but it is one of the most important issues that requires our reflection and work. What we need to do in achieving the goal of the common good rests in the narratives at play.

Here are a few that I have encountered over immediate time.

1. The problem of race is a problem of human sin. Racism will not be resolved until Jesus returns. In the meantime, we (Christians) should try to live a Christian life grounded in prayer, salvation of the non-Christian, works of love to and for the needy, and developing discipleship until Christ's return.

While I am a Christian and I agree that racism is a result of human sin (hamartia, defined as 'missing the mark,') I believe this attitude fails to capture fully the incredible phenomenon of racism. This narrative tends to reduce racism to the personal level (let's just all get along) and refuses to address the systemic and institutional presence of racism and the social, economic and psychological effect on all of us as American citizens.

Plus, I believe God has placed in every person's hand (not just Christians) the tools to destroy the power of racism such that systemic and institutional racism become a thing of the past. Waiting on Jesus' return is to wait too long when the power is within us.

The question remains: Will we use what we possess to make the promise of oneness a reality? Or shall we hide behind the promise of the Parousia (Second Coming) as an excuse not to do what we ought to do?

2. The problem of racism is overblown. There may be some racist acts here and there, and there may be some racist people among us, but racism as a social phenomenon is blown way out of proportion. It is an excuse black people (and other people of color) use if they don't get their way. In other words, if we quit talking about racism all the time and stop blaming problems on racism, racism will disappear.

However, I do not think people of color are imagining racism. It is not an excuse or an illusion. It is real.

3. Racism is the fault of black leaders. They get black people stirred up and create division. If black leaders would stop inducing black people to hate white people, we can be one nation.

This seems like avoiding the issue to me. Black people do and can think for themselves. I think leadership is important, but these days most folk I know are trying to be leaders of their own mind.

4. Racism is a social construct devised by white people. As reasonable white people we need to take on the responsibility of deconstructing racism.

I understand this narrative. My only addition is that all of us are now responsible for the perpetuation of racism and it will take all of us to eradicate it. One group may have constructed racism, but that is a column for another time. For now, however, all of us must be part of the solution to the problem of racism.

There are other narratives, of course, but space does not allow me to address them. This one thing is sure and true: the narratives we employ determine our reality and our actions. My hope is that we employ a narrative that promotes unity, equity, justice and love.

Remembering James Baldwin

August 8, 2018

"I imagine one of the reasons people cling to their hates so stubbornly is because they sense, once hate is gone, they will be forced to deal with pain." — James Baldwin

James Arthur "Jimmy" Baldwin was born Aug. 2, 1924. In my estimation he was one of America's greatest thinkers and social critics. He was a novelist and essayist. His writings addressed issues of race, sexuality and life in an articulate and powerful way.

His mastery of the English language and ability to capture the human imagination is unparalleled. Baldwin was a genius and a literary giant. If he would have lived, he would have been 94 years old on his birthday. He died Dec. 1, 1987, in Saint-Paul-de-Vence, France.

I first became acquainted with Baldwin later in life. My education in America, like most of us, was filled with white writers but absent of African American thinkers. I stumbled upon the book, "Nobody Knows My Name," and I became an avid reader of Baldwin's works.

Baldwin stated in "Nobody Knows My Name," that "any real change implies the breakup of the world as one has always known it, the loss of all that gave one an identity, the end of safety." Over the years I have found that Baldwin is correct in this assessment.

Change requires breaking up the world as we know it. We are comfortable in the worlds we have created. Therefore, change requires the acceptance of pain. But the pain we experience will lead to growth, or, as Betty Wright would sing, "No pain, no gain."

Baldwin loved an America that most often did not love him. His frustration with America's racism and homophobia caused Baldwin to ask in his book "The Fire Next Time": "Do I really want to be integrated into a burning house?" Baldwin saw the America of his time as a house on fire. He was disillusioned by the hypocrisy and racism of the American church and rejected the compartmentalization of himself by the status quo as "a negro writer."

At age 24 he moved to France and there he lived most of his later life.

While I love Baldwin's work, I disagree with some of his ideas. While I agree America is a house on fire, I cannot leave it. I believe we are called to be firefighters in this house. We have babies in this house that we cannot leave. I believe the fire can be extinguished if we are willing to do our job.

People ask me on a regular basis to recommend African American literature. I strongly recommend the works of James Baldwin. For those who wish to hear an African American perspective on sexuality and particularly male bi-sexuality and homosexuality read "Giovanni's Room."

If you did not catch "I Am Not Your Negro" during the Columbia True/False Festival, please make it a must-see for the future. I remember James Baldwin and I thank him and God for his tremendous gift and for sharing it with us. I leave you with a Baldwin quote that has influenced my life, my work, and thought:

"I love America more than any other country in this world, and, exactly for this reason, I insist on the right to criticize her perpetually."

Angry citizens, stressed police equal a dangerous situation

August 21, 2018

Over the past few weeks, several shooting incidents have been reported in downtown Columbia. In response to these events, the Columbia Police Department has decided to increase the number of police officers in the downtown area, particularly during evenings and on weekends.

I believe the logic of the CPD is that if they increase police presence, the threat of violence will significantly decrease. Some Columbians believe this is an appropriate response by the CPD — saturate the area, and criminals will flee.

Others in Columbia, however, believe the actions of the CPD are simply a police occupation. They claim that police saturation is an attempt to intimidate certain groups of people, namely people of color, and thus make downtown Columbia an "elitist whites-only" space and place.

What I know is that violent acts, particularly shootings, have spiked in Columbia. We hear about it on the news, and people outside Columbia believe the city is becoming a dangerous place to live.

The violence arises out of anger and frustration. Many people of color and poor people in Columbia are angry. They are angry because of the constant experiencing of economic disparity (it is true that 25 percent of Columbians are below the poverty level).

They are angry because of substandard housing and tyrannical property owners. They are irritated with schools that marginalize students based on color, family of origin and economics.

They are frustrated about being second-class citizens in a city that looks idyllic. Many people in this town feel hopeless and are seething. Given these dynamics, violence springs forth.

I know that community-oriented policing is nearly nonexistent and is not wholeheartedly embraced by many members of the CPD. That is a shame. When you do not know the people you pledge to protect and serve, you operate with stereotypes and prejudices.

We need to adopt a community-oriented policing philosophy before something seriously bad happens in Columbia.

My further concern is that the police being called in to saturate the downtown area are overworked, stressed out, underpaid and frustrated. I know some good cops in the police department. They are good people, very professional, and they work hard to see people as people. But now even they are tight and irritable.

The hours they work are too long, and the department, by every informed criterion, is a toxic work environment. We know the police department is understaffed and many of the police on patrol in downtown Columbia are younger and inexperienced.

I do not know about you, but I am very nervous around a person who is tired, frustrated and has a gun. I am especially concerned that one of the angry people in this community will be confronted by an exhausted police officer and the situation will escalate to a point that someone will be badly hurt or killed.

We need to find a way to address the reality of living in Columbia, the good and the bad. I believe there is a way we can meaningfully address the increased violence in Columbia and have a strong police department that is sensitive to the total Columbia, not just to the rich and privileged.

We all must work together to achieve this goal. And perhaps we are here in Columba because we have been called for such a time as this.

Two great individuals were honored last week

September 4, 2018

I intently watched the funerals/homegoing of Aretha Franklin and Sen. John McCain. As an ordained minister of 41 years and a citizen of Black America, I observed these events expecting to learn and celebrate the life of two individuals that have influenced my life in meaningful ways.

The music at the homegoing of Aretha Franklin was as expected. While Ms. Franklin was the "Queen of Soul," she was first and foremost a gospel singer of supreme magnitude. Most of the vocalists at her funeral sang with intent and passion.

The funeral of Sen. McCain was indeed impressive. His homegoing was more like that of a president. While I disagreed with most of McCain's political stances, particularly his stance on war, I respected his integrity. He spoke his truth and challenged wrong when he saw it. He was not intimidated by the rich and powerful.

I also learned some things in watching these two events.

I learned not to make a funeral ceremony a time for self-aggrandizement and purporting one's own socio-political agenda. I was greatly disappointed in the eulogy given by the Rev. Jasper Williams. Not only was it disrespectful to all single mothers, it articulated an archaic metaphysics grounded in sexist rhetoric. Christian eulogies ought to do three things: honor the deceased, comfort the mourning and glorify God. The Rev. Williams did none of the previous. It was simply self-glorification.

I learned that we still do not understand what it means to say that "Black Lives Matter." If all lives matter, then black lives matter, too. Too many people of color experience a world where their lives do not seem to matter. In saying "Black Lives Matter" it affirms that Black Lives Matter, too. Thank you, Stevie Wonder, for making the point.

I learned that it is still possible for conservatives, moderates and liberals to come together in harmony — if only for a moment. To see politicians from both sides of the aisle come together on one accord at the ceremony honoring John McCain was a moment of hope.

It is a shame that only tragedy and death make us see ourselves as one. I hope the spirit of unity will continue with legislators after the funeral of John McCain.

Two great individuals were honored last week. That taught us that if we use our gift for justice and unity, our gifts will make room for us. I honor Aretha and John. Let us all honor and learn from their lives.

Sept. 11 has become the symbol of my life

September 11, 2018

On Tuesday, Sept. 11, I celebrate my 41st year as an ordained minister. I was first ordained in my father's church, The Second Baptist Church of Slater, Missouri. I was also ordained later in the former United Presbyterian Church, USA.

My mother used to tease me by saying that the only reason I wanted to be an ordained Presbyterian minister was so I could drink alcohol without a guilty conscience.

Seventeen years ago, on Sept. 11, two of my Princeton classmates were killed in the attack on the Twin Towers. We had just spoken earlier that week and laughed about the funny experiences we had shared at Princeton. It was a great talk. Who would have thought that just a few days later I would be mourning their deaths?

Sept. 11 has become the symbol of my life. It is a bittersweet day. It reminds me that life is a constant flow of zeniths and nadirs, heights and depths, mountaintop events and valley-type occasions. It is interesting to me that one learns his or her best lessons not on the mountaintop but in the valley. For this time of reflection, I share some things I have learned along life's way.

Good leadership is grounded in good follow-ship. It is amazing to me how many young pastors want to lead churches and academics to be administrators but refuse to sit under someone to learn how to lead.

Leaders are not born — they are developed. Anyone who thinks they do not need to listen to someone, commit to taking the low seat sometimes and just be humble will never be a great leader.

Never let blind nationalism or zealous denominational doctrine keep us from the true test of leadership: Does your leadership demonstrate love, and does your leadership set people free?

Be slow to anger and quick to reconcile. I used to have a terrible temper. I would fly off at the drop of a hat. An old preacher once told me, "If you get mad quickly, you have to apologize a lot."

He was right. When one becomes angry quickly, you make mistakes. Some mistakes take a lifetime to overcome. Be slow to anger.

Some things are more important than money. We all need and want money. We were born in a capitalistic system that trained us to believe that success is determined by materialism. It particularly applies to those of us who struggle with the huge economic disparity apparent in this society.

But time and tragedy teach that integrity, friendship, family, vision, justice and hope are much more precious than wealth. Living well is good, but sleeping well is better.

Commit yourself to something bigger than yourself. Our social commitment to individualism has made too many of us selfish and self-centered. Our music reflects it, and so does our worship.

Church too often is about my blessings, my anointing, my miracle, my, my, my. ... We can only be our authentic self when we commit to something larger than we are.

I have committed my life to overcoming racism. It is especially frustrating when I hear people blaming the victims of racism for the presence of racism or watch institutions, especially academic and ecclesiastical ones, talk the talk of diversity but practice tokenism. But, in the end, it is the work and faithfulness to the struggle that makes life worth living.

Be your own person. Live your life your way. When I first began in ministry, parish and teaching, I tried to be like those I admired. I tried to preach like others, teach like others, pastor like others, etc.

I suddenly realized that God had called me to preach and teach like me and not like them. If we live our lives by other people's opinions and structures, we will never know the joy of authenticity. When I die, I want people to say, "He did it his way."

Be happy. At age 64, I can truly say I am happy. I wonder why it took so long to get here. Perhaps it was because I thought happiness came from the outside. Now I know happiness comes from the inside.

I urge you to be happy. My friends who died on 9/11 were happy because they were doing their thing. They were in touch with who they were.

It is hard to be happy given the division, violence and struggle all around us, but be happy because, in the words of the old black spiritual, "Trouble don't last always."

Why it's so important right now to vote

September 25, 2018

Over the past few days, I have had numerous conversations with students at Moberly Area Community College-Columbia and Columbia College and Columbia residents about the need to vote in the coming November election.

I am both saddened and shocked at the number of people, particularly of color, who have little or no interest in registering to vote ... and subsequently voting. When asked, "Will you be voting in the November election?" the most common response I have heard is, "What difference will it make?"

Somewhere along the line, the right and responsibility to vote has been lost. Some people think that the system is corrupt and that the voice of the common person represented by voting has been and is being ignored.

Others are turned off by the mudslinging and negative campaigns that dominate the media. Some others are disillusioned by the way the wealthy and special interest groups control American policy and practice. The bottom line is that many people are so fed up with the way things have become in America that they just have given up.

Yes, the system is corrupt. Yes, big money has polluted the system and poisoned the political waters. I suggest, however, that the way to change the course of this society and clean up the corruption is not to withdraw from the process but to actively engage in it. One way to make a change is to vote.

Voting is a moral obligation. Too many of our fore parents fought and died for the right to vote. No woman or African-American with a sense of history can stand by and refuse to vote. We have fought too hard and too much blood has been spilled not to vote.

As a child, I watched African-Americans practice reciting the Gettysburg Address or the preamble of the Constitution for weeks because they were aware of how the oppressor would make them take a "voting literacy test" before they could cast their vote.

I witnessed tactics of intimidation and beatings of black men and women who courageously prepared other African-Americans to vote. So, when I hear a person of color say, "I am not voting," it saddens and angers me tremendously.

Voting is also an American obligation. If we are to make this American democratic experiment work, we must raise our voices with the vote. The Trump supporters know that moderates and liberals vastly outnumber them. If we combine our efforts and work for the common good instead of allowing the good of the wealthy and privileged to be the rule of the day, we can make significant change in how things operate.

We can determine our course in history. We can make a change and stop business as usual if we vote in large numbers. It is our opportunity to be the country we ought to be: united and free.

Many groups — including Race Matters, Friends; Faith Voices; NAACP-Columbia Chapter — are registering people to vote in the upcoming election. We must take advantage of this opportunity to change the course of this country. It is too important to let this chance pass us by. We must not let the sacrifices of our fore parents be for naught. As citizens of this country, let us exercise our right to vote.

The crippling effects of sexual violence

October 2, 2018

The Brett Kavanaugh saga has presented all Americans with more than political wrangling about whether he should be the next Supreme Court Justice or not.

But last week was bigger than which political party is right or what procedural process is the best. Last week caused all of us to come face to face with the debilitating effects of sexual violence that permeates our society.

Whether you believe Dr. Christine Blasey Ford or not, the fact is that all of us have known and loved women who have had to endure the horrible experience of sexual assault. They are our wives, mothers, sisters, children, aunts, cousins and friends.

I am encouraged that so many Anglo women have come forward to share "their truth." However, I am reminded of the long history of violence to black bodies that most Americans have either ignored or refused to acknowledge. I am convinced that sexual violence is evil regardless of who has been victimized.

What we know is that sexual violence is crippling to the individual psyche: One may survive it, but one never gets over it. It places a hole in the soul of a person that is never filled or totally comforted.

In one of my ethics classes last week, I heard the spontaneous reports of women who shared their own experiences of sexual violence at the hands of date rapists, unknown attackers and even family members. I listened to their pain as they talked about the dehumanizing process of reporting the attack.

I agonized as they talked about shame, not being believed by family members or friends, anger and fear. I also watched how male members of the class reacted to the waves of emotion that filled the room. Some men openly wept, some deflected, but all were moved.

One woman who works with women who have experienced sexual violence told us that some experts in the field estimate that one-third of college women have experienced sexual assault.

She said it is difficult to get an actual count since so many women refuse to report the incident for myriad reasons. One woman in my class said the process of reporting her incident made her feel as if she were being raped again.

Have you wondered why no men have come forward and talked about how they have been sexually assaulted? Obviously, women are not the only ones who have had to endure the hideous violence of sexual assault. Where are the men?

Perhaps it is because as men we are taught not to vent our pain. As men, they say, we are to bear our burdens and move on with our lives. Such is a recipe for self-destruction.

I wonder if men would also come forward, would our society take the crippling effects of sexual violence more seriously? It is at least worth consideration.

In a reflection of the many women I have known who have experienced sexual violence, not all of them are survivors. Most of the women are alive, but the lives they lead have been shattered.

Many of the women I know have turned to drugs and alcohol to self-medicate. Some cannot have meaningful relationships because of overwhelming fear and distrust. Such experiences can transform a well-adjusted individual into a shell of a human being.

Sharing the stories of those who have endured sexual violence makes us aware but does not confront the issue. In one of the numerous polls that have been conducted in the last week, a clear majority of women believe Dr. Ford's report, but many men do not, according to the poll.

Aside from the ideological and political foolishness that surrounds the Senate hearing, is it true that most men do not believe women who state their pain? I hope not. I pray not.

Sexual violence is real. And we (especially men) must find a way to end it.

How we set the stage for a Trump presidency

October 9, 2018

This weekend, I watched former Republican statesman and retired four-star Gen. Colin Powell and former Secretary of State Madeline Albright on GPS. I have always held Gen. Powell in the highest regard, even when I did not or do not agree with his political affiliation.

There is no question that he is intelligent and articulate. He is one of many African-American men and women in this country who make me proud to be both African and American.

His comments about how the Constitution of the United States has been interpreted by President Trump as "Me the President" as opposed to "We the People" were powerfully poignant. While I agree that Mr. Trump sees himself as the king of the United States instead of its president, this news should come as no surprise to anyone.

If the Nazarene is correct that you "judge a tree by the fruit it bears," clearly Mr. Trump has borne fruit that demonstrates he has little or no regard for anyone that does not agree with him, whether they are Cabinet members, international allies, African-Americans, Latinos, members of the LGBTQ community, women, on and on.

Only kings believe they are always right and their word is law. Mr. Trump has appointed himself emperor, and his supporters in unison exclaim, "Hail Caesar!"

However, my thought today is not about Mr. Trump, per se. Trump is merely being Trump. Maya Angelou warned us that "when a person shows you who they really are, believe them!"

Many Americans hoped Trump would be what they wanted him to be. We should have believed him. This column is about how we the people have created the conditions for someone like a Donald Trump to become POTUS.

As Americans, we have taken our liberties for granted. America was to be a democratic experiment made up of immigrants committed to creating a unified society that would provide for all, life, liberty and the opportunity to pursue happiness.

Instead, we have allowed our commitment to individualism to make us callous and self-centered. We have created capitalism that only serves the few and denies the many. We have immersed ourselves in petty ideological demonology and neglected the call to create the common good.

Because of our lust for materialism, we attempt to have fairy tale lives swallowed by debt, self-righteous in character and hateful to others.

I listened to Sen. Mitch McConnell brag, in reference to the protestors regarding Brett Kavanaugh's confirmation to the Supreme Court, about how he "overcame the mob" in getting Kavanaugh confirmed.

Obviously, McConnell does not understand the meaning of "demos" in democracy. Demos means mob. Thus, a democracy is "mob" or "people" rule.

If one thinks he or she is more important than the mob, you think you are more important than the people. This country belongs to the people, not some self-appointed emperor or elitist politicians — Republican or Democrat — who merely want to be princes and princesses at the royal ball. This country belongs to we the people.

While I am painfully aware that many of the framers of the Constitution were racist and sexist, even the foolish can create something greater than themselves. The Constitution is a living document greater than the flawed people who created it. Its greatness is not because of its amendments. They are proof that it is a living document.

The greatness of the Constitution lies in its beginning: "We the people." And who are the people? As Madeline Albright pointed out in the GPS interview, "We are all immigrants." All of us, minus Native Americans, came here from somewhere else.

We are farmers, construction labors, waitresses, refuse collectors, bank tellers, factory workers, small business owners, educators, members of the military, janitors, hotel/motel workers, cooks and customer service personnel.

We are different colors, genders, sexual orientations, people of faith, atheists and agnostics. We are the people, and it is time for all of us to take our country back.

We cannot let those in power divide us anymore. Where there is unity, there is strength, and now is the time to unify — not by political party, but for the common good of this society.

If this democratic experiment is to survive, we the people must control its destiny.

Members of Congress should live like the rest of us

October 23, 2018

This weekend, I was reminded once again of the power of language.

I listened to U.S. Sen. Mitch McConnell, R-Ky., talk about the need to cut Medicare, Medicaid and Social Security to trim the federal deficit. This conservative, Republican thinking is not new. What is new is the labeling of Social Security as an entitlement program.

Really? It seems odd to me that anyone would call Social Security an entitlement program given the fact that hard-working Americans have paid into Social Security for many years with the anticipation of drawing off their money in their retirement years. That not an entitlement; that's our money.

But by calling it an entitlement program, it conjures up negative sentiments that cloud the facts. And let's face it, most people operate by their feelings and not their brains. McConnell is smart. He knows that if you change the language, you change the perception. And perception is reality.

Both sides of the issue regarding the budget and care for the citizenry are correct. The conservatives remind us that we must get the national debt under control. We must quit spending money we do not have. Truth. Liberals are also correct that we cannot keep breaking the backs of the economically disadvantaged (underclass, seniors, children) in order to handle our budget woes.

It is immoral, and it is already haunting us. The violence, mass incarceration, increased drug use and lack of proper medical care are greatly tied to economics. We cannot continue to hurt the poor to fulfill the agenda of the wealthy. Both sides are correct.

Here is one option I have not heard: What about the language that says we need to cut the salaries and benefits of those in the U.S. Senate and House of Representatives? I wonder what they would do if they had to pay for their own health care? Or ride public transit to work?

Let us outlaw gifts, privileges granted by corporations, etc., and make members of Congress live on what they earn just like the rest of us. They should make $100,000 per year because it is a lot of work to represent the common good. But they should not become millionaires with taxpayers' money.

This should hold true for Democrats and Republicans. We need representatives of the people, not barons and baronesses. For example, Rep. Paul Ryan, R-Wis., will retire from the House at age 48 with full benefits and approximately 90 percent of his salary. That's an entitlement program.

If we really want to do something about the fiscal nature of the republic, let's start with those in office. When our representatives in Congress have to live like us, face financial difficulties like we do, and feel the economic pressures we do, their language will change. Instead of calling programs that benefit society "entitlements," they will talk about them as programs to help all of us live better.

Then, fellow citizens, we will be keeping America great.

Who and what I'm voting for on Nov. 6

October 30, 2018

It will be a very interesting couple of weeks as the midterm elections get underway. Many pollsters are predicting a "blue wave" that will result in a change in the U.S. Senate and perhaps in the House of Representatives.

I am cautious about polls; after all, polls predicted that Donald Trump would not be elected president of the United States, and he was. My hope lies, however, in the reasonable people of this country who have come to realize that the Trump administration is bad for America. I hope they will begin the change in the direction of our democratic society, starting with the midterm elections.

Because the readership of this column has expanded tremendously, many people are asking me who I am supporting Nov. 6. I am supporting candidates who will put people ahead of profit.

Most are Democratic. One is a moderate Republican who has a heart for the people and wants to make the judicial system fairer.

We all know that the judicial system in this country needs a complete and total overhaul. Yet, we must also be wise enough to realize it is not going to happen overnight. Because I believe his heart and mind are in the right place, I am supporting the Republican candidate for associate circuit judge, 13th Circuit: Josh Devine.

My other choices:

U.S. Senate: Claire McCaskill

U.S Representative: Renee Hoagenson

Circuit judge: Finley Gibbs

County clerk: Brianna Lennon

Amendment 1: No

Proposition B: Yes

My fear is that if a change occurs in the makeup of the Senate and the House, white nationalists will increase their irrational assault on minority folks in this country. The insane killing of Jewish worshippers at the synagogue in Pittsburgh and the sending of pipe bombs to visible black and white leaders who promote the common good demonstrates how far white nationalists will go to "make America white again."

They know that while we continue to see America as a white nation, the fact is that America is becoming blacker and browner every minute. Their attack on the minorities in this society is vicious and without moral conscience. My fear is that it will increase after this election, not decrease. My hope is that it will not.

One caveat I must postulate. While Mr. Trump may fan the flames of division and hatred in this country, he is not the cause of the violence we are experiencing. The racial hatred we see was present before Trump was elected; it has just become emboldened by his rhetoric.

Some of us were fooled into thinking that we had become a post-racial society after the election of Barack Obama. The fact is that we are becoming more polarized every day, and the seeds of the polarization were lying under the surface all along.

Trump could help the situation become better, but he didn't create it. It was always there; we either refused to acknowledge it or failed to see it. Despite Tom Sowell's sentiment, racism is not on life support; it is alive, well and going.

Again, my hope is that this election will result in a turnaround in policy, practice and conversation in this country. Regardless of your choices, please do get out and vote. This is an important election, and it is our right and responsibility as citizens to voice our aspirations through the ballot.

Please vote Nov. 6.

The election is over. Now what?

November 13, 2018

For the past few months, we have been bombarded with campaign ads and political rhetoric. Candidates have promised to protect our values (whatever that means) and work to solve the problems that plague American society.

We will see. There is no question that America is divided. Liberals turned out at the polls in record numbers, but so did conservatives, particularly Trump supporters. The result is that the Republicans continue to control the Senate, and the Democrats will control the House of Representatives.

Some see this as providing balance in Congress. My optimism is very cautious. These next two years provide the opportunity to work collaboratively on serious issues that will advance the common good of the country, heal wounds and move us toward unity. But my fear is that our political officials will do nothing but bicker and play foolish partisan games.

If both conservatives and liberals are willing to do the right thing (that is, work for the common good of America), there are issues that truly threaten this country.

1. We must do something about health care. Conservative white nationalists made health care a discussion about black Americans in the urban setting. The Affordable Health Care Act became a personal attack on America's first black president.

Alas, that is why the plan became known as Obamacare. It was code for "N-word care." But the facts are that many white citizens of this country are in desperate need of affordable health care. Rural medical facilities are closing each month, and the farmers who feed us cannot afford to get proper medical care.

Yes, black Americans in the urban setting need health care, but so do white rural Americans and others in the work force. America needs affordable health care.

2. The violence in this country is out of hand and has been so for a while. We are afraid to send our children to school, take our beloved to the bar or club, watch a movie with our kids at the theater, attend the worshiping house of our choice, or go to a concert with our friends, all because some maniac might decide "it's killing time" at the spot we occupy.

Even in idyllic Columbia, all of us have noticed the increase of violence in our community. The lie that all bad things happen in Douglass Park has come to an end. Violence in Columbia can happen anywhere. What we are experiencing in Columbia reflects the national scene. Violence is rampant.

It is too easy for the violent to have a gun, and the lack of community policing and cooperation has provided the material conditions for the phenomenon of violence to expand. We are being killed by our own, not by some foreign entity from the outside.

3. We need to seriously address the economic disparity in America. Everything is too expensive: food, gas, clothes, utilities, housing, on and on. You might go to the store praying, but you will come out cursing.

There used to be a time when, if you were an educator, you were a member of the middle class. Now teachers on every level are in the lower class. I know teachers who must apply for food stamps just to make ends meet.

The wealthy might not have a concern here, but that is the problem in a nutshell. The rich are getting richer, and the poor are becoming poorer. The vast number of Americans are not looking for a handout; they need a hand-up. If the economic condition of the country is not addressed soon, the seeds of rebellion might come to bloom. That is something none of us want or need.

I hope that, with so many women in political office, perhaps a change will come. I hope so. Maybe we can start having meaningful conversations between conservatives, moderates and liberals that will put the country first instead of the divisive rhetoric we have experienced in the past.

History records that no great country fell because of the threats from the outside. It was the internal problems that caused those great nations to fall. My prayer is that we learn the lessons of the past and be the nation we can be.

As Yahweh said to Moses at the banks of the Red Sea, "The power is in your hand."

A heartfelt tribute to John C. "Babe" Martin

November 20, 2018

On Nov. 8, mid-Missouri lost a tremendously talented bluesman by the name of John C. Martin, affectionately known as "Big Babe."

Residents from far and near loved the Chump Change band and to hear Babe play his guitar and sing the blues. If you ever heard Babe Martin hit a "lick" on his guitar or soulfully sing one of his favorite blues ballads, you knew you were experiencing something special.

He would sing in such a way that it would penetrate your psyche. You felt like he was singing your song and telling your story.

I met Babe Martin and Chump Change over 30 years ago. While working as cultural affairs coordinator for William Woods University, I had

Babe and Chump Change Band perform at the university during Black History Month.

They "turned it out." Old and young, Fulton community members and residents of the university laughed and cried, swayed and moaned as Babe played and sang.

It was obvious that great guitarists and bluesmen/blueswomen heavily influenced Brother Martin's musicianship. One could hear echoes of Muddy Waters, B.B. King, John Lee Hooker, Betty Wright and Eric Clapton in his lyrics and his playing.

He once told me Jimi Hendrix had a great influence on him and how he wished black people would have received him like the white community did. He concluded by saying, "It's about the music, Reverend, not the person."

True, Brother Martin. True, indeed.

Babe loved the blues, and he loved those men and women who played and lived the blues. He did not just play guitar; he knew his instrument. It was a part of him, and thus improvisation was natural for him.

Improvisation was simply allowing his creative imagination to soar through his guitar. His passion for the music was contagious.

If you caught Babe and Chump Change on a night when they didn't just play well, but together were "caught up" in the music, you realized that you had witnessed a spiritual experience that had produced a divine ecstasy.

God had placed a tremendous gift in John C. "Babe" Martin. His gift to us was his music.

I shall miss Babe Martin. We shall miss his great gift to us. I believe that somewhere in eternity, Babe Martin and all the other great musicians that have gone on before are engaged in a celebration of gifts because, "it's about the music, not the person."

Columbia needs a visionary as city manager

December 4, 2018

With the resignation of Mike Matthes, Columbia finds itself in need of a city manager. As the search committee reviews and interviews candidates, my hope is that it will strongly consider the following: Columbia needs a city manager with vision and commitment to the common good. We need more than an administrator; we need someone with good ideas.

Our city has some major issues that need to be addressed in a manner that does not just place a Band-Aid on the problem but has the possibly of long-term results. The need for the Columbia Police Department to embrace a community-oriented philosophy is painfully obvious.

The growth of the city makes all of us aware that infrastructure needs attention. City employees need a raise. Violence in the city is increasing. I like how The District looks, but there are other parts of the city that need repair.

These are just a few of the issues that need visionary leadership from the office of the city manager.

Columbia's new city manager must also be racially astute and sensitive. Columbia is a city of many ethnic and racialized communities. We are from different places and demonstrate different cultures. We need a manager who understands this fact and has the dexterity to speak meaningfully and act responsibly to a multicultural community.

The days of Little Dixie, good-ol'-white-boy politics is over. We need a city manager who thinks in terms of "all of us," not just some of us.

My friend and colleague Keith Simon, co-pastor of The Crossing, reminded all of us that the "ultimate" solution to the problems that we face, not just in Columbia but in life, will not be solved by putting the "right" people in office or having the issues analyzed by the smartest folks.

I agree. But the optimum solutions can benefit us greatly by placing the right people in the right positions. It can make us a better community if our city manager is one with a wholistic vision of Columbia.

I dreamed that the next city manager of Columbia would be a woman of color. I think women have a way of looking at issues differently. They tend not to be captured by linear thinking.

A woman of color, who hopefully has not sold her birthright to be acceptable, could help Columbia discover and receive a fresh perspective.

Who knows? Maybe dreams do come true.

True victims of a government shutdown are workers

December 18, 2018

As America braces for a government shutdown, one must question the common sense of both the president and Congress. Both sides are acting like little kids fighting over a toy. Both sides need to receive switches and coal for Christmas. The president wants his wall. Congress offered $1.3 billion to allow him to build a wall that will be meaningless and obsolete before it is built. The president wants $5 billion. All of us know that a wall will not solve the immigration issue. Once it is constructed, people will figure out how to go around, under or over it. Obstacles simply provide the opportunity for creative action. As Chicken George said to Kunta Kinte in "Roots," "If Plan A doesn't work, use Plan B." People from Latin America will find a Plan B.

On the flip side, the need to show congressional strength, especially with the Democrats, has brought all hope for compromise to a standstill. They are dug in because they know Jan. 1 is coming. With a Democratic House of Representatives, Democrats think they will be able to control Mr. Trump. They are wrong, of course, because Mr. Trump is irrational, and no one can control an irrational person. Mr. Trump shouts, "I want my wall," and the Democrats respond, "Na, Na, Na; you can't have it!" The situation would be almost funny except when we think about the victims of this insanity.

I am talking about the thousands of people who will not get a paycheck because of a government shutdown. Some will have to work without pay; some will have no pay and be temporarily laid off. Either way, it means no money. They will still have bills to pay, mouths to feed and obligations confronting them. But, no pay. Even if you say, "Well, it will just be delayed," the bottom line is no pay.

What really burns me up is that the people making the decisions, the president and members of Congress, have plenty of money. A government shutdown will not affect them at all. The ones affected are ordinary working folks who, like most of us, live from paycheck to paycheck. You know that to have your pay delayed puts you behind. Once you are behind, it is hard — if not impossible — to catch up. This is something that the wealthy and those who have access to privilege and power never understand. But you and I understand.

I hope the powers that be will get over their tantrums, work out a compromise that will avoid a shutdown and start thinking about the common good of America. Party politics and ideologically driven behavior are destroying our country. We may have enemies outside of America, but the enemies within are the most formidable and threatening to the common good. A house divided against itself will never stand. Mr. President and Democrats: Let's grow up and find a solution, so government workers can have a holiday, too.

2019

Challenges and promises ahead in 2019

January 1, 2019

Happy New Year. 2019 will be a year of many challenges.

On the national level we are amid a partial government shutdown where over 380,000 federal workers have not received a paycheck.

GM workers in Ohio are fearing a plant closing, and Wall Street continues to be shaky waiting for a deal between the U.S. and China. The Mueller case looms large, troops from Syria are coming home and the national debt continues to rise.

It will be very interesting to see how President Trump will deal with a Democratic House of Representatives, not only about "the wall" but other matters that will arise.

All in all, 2019 will be politically intriguing.

2019 will also be socially and politically fascinating on the local Columbia scene.

Who will be the next chief of police? Who will be the next city manager?

Will the new people be simply a recapitulation of the same 'ol thing, or will they be people who will take matters such as community policing and social equity seriously?

There exists a real possibility for positive and productive change in Columbia if the right candidates are selected for the two positions.

As a community, 2019 presents us with the opportunity to address the growing violence that is becoming a regular phenomenon in Columbia. No one social entity can combat this problem alone. It will take a cooperative effort of law enforcement, churches, civic organizations, neighborhood associations, schools, parents, and individual folk to stop the violence.

We all know the increase of drugs in Columbia is correlative to the increase of violence. The question is, what can we do about it? That will be a major challenge for Columbia in 2019.

I truly believe that every challenge is an opportunity for human genius to excel. There are many gifted people in Columbia who, when united, can bring resolution to the issues that confront us.

My hope is that the national level will figure out that united they can resolve many of our problems. I am not, however, optimistic about Washington. But I am optimistic about Columbia. Our problems are still manageable if we work together.

I wish you a very wonderful 2019. May you and your family be blessed.

May a spirit of cooperation and mutual respect for the "common good" return as the rule of law in Washington and may our communal life in Columbia be more greatly enriched by intentional inclusion and not mere cosmetic diversity.

The power is in our hands. Happy New Year.

Something must be done about economic disparity

January 8, 2019

According to Sunday's article written by Ellen Cranley in Business Insider, U.S. Rep. Alexandria Ocasio-Cortez, D-New York, has touted a plan that would tax multimillionaire Americans 60 percent to 70 percent on their income over $10 million to fund massive energy and infrastructure overhauls.

The plan aims to reduce the country's carbon emissions to zero and eliminate fossil fuels in 10 years. The New York representative said in a "60 Minutes" interview Sunday that a new marginal tax rate would affect Americans making more than $10 million to help pay for the "Green New Deal."

Such an idea is not new. Tax policies under former President Dwight Eisenhower reached 90 percent in the 1950s. Through the administrations of presidents John F. Kennedy and Lyndon B. Johnson, the rate sat at 70 percent. President Ronald Reagan then sliced the top rate to 50 percent in the early 1980s before it eventually fell to 38 percent in 1986.

Some estimate that of the 16,000 Americans whose income is $10 million or more, a taxation of 60 percent to 70 percent would add an additional $72 billion to the federal government each year. Not only would the money benefit our move away from fossil fuels, but other necessary programs that help the neediest among us would have substantial assistance.

The plan makes sense, but we all know that Ocasio-Cortez's plan will not see the light of day. The wealthiest Americans will use their access to privilege and power to squash any plan or idea that would increase their taxes.

Their concern is not the common good. Their concern is how to acquire more wealth.

The real issue is how do we overcome the economic disparity that is currently tearing our country apart? The rich are getting richer, and the poor are being forgotten. The middle class is almost nonexistent.

Too many Americans are shackled by debt and subsequent poverty. The gap between the rich and the rest of us is staggering.

Economic disparity, locally and nationally, breeds violence and unrest. If we do not address this issue seriously, we will all be in trouble. None will be exempt; none is immune.

Higher taxation of the wealthy will help, but it is not the solution. A radical redistribution of wealth is the ultimate solution. Perhaps Thomas Jefferson was correct that inheritances should be outlawed or at least restricted. I leave that debate to you.

We know, however, that something must be done about economic disparity. For the good of the republic, and not just the few, a radical redistribution of wealth is paramount. A redistribution of wealth must take place if we are to survive.

Remembering the life and work of Dr. Martin Luther King

January 15, 2019

Today is the birthday of the Rev. Dr. Martin Luther King Jr. While we will celebrate his birthday next week as an official holiday, the fact is that he was born Jan. 15, 1929. One can read all the achievements and accomplishments Dr. King received during his lifetime in books and online. Many pontificators will promote them next week in churches and gathering places all around the country. I would be surprised if POTUS says something honorable about Martin. Such is the lip service most will give: same old statements; same "Dream" speech; same old "We Shall Overcome"; same old, same old.

As we look at contemporary America, Dr. King's message may be more important than ever before. I always laugh at how many Anglo (white) people hesitate to refer to him as Dr. King and gravitate to calling him the Rev. King; it is a way of demeaning his intellectual prowess. However, Dr. King had something to say that is pertinent for today.

King began to see that if we do not put workers and common people at the center of all discussion and strategy of what is the common good for society, we will never be able to draw this nation together. We need fewer think tanks, favorites of the status quo, and more working common people at the table making decisions. Instead, what we have are oligarchs who care nothing about plain ol' ordinary people. My proof is that we are still experiencing a government shutdown, with 380,000 to 800,000 government workers not getting paid because of a southern border wall that will not solve the immigration problem one iota. When we have leadership that does not care about working people, the underemployed, seniors, children or anyone else but the rich and powerful, the result is a threat to the common good — and this society. Martin Luther King knew it. We have not learned it.

King believed that Americans were people who had the capacity to commit to something greater than themselves. The "I Have A Dream" speech has no meaning if we do not understand what King's assumptions are: 1) To dream, one must care for the "other" like one's self; and, 2) Dreaming is the willingness to make the impossible possible. What former slave's child would want to love a slave owner's child? The children who care enough to commit to making the impossible possible. Can we commit to making the impossible possible in contemporary America?

With the divisive nature of American society today, I wonder what Dr. King would say about our current state of affairs. I hear people say that the dream is turning into a nightmare. If that is true, it is our fault. We can, like Martin Luther King, commit to a vision of being something better and greater than we are. To do so will take courage: the willingness not to be cowards in the face of racist, sexist, homophobic ideologies nor foolish when confronting the Goliaths of privilege and power. Courage is the mean between two extremes.

Dr. King also reminds me, and us, not to let the rhetoric of the oppressors break my connection with the God of my ancestors and history. It is the God of Africans that survived the middle passage and of Sojourner Truth, Nat Turner, Frederick Douglass, Mary McLeod Bethune, Howard Thurman, Wyatt T. Walker and others that grants wisdom, courage and power to confront the challenges of the day. Some people will never understand this, but our being as people of color can never be dependent on what someone else thinks we should be as a people. Martin's God was one that invested in the human condition. Because I believe the God of becoming has invested in the human condition, if we fight the "good fight," we will be victorious. "For mine eyes have seen the glory ...."

We've forgotten what it means to be rational

January 22, 2019

"The will is a kind of causality belonging to living beings insofar as they are rational; freedom would be the property of this causality that makes it effective independent of any determination by alien causes." - Immanuel Kant

This weekend, I watched a white female college student at the University of Oklahoma perform in a video in blackface, laughing and using a racial slur.

Later in the news broadcast, I watched white high school students in Kentucky disrespect and taunt a Native American while proudly wearing their red "Make America Great Again" hats.

My question for us today is simply this: Have we lost what it means to be rational beings?

In the simplest form, to be rational is to employ good critical thinking, be compassionate and respectful of others, rid ourselves of bias and prejudice and seek the common good.

But irrationality rules the day. What saddens me most is that too many folks are quite proud to be irrational. Clearly, the POTUS is irrational. If he really believes that a fifth-century solution (the wall) is the answer to the 21st-century problem of immigration, he is irrational.

When Democrats refuse to communicate with Republicans to seek the best for society as the solution to our domestic problems, that is also irrational.

If all matters are reduced to who is liberal, conservative or moderate and the subsequent demonizing of each group, the hope of a united democracy is lost. Contemporary religiosity will not save us. It has become, in too many circles, the epitome of irrationality.

I asked a group of students one day, "If you must make a major decision, which would you allow to guide you, your feelings or your reason?" The majority stated, "My feelings!" How sad!

The problem is that feelings are fickle — they change based on "alien causes." Our rationality is based on justified beliefs. We have evidence to believe X, Y or Z. The lack of reasonable thought is rampant and is shredding our society.

The lack of rational thought is hurting us in immense ways. At least 800,000 people have not seen a paycheck in a month. Food stamp allotments and Section 8 benefits are being threatened.

Most people I know and see are angry, disappointed and frustrated. We may have formally celebrated Dr. Martin Luther King Jr. Day on Monday, but many folk believe "The Dream" is dead or on life support, both in the U.S. and around the world. The idea of a beloved community has been swallowed up by xenophobic nationalism.

The result of our irrationality is a loss of freedom. Rational people can disagree without being disagreeable. Irrational people seek the death — whether actual or death of personhood — of the other because of their disagreement.

Our freedom is too precious to throw away. Our society demands we become rational again.

As parents, we must teach our children that every person is of ultimate worth regardless of color, sexual orientation, gender, economic level and education. Educational institutions must be intentionally holistic in pedagogy. Universities, colleges and financial institutions need to stop talking about the need for diversity and be inclusive.

Why is it that on every college campus in this town most black and brown people are in food service and custodial positions, with so embarrassingly few in administration or on a faculty? Rational people know this is wrong, and that is an impediment to our freedom to create the common good. It is time to exercise our common rationality and be the change we want to see. Our freedom depends on it.

Don't impeach Trump. Avoid the ugly consequences

January 29, 2019

"No man will make a great leader who wants to do it all himself or get all the credit for doing it." - Andrew Carnegie

About a week or so ago, a few of my friends and I discussed the plight of Donald Trump and whether he will be re-elected as president of the United States. According to polls taken after the governmental shutdown, the answer is no.

Of course, things can change. Americans have episodic amnesia. If the stock market does well, a third-party presidential candidate splits the vote or a weak Democratic candidate is presented, America may forget the insanity of this presidency and re-elect Mr. Trump.

Many of us did not think he would be elected the first time. If Carnegie is correct, he should not be re-elected in 2020. But we shall see.

One person in the conversation proposed that the best move Congress could make is to impeach Mr. Trump. Others in the discussion thought this was a great idea. They were aghast when I declared that impeachment is a very bad idea.

Everyone who reads this column and who takes the time to know me knows that I am not a Trump supporter by any stretch of the imagination. He lacks what Aristotle called "arete," or excellence of character. He is immoral, he lies, he promotes division, he is a racist, he lacks the ability to think beyond the obvious and he is impulsive.

But impeaching Donald Trump would be a huge mistake, and here's why:

If Trump is impeached, Mike Pence would become the POTUS. If you think things are bad with Trump, they would be worse with our vice president. Pence is well-connected in the Senate. He is crafty and smart.

His conservatism is vicious. He is eloquent and poised. His rhetoric would sway people who operate by their emotions instead of their rationality in a heartbeat. Impeaching Trump would give this country someone worse: a cold, calculating oligarch.

Also, impeaching Trump would enrage his radical base. By radical base I mean white supremacists who are not above violent conflict. White supremacy groups are growing in every part of America. They truly believe that to make America great again is to make America white again.

They are not above violence, as evidenced by the 2017 gathering of white supremacists in Charlottesville, Virginia. They believe Mr. Trump is leading them to the "ivory" promised land, and it doesn't take a rocket scientist to understand that impeaching Trump would give the Ku Klux Klan, neo-Nazis and others of that sort motivation to lash out in horribly violent ways.

We have seen this happen in the past. I do not want to experience it in the future.

The talk about impeaching Donald Trump is being promoted by liberal members of Congress, by many in academia, by angry farmers and factory workers. It is being raised by frustrated LGBT community members, social activists, black and brown community leaders and just ordinary folks who are tired of Trump's antics and selfish behavior.

Just check social media if you have doubts. What we must not do is allow our frustration to cause us to make a bad decision that will result in tragic consequences.

What should be done? How about censuring Mr. Trump and taking away his Twitter account? That would be a good start.

If Republicans and Democrats would stop getting caught up in the "Trump hype" and pledge to work together for the common good of this country, that could hold Mr. Trump at bay.

And, of course, we must elect someone as president who cares about America more than him or herself.

Black history is American history — good and bad

February 5, 2019

A young white professor asked me if I still celebrate February as Black History Month. In his kindest, trying-not-to-be-offensive voice, he suggested that since there is no more legal segregation in America and that the racial problems in America are minimal at best, didn't I think that celebrating black history was now passé'?

"After all," he said, "white people are tired of blacks trying to make us feel guilty about the past. Let's just move on."

I took a deep breath and stated that I celebrate the history of black people in America every day, not just in the month of February. I continued by saying, "Celebrating February as Black History Month is important because black history is American history — good and bad."

He looked puzzled, and I realized that he was a degreed fool who never took the time to get an education, so why continue the conversation? I got my cup of coffee and went back to work. After all, it is more important for me to contribute to the narrative of black people in America than to convince someone who doesn't want to learn.

It seems to me that the enthusiasm to celebrate February as Black History Month has waned. I no longer see large gatherings to discuss and remember the contributions black people have made to the United States of America and the world.

Churches no longer have interracial worships like we used to do. Too many of our black churches are remiss in celebrating. One black pastor told me he didn't have time to celebrate black history because he was too busy celebrating Jesus.

Far too many schools act like the only people worthy of reflection are Martin Luther King, Rosa Parks and Frederick Douglass. What happened to reading Toni Morrison or Zora Neale Hurston or reviewing the work of George Washington Carver?

There are three reasons we should take time to celebrate February as Black History Month.

First, it presents to us a narrative that is both painful and productive. It will make all of us acknowledge that we can be horrifically cruel or compassionately kind. It will teach us how religion was used to opiate people but how it was also instrumental in the quest for liberation (ex.: the Quakers and the historic black church).

It demonstrates how our prejudices enslave and how a group of people who refused to give up can rise above the most oppressive circumstances. Black history is a lesson of what can happen despite the odds being against you.

Second, celebrating black history is a lesson for the present. While in some ways we as a nation have progressed, in many ways we have regressed. The slavery of the past no longer exists. Instead, we have the new slavery known as the prison system. I do not have to deal with black "man-catchers" who return African-Americans to the plantation.

Today's man-catchers encourage black youths to be professional athletes or entertainers who cannot even read the contracts they sign or handle the money they receive. What the history of black people teaches is that the "game" in the present is the same "game" of the past and that, if we are not vigilant and wise, we will fall for the game again. Knowledge is power, not merely money.

Third, black history equips me for the future. It teaches that the fundamental new in society and within politics is achievable. We can be an inclusive, multicultural society. Economic freedom and development literally lie within our own hands.

No black community or any community of color needs to be shackled by predatory lenders or dependent on slumlords to live. We have the economic power to develop and grow. This is what Brother Malcolm was saying to us in the past. It is also why white supremacists do not want us to read Malcolm X or anyone else who can teach us to be self-reliant.

I celebrate February Black History Month not because I want to rehash old wounds or make white people feel guilty. I celebrate the narrative of black men and women because it gives me strength for the present and hope for the future.

Join me in celebrating February as Black History Month.

Celebrities forget that talent without discipline can be disaster

February 26, 2019

Talent without discipline is like an octopus on roller skates. There's plenty of movement, but you never know if it's going to be forward, backwards, or sideways. - H. Jackson Brown Jr.

What a week for the American entertainment industry. The Oscars were a delight as we watched more women and people of color win awards. Hooray!

The week was also a spectacle of sadness and disappointment. Jussie Smollett's claim of being the victim of racial and homophobic attack is being seriously questioned by the Chicago police.

Robert "R." Kelly is being charged with 10 counts of sexual abuse. Three of the women testifying against him claim they were underage (under 16) when Kelly abused them. If convicted, Kelly could serve 70 years in prison.

There is plenty of discussion about what is the truth in both of these instances. There will be speculation from now until Shiloh comes. Some things, however, are indisputable.

Mr. Kelly has been suspected of pedophilia for many years. This is not the first suggestion that something is very wrong with R. Kelly's sexual choices.

My problem is that it doesn't seem that anyone wanted to help him work through his issues and get him the help he so desperately needs. People wanted to help him spend his money, be in his entourage and live the high life. But it is also clear that no one wanted to help him be a good man. And that is a shame.

In the case of Jussie Smollett, I hope he is telling the truth, but it is not looking good. If Mr. Smollett lied about his assault, it hurts two communities — the black community and the LGBTQ community.

The problems both communities face are real. A lie only exacerbates the problems. There are enough haters shooting at the black and gay communities. We need not give anyone ammunition to shoot with.

In both cases, one thing is evident for me. If a person of color in America forgets who he or she is and thinks fame or money will exempt them from reprisal and repercussion, that person is a fool.

Both men are very talented. Both men are black. But both men forgot that talent without discipline is a recipe for disaster. The more we have been given, the more is required.

Now because of an undisciplined act(s), one talented man may die in prison and another may never act again. Pedophilia and filing false reports are crimes. You may think your popularity and wealth make you untouchable. Not so, Mr. Kelly and Mr. Smollett. You are still black men in America.

My hope is that R. Kelly and Jussie Smollett learn valuable lessons from these issues. I also hope that young talented black men and women will awaken and realize that if you abuse, lie and live as if you are the center of the universe, you will reap what you sow.

The time of foolishness must come to an end. It is time for all of us to be about the task of building mutually respecting communities.

Ron Stallworth gave us a reason to talk about police and race

March 12, 2019

Last week, Ron Stallworth, author of "Black Klansman," visited the Columbia College campus to engage administrators, faculty, staff, alumni, students and others in the community in a conversation about his No. 1 best-selling book, the movie directed by Spike Lee that won an Academy Award and contemporary American life.

Stallworth, a graduate of the Salt Lake City campus of Columbia College, was this year's annual Schiffman Ethics in Society guest lecturer.

Mr. Stallworth, a retired police officer with over 30 years of service, held an afternoon Q&A session, followed by a 7:30 pm "conversation" led by Columbia College President Scott Dalrymple.

Mr. Stallworth was very approachable and straightforward. He was entertaining and enlightening.

His wife was also a joy to meet, and it was obvious that she was his "boo!" When asked tough questions, he did not back away nor worry about who affirmed or rejected his response. He told it as he saw it.

Two issues came up that I think are worthy of reflection. Stallworth was asked if it was harder or easier to be a police officer of color today than when he started his career. His response was that he believed it was harder now than ever.

He pointed out two issues that need to be understood. The first is that none of us understand what police officers go through daily. Because they are putting their lives on the line every hour on the hour, they build what Stallworth calls a "blue veil" to surround and protect their fellow officers. That is why, Stallworth said, police officers sometimes resent community criticism.

On the other hand, he said that there are "bad cops" among the rank and file who should never be police officers. When police departments refuse to remove "bad cops," it hurts not only the departments in question but the whole of law enforcement and the community.

It is in these situations where community-oriented policing is most needed. Citizens ought to point out bad policing and demand that bad police officers be fired. The community deserves good policing.

In the same conversation, he noted that the pressure on police officers of color is tremendous. For some in the black community, a black cop is "too blue." For many white cops and those in the white community, a black police officer is "too black and not blue enough."

When we think about the Columbia Police Department, could the dynamics mentioned above be reasons we are not attracting qualified officers of color? It is worth thinking about.

The second issue concerns the ending of the movie "BlacKkKlansman," based on Stallworth's book. He has been told that while people liked the movie, some had a hard time relating to the ending, which is a scene from the Charlottesville, Virginia, clash with white supremacist groups.

When asked about it, Stallworth simply stated, "It is real, and it is today." I found this odd. We like thinking about a black man who infiltrated the Ku Klux Klan 40 years ago, but we have a hard time relating to the racism that is prevalent today. Why?

Groups of white nationalists and white supremacists have grown in numbers over the last 10 years in the U.S. Systemic racism has grown in girth and breadth, while institutional racism still acts as the vanguard of white privilege and power.

While Mr. Trump fans the flames of hate and division, he is not the cause of it. He is merely an example of how far backward we have gone in the quest for racial equity and the common good.

Stallworth's comment that the scene from Charlottesville "is real" gives rise to another question: Is it too real? Are we so committed to being socio-political ostriches who place our heads in the sand of fantasy that we no longer wish to work for justice and equality?

Do we really think that racism doesn't exist? I hope not.

I appreciate Mr. Stallworth's visit and sharing of his story and thoughts. He should make all of us think and reflect on what kind of America we want and how hard we are willing to work to make it a reality.

Mueller Report holds too many secrets to worry about

March 26, 2019

After two years of investigation, the Robert Mueller Report regarding possible collusion between the Trump administration and Russia is in the hands of Attorney General William P. Barr.

Barr has given a summary of the document, suggesting that while it does not completely exonerate President Trump, there seems to be no strong evidence for wrongdoing, collusion, or Russian interference in our last election.

The president and Sarah Huckabee Sanders emphatically claim that the report completely exonerates the Trump administration. No surprise here.

The Republicans claim that the Democrats pushed the investigation simply to "smear the president with innuendo and false conspiracy theories."

The Democrats state they were only demanding greater transparency into the workings of the Trump administration and his campaign.

There are three sides to every story: The Republican version, the Democrats' version and the truth. I don't think we can ever know the truth about this matter.

What bothers me most about the Mueller Report is that we the people have not had an opportunity to examine the document for ourselves. Most Americans can read. Many Americans can read very well.

Don't tell us what the report says, let us have an opportunity to exercise our own exegesis (what the text says) and hermeneutics (what the text means). Mr. Barr let us read the report for ourselves and stop shrouding it in a cloud of mystery.

Do most Americans really care about the report? Probably not. Would we be surprised to find out Mr. Trump did have some dealings with the Russians? No. It would not surprise us because after being lied to about who is going to pay for building the Wall, the Stormy Daniels affair, and that the leader of North Korea is a good person, none are that naive.

The fact of the matter is that far too many Americans have other things to think about. Most people in this society are overworked and underpaid. They have a hard time making ends meet.

We worry about school safety for our children. We pray every night that we, our children, and our parents can remain relatively healthy because of the non-existence of affordable health care. No one can afford to be seriously ill.

Please spare me the Obamacare rhetoric — if Republicans and Democrats wanted to make affordable health care for Americans a reality, they could do it. They just will not do it.

And thus, I blame both parties for caring more about maintaining their wealth and congressional seats than the well-being of Americans, the common good of this nation and the people in this society.

I hope we see the Mueller Report someday soon. I hope more that government officials will take seriously their tasks: Serve we the people, lift the society and promote the common good.

Clean up Columbia — because it's the generous thing to do

April 9, 2019

On Saturday, the city of Columbia will sponsor its annual Cleanup Columbia Day.

Last year, more than 1,500 people volunteered to help beautify our city. It was a great time of meeting new people and gathering together for the aesthetic good of this community.

We worked together: black, white, Asian, Hispanic, older, younger, gay, straight, etc. None gathered because of religious or political positions. All gathered simply to give our time and effort in the spirit of appreciating the beauty of Columbia.

If you have ever lived in a large urban setting, you appreciate Columbia's attractiveness. Even the not-so-attractive places in Columbia are 100 times better than the painful parts of Chicago, Cleveland, Detroit, Washington, Baltimore and other cities.

Columbia is a place worth caring about. I am not overlooking the real problems and issues we must deal with in Columbia, but sometimes I think we must appreciate what we have and not just complain about what we do not have.

We have one of the best-looking small cities in America. That, I think, is worth celebrating and maintaining.

I asked one resident if he was going to participate in the cleanup day this year. He strongly told me "NO!"

He proceeded to tell me that Columbia hadn't given anything to him, so why should he give up his free time to clean up Columbia?

How sad. If we only do something in order to get something, we are pathetic human beings. Sometimes we ought to commit to something bigger than ourselves.

I am pleased to say that many of my ethics students at both Columbia College and MACC-Columbia are volunteering to help clean up Columbia. Most of them do not live in Columbia; they just want to do something ethical and not just talk about being ethical.

I encourage all my readers to participate in the Cleanup Columbia effort Saturday. The work begins at 10 a.m. The city has information on its website. Check it out, and in the spirit of the beautiful, come out and participate.

A tribute to groundbreaking filmmaker John Singleton

April 30, 2019

The influential film director, screenwriter and producer John Singleton died Monday after suffering complications from a stroke he experienced April 17.

Singleton was the first African American and youngest person ever nominated for an Oscar for best film director. He is best known for his movie "Boyz N the Hood." Many of us also remember his brilliant artistry with the films "Baby Boy" and "Poetic Justice."

He was a genius who gave life, humor and depth to the characters in his movies.

Those who knew him speak about his humility and his willingness to see potential in others. It was Singleton who employed and promoted Ice Cube, Cuba Gooding Jr., Taraji P. Henson, Tyrese Gibson and others.

Henson, when reflecting upon Singleton's ability to see the potential in others, stated, "He saw something in me that I did not see. His 'seeing' changed my life."

Three things come to mind when I think of John Singleton. The first is how paramount it is to possess the courage to see with one's own eyes. Hollywood was trapped in the mode of producing movies about black life that entertained but did not capture the essence of black urban life.

Singleton forced us to change our perspective about what it means to live and grow as a black person in urban America. He shattered the Hollywood stereotypes we had become accustomed to and saw black people in the urban setting as real people with hopes, dreams, fears and courage.

Second, Singleton epitomized what it means to believe in others. Too often in this self-centered society, we forget we can never be all we should be unless we are willing to invest in someone else. He knew he had a gift, but he did not allow his gift to blind him to the gifts in others.

In Ubuntu philosophy, there is a saying that fits the life of John Singleton well. It goes, "I am because we are." The way Singleton invested in others states that he took this motto to heart. All of us should. I hope more of us will.

Third, the tragic end of Singleton's life at age 51 from a stroke reminds us, particularly black men, that we need to take the care of our health seriously. Many men do not go to the doctor as we should.

We need to watch our diet, and we must exercise. Too often we do not care for ourselves as we should. All of us need to promote health care and make our health a priority. We owe it to those who love us to take care of ourselves.

I thank the Ultimate Reality for the life and shared gifts of John Singleton. His work will stand as a monument to his genius. His humility and willingness to invest in others grants him a place of peace in eternity.

A mother's love deserves all the honor it can get

May 7, 2019

Sunday we will celebrate Mother's Day. Many people influenced by Christianity will attend houses of worship with Momma. This is particularly true in the African American community.

It is the one Sunday when every black person made sure they went to "church with their ma dear." Most of us will share a meal or give flowers or candy, or both, to the woman who loved us and nurtured us. A mother's love is special. It deserves all the honor that can be given.

A mother is more than just a female parent. She is the person who loves us despite our faults and idiosyncrasies. Most times, she is the person who birthed us. Sometimes, however, she is not our biological parent but the woman with the capacity to love and empower us along life's way.

It may be a grandmother, an aunt, a family member, a foster parent or someone who adopted us. Whatever the connection, we recognize this person as a mother in our lives.

I was very fortunate to have a good mother. I joke that she was 5 feet by 5 feet. She had a contagious laugh that infected all in a room. She loved all children.

Even when the society was staggering from Jim Crow stupidity, on many occasions our house looked like a gathering of the youth delegation of the United Nations. Gladys Dawson welcomed everyone. She saw it as her calling to encourage, discipline and empower the kids she met.

She taught us to love all kinds of music and have compassion for each other, and she told all of us that we're "somebody" — no matter what anyone in society might say.

She was not perfect, but she was a perfect lover of people. One of her songs of life was, "If I can help somebody along the way, then my living will not be in vain."

When I preached her funeral in 1989, I rejoiced in the fact that she was my mother.

Mothers who love and nurture not only their own children but other people's children have a huge impact on a community. Their actions teach us not to be selfish and self-centered. Their wisdom helps develop our humanity.

Their spirituality allows us to touch and connect to an Ultimate Reality and realize that we are not in this battle alone. Their love is greater than death and the grave.

It bothers me when I observe a female parent who acts like she cannot stand her child. I once heard a woman say to her daughter, "I can't stand you because you look like your damn daddy."

I thought to myself, "What a horrible thing to say to a child." With mothers like that, it's no wonder so many of our children have poor self-esteem, an acute sense of hopelessness and despair, and a propensity to violence.

They are angry, and they have a right to be. If you don't want to be a mother, stop abusing that child and give the child to someone who will rear him or her with honor, love and respect.

We need mothers who are willing to reach out and positively influence their children and others. And we need men to stand by and support good mothers.

To all the women who have taken the bold step of faith to be mothers, I — we — honor you. Happy Mother's Day.

Invest in black college students for America's future

May 21, 2019

Commencement speaker Robert F. Smith announced to the 2019 graduating class of Morehouse College that he would create a grant to pay all their school loan debts.

The estimated cost of such graciousness is $40 million. Ranked by Forbes as a billionaire, Smith is known for such acts of kindness. He has given large sums of money to Cornell University and other academic institutions.

The cost of a college education has risen substantially. Students are incurring more debt than ever before.

Another problem they face is a lack of high-paying jobs. I know students who leave college $100,000 in debt and take jobs paying $30,000 to $40,000. Such huge debt handicaps our young people.

The financial hardship for students at historically black colleges and universities is particularly harsh. Many students at HBCUs are first-generation college students whose families do not have the economic resources to aid them.

HBCUs do not have the wealth of white academic institutions, and thus they cannot assist students as well as their fellow white institutions. Black students are dependent on loans to continue their education. If they are seduced into credit card debt as well, their battle is enormous.

I am happy and proud of African Americans who take on the task of investing in black college students. Tyler Perry and Oprah Winfrey have done the same.

While the pool of wealthy black people in America is much smaller than their Anglo counterparts, more African Americans need to invest in black college students. I hope that more Anglo Americans will also invest in HBCUs and black students attending private or public white institutions.

One of the ways the economic disparity that exists in this country between black and white Americans can be overcome is through the education of African American students.

They need, however, a way to garner an education without experiencing huge financial debt. We may not be billionaires, but all of us can help.

The United Negro College Fund is one method of giving help. No one wants a handout, but all of us need a hand up. Investing in black college students is investing in America's future.

Compassion after tornado is proof of human kindness

May 28, 2019

"Do your little bit of good where you are; it's those little bits of good put together that overwhelm the world." – Desmond Tutu

In the wake of the tornado that hit Jefferson City, I have watched Missourians come together to assist fellow Missourians in need. Human beings, black, white, Latino, gay, straight, Christian, non-Christian, Republican, Democrat, urban and rural have donated items, money and time to help those who became victims of the storm.

It is heartwarming to me to watch us come together to help someone. Given the social, political, economic and racial divisions in this country, such acts of kindness and love should renew our belief in the goodness of the human spirit.

Sometimes it is hard to believe in the goodness of the human spirit. We are constantly bombarded with bad news from various arenas: news media, social media, the barbershop, the beauty salon, the gym, everywhere. The result is that we are tempted to commit two intellectual, social-ethical errors.

The first error is to turn off all media and withdraw from the external world of activity. We adopt a mindset that if we just ignore all the negativity around us it will go away.

Such a mindset is an error because only our collective actions will overcome the evil in the world, and to be informed is to be empowered. No matter how painful the media is, we must stay informed. It is our duty and our right.

The second error is to believe that everyone is only out for themselves. The psychological egoists state that "all people always do what is in their own best interest." They believe all acts of altruism are merely "self-centered" thus to believe that people have compassion for others is simply a flight into fantasy.

I refuse to believe that the people in Jefferson City who went door to door to make sure their neighbors were all right or those who volunteered to clean up neighborhoods, served meals, helped give clothing and baby food to those who are now homeless did it only for themselves.

That kind of thinking confuses the resultant good feeling of doing for others with motivation. Are there selfish people in the world? Of course. But I believe more people believe it is a good thing to be part of a solution instead of the problem.

I believe most people can exercise and demonstrate compassion without a hidden agenda.

I am proud of my fellow Missourians who reached out and are still helping victims of the storm.

I am also proud of people who not only help after a tornado but help the poor, the homeless, the disenfranchised and the socially forgotten every day.

You remind me that the goodness of the human spirit still exists.

Why everyone needs to celebrate Emancipation Day

June 11, 2019

Throughout the United States, and some places in Canada, African Americans will celebrate Juneteenth as Emancipation Day, or Freedom Day.

The story goes that on or around June 19, 1865, the abolition of slavery was announced in Texas and throughout the Confederate States of America.

Since the exact date is still somewhat questionable, most African Americans celebrate the dates from June 13 to 19 as Juneteenth. It is worth noting that in Missouri, many African Americans celebrate Aug. 4 as Emancipation Day.

This is historically true in Cooper, Howard and Jasper counties. That is the date in 1863, passed from generation to generation, that former slaves in Cooper, Howard and other counties became aware of the emancipation proclamation.

As a young man growing up in Joplin, Aug. 4 was a time of reunion, celebration and reflection. Black people from far and near would gather together at the "Negro Park" (Ewert Park) for a time of fellowship and remembrance.

Some people argue that emancipation celebrations should end. Opponents suggest that these celebrations only fan the flames of racial hatred and division.

I heard a broadcaster on a local talk show declare, "African Americans should just be Americans. Slavery and segregation are over. Everyone who is an American is equal. Black people need to just move on."

What this dear fellow needs to remember is the historical narrative of African Americans is the narrative of America. We cannot pick just the parts that make us comfortable; we must reflect upon it all.

I realize that the abolition of legal slavery was not an act of Anglo-American goodwill and compassionate feelings by common humanity. All of us know that President Lincoln did not want to abolish slavery as a once-and-for-all final act. His plan was a gradual process that would conclude in about 1920.

In a letter written to Horace Greeley, Lincoln stated, "If I could save the Union without freeing the slaves ... I would."

We all know that northern industrial interests fueled the abolition of legal slavery. They were drooling for those black bodies to be workers in the new northern factories. Economics, not a heightened sense of morality, pushed the emancipation of African Americans.

And yet, I still believe we should celebrate Freedom Day. Why? Because we have many African American youths who know little or nothing about their ancestors. They are ignorant of segregation and fail to grasp the horror of lynching.

The result is a new slavery to crass materialism, confused identity, violence and self-centeredness. Our youths are not the only ones enslaved. The same is evident among many black adults.

One of the possible solutions to the problem of our new slavery is education about who we really are. Frederick Douglass wrote, "Education makes a child (and an adult) unfit for slavery."

His words are true today. To celebrate our history is to learn about who we are and what we can be as black people in America.

It is also important for Anglo-Americans to join in the celebration. History records that many white Americans fought against slavery and segregation. Quakers and Unitarian Universalists are the most prominent in my mind.

The celebrations remind white people that the position of friend or foe is not reduced to color, but to character. Whoever stands against oppression is my friend.

White Americans will receive an education that can liberate them from the bondage of privilege. Sojourner Truth once said that one of the hardest tasks she faced was convincing a slave that he or she was a slave and that it was all right to be free.

The same is true for many white people in America. Celebrating the emancipation of black people is the opportunity to celebrate the possibility of white (Anglo) liberation.

Several Juneteenth celebrations are happening in the Columbia and Jefferson City area. Take time to celebrate the possibility of our mutual emancipation.

The benefits of a loving, engaged father are lasting

June 18, 2019

"Say not in grief 'he is no more' but in thankfulness that he was."- Hebrew proverb

Last Sunday, many of us celebrated Father's Day. It was a time to reflect and ponder what it means to be a to be a father and to have experienced the love of a father or the father figures in our lives.

Those who had a loving father in their lives are blessed particularly when we think about how many children do not have a father or have experienced the horror of a bad father.

My father died in 1995. He was a career military WWII officer in the segregated Army. He was one of the first educated clergy west of the Mississippi and served as a pastor throughout the United States.

He served as an NAACP president and marched with Dr. King in Illinois. He was not a perfect man, but a man who perfectly loved my mother and me.

As a young man, I did not appreciate his wisdom and courage. I thought his old-school thinking was out-of-date and too simplistic.

When I became 25 years old, I realized that he was brilliant. He hadn't changed, but I had.

When I preached his funeral in 1995, I was aware of what a good father he was. Sometimes we do not fully appreciate the people in our lives until they are gone.

Fatherhood demands the strength to "stand with" despite the obstacles that confront us. No child is perfect. All children act out, have periods of insanity and do things their own way.

But fatherhood demands that that we stand with our children regardless of what they may do. We must love them even when we do not love their actions.

Regardless of my episodes of failure, egocentrism and disappointment, I knew my father had my back. The same was true of my mother.

We need fathers to parent their children. The degree of absentee fatherhood we are experiencing in America is destroying our communities.

Too many men are walking away from their responsibilities as fathers. The result is that too many of our sons and daughters are going to the penitentiary and are fooled into thinking that street life is authentic life.

It is a crippling fallacy that is killing us. Too many women are having to be father and mother in their homes. The saddest part of this fact is, now, many people think that this circumstance is normal.

This phenomenon must stop. Dads, we need you to be dads.

I am also aware of the men who are attempting to be good fathers. They do not get the recognition they deserve. Many of them are being fathers to their biological children and to children who are theirs by love and not blood.

There are men who are acting as father figures to young men and women all around.

They are teachers, coaches, clergy and plain old ordinary men who are willing to listen, encourage and spend time with a young person.

The problem is there are not enough men picking up the challenge. We need more men to be proper father figures in our communities.

Thank God that I had a good father. I am also thankful for the men who stood as fathers in my life and served as role models to me and many more.

Most have gone from here to eternity, but their witness of fatherhood resonates forever.

"A great soul serves everyone all the time. A great soul never dies. It brings us together again and again." - Maya Angelou

Crisis for children at the border is alarming

June 25, 2019

The situation at the southern border has become alarming. The reports of children being separated from their families are horrifying enough. But now it has worsened.

Last week, we were told that necessary personal hygiene items like soap and toothbrushes are being denied to these children. The immigration policy that is plaguing our country is quickly moving from ridiculous to insane.

According to Lyndon Haviland, guest contributor for The Hill, "The public health crisis facing migrant children at the southern U.S. border is at a boiling point. Detained kids are sleeping on concrete benches because the government is running out of room, and out of money. Thousands have been sexually abused. And six have died in U.S. custody over the past eight months alone."

Instead of acting in a more humane manner, we continue to play the blame game. Mr. Trump and Mr. Pence blame the Democrats for this catastrophe. The Democrats blame Mr. Trump and his administration. The well-being of over 10,000 children is being left in limbo ... or worse.

There are laws in place that assert humane treatment for immigrant children. These laws are decades old. They have been the guide for action and have served as protection for children, whether from Guatemala or Georgia.

The problem is that the laws are not being enforced. The cause is either benign neglect or ignorance. Either way, the problem continues to grow.

One thing that is crystal clear is that the system in place to handle the issue of immigrant children at the southern border is antiquated and inadequate to handle the crisis.

We need a new system that is compassionate and moral. The answer is not to "let Mexico handle it" or rely on massive deportation. These ideas may pacify the conservative base, but they do not help the children who are suffering.

We, as Americans, when committed to the common good, have always held children in high regard. We have always proclaimed that the well-being of children is a moral obligation to which we must comply as rational people.

Something in us would motivate us to ensure their well-being was intact. We have been acutely aware that children are not responsible for their circumstances nor capable of changing them.

At our best as adults, children have moved us to be compassionate. Our compassion, in the past, has known no limits.

The question is, "What has happened to us?"

It is one thing to label adult Latinos "murders and drug dealers" (even though we know this is not true).

It is quite another thing to demonize the children.

Surely, we as citizens of these United States have not completely lost our moral conscience.

Regardless of political affiliation, we must care for children at the southern border. History will hold us accountable for our actions. I am convinced that the universe bends toward justice. I fear that if we do not treat these children with compassion and love, we will reap a horrible consequence. It is universally true — we reap what we sow.

Proud of U.S. women who triumphed on the world stage

July 9, 2019

The past week has given us several occasions to celebrate our common way of life.

I am not talking about the military parade in Washington, D.C., orchestrated by President Trump or the usual fireworks displays seen all over the nation. Those things are good and necessary, one guesses.

No, the occasions that should have captured our joy and sense of national pride came from sports. The winning of the World Cup by the U.S. Women's Soccer Team, and the outstanding tennis of 15-year-old Cori "Coco" Gauff.

Everyone who follows soccer, and particularly women's soccer, knew that the women's team had the individual skill and talent to do well in the tournament. The question: Could they play together as a team and focus on their common goal? The victories over France and the Netherlands proved they could become one team, with one purpose.

Gauff proved that one's gift is greater than notoriety. Winning against the great Venus Williams put the world on notice. Gauff has the athleticism and speed to do very well in tennis. She, like the women's soccer team, reminded Americans that we are all ages and colors. To deny our national diversity is to deny who we are.

I realize that not everyone is a sports fan. I have a very limited knowledge of both soccer and tennis. But I understand perseverance and commitment to something greater than ourselves. These women overcame obstacles. They worked on their craft even when they didn't want to do so.

The women's soccer team taught us that you don't have to look alike to garner something great, but you must work together. As a country, we are failing to remember that.

I was also elated that the best of us was represented by women. It was American women doing their thing before the eyes of millions.

Even though they are not paid like their male counterparts, they did their thing. Painfully, we observed talented women once again be the victims of economic disparity.

Neither women's tennis nor soccer players earn the money that men do. It is a shame, because women can perform at the highest level, and yet (like most places in America) women are paid less than I am.

Someone said to me this week that there is not much to be joyous about these days. I agree that there is a lot to be upset about, but there are still many things to celebrate and have a sense of pride.

How about those women who represented us on the world's biggest stages and represented us well.

Actively resist the ugly politics of ignorance and hatred

July 16, 2019

"So interesting to see 'Progressive' Democrat Congresswomen, who originally came from countries whose governments are a complete and total catastrophe, the worst, most corrupt and inept anywhere in the world (if they even have a functioning government at all), now loudly and viciously telling the people of the United States, the

greatest and most powerful Nation on earth, how our government is to be run." - Donald Trump

Just when you think the current president has exhausted his demonstrations of ignorance and hatred, he hits you with another whammy.

The above tweet comes from the man we allow to be president of the United States. His target(s) are four women of color who serve in the U.S. House of Representatives, Democratic Reps. Ayanna Pressley of Massachusetts, Rashida Tlaib of Michigan, Alexandria Ocasio-Cortez of New York and Ilhan Omar of Minnesota.

Known as "The Squad," each has called for the impeachment of Donald Trump.

The tweet is embarrassingly ludicrous. The law requires that one must be a citizen of the United States to serve in Congress, yet Mr. Trump urges them to go back to the countries they originally came from.

Is Mr. Trump not cognizant of the fact that three of the women of his disdain were born in the United States and one came to this country at an early age and is legally a U.S. citizen? Their country is this country.

Perhaps he became confused because they can speak multiple languages and have the courage to express a faith tradition that is not white, Western European and Anglo-American?

Is his anger grounded in political difference or on the fact that these women are smarter than he could ever become and refuse to allow him to grab them by their genitals? One wonders.

The second thing that illustrates the president's old-fashioned stupidity is the logic behind the tweet. It assumes that some of us are more American than others. Is this idea based on color, language or dress?

The fact is that the only people from here per se are Native Americans, and they, too, came from somewhere else. All of us came here from somewhere else.

I love reminding so-called white people like Trump and his base that they originally came from Africa. All people originated in Africa!

The overt racism Trump expresses is troubling but not surprising. Maya Angelou once said that when people show you who they really are, believe them.

Mr. Trump has repeatedly shown us who he really is and that we should believe him. The more sensible people who voted for him (all of his base are not idiots!) in the last election are embarrassed by his tweet.

I may be naïve, but I do not think everyone who voted for Mr. Trump is a racist. I think some who voted for him wanted a dramatic change in government as usual and believed Mr. Trump would be the great white hope bringing constructive change and a voice for the "little people" in America.

Some voted for Trump because they didn't like Hillary Clinton. Some voted for him because of a twisted and pseudo-theological xenophobic perspective that maintains the God is for everything white.

Some voted out their anti-black anger directed at President Obama. Whatever the reasoning of those who voted for Mr. Trump, it is undeniable that if you vote for him again, you are willfully voting for a racist who is anti-diversity and pro-divisiveness. The subsequent result is that no country divided against itself can stand.

All politicians make mistakes in speech and action. The Squad has made some errors in speech and action that must be admitted. The Squad needs to make some adjustments.

Stop being vulgar in speech. You are educated women with expansive vocabularies. Don't sink to the lowest common denominator like Mr. Trump.

Just because someone calls you a socialist or anti-Semite doesn't make it true, but don't give people ammunition to shoot you with. Be bold and wise.

All people of color who attempt to speak truth to power get labeled and ridiculed. 'Tis the nature of the beast. If you happen to be a woman, it is worse.

Racism, sexism and homophobia are bastard triplets birthed in a cradle of ignorance and fear. We who truly love the idea of this democratic experiment must not allow division, the insanity at the border or the calculated efforts to limit personal freedom to destroy our country.

We can stop the madness if we are willing to intentionally stand together for the common good and not just for the good of some.

If we fail to stand with and for all Americans, we shall surely face doom together. The power is in our hands.

Conquering the seductive menace of distraction

July 30, 2019

Distraction: Something that prevents someone from giving full attention to something else.

One of the things you must give Mr. Trump credit for is his superb use of distraction. He is a master of making America give full attention to something that is either ridiculous or outrageous and ignoring what is important. The recent tweets by Mr. Trump illustrate my point.

Trump has launched a barrage of attacks against Maryland Congressman Elijah Cummings. Trump has now accused Cummings of being a racist and improperly using federal and state funds given to improve Baltimore.

He declared that Baltimore is a "rat-invested" city that no one would want to live in. Ben Carson has now echoed the president, saying that as a neurosurgeon he was hesitant to send children back to "infested" homes in Baltimore.

For the record, every major U.S. city has problems with housing in low-income areas. All have problems with rats, roaches, etc. Baltimore is no better or worse than Kansas City, St. Louis, Detroit, New York or Washington, D.C.

There are some very good areas in Baltimore, and there are some horrific areas there, too. Let us note that one of the best research institutions in the world, Johns Hopkins, is in Baltimore.

It is interesting that Mr. Trump would make such comments about Baltimore given that his son-in-law, Jared Kushner, is one of the major slum lords in Baltimore.

If the economy is doing so well, why isn't the Trump administration fixing the problem of poverty and housing in America instead of padding the pockets of the rich?

However, Mr. Trump's tweets do not alarm any thinking person. He did reveal, however, that he does not know what racism is if he thinks Cummings is a racist.

Black people can be prejudiced and/or biased, but they cannot be racist. White America constructed racism.

Racism is a three-tired phenomenon that is individual, systemic and institutional. Since people of color did not construct racism in America and do not have access to the privilege and power of deconstructing racism, only white

America can either dismantle racism or continue to perpetuate it.

My main concern is not Mr. Trump's propensity for divisive rhetoric. Mr. Cummings, the Rev. Al Sharpton and members of The Squad are big boys and girls.

They, like all of us who speak our minds, have learned to grow thick skin. My main concern is that Americans who truly love this country not get distracted by this nonsense and lose sight of what is truly important.

The situation in the Middle East, particularly Iran, is of massive importance. War in the Middle East will have devastating consequences to our society.

Perhaps we should stop being the "police force" of the world and recognize the rights of sovereign countries.

We have plenty of issues to tackle here at home. We need Republicans and Democrats to focus on them and stop being distracted.

The situation at the southern border demands immediate attention. We created the problem by our interference in Latin America. Suddenly, we withdrew funding, and a bad situation became worse.

People fled Central America for a better life. Now, we have nearly 100,000 people in detention centers.

Why can't a bipartisan group from the Senate and the House of Representatives tour all the facilities as one fact-finding assembly and report to us the truth of what is happening there?

It is reported that people are sick and dying. We are told children are in cages. Shouldn't we find out what is true in a bipartisan manner and forget about Trump's lunacy?

Robert Mueller's comment during his hearing before a House committee is important. When asked whether he believed the Russians interfered with our political system, he replied, "They are now!"

Regardless of how much Trump loves Mr. Putin, we cannot continue to allow foreign powers to interfere with who we are as a democratic republic. What the Russians are doing is far more important than what I am called by a racist.

Finally, we need Democrats to stop acting like chickens with their heads cut off. They need to unify and present a way for us to be united again.

Their infighting will result in Trump being elected again. I am not anti-Republican, but I am anti-Trump.

Four more years in office for him will put this country in a situation we may not recover from for a very long time.

We are being distracted, and it is hurting us. As a nation, we are more divided than we have been in a long time.

It is time for us to be about what is important for the common good, not simple-minded ideological agendas.

How can we unite the Anglo population and people of color, the wealthy and the poor, urban and suburban, the working class and the rural community?

That is the vision and goal of the common good. It should be the goal of every American who wants us to be truly great.

Mr. President: We must stop killing each other. Now

August 6, 2019

The speech Mr. Trump gave Monday in the aftermath of the tragedies in El Paso and Dayton was moving.

For once, he sounded like the president of the United States of America by denouncing racism, bigotry and white supremacy.

Of course, he did not address how his prior rhetoric fanned the flames of racism, bigotry and white supremacy ideology in America. Perhaps that is a speech or tweet coming in the next few days.

Suffice it to say that he did acknowledge that racism is real and that the growth of the white supremacy movement is a serious threat to this country. Domestic terrorism is not a figment of the imagination of a few.

Now we see if the president means what he says and will do something to unify instead of dividing the nation. We shall see.

The other major issue we must address is the problem of guns and violence in America.

Reportedly, there have been 251 mass shootings in the U.S. this year. The death toll has reached over 8,700 people, with 17,300 or more injuries. A total of 33,237 shooting incidents have been reported across the country.

We know that many shootings are not reported. We cannot ignore the presence of gun violence in our society.

Clearly, there are no easy answers or solutions to the problem. Yes, we need to prevent the mentally ill from having access to assault weapons. Yes, violent video games seem to numb us to the horrific reality of violent death. Yes, we have some problems with social media.

But these alone fail to address the problem in its totality. Somehow we must break from our propensity to think all problems can be settled by violence.

From the old Wild West personae to the prominence of "gangsta" rap, one thing is painfully obvious: There is a hole in America's soul.

We are killing one another. Our violent character has led us to disaster.

The time for talking about gun violence and gun control is over. There have been enough seminars on communities and violence, books suggested and prominent speakers pontificating about the problem.

We need our national, state and local leaders to act. It is too easy to get a gun in America.

I have grown up with guns all my life. My father (and later me along his side) would hunt every winter.

We filled our freezer with wild game. But never did we use an assault rifle to hunt. We hunted rabbits and deer, not Bigfoot or Godzilla.

My point is the availability of semi-automatic and automatic assault weaponry is unjustifiable. Common sense states that we must change our thinking about guns if we are going to survive.

I am learning, however, that common sense is not all that common.

It is interesting how tragedies bring us as Americans together. I hope that we will come together about gun violence and violence in toto.

To build the common good, we must enact laws that keep us from killing each other while we work on methodologies that can teach us how to love each other.

So, Mr. President, I hope you are being real with what you said Monday and pull Republicans and

Democrats together to reform gun laws in America.

Our condolences to the families who mourn in El Paso, Dayton and Chicago.

May we one day learn to beat our swords into plowshares and study war no more.

A tribute to Dr. Joseph Bien, my teacher and friend

August 13, 2019

On Monday, Aug. 5, Dr. Joseph Bien died.

Dr. Bien was a professor of philosophy (retired) in the MU Department of Philosophy. He was my dissertation director and my friend.

He and some others in the department, like William Bondeson and Peter Markie, made me feel comfortable and capable.

At that time, I was the only African American in the graduate program. Yet he never treated me like the "department's token Negro." I had already completed a master of divinity degree at Princeton, but now I was part of a different discipline, one that was challenging and often intimidating.

Joe Bien reminded me that I could do the work ... and I belonged.

You can read about Joe Bien's many accomplishments in various places but allow me to share what Dr. Bien meant to me.

Joe pushed me to think in an informed, inclusive manner. He was an atheist; I am a Christian and was pastor of the Second Baptist Church in Columbia. He was a Marxist; I am not. He was Anglo; I am African American.

Joe allowed me the freedom to think about the world as bigger than the parochial religiosity I had known. With Dr. Bien, I read Karl Marx and did not rely on what people said Marx or Marxism is about.

Being with Joe, I both understood and appreciated why many good people do not believe in God. He allowed me room to disagree with notions and ideas without being disagreeable.

So many people attempt to put me and others in a box. Joe affirmed my right to think my own thoughts and speak my own mind.

Dr. Bien demonstrated what true forgiveness is all about. During my tenure as a Ph.D. student at MU, I developed a problem, an illness. In most barbershops, beauty parlors and gathering places, people talked about my problem and ridiculed me.

They stated that I would never be whole again and spoke of me as an embarrassment to my race, my calling and the University of Missouri.

But Joe never gave up on me. He was disappointed but believed that I would recover and go on to be the philosopher and theologian I am today.

The point is that Joe Bien believed in me even in the times I didn't believe in myself. Today I am strong, whole and full of vinegar. Thanks, Joe, for believing in me.

Joe encouraged me to love life. He loved the opera, classical music and movies. His love for aesthetics and life stirred my own love of music and life.

Life is not easy. He was with me when I preached my mother's, father's and only sister's funeral. He affirmed life amid death.

With him, I affirm life, despite the divisive, violent events that are happening all around us. I still believe in people, and I love life.

Joe was not perfect. Like all of us, he had his shortcomings. He could be snippy at times.

But knowing him made you love and admire him. I shall miss you, Joe. Though you did not believe in God, I have a big God that believes in you.

Rest in peace my brother, and I will see you again.

Brazil's stubbornness has worldwide impact

August 27, 2019

"We cannot accept that a President, [Emmanuel] Macron, issues inappropriate and gratuitous attacks against the Amazon. Nor that he disguises his intentions behind an 'alliance' of the G-7 countries to 'save' the Amazon, as if it were a colony or no man's land." - Jair Bolsonaro, President, Brazil

Before the conclusion of the G-7 Summit, member countries voted to give Brazil $22.2 million to fight the fire raging in the Amazon rain forest.

President Jair Bolosonaro, a skeptic of climate change, then rejected the much needed aid. He seems to believe that the assistance is an attempt to colonize Brazil. Hmmm.

The fact of the matter is that the fire in the Amazon affects not only Brazil but the entire world. Approximately 20% of the world's oxygen is supplied by the Amazon rain forest.

The destruction we are witnessing will impact the Earth for centuries.

Not only will the world's climate be impacted by the fire, animals and tribal communities that live in the Amazon are being directly affected now.

The pictures on social media of people and animals burned by the fire are heartbreaking.

Adults and children are experiencing death and destruction. Though we may be living in an anti-Latin/South American period, it is undeniable that as a world community we have a moral obligation to save the people and animals ravaged by the fire in the Amazon.

We share the world. Our duty is to help those in need. Truly, people and animals in the Amazon need to be rescued.

How sad it is when petty politics interferes with doing good. Brazil is incapable of fighting the fire alone. Brazil needs the resources offered by the G-7 to help during this tragedy.

But Bolsonaro is too proud and irrational to receive it. I am always wary of small-minded people with too much power.

This is just another example of why we should be wary. White Western Europeans have a long history of colonization and raping lands of their natural resources (of which Brazil has plenty), but I believe this gesture of good will from the G-7 countries is genuine.

The world has something at stake with this tragedy, and, again, it is the world's moral obligation to assist Brazil. It is Brazil's obligation to accept the help.

The effects of climate change are real. All of us have already felt them: weird winter patterns, strange summers, floods, weather disasters, and on and on.

Beginning with elementary school science class, we learned how plant life gives us the necessary oxygen to survive on this planet.

The destruction of forests of great size, like the Amazon rain forest, will not only affect us, but also our children and our grandchildren.

My hope is that Bolsonaro will come to his senses. A change of heart and mind by Brazil's president will not only help Brazil, it will bless the whole world.

My prayers this day remember Brazil.

Bullets are equal-opportunity destroyers

September 3, 2019

I awoke today to another report that a shooting happened in Columbia.

Allegedly, individuals in two cars engaged in a gunfight on southwest I-70 near the Stadium exit.

Currently, the police believe that the occupants of the vehicles knew one another.

The preliminary report stated that two individuals sustained non-threatening gunshot injuries. Fortunately, no one else was injured.

As I listened to the news report my heart broke, again. What if some innocent family member driving along I-70 had been struck by a stray bullet?

What if it had hit some child?

Living in Columbia has given many of us a false sense of security. We feel immune from danger.

Domestic terror is a reality for other places, like Texas, Florida or Ohio, but not here.

Too many Columbians believe that violence only happens in "those communities." This incident painfully reminds us that it can happen anywhere.

One fact is undeniable: Bullets are equal opportunity destroyers. They can kill anyone.

They are not influenced by whether you are white or a person of color. They will kill a person who is straight, a member of the LGBTQ community, Republican or Democrat, male or female, atheist or theist.

Money, education and occupation cannot stop a bullet from killing. Clearly our political utterances have not curbed the problem.

The problem is not Republican or Democratic. It is not conservative or liberal. It is an American problem.

We are at war with ourselves and the core of our common good is being threatened.

When did our disregard for human life become so prevalent?

We live in a society where we are willing to kill one another over any disagreement. The easy answers are that the violence we are experiencing is due to either drugs or mental illness.

Indeed, these are components of the problem but fail to explain the phenomenon fully.

Do we hate ourselves so deeply that we are willing to kill others so readily?

I remember while at Princeton hearing the great George Hendry lecture on the death of the Roman Empire.

One phrase that has always stuck with me is his comment that the Roman Empire did not fall because of enemies outside its borders. It fell because of enemies within.

I wonder if the enemies in our society are more of a threat to our survival than any enemy outside the U.S.?

We cannot avoid the fact that it is too easy for anyone to acquire a gun. We need reasonable gun control.

I do not want to restrict responsible people from possessing a gun. I want to stop irresponsible folks from having a weapon. No ordinary citizen needs a weapon that fires 100 rounds or more.

I know common sense is not common, but surely, we can agree that something dramatic needs to happen.

There have been too many mass shootings as well as too many isolated shootings.

All of them endanger us. All of them need to be stopped.

As Americans we must end the violence for our sake, for the sake of our children and for the sake of this republic.

Let's break away from exclusive language about God

September 10, 2019

On Feb. 1, 2018, the Episcopal Church Diocese of Washington, D.C., voted to stop using only masculine pronouns in referring to God.

The decision was made while preparing to update its Book of Common Prayer, as well as fostering the conscious use of male, feminine and neuter terms in preaching, prayer and teaching.

The diocese believed that inclusive language would be a way to broaden our understanding of God and create an atmosphere of respect for the entire human family.

I agree.

Sept. 11 represents my 42nd year as an ordained minister. During most of my career as a preacher and teacher, I have intentionally used inclusive language about God.

Anyone who knows me will attest to this. It just makes good theological and philosophical sense.

If God exists (which I believe God does), and the human family is created in the image and likeness of God, then to think about God as both male and female is without question.

To speak about God must include both masculine and feminine concepts and terms. At the root, what I posit is an antinomy: God is male and female ... and neither.

The insistence of using inclusive language when speaking about God has caused great debate in the church.

Fundamentalists see such a move as heresy. They claim that all referents about God in the Bible are male. Since Jesus refers to God as Father, then God must be male. After all, they say, men are made in the image of God, and women are made in the image of men (the rib story in Genesis).

Many liberal churches object to the conceptualization of God as male but fail to do their exegetical homework. They want to decry the injustice of such a conceptualization but on social grounds, and not on theological grounds.

Exclusive language about God lends itself to the denigration and oppression of women.

If women are made in the image of men and not God, then they are second class to men.

Historically, this idea has been used to prevent women from participating as clergy and holding major offices in the church, as well as separating learning experiences by gender.

It has socially promoted discrimination and sexism. It has not been that long ago that women were prevented from the opportunity to learn philosophy, systematic theology, mathematics and science simply because they were women.

Exclusive language supports a toxic masculinity that can no longer be tolerated.

My greatest angst comes from women clergy and laity who only use masculine language about God. These same women object to sexual discrimination in the church but employ the language of discrimination and exclusivity.

Tradition has taught us to refer to God in the masculine only. Traditions forged by social constructs tend to be rigid. They are slow to change.

However, they can be changed. For me, part of the problem lies in our forgetting the Second Commandment: "Make no graven image of me." Graven means serious, inflexible and permanent.

A graven image can be made of physical materials or intellectual concepts. I think God was trying to teach us that none of our images can capture the totality of God as an ultimate reality. To act as if only male concepts are correct is hubris.

So, hooray for the move by the Episcopalians. I hope other denominations will join the movement toward inclusive language about God. Then I think we will hear Her (God) say, "Well done!"

Violence in Columbia — and a way forward

September 24, 2019

The shootings that we have experienced in Columbia the last few weeks have all of us baffled, concerned and frustrated. Many experienced and learned people are speaking out about how to stop the violence.

Some see the events as nothing more than the activities of criminals in our community. The solution, for them, is simply to lock black folks up and systematically rid ourselves of these lawbreakers. The problem is that imprisonment has not solved the problem in our society. We keep building more and more prisons, yet the propensity for violence increases. It is simply a temporary solution to an ongoing challenge.

Some have articulated the various systemic and structural barriers that have perpetuated the problem of violence. Unfortunately, the phenomenon is deeper than theoretical analysis can adequately address.

Some attribute the cause of violence to a spiritual lostness that can only be conquered through prayer, preaching and supplication. Again, while I believe in spiritual action, preaching at the problem and quoting scripture will not stop the tragedy.

I believe that the root of the problem is anti-black hatred within the black community. It is "the elephant in the room" that no one wishes to acknowledge. This problem has been with us since our days in slavery. Many black leaders and thinkers have addressed it: Garvey, Malcolm X, Gordon, Angelou, King and Cone just to name a few. Somewhere along the line we have allowed ourselves to be fooled into 1) hating ourselves and 2) hating other black folk and people of color.

While white people do kill other white people, black-on-black crime is a major problem within the black community. Our failure to work together for a common cause; our non-support of black entrepreneurship; the foolishness of light-skin, dark-skin rivalries; the downplaying of education; and, of course, the killing of one another all point to the power and prominence of anti-black hatred within the black community.

The black community in Columbia has changed. Once, we had the people like Beulah Ralph, Sarah Belle Jackson, Almeta Crayton and others who encouraged and inspired us to think of ourselves as one people while fighting against the systematic racism that plagued Columbia. We were a community of families that watched out and cared for one another.

Now it seems that we operate by a mantra that goes: "Every person for themselves."

Something fundamentally new (and yet old) must emerge if we are going to stop the violence in Columbia. We must insist, loudly and clearly, that gun violence in the black community will not be tolerated by black Columbia. We can and must police ourselves. We must stop quoting how "snitches get stitches" and proclaim, "Put down the guns, and stop the violence or you will have to answer to us!"

We must unite for positive change in our community. The NAACP, Race Matters, Friends, black Churches, black Muslims, the Minority Men's Network, black university and college faculty and others must form a think tank and action group to address the problems black youth (and the black community in toto) are experiencing. The need for decent jobs and affordable housing, as well as positive self-identity, is real. If we continue to act as if it is someone else's problem, we shall continue to see our children die before our eyes.

We must become merchants of hope and not despair. We decide if we will be victims or victors.

The power is in our hands. Use it.

My sincere condolences to all the families that experienced death because of senseless violence in our community. It is time for a change. Some things black people must do for themselves.

overcoming anti-black hatred in the black community has to be a top priority.

United, we are mightier than the giants standing before us

October 6, 2019

Some of the critics of my last column mistakenly believed I was advocating a "pull yourself up by your boot-straps" ideology. Such thinking could not be further from the truth. Indeed, black self-hatred is the residue from slavery and segregation, perpetuated by the systemic, structural and institutional racism experienced in contemporary America. Black people did not establish the systematic and structural racism that exists. White America constructed it and benefited from it. White people must recognize this fact, and white people need to dismantle systemic and structural racism if we are going to move from chaos to community (à la Martin King). Agreed.

What I am positing is the revisioning of the psychological, spiritual, economic, social and political emancipation of black people. We must find a way to establish a sense of black pride and solidarity that promotes well-being while rejecting and resisting the murdering of ourselves. The questions are: How can black people become black people's best supporters? How can black people start to see each other as brothers and sisters in a common struggle for liberation and the good, and not enemies? How can we overcome pettiness, classism, sexism and homophobia in the black community so that all of us may rise to the destiny envisioned by our fore-parents?

White America must take on the onus of deconstructing racism. Black people must take on the task of promoting self-love.

I was encouraged to hear both Columbia's mayor and police chief acknowledge last week that the problem of recent gun shootings and violence is not a phenomenon that we can arrest away.

They are correct. The violence we are experiencing is a multifaceted issue. The violence in the black community, here and across this country, is an internal and external phenomenon. The systematic and structural racism in play in our society has promoted black self-hatred, particularly in the form of murder. The same violence is also tied to the insidious economic disparity citizens in low-income communities confront every day. Since most of those citizens are black and brown, black-on-black and brown-on-brown violence is more prevalent in said communities. The lack of finances to meet basic needs results in violence against others, even those that look like you. As a caveat, please remember white-on-white crime happens as well.

Lack of education and the absence of the middle class within the communities where violence is high leaves young people without role models who can relate to their experience. The continuous otherworldly posture of too many black churches raises anger and disappointment. The black church — the one institution born of struggle and owned by black people — is woefully absent when the need for its presence is so evident. The need for psychological resources is at an all-time high in our community. These socio-economic factors cannot be overlooked. Yet articulating these factors alone does not answer the question: How do we stop the violence here and elsewhere in America?

There is a hole in the soul of black folk in America and in Columbia. We have learned that social integration, the pontification of political parties, crass materialism and well-intentioned educational institutions were nothing more than empty promises grounded in greed, wealth and power. It has left us in despair, drowning in anger and often hopeless. After generations of hurt, the result is violence. Yes, criminals need to go to prison. But they also need education and training while they are there so they can create their own dreams, instead of destroying others'.

Our fore parents envisioned something greater than what is happening in our communities, both black and white. It is time to be about the business of constructing a society that illustrates our greatness and does not foster the worst in us.

I believe we are greater than our circumstances, and mightier that the giants that stand before us. I believe in human autonomy and the ability to choose and create the fundamentally new. The promise was never that the road would be easy. The promise is that we can be victorious. Our ancestors knew why the caged bird sings. We must rediscover it, too.

There are hints that the city may reorganize the Mayor's Task Force on Community Violence. Five years ago, the task force made recommendations to the city about how the address the problem of violence. Some things were implemented, some were not. I hope a new task force will come into being. I hope it will include many stakeholders. We need the hard, penetrating social analysis of a Traci Wilson-Kleekamp, the experience of a Mary Ratliff and the progressive conservative knowledge of a Josh Divine. We need some clergy with backbone to mobilize our people for change. But we also need the real folk who know and live in Columbia and who know firsthand the challenges they face every day. We need people who love and care about the whole of Columbia.

The greatest task will be remolding dreams and filling the vacant spaces of the human heart with hope — a real hope. Not just for our children, but for all of us.

An appeal for just uniform punishment for murderers

October 8, 2019

"And forgive us our trespasses as we forgive those who trespass against us." - Jesus

"To understand everything is to forgive everything."- Buddha

In September 2018, Amber Guyger, a white, female Dallas police officer, entered the apartment of Botham Jean, a 26-year-old black man, and shot and killed him.

Guyger claimed that she believed she was in her own apartment (which was one floor below Jean's apartment) and thought he was an intruder.

She was sentenced to 10 years in the Texas State Penitentiary. At the sentencing hearing, Botham Jean's 18-year-old brother told Guyger, the court and the world that he and his family forgave Guyger for killing his older brother.

Two questions arise from this incident. First, what is proper forgiveness and are there some people and states of affair that we ought not to forgive? And, second, does forgiveness exonerate injustice?

Forgiveness relieves the person (or family) victimized by violence (or any offense) from the weight of hatred.

Forgiveness is not about the recipient; it is for the forgiving party. It is not tied to the confessional nature of the offender, because no one can be certain about the sincerity of the confessor.

After all, we live in a culture that has taught all of us how to "fake" it.

Forgiveness transforms the offended from the burden of hatred and malice to the power and opportunity of forward movement.

Forgiveness prevents the offended from being handcuffed to an event of the past, no matter how heinous the event might be.

What Botham Jean's younger brother did in declaring the family's forgiveness of Amber Guyger's murderous act was to declare before humanity and God that the action will not shackle us to hatred or prevent our movement forward into the future.

We will not be slaves to madness. Such is the power of forgiveness.

What forgiveness does not do is excuse or exonerate injustice. In the case of Amber Guyger, injustice was demonstrated at multiple levels.

It was wrong to investigate officers to attempt to find marijuana in Jean's apartment to discredit him.

It was wrong to leave Guyger at the crime scene alone. And paramount to all of this is the fact that Guyger was sentenced to only 10 years, which means she is eligible for parole in five.

If I walked into an Anglo person's abode and murdered the occupant, please believe I would receive a sentence of more than 10 years.

For clarity's sake, let me say that I do not want Amber Guyger to receive an unjust sentence because of the long history of unjust sentences black people have received throughout American history.

That would not be justice. That is simply revenge, and revenge is the bastard twin of hatred.

I want the judicial system to treat all people fairly and not give preferential treatment to those who enjoy access to privilege and power.

If judges are going to give hugs and Bibles to Amber Guyger, then give hugs and Bibles (or Korans, Vedas, Tanakhs, Tao Te Ching, etc.) to everyone convicted of a heinous crime.

I want murderers to be convicted whether they live as parasites in the black community or wear blue uniforms. No one should be allowed to murder the innocent without just punishment.

This is not advocacy for the death penalty (that is another form of injustice). This is an appeal for just, uniform punishment.

Dr. Martin Luther King Jr. once wrote, "He who is devoid of the power to forgive is devoid of the power to love." I would add from author Bell Hooks, "There can be no love where there is no justice."

e must become better at practicing forgiveness, love and justice if as a society we are to live as we ought. One without the other is merely an invitation to destruction.

Another Christian perspective on the sermon about gender

October 18, 2019

"For now we see through a glass, darkly; but then face to face: now I know in part; but then shall I know even as also I am known." - Saul of Tarsus

"God alone is Lord of the conscience." - basic Presbyterian principle, 1877

Last Sunday, Keith Simon, co-pastor at The Crossing, preached a sermon at the church in Columbia that has ignited serious discussion and controversy in the community.

As part of his sermon series entitled "Genesis: The Strange but True Story of Everything," Simon addressed the issue of transgenderism.

For purposes of introduction, allow me to state that this column is not a bashing of my friend and brother, Keith Simon. Instead, it is a response to what I think is a theological error in thinking.

My goal is to state that all Christians do not think the same about LGBTQIAA+ issues. There is another Christian way of thinking that is also legitimate.

What I know is that Keith Simon is a good man and The Crossing is a good church. It supports many projects in Columbia, including Ragtag Cinema, the True/False Film Fest, Fun City, drives to feed the hungry, the repair of senior citizen homes and the payment of medical debts that crush the working poor. All of these acts are unquestionably good.

The Crossing is a good church, but it is not a perfect one. No person or organization, including churches, is perfect. All of us, conservatives and progressives, "look through a glass darkly."

We should not demonize Pastor Simon, the ministry team or The Crossing. We should agree to disagree.

Since we all make errors in thought and action from time to time, we should speak to one another, in love, about our disagreements and affirm our common humanity. Humility and forgiveness are key.

Keith Simon is a Christocentric, evangelical Christian committed to a white, western European, Anglo-American understanding of God, the Bible, salvation, authentic living, etc. Such is the paradigm out of which he operates, and I respect that.

I, however, am an African American, theocentric Christian committed to an African American understanding of God as Mother and Father, a black hermeneutical method of interpreting the Bible that affirms and includes the whole human race as the children of God and not just Christians.

I believe the goal of Christianity is liberation from all forms of oppression (economic, gender, racial, spiritual, social, political and physical) and that engaging in such efforts is superior to personal piety and doctrinal commitment.

I believe social justice is authentic Christianity, and without work toward justice, we are merely sounding brass and tinkling symbols. Having said all that, in love, I come to publicly disagree with my brother regarding the phenomenon of people who identify as transgender.

We must acknowledge that gender dysphoria is a condition where a person experiences discomfort or distress because there's a mismatch between their biological sex and gender identity.

It's sometimes known as gender identity disorder (GID), gender incongruence or transgenderism.

It is not, however, the same as anorexia neurosis. To equate the two is mixing apples and oranges.

People who identify as transgender do so in many ways. Some remain "stealth" or incognito to the outside world, while some take large amounts of estrogen or testosterone to alter their physical appearance. Others have partial surgical procedures.

All people who identify as transgender do not have full surgical transitions as Caitlyn Jenner did, nor do they want to do so.

Such thinking is erroneous, and portraying transgenderism as only surgically transitioning is misleading.

What Pastor Keith suggested is that God has provided a "divine design" for authentic living, found in Genesis 1:27 and reiterated by Jesus in Matthew 19.

The "design" is for people to be male and female. The sermon alludes that not following the design, particularly as a Christian, is to live an inauthentic life outside the authority of God and Jesus.

While I do not want to engage in a Bible study, I suggest that members of the queer community, including transgender people, are still male and female, they are just LGBTQIAA+ males and females. They are not another species; they are still human and part of the divine design.

To state they are violating the profile for what it means to be authentically human is a much too narrow biblical position, grounded in patriarchy. As a Christian and a human being, it is a position I cannot and do not support.

The sermon offered statistical data as evidence that transitioning people who elect to surgically transition are at a higher rate of suicide than those who do not.

Such data is suspect, given the absence of reports of people who identify as transgender, surgically transition and live healthy, flourishing lives.

Surely there is some evidence to support the election of surgical transition that leads to flourishing, well-rounded lives. Without showing the other data, the argument suffers from the fallacy of begging the question.

The decision made by people who identify as transgender is their God-given right. What I know about God is that God created us as autonomous beings. We have the freedom to exercise our choice as to who we are.

That is the point of Rachel Dolezal. If we can do so racially (biracial persons have been trying to educate us on this point), we should have the right to do so when it comes to gender.

To deny that right is slavery, not freedom in Christ.

"For they that the Son sets free are free indeed."

We all accept dirty money. Let's clean it with noble acts

October 22, 2019

Some interesting conversations have arisen since the fallout over The Crossing church co-pastor Keith Simon's sermon on transgenderism.

My response was published in Sunday's Missourian, and I really don't want to address the sermon any longer, other than to apologize that my comments did not include or address the issue of nonbinary gender.

No writer can say everything in one column. Please hear this: I do think God also created people who affirm nonbinary gender.

I am still a student in the process of learning about the nuances of gender, and I try not to talk about what I do not know.

We are engaged in a new field of study when we explore sexual fluidity, and we will discover more as the research continues to grow and expand. Thanks to those who called my attention to the phenomenon of nonbinary gender.

With the Ragtag Film Society deciding to no longer accept financial sponsorship from The Crossing, the conversation about money has become fascinating to me.

My understanding is that over 1,000 people signed a petition asking Ragtag Cinema and the True/False Film Festival to give up funding from The Crossing because many consider it "dirty money."

This does not come from the Ragtag Film Society. They are refusing the money because of a difference in core values.

But here is my question: Given that we live in a capitalistic society, where may I find "clean money"?

Isn't all money under a capitalistic system dirty money? If you put your money in a bank, that bank probably invests in all kinds of enterprises in order to produce a profit. That may include the sale of weapons to enemies of democracy or investments in sweat shops in various parts of the world.

If you have a 401(k) plan, you also may have no clue where your money has been invested.

Here are other possible scenarios:

If I sell artwork to a drug dealer because his daughter fancies it, have I acted complicatedly by accepting his money?

I have a Ph.D. from a historically racist, sexist, homophobic academic institution. Have I benefited from dirty money if my degree is fruit from a poisonous tree?

Again, what constitutes dirty money?

When I pastored a church in Detroit, I would put the hymn numbers on the wall for congregates to easily find the hymns. It's a common practice in many churches.

I suddenly noticed an increase in attendance increased, as well as the offering. I subsequently learned that some people who attended the worship services were playing the numbers (Pick 3, Pick 4, or a street numbers game) and hitting on a regular basis.

Not only were they hitting, they were "tithing" (10%) their winnings! When I discovered what was happening, I stopped putting up hymn numbers, but the question remained: Was the tithing dirty money?

One of the most ardent and strident critics of my columns, Cam Neal, said something that I think is unquestionably correct: "We must not accept false premises."

To believe that clean money and dirty money exist is a false premise that leads to an invalid argument.

It leaves two choices: Refuse all sponsorships and money of any kind because it could be dirty money. Or clean dirty money with noble action.

Because of the way the world of economics works, we can never know how or where money is generated. I therefore suggest we clean the money with noble action.

Use the money to get inmates out of jail if they are in danger of losing their homes and jobs because they have been incarcerated for much too long.

Take the scholarships from Shell, Exxon, and Mobile oil companies and use them to help students become engineers and make the world a better place to live.

It has been reported that The Crossing gave True/False $35,000 in financial contributions, while Ragtag Cinema received $8,000. If people consider it dirty money, give that money to me.

I could develop a theological education program in conjunction with Columbia College or Stephens or Moberly Area Community College to train black clergy who cannot afford it because they must feed their families.

Use the money to bless organizations like the Turning Point and the Voluntary Action Center.

Organize a network to help women and men escape human trafficking or have ongoing Christian-LGBTQIAA+ conferences so we can all learn and not just rant.

Fund workshops on nutrition and mental health needs in the black community.

If all money is dirty money, let's clean that money with noble acts. Is anyone out there willing to help me?

'Harriet' is a movie that everyone should be sure to see

November 12, 2019

I had the good fortune of seeing the movie "Harriet" with my wife and friends the Revs. Brenda and Jim West. If you have not seen this movie, you should.

It captures not only the fire and passion of a woman determined to be free of the shackles of slavery, but it makes us feel afresh the enormous hardship and pain African American families endured.

The movie about the American abolitionist and political activist Harriet Tubman is not another "slave" movie with black actors who ultimately end up affirming and honoring the "good white people" who set colored people free.

Instead, "Harriet" points to the noble work of black people who gave all they had to liberate black people from the tyranny of slavery.

White abolitionists are noted in the movie. In one of the most touching scenes, a white farmer takes Harriet to the Pennsylvania state line and asks her, "Shall I take you across, or do you want to walk into your freedom?" Harriet walks.

Scenes in the movie show actual sections of the Underground Railroad. It was almost surreal to see how both beautiful and diabolical the terrain was for those who wanted freedom. The river scenes were spectacular.

I appreciated that the movie also showed that not all black people stood behind the liberation of enslaved folks. There is a vicious black Uncle Tom slave-catcher in the movie who will bring your deepest disgust to the surface.

Again, it is a reminder that not everyone who is your color is always in your corner, both then and now.

The movie is not an attempt to create "white guilt" or "black shame." It is a movie that honestly reflects American history and presents to us a real American heroine: a black woman named Harriet Tubman. To remain ignorant about our history is the first step toward repeating it.

I am very surprised how many people, black and white, don't know who Harriet Tubman is or was. As children, we were as acquainted with Tubman, Sojourner Truth, Frederick Douglass and Nat Turner as we were with Betsy Ross, Patrick Henry and George Washington.

It demonstrates how inadequate public education is to equip our children with culturally diverse and informed education.

Again, I encourage you to go see "Harriet."

The American dream remains a nightmare for many

November 19, 2019

Once upon a time, Americans possessed an idea of the common good. It was not only political in character but social and economic.

Our sense of the common good we inherited from antiquity. From Plato to Adam Smith, we have envisioned the common good as both a responsibility and a right of every citizen.

Indeed, our history has demonstrated that often we are seduced by a quest for privilege and power. One needs to only think about our mistreatment of African Americans, women, Indigenous Americans, the queer community, etc., and the proof looms large before us for those who have eyes to see.

Yet, despite our mistakes, our collective spirit has believed and yearned for the fruition of our ideal of the common good. We sense its reality even if we are not able to articulate it or concretize it.

We simply know that the quest for the common good is necessary.

Somewhere along the line, our sense of the common good has been shattered into pieces. Our social, political, economic, intellectual and spiritual pursuits have become individualistic and selfish.

In the words of Adam Smith, "All for ourselves, and nothing for other people." We are so ideologically driven that conversation between opposing proponents has become almost impossible.

Conservatives and liberals are more interested in some warped sense of "ideological purity" than the prosperity of the neighbor and, subsequently, of the society.

Democrats and Republicans have demonstrated no sense of the common good. Instead, we are being force-fed their agendas.

Whether leftist or rightist, their agendas have missed the needs of the real people of America.

Teachers in America cannot make a living wage. Farmers who have fed us for generations cannot afford to farm. Labor is being forced to do more for less.

Hardworking citizens are no longer the middle class. They are now the "working poor" who cannot pay for rent, food, gas, insurance, utilities, children's clothing and medicine all in the same month.

The American dream is a nightmare for many, many people. And no one — not the president, not the Senate, not the Democratic Congress — is asking us what we need.

Yet the rich are becoming richer and are increasingly immune from criticism and reproach.

Is this the America we hoped for? Of course not. America is greater than the divisive, elitist, racist, sexist, homophobic, pseudo-intellectual demagoguery we are experiencing.

All of us need an America that is by and for the people, instead of against the people. No senior should have to decide whether to buy medicine or food.

No parent should worry about whether little Nathan will be shot on his way to school, in school or coming home from school.

No generational framer should have to worry about losing the farm because she can't compete with corporate farming nor governmental tariffs.

If our elected officials, Democrats or Republicans, are not going to invest the time and talent necessary for the creation of the common good for all Americans, then we the people need to take them out of office. The same is true up and down the political hierarchy: national, state, county, local. We do not need more ideologues; we need persons that love and care about the people.

If we who are black, Anglo, Latino, Asian, LGBQIAA+, Christian, Muslim, Jewish, atheist, agnostic, well-educated, working class and/or whatever do not rediscover the common good, we shall surely see the American dream destroyed and not just differed. The Nazarene is correct. A house divided against itself cannot stand.

Expressing gratitude may be the simplest way to feel better

November 26, 2019

"I am grateful for what I am and have. My thanksgiving is perpetual." - Henry David Thoreau

Thursday we shall gather with family and friends to give thanks for all the good things we have experienced this year.

While Thanksgiving has strong religious and cultural roots, it is celebrated more and more as a secular holiday.

Modern society confronts us with chaos daily. We live hustle-bustle lives, bombarded with demands of various kinds — vocational, personal, economic, social, political.

The opportunity to pause, to give thanks for who we are and what we have, provides us with the occasion to center ourselves, be humble and bask in the light of love and joy.

I am learning to delight in the little things. A smile from a stranger, an encouraging word from a colleague, the greeting wave of a child or the embrace from a senior citizen raises my sense of gratitude.

I am convinced that if one does not give thanks for the little things in life, one will never appreciate the "big" things.

We live in a materialistic world. We are judged by what we have. Sometimes, this same materialism seduces us into an artificial sense of self: I am better if I have more things.

The reality is that who we are cannot be measured by our acquisitions or our positions, but by our character. After all, none of us gets to keep what we have when we die.

I live in an area where I see many homeless people every day. I am surrounded by the working poor, who must grind daily just to make ends meet. A cloud of despair hangs over many people, young and older.

Circumstance can make one, in the words of Marvin Gaye, "want to holler and throw up both your hands." And yet there is much for which we must be thankful.

Allow me to name just a few.

We can give thanks for family and friends who love us for the right reasons. All of us have haters, but the fact is that we also have people in our lives who truly love and cherish us, and they do so for the right reasons. They recognize that there is something in us and about us that is worthy of love.

We can be thankful that we are alive. Life is sometimes hard and frustrating. Yet if we live, we can change our lives. If we are in debt, get rid of it. If we are surrounded by negative people, change acquaintances. Our circumstances need not be our conclusion. You have the power to change your world. And for that, be thankful.

We can be thankful for those who are praying for us. I still believe that prayer changes things. I know that I am here because someone prayed for me. I am not just talking about Christian prayer. Muslims, Jewish practitioners, Buddhists and Hindus all pray for the community of humanity. I am grateful for their prayers.

I am grateful for a deep sense of justice, faith and love. I realize that injustice seems to be winning and common sense is at an all-time low. But there are justice warriors among us who are fighting the good fight. My grandmother once said that she believed "trouble won't last always."

My faith affirms her belief, and my sense of love is that all systems and people can and will be transformed for the good. Hope that is seen is not hope.

I am thankful that "weeping may endure for a night, but joy will come in the morning."

As we feast this Thanksgiving Day, let us commit ourselves to a perpetual thanksgiving that works within us every day.

The writings of James Baldwin are important today

December 10, 2019

December 1 marked the death in 1987 of one of America' greatest thinkers, James Baldwin.

For those who are not familiar with Baldwin, he was a novelist, playwright and social activist. His mastery of the English language and his penetrating social analysis captured the imagination of millions.

Three Baldwin essays/books that are must reads are "The Fire Next Time," "Giovanni's Room" and "Notes of A Native Son."

His commentary on American life is just as pertinent today as it was at the time of his death.

Baldwin forced us to examine the interconnection of race, gender and class. A man who bore the double crucible of being black and gay, Baldwin understood how these three social phenomena affected life in America.

In response to America's desire to have fruitless polite conversation regarding race, class and gender, Baldwin wrote, "We can disagree and still love each other, unless your disagreement is rooted in my oppression and denial of my humanity and right to exist."

Baldwin was keenly aware of how America's call for gradualism contributed greatly to the perpetuation of racism, classism and homophobia.

Baldwin, with others such as King, Malcolm, Nikki Giovanni and Alice Walker, realized that the call for gradual social change was a call for no change at all. Baldwin realized that a system that denies my right to exist and my humanity must be confronted and changed immediately and that the sentiment of gradualism was an appeal to death for people of color, the queer community and the poor.

Baldwin's debate with William F. Buckley demonstrates Baldwin's clarity of thought and the dual nature of systemic racism in America.

Buckley's staunch opposition to "integration" and support of white supremacy is haunting. While Buckley's rhetoric is representative of conservatism both then and now, Baldwin was also aware of white liberal racism that sees itself as the savior of black people.

By participating in the 1963 March on Washington, Baldwin saw how white liberals would support a narrative that made them feel good about themselves but reject the notion of black power.

Why? Because the call for black power threatened white privilege, a privilege that white conservatives and white liberals share.

There are several good, informative books available in the contemporary market. However, sometimes I think we are so fascinated by what is "new" that we forget the wisdom contained in "the old."

One day while returning to Columbia by plane, a young black man noticed that I was reading "The Fire Next Time." He said to me, "Wow, it is nice to see a brother reading old books."

I smiled without comment. But I thought to myself maybe part of the reason our social progress as black people has not gone further is because we have discounted old thoughts and old wisdom.

We no longer listen to Frederick Douglass or Marcus Garvey. We have forgotten womanists like Alice Walker. We ignore black, gay geniuses like Baldwin and Langston Hughes.

Perhaps that is why so much of contemporary social justice speech is superficial and pale.

I encourage you to read some of Baldwin's work. I invite you to see "I Am Not Your Negro." It will enliven your spirit and resolve to declare your humanity and your right to exist.

Amid all the celebrations, please remember Kwanzaa

December 24, 2019

As we engage in many types of celebration during this holiday season, I urge you to please remember Kwanzaa.

Though not as popular as Christmas or Hanukah, a remembrance of Kwanzaa is as important today as ever before. Perhaps, even more so.

For those who are not familiar with Kwanzaa, it is an annual weeklong celebration beginning Dec. 26 and ending on Jan. 1 with gift-giving and a feast.

It is celebrated in the United States, Canada, the Caribbean and other countries of the African diaspora.

It was conceptually birthed by Dr. Maulana Karenga and first celebrated in the U.S. in 1966. While the celebration is Pan-African in both style and content, it is a celebration that all people can participate.

Kwanzaa stands on seven main principles.

1.Umoja: Unity. We are to unify the family, community, nation, and our people, if success is to ever be a reality. Parents need to be parents, community leaders must lay aside petty issues and unite the community, and education must become more than learning answers for a standardized test. Umoja understands that united we stand, divided we fall.

2. Kujichagulia: Self-determination. We have the responsibility and power to create the fundamentally new in our lives. We may have been victimized by systems and powers, but we can re-create our own destiny. Our corporate and individual motto must be 'I can do all things.'

3. Ujima: Collective work and responsibility. We must build and maintain our community together. Clearly, we have a call stop the violence and dehumanization we experience our community.

If city budgets don't include community-oriented policing and community building, build our own protocol and demand that it be observed.

If poor and children of color are behind educationally, set up our own tutoring programs in these churches that keep asking for offerings for the "building fund."

Feed ourselves, grow our own food. Build co-ops for child-care and health resource centers.

We have the talent. Do we have the desire?

4. Ujamaa: Collective economics. Most black dollars leave our community and support our communities.

This principle encourages the communities of color to invest black and brown dollars in the community and build and grow national and global networks of economic opportunity.

For example, one of the first things the black community did after slavery was to build black educational centers and black businesses. Education and economics make a once-enslaved people free.

5. Nia: Purpose. We must regain the purpose of our lives. It is not to be gangsters and drug dependents.

Aspiring to be the "black bourgeoisie" cannot the goal. Our purpose is to live in a manner that honors our ancestors and inspires our children and their children toward greatness.

Our purpose must be to live with moral integrity and reject the seduction of racism, sexism, homophobia, ageism, materialism and militarism.

6. Kuumba: Creativity. This principle is obvious: we are compelled to make the community, nation, and our people better than how we found them by employing the best of our creativity and imagination. If what we have used before has not worked, try something else. Imagine the unimaginable.

7. Imani: Faith. I believe that faith is the substance of things hoped for, and the evidence of things unseen. It was the faith we possessed by the Christianity of Africa and not of the oppressor, that caused us to believe that trouble will not last always.

Because we realized that "I am because we are," we maintained a faith in others who were our color and those that were not, in other faith practitioners (some Christian and some who were not).

The only criterion was, 'do you dared to catch the vision of a fundamentally new society?' If so, faith will take us through.

We had a faith in the God of our weary years and our silent tears, not prosperity ministry, exclusion and privilege. It was and is the faith that empowered us in our worst times and keeps alive the hope of better days to come.

This same kind of faith calls us to hold on to it today.

In this time of division, hostility, and despair I believe celebrating Kwanzaa can give us the occasion to re-capture a greater sense of self, purpose, community, and the God who sets at liberty those who are oppressed.

In doing so we may re-imagine ourselves as victors and not victims, as an empowered, united community, and not each other's mortal enemies.

2020

Let the new year bring unity and justice for all

January 7, 2020

We have now entered a new year. Most hoped for a new year different from 2019.

We have yearned for a time of peace, unity and progress toward the building of a common good for all Americans. Instead we find ourselves in the center of chaos.

War with Iran could be on the horizon. The impeachment initiative by the Democrats is a grandiose illustration of folly, given the ideological rigidity of Senate Republicans.

We are more divided as a nation than ever before. Racial, economic and gender disparity is a common reality for far too many people in this society.

Our infrastructure needs drastic repair, and our justice system has become simply the means by which we can imprison black, brown and poor whites in such record numbers that it is now the new slavery in America.

Senseless violence in our schools, malls and churches haunts us every day. And the opioid crisis continues to worsen.

Farmers now encourage their children not to make farming their profession, and the educational system seems more concerned about money than enlightening our future generation.

Fresh water and clean air are no longer a priority. The only ones happy about the way things are at this point in 2020 are the pharmaceutical companies, the wealthy and the weapon producers. We are in the center of chaos.

Yet I have hope.

I, first, have faith in a God who specializes in transforming chaos into the creative good.

Second, I have faith in the ideas of the Constitution of the United States. While No. 45 desires to be king, the Constitution reminds us that we are a democratic republic and no self-indulgent despot shall, in the end, be victorious.

Third, I believe the vast number of Americans are not white supremacists, nor are they gangsters, sexists, homophobes or terrorists.

Most Americans are fundamentally good, average citizens who want safe schools, a clean environment, meaningful places of employment for themselves and their children, access to proper health care and the good life for themselves, their children, their neighbors and their neighbors' children.

Most Americans are not self-righteous, navel-gazing creatures of blind faith, hungry for blood and thirsty for war. They do not want their children or other children engaged in senseless wars manufactured to boost a president's ego.

They do not want a wall to be the answer to our immigration problems or see immigrants' children locked in cages.

Most American Christians do not care who in the congregation or in the pulpit is gay or straight. Real Christians are about love and justice, not hate and divisive pseudo-biblical posturing.

When things in a society are as chaotic as they are now, the populace will rise and declare that enough is enough.

Not with violence, but with nonviolent direct action. My hope is that we do not wait too long.

The need to return to sane political and social action is now, not later. My hope is for a just society, where we study war no more and live in a unified America.

Closing off our minds to new thoughts thwarts our ability to grow

January 14, 2020

I was poignantly reminded last week of how we as Americans have loss the art of disagreement. We no longer gather to debate issues, whether secular or religious, with the goal of perhaps finding mutual ground that leads to a common good. Instead, we viciously attack one another with the hope of destroying "the other," self-righteously convinced that "we are right because we believe it, and if you don't believe like me you are wrong, vile and beyond redemption."

This phenomenon has been pervasive in our culture for a while. Think about how many brilliant proponents of ideas worthy of reflection have been uninvited to speak at galas, churches and college campuses simply because we disagree with his/her position. The list is extensive but it includes former Secretaries of State Henry Kissinger and Condoleezza Rice, former Harvard University President Larry Summers, actor Alec Baldwin, human-rights activist Ayaan Hirsi Ali, DNA co-discoverer James Watson, Indian Prime Minister Narendra Modi, filmmaker Michael Moore, conservative Pulitzer Prize-winning columnist George Will and liberal Pulitzer Prize-winning columnist Anna Quindlen, to name just a few.

I was scheduled to teach a course in February in recognition of Black History Month on Black Hermeneutics, Black Liberation Theology and Womanism at Columbia's largest white, evangelical church. The course was to demonstrate how African American Christians have read and interpreted the Bible from their lived experience(s) given the reality of racism and sexism in America. Long story short, I was asked by the senior pastors not to come and present my research because of our theological differences. In fairness to the pastors, they did pay me for my intellectual work, though they withdrew the opportunity to speak. I guess their Bible did not include the Nazarene's statement to his disciples, "They who are for us (in principle) are not against us."

One of the worst results of the Trump Era is that it has become acceptable to be closed-minded. Republicans brag about how they will not entertain any Democrat idea, and Democrats pride themselves in discounting all Republican discourse. Conservative Christians dismiss Progressive Christians for being too liberal, and Progressive Christians denounce Conservative Christians for being far too rigid and trapped in patriarchy. The Black-White divide is widening, yet white nationalists are screaming for more racist policies. Sexism is still a reality for most women in America particularly in the arena of economics. The systemic oppression of the LGBTQIAA+ community is becoming more entrenched and more frightening.

When our society closes its mind to other thoughts and ideas, we lose our ability to grow and develop. All of us need to stop and listen to each other instead of operating out of our fears and prejudices. We need each other if this great democratic experiment is to survive. If we do not recommit to finding common ground and establishing the common good for every American, I am afraid America will be lost beyond the point of salvation. We cannot defeat the real enemy we all face if we continue to fight among ourselves.

Impeachment could be an exercise in futility for our nation

January 21, 2020

At the close of celebrating Dr. Martin Luther King Jr. Day, the Congress of the United States of America begins the impeachment proceedings of its 45th President, Donald Trump. Ironic, isn't it, that the day after we celebrated a prophet of unity, we are now engaged in trying to remove one of America's most divisive presidents. It is quite clear that if Sen. Lindsey Graham is the voice of the majority Republican Senate, the impeachment process is dead in the water and Donald Trump will remain president.

When the rhetoric of impeachment came to a head, I suggested in my column that we ought not impeach Trump. It is not that I believe Mr. Trump deserves to be president. He has fanned the flames of hatred and division more than any president on record. The fact is that most Americans did not vote for him. The Electoral College (and the Russians?) elected Donald Trump. My argument was grounded in the fact that if Trump is impeached, Pence becomes president, and, in my estimation, Pence would be worse than Trump. I know that for the good of the country and the common good, Mr. Trump should not be president. Given the political realities in the Senate, however, impeachment is not the way.

I sometimes think that liberals, moderates and progressives operate under the illusion that removing Mr. Trump from office — alone — will create a society of mutual respect and oneness. Reality states that there is a sickness in our society that Mr. Trump heightens but did not cause. The sickness looms larger than him. White supremacy has grown in the last 10 years or more. Mass incarceration and mass deportation has created a mindset that "white is right" and America is better without people of color. The oppressive systems of sexism and homophobia have not disappeared but have become more deadly and sophisticated. The economic ocean (Can we still call it a gap?) that exists between the rich and the poor, perpetuated by classism, grows ever larger each day. And have we forgotten that we still have children in cages and unsanitary conditions at our southern border? America is suffering from a sickness of the soul that removing Mr. Trump from office alone will not heal.

For our country to be healthy and whole again, a moral transformation must take place that affects our thinking, our actions and our policies. If such a moral transformation does not take place, not only will Donald Trump be reelected for four more years, but the destructive nature of the malaise will continue to decimate our communities and our country. To be moral must become more important than to be rich and powerful. How we treat one another must take precedence over ideological commitments. This is not about which political party is right; the task is how can we begin to do what is right.

How, then, do we begin the arduous task of doing what is right? Here is one starting place that is superior to religious preference, racial analysis and socio-political systematizing: "Love your neighbor as yourself."

Overcoming history's patterns takes action, not just lessons

February 6, 2020

"Those who have no record of what their forebears have accomplished lose the inspiration which comes from the teaching of biography and history." - Carter G. Woodson

For the last couple of years, I have attempted to encourage Anglo Americans in Columbia and nationally to embrace Black History Month with a sense of fervor and intellectual hunger. After all, Black History is American history, and a failure to observe and learn our history promises a certain social end: We are doomed to repeat past catastrophes. With the rise of white supremacy, public school systems refusing to incorporate black historical narratives in their curricula and the smug dismissal of Black thought, art and culture by white academic power merchants, however, this year I refuse to engage in Black apologetics with those who don't get it or who don't want to understand.

Instead, my efforts have turned toward emphasizing the need of Black historical study for and by Black people (which includes biracial persons). I appreciate the commitment of Anglo Americans who hunger for knowledge of the struggle and victories of Black people in America. But the importance of immersive study into the history of Black people in America is first and foremost for Black people. Without a clear understanding of our history, we will continue to be seduced by the fallacious arguments of white supremacy: Individualism is better than community.

Black history is both descriptive and normative. It is descriptive of the struggle Black people have endured since our arrival on these shores in 1619. Ever since then Black people have had to bear what my friend Steve Weinberg calls "the crucible of race." Black history describes the victimization of Black people during slavery, Jim Crow segregation and contemporary manifestations of racism that infect our individual interactions, the systems we live under and the institutions that we are part of in American life.

But Black history also demonstrates how a victimized group of people were able to first survive and then become victorious despite the odds against them. It illustrates how Black women were and are the glue that held together family and community in the face of lynching, torture, dehumanization, lack of resources and second-class citizenship. The history gives a portrait of Black men, though beaten and ostracized, who invented the fundamentally new, from the cotton gin, the stoplight and advanced open-heart surgery. It gives the narrative of how united Black communities fought off drugs and violence when they envisioned themselves as an "us" and not simply an aggregate of "I."

Black history is also normative. It tells us what we as Black people in America ought to do. It was not by accident that two of the first things former slaves did after Emancipation was to build institutions of education and vote in elections. They realized that voting was one way of changing the status quo.

They heard Frederick Douglass say that "education makes a child unfit for slavery," and they believed it and excelled academically. Black History teaches us that education is not merely garnering a degree — it is the ascertainment of knowledge that makes us a stronger, better people.

Black history proclaims in a powerful way that if we stand together, we can accomplish anything we set our corporate will to do. We can build another Black Wall Street, great communities with affordable housing, our own grocery stores, a Black hospital and on and on. Black history instructs us that dependence on white institutions with no belief in, or movement toward, Black collective power is simply another form of slavery. Aren't you tired of singing, "We shall overcome" and remaining in the same or worst economic, educational, social, spiritual and political state? Black history teaches those who will operate by its lessons that overcoming is not a song, it is an action.

Black church could save soul of America

February 11, 2020

"Black churches are very powerful forces in the African American community and always have been. Because religion has been that one place where you have an imagination that no one can control. And so, as long as you know that you are a human being and nobody can take that away from you, then God is that reality in your life that enables you to know that."- James Cone

Since her birth in America, the Black Church, at her best, has been engaged in the activity of social justice. The reasons might seem obvious to those who are acquainted with the history of black people in America. The Black Church is the church born of struggle. She was birthed in the context of slavery and white oppression. From her inception as the center of worship, education and identity formation for black people, the Black Church understood that being authentically Christian demanded sociopolitical activism.

The Black Church was the memory of Africa encased in the rhythms of her speech and song and the hope for the future despite the cruel realities of its present. The white, western, Euro-American church used Christianity to suppress black protest, give legitimacy to slavery and segregation while proclaiming racial oppression as fulfillment of the will of God. The Black Church understood the importance of reminding black people that the Christianity practiced by slave owners was apostasy and, though enslaved, that they were not three-fifths of a person but full human beings made in the true image and likeness of God.

Second, as the primary institution owned and operated by black people, it was painfully clear that the church had to stand against the systemic racism that the white mainline and evangelical church, either tacitly, or fully, supported. Cornel West stated, "If the (Black) churches don't move, much of the community won't move. We've got a situation in which a black church is still a major institution in the black community where 55% of the black folk attend and over 75% pass through its doors."

The questions worth pondering during Black History Month are, "Does the Black Church still exist, and is it still necessary in contemporary America?"

I will address this issue more thoroughly in a presentation next week at MU for Black History Month. At this point, let me say that the Black Church still exists and is necessary in America today. Given the division and strife evident in every quarter of our society, the Black Church may be the only institution that can save the soul of America.

When the Black Church embraces its role and responsibility in America, the violence in our communities will take a dramatic turn for the better and the deconstruction of racism will take on new vigor. Black clergy must accept the role of being both prophetic and priestly. The Black Church should begin interpreting the biblical text from a black-awareness instead of a white theology that maintains the status quo.

If Black History Month is to honor what is great about us, then we must honor the Black Church — she belongs to us.

Improving financial reality for blacks means investing in ourselves

February 18, 2020

"Considering the myriad problems facing the Black community, both here in America and throughout the African diaspora, it is time for Black people to think in terms of economic development and self-determination. A form of predatory economics is

destroying Black people, and we must begin to pursue cooperative economics in which we control our communities if we are to succeed." - Us Lifting Us, Atlanta, Georgia

In his State of the Union address in January, President Trump cited the historically low black unemployment rate as an indicator of America's economic success and growth during his presidency. Brookings experts Marcus Casey and Bradley Hardy, however, note that "the unemployment rate alone presents a revealing but incomplete picture of economic well-being within any community." Two major factors are left out of the Trump analysis that need accentuating. First, the unemployment rate for African Americans (6.0%) is still almost double of Anglo Americans (3.1%). Second, the median household income for African Americans is nearly $30,000 less than it is for Anglo families: $41,361 to $70,642.

Outside of retirement accounts, only 37% of African Americans own wealth-building products such as stocks and mutual funds.

Only 35% believe they are doing a good job of preparing for retirement.

About 33% have less than one month of funds saved for a crisis and less than 25% have amassed more than six months of emergency savings.

And, 58% are actively involved in educating their children on finances, versus 48% of Caucasians. Forty percent rely on family members for information (from African American Economics: Real Facts, Black Enterprise, 2019).

"The study shows African Americans want to improve their financial situations and are hopeful about the future," said Evan Taylor, African American market director, MassMutual. "At the same time, it sheds light on the financial struggles and inequities that the African American community continues to battle. Those contradictions indicate a need for greater financial education and discipline for the whole family to achieve economic success. In fact, the biggest financial regret expressed by respondents was that they wished they had started saving and investing sooner." Sixty-three percent of African Americans believe the American Dream of financial security is achievable, while 33% believe the American Dream no longer exists.

The State of the American Family survey consisted of 3,235 total interviews with Americans, including 482 African American respondents. Most of these interviews (2,730) were conducted with men and women ages 25–64 with incomes equal to or greater than $50,000 and with dependents under age 26 for whom they are financially responsible. Respondents had to contribute at least 40% to decisions regarding financial matters in their household to qualify.

In this survey, 63% of African Americans believe the American Dream of financial security is achievable while 33% believe the American Dream no longer exists. Clearly, many African Americans still cling to a hope that the economic system in this country will one day benefit them despite the counterevidence. Notice that the respondents in the above survey had an average income of $50,000 or more. No doubt that those who have a median family income of $41,000 or less would have a much different narrative to tell.

I disagree with Evan Taylor's assessment of the problem. Taylor's "pull yourself up by your bootstraps" approach cannot be the answer given to the huge economic disparity African Americans face. I agree with the Atlanta self-development group that "the need for Black people to develop a comprehensive economic and political strategy has become overwhelmingly and undeniably clear. Now more than at any other time in our history since 1865, Black People must organize for real power to ensure the safety and welfare of its people." By collective investing and self-determination, we can reconstruct the economic situation the majority of African Americans currently live under.

Black History Month is, again, descriptive and normative. Since the days of Marcus Garvey, and later Malcolm X, we have been instructed to invest in ourselves. So far, we have ignored the lesson. Perhaps the present economic realities will motivate us to build and grow.

A tribute to womanism during Black History Month

February 25, 2020

As we conclude the official celebration of Black History Month and move toward March as Women's History Month, I pause to celebrate the undeniable contribution black women have made to the black community and American society.

When one thinks about the bold, assertive black women who gave voice to the black struggle from a woman's perspective, we are thinking of womanists in our midst. Alice Walker's definition according to Encyclopedia.com defines a womanist as a "'Black feminist or feminist of color' who is bold and assertive, who relishes African American culture, and is committed to the flourishing of the entire African American community."

Womanism arose as a movement in the 1980s. The term womanism/womanist was first coined by Alice Walker in 1979 in her short story "Coming Apart." Since then, womanism has grown as a social, religious and political critique of oppressive systems that affect black women in a unique manner. The womanist analysis is both historical and contemporary. It gives voice to the concerns of black women, as well as celebrating their strength and creativity. Womanism, therefore, is a resistance to the injustices black women have experienced and are experiencing.

You can find three main critiques in the womanist analysis. First is a critique of the patriarchy found in the black community. It draws attention to how black men called for equal justice and liberation from oppressive systems but have practiced patriarchy in various arenas of black life — within the family and the black church in particular.

Second, womanism challenged white feminism for its racism and its failure to understand that America treats women of color differently than white women.

Third, white power structures reflect a lack of appreciation of class struggle women of color endure and experience. The oppression black women experienced is qualitatively different than that of white women. Womanists point to the three-headed monster they face daily: racism, sexism and classism.

The goal of womanism is developing a strategy that will lead to justice, revising the "narrative" (social and religious) by making it more inclusive and connecting with other oppressed communities.

We all know of the great womanists of history: Ida B. Wells, Harriet Tubman, Sojourner Truth, Mary McLeod Bethune, Toni Morrison, Zora Neale Hurston and so many more. I think however that we ought to celebrate the womanists in our own community, like Muriel Battle and Almeta Crayton, just to name two. Columbia has known some powerful black women who were assertive and bold. They loved the black community and hated the systemic racism that plagued "Little Dixie." They tirelessly worked for the common good of black people in this community. We remember you, sisters. Thank you for your work to make Columbia and America better.

A tribute to McCoy Tyner

March 10, 2020

"McCoy was an inspired musician who devoted his life to his art, his family and his spirituality. McCoy Tyner's music and legacy will continue to inspire fans and future talent for generations to come." - From Tyner family social post

Alfred McCoy Tyner was one of America's greatest jazz pianists. He died last week at age 81. He was known for his work with the John Coltrane Quartet and a long solo career. He was an NEA Jazz Master and a five-time Grammy winner.

Not a player of electric keyboards and synthesizers, he was committed to acoustic instrumentation. Tyner, who was widely imitated, was one of the most recognizable and most influential pianists in jazz history. I had the privilege of meeting Mr. Tyner during my years as a student at Cornell College. His warmth and graciousness made a huge impact on me. Upon meeting him, I knew at once I was in the presence of greatness and humility.

As a musician, many people suggest McCoy Tyner revolutionized jazz piano playing. His fearless call-response playing provided an avenue not witnessed before in jazz. He could play at the level of a whisper and suddenly respond with a fortissimo that was both arresting and moving.

In a 2006 interview with the Union-Tribune, Tyner shared something that characterized his life as a musician. He said: "Don't be afraid to take a challenge and go into new territory. If you know what you're doing, it's very inspiring. Fear itself can stop you. But if you're not afraid, you have a chance."

Indeed, he was fearless as a musician. He found his voice and was not afraid to express it on his own terms.

In listening to Tyner over the years, I now realize what it was that captured my imagination: the spirituality that would spring forth in his music.

There are hints of his respect and love for his African roots. Some attribute it to his acquaintance with African music and rhythms he learned in his youth taking African dance lessons. Perhaps. But clearly the call of the motherland is evident in his style of play. There also is an obvious traditional African American influence present.

Tyner not only listened to the jazz giants before him but also the great gospel sounds of the traditional black church. He learned how to blend these influences and make them his own.

I shall miss McCoy Tyner's music. If you have not experienced his music, you should listen to his "Inception" album or his work with the John Coltrane Trio. You will be inspired and impressed.

See you later, McCoy Tyner. May you rest in peace.

Facing the coronavirus quarantine with the right tools

March 17, 2020

The coronavirus is upon us. Each day, we are constantly reminded that we are amid a global pandemic.

The news media communicates tales of woe. We cannot avoid listening to the growing number of people infected by COVID-19 and the rising death toll caused by the virus here and abroad.

Our world has changed.

The closing of restaurants and bars, schools and educational institutions moving to online/virtual education and the requests from national, state and local officials to practice voluntary quarantining and social distancing remind us that the pandemic is real.

Pandemics affect us not only physically but also emotionally and spiritually. One can feel lonely, isolated and afraid during times like these. The goal for all of us is to survive this threat. We can survive well, or we can survive not so well.

I choose to survive COVID-19 well. If you are of a similar mindset, I give some suggestions (from other survivors) on how we may survive well.

Eat and drink well.

Now is the time to forget about being a Size 1 in a swimsuit and think about foods that comfort the body and the mind. It's time to cook like Momma and Grandma used to cook. Eat lots of green vegetables, rice, beans and fruits. Drink lots of water and herbal teas. Go easy on the alcohol because it can increase depression and despair. Feeding the body feeds the mind. Endurance food is important in times like these.

Exercise.

Exercise will strengthen the body and release endorphins in the brain. I am not talking about exercising like you are training for the Olympics (unless you want to). Try stretching, walks or some tai chi movements. There are lots of exercises we can do at home. Put on some music and strengthen the body.

Meditate and pray.

Meditation demands deep breathing. Prayer grants centering. Together one can experience calm during the storm. The ancients have tried to encourage us to meditate and pray for centuries. Since most of us will have to work from home, now can be a good time to increase our inner strength through meditation and prayer.

Laugh, laugh and laugh some more.

Intentionally seek out humor. Spend more hours checking out your comedians and less time watching garbage on social media and TV. Laughter can change your perspective, move you from being self-centered, and increase your sense of well-being.

Help someone else.

I am very concerned about two groups of people: the homeless and the elderly that live in their own residences. Though we are encouraged to stay home, the homeless have no place to call home. Sister Jones has a place to stay but no one to check on her. I am proud of how many Americans are finding ways to help our most vulnerable citizens. We, too, should have such a spirit. Call, share, help someone else. The old Black spiritual states, "If I can help somebody as I pass along, then my living will not be in vain."

Maintain hope.

They tell us the pandemic will get worse before it gets better. Well, maybe. But my hope is grounded in the reality that, "Trouble won't last always!" There will be an end to this situation. We must hold fast to our faith and hope. Stand on your hope and be like a tree planted by the rivers of water, "I shall not be moved."

I hope these ideas help you to survive well. We can and will make it through.

What have we learned in the midst of a pandemic? Work for common good

March 31, 2020

If you took the time to read last week's column, you noticed how my conservative critics vehemently objected to what I had to say about "The Donald" and his ineptitude in handling the COVID-19 threat.

They missed the kudos to those who have sacrificed their lives and families to serve on the front lines to protect us and immediately went to (a) defending 45 and (b) blaming and bashing President Obama.

Why are these folks so obsessed with Barack Obama? Maybe they realize that history will record him as a great statesman and list Donald Trump as a buffoon. Indeed, they got their underwear in a knot ... again. Of course, that happens when you think with the wrong part of your anatomy.

There are certain things we have learned during this period of COVID-19. They loom large, despite the ideological rantings of the "Trumpeters."

We acted too slowly. As of Tuesday morning, we have over 1,000 cases in Missouri, with approximately 3,000 deaths nationwide. Medical experts are predicting that we could reach the 100,000-200,000 mark as a nation. I hope they are wrong.

I am thankful for Dr. Anthony Fauci for keeping "The Donald" from making dire matters worst. Clearly Dr. Fauci and the rest of the coronavirus team convinced "45" not to end the distancing restrictions too soon. Finally, some common sense for the common good in the White House.

We have learned it is possible for Congress to work together. They passed the stimulus bill, which will help small businesses and individuals in the short run. Now if we could get them to work on other issues to improve the common good, how wonderful would that be? At least we learned that they could work together if they want to.

There are other things we have learned. There are some people in this country who truly care about their fellow Americans ... and some who do not. There are hundreds to thousands of volunteers helping medical teams, serving food to the elderly and children, entertaining online and all around reaching out to others prove that some people care. Not only is the disease a threat, but loneliness, despair, and doubt can have adverse effects on the populace. But many people are trying to help lift the burden by showing that human compassion is not completely dead.

We learned that some people do not care about others at all. How about the governor who said that many seniors would be willing to die in order to save the economy. What seniors is he talking about? One of my social justice acquaintances said that the comment and others like it are the epitome of Christian patriarchy.

No.

It is the epitome of small-minded white men who only care about their profits, their privilege and maintaining their power. Christianity has nothing to do with it. Narrow-minded capitalism does.

We have learned that most people are taking the virus seriously and some are not. Most folks are practicing social distancing; others not so much. I was in the store the other day, and a woman started running toward me saying, "Oh, Reverend. Good to see you. Let me give you a hug!" I quickly responded, "Uh, I love you, but 6 feet. Back up, darling. Six feet."

We still have churches that are meeting, young people having parties, on and on. What are we doing? Everyone must think about "the other." We must all practice social distancing and not use religion or pleasure as an excuse to be irresponsible.

We are learning that people are praying for the world. I was quite pleased that news networks asked Bishop T.D. Jakes to pray for the world on live TV. But I also know of Muslim, Jewish, Christian, Baha'i, Wiccan and Hindu folks who are praying for the world as well. I have a big God and don't concern myself with what faith community an individual represents. No faith community has all the answers, because all of us can see and know only a portion of the ultimate reality. I am just happy that, in the words of a black gospel song, "Somebody prayed for me, they had me on their mind. They took the time to pray for me. I'm so glad they prayed, I'm so glad they prayed. I'm so glad they prayed for me."

My fellow citizens, I am praying for you. Let's pray for each other.

COVID-19 affects African American communities harder

April 14, 2020

The world has changed. COVID-19 has affected America and the world in ways we could not anticipate or imagine. Coronavirus has changed our interaction, the way we worship and the way we think about our bodies, our environment and our future. The pandemic is for real.

We have become increasingly aware of the disparity between African Americans and the Anglo community about infections and death because of COVID-19.

Nationally, more African Americans proportionately have become infected and died as a result of the pandemic than whites. I am curious to know the numbers in Missouri. My fear is that the same will hold true in our state.

Several issues come to the fore regarding the disparity. First, all Americans that suffer with preexisting medical conditions are at a higher risk of infection and death than those who do not. Suffering with conditions or diseases such as high blood pressure, lupus, diabetes, etc. makes us more susceptible to infection from COVID-19. Many African Americans suffer from these conditions.

This medical disparity, however, is directly tied to the economic disparity in America. African Americans lack access to the medical help white America often takes for granted. The cost of pharmaceuticals is outrageous. I know many African Americans who do not receive the medical treatment or medications they should because of cost.

We could have remedied this problem if affordable health care was made available, but our administration's obsession with President Obama killed what was needed to allow people of color and the poor to have what is necessary to live better, or at least not be so vulnerable to COVID-19. Once again, we are the victims of throwing the baby out with the bathwater.

It is amazing to me that so many people are not aware that many of the medical conditions African Americans suffer from are not due to genetics but are due to the environments in which we grew up. We all know that too often corporations drop their chemical waste and pollute the air and water in the areas where black people live.

I wonder how many children who were diagnosed with juvenile asthma really were victims of the waste dumped in their communities; how many other preexisting conditions were exacerbated by corporate insensitivity and lack of concern? I hold Flint, Michigan, as an example.

Second, African Americans must seriously observe the social distancing and face-covering mandates. I realize lots of Americans ignore the mandates, but we cannot allow ourselves to copy such foolishness. One of the problems with face-covering is that in many communities, face-covering by black people is seen as suspected criminal activity and not social prevention.

When the surgeon general (a black man) talked about using a bandana as a face-covering, I thought to myself, "Yeah, right; you want black folks to walk in a grocery store or liquor store or bank with a bandana tied around their face? You must not know where we live. That can get a black person killed in America."

Like D.L. Hughley, my advice to African Americans is not to be surprised if you are treated rudely or suspiciously in the gas station or grocery store because you are black and your face is covered.

Racism doesn't stop because we are in a pandemic. In the vernacular of many black folks, be "woke" but be safe.

African Americans have always had to care for ourselves. We cannot look to government to protect us. We must protect one another. We can't use bad religiosity or recklessness to control our action. These are serious times.

While I want all people to make it through this pandemic, I am particularly concerned about black America. Though "this too shall pass," we must ensure that we survive and survive well. Black America, be "woke."

How COVID-19 has revealed the best and worst in us

April 21, 2020

The pandemic has brought out the best and the worst in us. We can never thank front-line essential workers enough for all they have done to take care of America during this crisis. A huge thank you goes out to medical personnel, grocery store employees, police officers and firefighters, sanitation employees, postal workers and many more who risk their lives to provide what we need to make it through this time.

I am also impressed with folks who go out of their way to help seniors, children, the unsheltered and all the most vulnerable among us by picking up medicine and supplies, preparing meals and giving essential items. I watched a man buy over 200 sandwiches to give to nurses who had to work long shifts in a critical care facility. How about school bus operators taking meals to school kids, food pantries providing for folks to help make ends meet or restaurants banding together to give meals to the unsheltered? Some of the best in us is showing all around us.

Some of the worst in us shows up as well. We now have protesters dressed in battle gear, carrying weapons and brandishing Confederate flags and signs like "Don't Tread on Me" defying the stay-at-home orders aimed at keeping us healthy and alive. To have "the Donald" and White House Adviser Stephen Moore support such madness is beyond imagination. Moore went on to compare the protesters to civil rights activist Rosa Parks. What?

If a group of black and brown people wielding weapons would have conducted these protests, they would have been arrested on sight and Trump would have called them "bad people." Rosa Parks was protesting over 200 years of white supremacy. These people are protesting having to stay home for less than 200 days. The stay-at-home order was to protect us. People are still getting sick and dying. We don't even hear about how the virus is affecting Native American communities. The virus is serious, and the actions of the protesters are reckless and dangerous. They ignore science and simply want their way like spoiled children... with guns.

People have rights, but not the right to expose the rest of society to COVID-19. If they want to ignore the orders, stay away from the rest of us and sign a waiver stating that you and your family will not receive medical treatment if you contract the virus. Old folks said, "A hard head makes a soft behind." If you want to be obstinate, suffer the consequences. But don't infect me and the rest of us who are trying to be responsible.

At the end, I believe that more Americans will demonstrate the best in us than those who portray the worst in us — or at least I hope so. Everyone please stay safe and stay sane.

Reopening requires caution, maintaining a sense of responsibility

May 5, 2020

As of Monday, Missouri is in Phase 1 of reopening businesses and recreational facilities and returning to daily life. The reopening during the pandemic creates mixed emotions.

On one hand, we are aware that more than 70,000 people in the U.S. have died of COVID-19.

People are still being infected and dying. Almost every community that has eased the stay-at-home order has seen a spike in cases of the disease. The reports on people infected who work in the meat industry is alarming, to say the least. Many fear that we are opening too soon and doing so may result in terrible consequences.

On the flip side, approximately 30 million people in the U.S. are out of work. We have not seen these numbers since the Great Depression. Small businesses are on the verge of collapse, if they have not closed already.

The virus has greatly hurt the economy. We are all in the same storm, but we are not all in the same boat.

A few of us are fortunate to be able to work from home, receive a paycheck and keep our heads above water. But if you are unemployed (whether terminated or furloughed), the financial survival issues loom large. I understand the frustration of those who want to go back to work. They have bills to pay and mouths to feed.

I also understand that when you get financially in the hole in America, it is exceedingly difficult to climb out of it.

Because we are reopening, we must remain vigilant. We must wear masks. I do not understand people who will not cover their faces. Gov. Andrew Cuomo in New York is correct: To not wear a face covering is just disrespectful. It amazes me that many of the protesters who cried about their "freedom" being denied have acted with a total disregard for the common good by not covering their faces with a mask.

Freedom comes with responsibility to the common good. Freedom without responsibility is anarchy.

We must continue social distancing. I like to hug as much as the next person, but we must observe the 6 feet rule for our survival. This is a time to listen to the medical, scientific experts and not politicians. Keep social distancing for our survival.

We must be honest. If we are sick or have the virus, tell somebody. We are all familiar with the symptoms. If you have the symptoms, stay home. If you are asymptomatic and have the virus, do not pretend that you are OK. You are endangering others.

I became painfully aware of how important the above precautions are last weekend.

One of the former members of Dawson Journey Ministry died last Saturday from COVID-19. She was observing the stay-at-home order diligently.

But she allowed a visitor to enter her home, and the visitor had the virus. The saddest part of this narrative is that the visitor knew she was infected, but she refused to tell anyone. Subsequently, the visitor infected my former member, and my member died of COVID-19 — all because one person was not honest.

COVID-19 is not the flu. We cannot get rid of it by wishing it away or pretending "it is not that serious." We have a moral responsibility to each other. That moral responsibility is to keep each other safe. This problem is bigger than politics, race or gender. The coronavirus is an equal-opportunity destroyer. If we are going to reopen, let us please be wise. It is a matter of life or death.

Living in a society with two sets of rules makes everything unfair

May 12, 2020

"American rhetoric and law have been hypocritical since their inception, and nowhere has this been more evident than in legal protections and law enforcement for black people. Black Americans have, for the entire history of this country, faced a legal system that treats them differently than white citizens. It has gotten better, sure, but this enduring legal double standard demands closer examination." - Jonathan Blanks

If Americans have learned nothing else during this pandemic, we have learned that we live in a society with two sets of rules. There are rules for those who have access to power and privilege, and there are rules for those who do not.

There are rules for those who promote white supremacy, systemic racism and patriarchy and rules for those who attempt to be progressive advocates of justice.

There are different rules for white Americans and another set of rules for people of color. I realize that those who are "woke" will say that I have done nothing more than state the obvious.

Clearly, the knowledge of two sets of rules is not as obvious to white Americans as it is to people of color. Black Americans have been aware of the history of the double standard since our arrival to this country.

Through slavery, Jim Crow laws, discrimination in housing, employment, education, etc., black people have had to bear the burden of two sets of rules.

It is undeniable that many white people claim that all are equal under the law and they muse about how black people are just being overly sensitive, are making excuses or are stuck in the past.

Two recent instances, however, prove my point. Ahmaud Arbery, an African American young man, was shot and killed by two white men in Georgia. The incident was perpetrated by assailants two months before the men were arrested. Two Brunswick, Georgia, district attorneys sat on the case and, using "good ol' boy" politics, allowed the men to be free.

Two months later, they were finally arrested. They are now in jail without possibility of bail. The video of the shooting is conclusive and clear: The men murdered Ahmaud Arbery. My point is not that white supremacists do bad things to black people. My point is that if two black men had shot a white jogger anywhere in America, they would be arrested immediately and placed in jail.

The second instance that illuminates the fact that we operate under two sets of rules in this country consists of the protesters arriving at state and federal buildings with semi-automatic weapons.

None of them has been arrested. If 10 black people would have showed up carrying high-powered weapons, the police would have arrested them in a New York second. But because they were white, no arrests. Such is life in the America of double standards.

We must make a change. If we are to truly become one nation, we must have one set of rules for all Americans. Double standards can no longer be tolerated at any level of this nation. From the White House to the jailhouse, we need uniformity of law, or else we will become more fractured and more divided.

Many white people say that we just need more time to change our attitudes and practices. In the flavor of James Baldwin, my response is: How much time do you need to get white America together? How many more excuses are needed to justify the actions of unethical, irresponsible people?

The time for excuses is over. The time for creative progressive action is now.

Pray for the family of Ahmaud Arbery.

Finding hope amid the pandemic

May 19, 2020

We are in the process of reopening the U.S. The coronavirus pandemic has had a devastating effect on this country, an effect no one was prepared for nationally, locally and personally. Over 90,000 people have lost their lives to the virus. Unemployed Americans have topped the numbers of the Great Depression. The stay-at-home orders have frazzled the patience of many. COVID-19 has taken a toll on all of us.

Now, we are reopening. My hope is most of us in the U.S., Missouri and Boone County will be responsible and sensible as we reopen. We must continue to practice social distancing and wear masks. Businesses and churches must respond in a manner that will help us and not hurt us. We understand many people and businesses are in tough economic situations, but we cannot let profit become more important than people. If we think economic recovery will happen overnight, we are simply fooling ourselves. The process of restoration will take time. We must endure with hope and not be reckless.

I have heard lots of people talk about "returning to normal." I hope we will not return to the normalcy of division and hatred we experienced before the pandemic. I hope we will be better people. Perhaps, the quarantine has transformed us to be more appreciative of community and activities we had taken for granted. I believe being forced to stay at home helped us garner greater respect and love for family and friends. We all are going through this pandemic together, so let us stay together in purpose for the common good.

We have learned some great lessons during this crisis. We have learned how we must never let politics and selfishness rule the day. We have learned the majority of Americans do care for other Americans, whether they are teachers, who have gone above and beyond the call of duty to encourage and equip their students, or essential workers, who have put their health and the health of their families at risk to care for us. We have also seen acts of kindness ordinary people have shown by sharing food, providing medication and essential items for seniors and others at risk and survivors of COVID-19 donating plasma to help others recover. We have learned some great lessons. If we remember the lessons, we will come through this better and wiser.

It is easy to be pessimistic and callous. There are a lot of things happening that, in the words of Marvin Gaye, "make you want to holla and throw up both your hands," but I choose to stand on hope. The virus will spike with the reopening, but this time, we will be better prepared. Or at least I hope so.

The future is uncertain, yet if we sally forth courageously and sensibly, we shall see a great new day. Be hopeful.

A religious response of faith and reason to the reopening

May 26, 2020

Memorial Day weekend was presented to us with a mixture of embarrassing awe and marvelous pride.

The president's announcement for all churches to reopen was embarrassingly hilarious. I realize the president has a god complex, but he cannot order religious leaders to act against the good of their congregates or society. To date, 98,000 people have died from the coronavirus.

As a pastor, I know how painful it is to have a member die of COVID-19 and not be able to give the proper homegoing to the deceased and celebration of life for the family. Fortunately, most religious leaders have ignored Trump and have operated during this pandemic with both faith and reason.

I am particularly proud of black church leaders, who have ignored the president and followed the advice of scientific and medical experts. I was proud to hear the president of the National Baptist Convention, U.S.A. Inc. advise National Baptist pastors not to open their churches for face-to-face gatherings until the science says it is safe. The convention represents the largest predominately African American denomination in the U.S. It, along with other predominately black denominations, realizes that African Americans are disproportionately susceptible to contracting the virus and dying from it than the white community. Staying closed and Zooming worships helps to keep our people alive. Again, this is another example of faith grounded in reason.

All of us were shocked at the irresponsible behavior of partying folks in Daytona Beach, on the beaches and party spots on both coasts and, of course, at the Lake of the Ozarks. Of the hundreds and thousands of people caught on video, very few, if any, practiced social distancing or wore masks. No rational activity was being practiced, only pure hedonistic egoism. Bad faith said to them, "just have fun and to hell with anyone else." May I remind us that the death toll is rising in this country?

I understand the argument of people who need to go back to work to save their families from financial ruin, but shameless disregard of social distancing due to a desire to have fun is both immoral and criminal.

The time is now for all of us to act with a sense of moral character. People need to realize that no one cares about your health and well-being unless you care about yourself. You cannot blame business owners if you do not practice social distancing and listen to the medical/scientific community. All people need to act with an acute social consciousness. As people of color in the U.S., we must be exceptionally vigilant.

One definition of faith is that faith is the substance of things hoped for and the evidence of things not seen. I have faith that most Americans understand the importance of being disciplined and responsible. I have faith that the religious community to which I belong, and others, will continue to engage in practices that empower us in these difficult times and not threaten our life. I have faith in the scientific community that the virus humans created will eventually be defeated. I have faith in a God who stands with us during this pandemic.

My reason tells me that I must protect myself and my family, friends, church members and students because we are our brothers' and sisters' keeper. Reason tells me survival is imperative, and the greatness of a society is determined by how it cares for the citizenry and not by the interest of the economy. If we take care of people, people will take care of the economy. That is just business ethics 101. Faith and reason confirm my belief that we will make it through this time but only if we are faithful to one another as fellow members of this democracy and reasonable in our actions. Be well; be safe.

Protests could be the start of dismantling racism, making change

June 9, 2020

We are witnessing protests in every region of this country. All of the protests begin peacefully. Some have ended violently, and violence is something none of us condone.

The murder of George Floyd simply was the proverbial straw that broke the camel's back. Black rage has been lying beneath the surface for a long time. America has never known how to deal with black rage. It has either viewed it as illegitimate or dismissed it as "blowing things out of proportion." And yet, when people think about the atrocities committed against black people for the last 400 years, it is incredible that incidents of violence have not exploded more. One needs only to think about Rosewood, Florida; the Tulsa Massacre; East St. Louis, Illinois; New York City; or that Missouri has the highest numbers of lynchings of black people outside of the deep South. Then you will begin to understand why black rage exists.

Some people talk about the beating of Rodney King as the beginning of the deterioration of trust between people of color and the police. But police brutality began in America hundreds of years ago. Before Rodney King, people of color have been mistreated, molested and killed by the police for hundreds of years in this country, and in Missouri. People talk about how there are some good police officers, but their presence is vastly overshadowed by racist cops who either willfully disrespect black lives and black bodies, or who are complacent when they witness injustice committed by their fellow officers.

I am encouraged by the protests in Columbia and nationally. It means that many in the white community finally get it. If you look at the thousands of people engaged in the protests, huge numbers of young and older white Americans are calling for justice and unashamedly shouting, "Black Lives Matter." One well-intentioned white friend asked me, "Why are they saying 'Black Lives Matter'? Don't all lives matter?" My response is yes, all lives matter, but white America for too long has acted as if black lives do not matter, and so we must proclaim that black lives do matter. Large numbers of white Americans, and people around the world, understand.

Many people in Columbia have been calling for community-oriented policing for a long time. Obviously, when you see the community, particularly communities of color, as your neighbors and not the "enemy," the incidents of police brutality will diminish. In our community, credit must be given to folks such as Traci Wilson-Kleekamp and Race Matters, Friends, Missouri Faith Voices, Steve Weinberg, Valerie Berta, Brittany Hughes, the Rev. Molly Housh Gordon, the Rev. Maureen Dickman, the Rev. Brad Bryan and many others who have called for community-oriented policing. Unfortunately, there has been resistance to their clarion call. Perhaps, the Columbia Police Department is now motivated to change their former posture. I hope so.

The crux of the problem is our failure to dismantle the continual systemic racism that is pervasive in the U.S. and in Columbia. Some of my critics have tried to convince me that racism is dead and that only liberals, or socialists or malcontents are keeping it alive. But with the recent deaths of George Floyd, Ahmaud Arbery and Breonna Taylor, such a response is both ridiculous and willfully insensitive. Those who make such an argument are people walking around with their eyes wide shut.

My hope is that after the protests here and across America, our politicians will be about the business of creating an environment of dismantling racism and making systemic change. We do not need the formation of task forces and committees that gather and analyze data, but have no power to enact transformative change. Diversity is not inclusion. Data gathering is not change. There can be no peace or love where there is no justice. Justice demands more than conversations about policing, employment, housing, economic disparity and a host of other issues that need to be addressed. We need real change.

Until then, protesters stand tall and strong until a change comes. Demand it. Insist on it. Let an older protest song from the Sounds of Blackness be your song, "Hold on, change is coming..."

It's time for reimagining policing in Columbia

June 16, 2020

Sunday represented the 20th day nationally, and the 13th day in Columbia, of protests.

While some attempt to degrade the protests as acts of lawlessness, rioting and the lot, the fact of the matter is that the protests demonstrate that people are wanting and demanding an end to police brutality and the dismantling of systemic racism in all American institutions, including the police departments across this country.

This is an opportunity that we as a community can begin to reimagine what policing in Columbia can look like for the present and the future.

How can we engage in community-oriented policing without over-policing neighborhoods that are already over-policed?

Is it possible to defund police departments in such a way that the resources needed for mental health, housing, medical health and other social needs can be better addressed and still maintain policing?

Can we imagine a community where the goal of policing is no longer domination and control, but actual protection and service? I think we can — and we must.

I believe that there are more good people in this community than bad people. I believe that most families want the same things: the best for their family members and the opportunity to grow and thrive without obstacles that discriminate and oppress.

We all have sons, daughters, wives, husbands, partners, nieces, nephews and grandchildren. None of us want any of these we love killed by police brutality.

The fact is that all of us could be victims of police murder, particularly if you are a person of color.

I also believe that while Columbia has the same issues and problems of larger cities, we have the capacity to solve more of these problems than larger communities. All cities have a long history of racism and police brutality. Columbia is no exception; after all we live in "Little Dixie."

But we can effectively dismantle racism in Columbia. The first illustration of this truth is that the protesters in Columbia are black, white, Latino, Native American, Asian, Christian, Muslim, non-Christian, older and younger, LGBTQIAA and non-binary.

The same is true of protesters nationally and around the world. They are a diverse group. They all demand justice. Why? Because they know that justice for any of us is justice for all of us.

Do not be fooled by thoughtless rhetoric. Some say that all of this is about the Democrats and their agenda. Others lament that it is socialism, or subtle communism.

Most black people who know their history realize that we can no longer place our faith in any one political party. Democrats and Republicans have sold out black people since we arrived in 1619.

We remember that white Democrats and Republicans organized and perpetuated violence against the black community. We remember how Democrats and Republicans enacted Jim Crow laws, instituted White Citizens Councils, promoted segregated housing, schools and restaurants.

Those of us who are "woke" vote for the best candidate to do the job, the candidate who will unite us as a nation and not divide us, and one who understands and believes in the common good, not the good of the rich at the expense of the poor.

For black Americans, it is about voting for someone with character, not political platforms. That point guides our decision-making.

As I told the crowd at last Sunday's protest, this is a time for creative imagination.

We must reject old paradigms and practices and create the fundamentally new.

The "new" must be grounded in justice, not profit. We must define what we mean when we utter, "we the people."

"We" must include all of us and not just some of us. We must challenge old stereotypes and old patterns of behavior and thought including brutality and racial, gender and sexual profiling.

The symbols of racial superiority must be removed because they not only point to a reality, but they also participate in that reality.

Miss me with the argument that it is just Southern history unless you are going to be honest enough to admit that Southern Confederate history is a history of murder, rape, and dehumanization of black, brown and Native American people.

I agree with Councilman Ian Thomas that one of the first things that we must do in Columbia is to ban chokeholds.

I hope the mayor and the City Council will concur with this idea.

I wish that the governor and the Boone County commissioners would do the same. It is time to reimagine what we can be as a community. I believe we can do it.

Living in the age of 'spin' and trying to decide what to believe

June 23, 2020

"This is the most important time for this generation, for this is the age of 'spin.' "- Dave Chappelle

One of the things I have done to maintain my sanity and spiritual power during this pandemic is watch lots of comedy. I know that laughter is good for the soul and body. I admire good comedians because they are brilliant. They take tragedy and transform it into humor and make us look at ourselves in a critical way without offending our hypersensitivity. While watching Dave Chappelle's "Deep in the Heart of Texas," he stated the above excerpt that has arrested my attention: "for this is the age of spin."

We are living in a time where truth is determined by the narrative(s) that accompanies said truth. The ancient question of "What is truth?" should cause us to pause and wonder. For example, is truth determined by political agendas, conservative versus progressive socio-economic analyses, racial history and the lot, or is truth determined by subjective feelings and emotions so that now one says, "This is my truth" and not "This is the truth"?

A case in point: Congressman Mike Gallagher R-Wis., joined by his colleague Ed Perlmutter D-Colo., introduced bipartisan legislation to require all medical providers, including insurers and drug companies, to publicly disclose costs for all products, services and procedures. The Transparency in All Health Care Pricing Act of 2019 requires all price disclosures to be available at the point of purchase, in print and online, and include all wholesale, retail, subsidized, discounted or other prices.

I think this is a great idea, but it is dismissed by Democrats and Republicans because of party loyalties. One fact that illustrates the problem is that many young families end up on the verge of bankruptcy simply because they had a baby, or how about the senior who was hospitalized for COVID-19 and, after leaving the hospital, was presented with a bill for $1 million. Should we not support legislation that provides for the common good? But alas, such ideas become the victim of spin.

The pandemic death toll is now more than 120,000 in the U.S. Is it because of more testing, or is it because of new infections? Should monuments of Confederate generals be removed, or should they remain because they are important to American history? Is wearing a mask and observing social distancing a violation of personal freedom, or is it an intelligent response to a pandemic and a sign of moral consideration of fellow Americans? Should one affirm that Black Lives Matter, or is it an affront to white Americans? The current answers to these questions, unfortunately, are grounded in spin.

Americans do not know what to believe. Spin doctors have a way of distorting reality in such a manner that good becomes bad and right looks like wrong. When we rejected the idea of objective truth and purported that truth is the product of subjectivity, we became slaves to spin doctors, who manipulate narratives of distortion and prejudice. The consequences are paramount.

We find ourselves forced into false dichotomies that are destructive to American life. Should we build the economy or protect the health of the citizenry? Should we respect the history of all people of color, or is white, male-dominated history the only important history? Should parents have a right to choose what school their children attend, or should we construct public education in such a manner that schools provide quality education regardless of ZIP code?

Instead of wrestling with the issues as people for a common good, we respond by spin: Democrat or Republican, white or people of color, Christian or non-Christian, male or female, gay or straight and on and on.

Somehow, we must take our minds back and break the seductive power of spin. We must decide to be thinking, rational people or be controlled by the hype. Our future depends on our decision.

Being Black in America on the Fourth of July

June 30, 2020

On Saturday, America will celebrate Independence Day. July 4 is a day of internal conflict for every enlightened African American. As Americans, we'll celebrate the ideals of this Democratic experiment. We are the one country in the world that consciously proclaimed that despite our differences we could form a "more perfect union" grounded on principles of justice, respect, meaningful life, liberty and equality. These noble ideals are what makes America great.

The U.S. Constitution continues to encourage us that what we have written, we can achieve. Though the Constitution was written by flawed men who were racist, sexist and probably homophobic, they produced a document greater than their weakness. The ideals of the Constitution have drawn people around the world to this place because they believed that we could live up to the promised American dream. The Constitution makes those who were captured and forced to be here hope that one day we will be one.

The African in me, however, remembers how we have failed to be the nation we aspire to be. Racism has been part of the American experiment from day one. White America stole the land of the indigenous peoples of America, infected them with disease, raped and looted them and broke every treaty it ever made with Native Americans. The enslavement of Africans and the subsequent historical acts of anti-black racism has placed an indelible stain on America. We have treated Asians and Latinos horribly. Racism in the development of America has become both systemic and institutional. It is not merely individual. We are witnessing its insidious character in acts of police brutality, indifference to the forced imprisonment of Latinos and the separation of their families at the Southern border, mass incarceration of the poor, Black, brown, and ignorant urban blight, coupled by shouts of "white power" by white supremacists. It is hard to celebrate when one feels like the country you love hates who you are.

Yet, I will celebrate the Fourth of July because I am African American. As African Americans, our families and community have helped build this country. Black people have made major contributions to America's prosperity and existence. We have fought in its wars, produced great inventions, entertained its populace and contributed to its greatness. We have been and still are its poets, teachers, inventors, merchants, farmers, clergy, scientists and business leaders. Despite harsh segregation, Jim Crow laws, lynching, rapes and murders, Black people produced for the America they believed in and loved. Black people have blood in the bricks and tears in the mortar of this nation. I celebrate our contributions to the hopeful actualization of the American common good.

I celebrate the idea of this democratic project. I am encouraged that more white Americans are realizing that racial injustice at every level is injustice toward everyone. Young and older white people are saying "enough is enough." Americans are tired of the division in this country. They understand that Black lives do matter and are tirelessly protesting to make the point clear. Americans want an America that includes all of us, not just the "white" part of us. I celebrate the cultural shift that is happening before our very eyes.

So, I will celebrate in hope. My hope is for an America that becomes what we imagine, "the land of the free and the home of the brave."

Wear a mask and support the safety of us all

July 7, 2020

On Monday night, the Columbia City Council voted to impose a mandatory mask-wearing ordinance for 90 days in most public and some private places.

Everyone age 10 and older will be required to wear a mask when around people beyond their household.

The penalty for failing to wear a mask is a $15 fine for individuals. Businesses face a $100 fine for each employee.

I realize that emotions run high about this issue. Some Columbians believe a mandatory face covering ordinance is an unnecessary imposition and a violation of personal freedom, an example of government overreach.

Perhaps, but is it a necessary one during a pandemic?

Masks are cumbersome and annoying. No matter how decorative we make them, they can be uncomfortable to wear, especially given Missouri heat and humidity.

Yet, we are compelled to do many things for our safety and the safety of others that are cumbersome, like buckling a seat belt, wearing a helmet while riding a bicycle and putting our young children in a car seat.

However, very few people complain about these rules. All of us must give up some personal freedoms to live in a democracy. It is called being committed to the common good.

For example, we have free speech, but we cannot carelessly yell fire in a crowded theater. We must be willing to do some things for the benefit of all of us, including health and safety demands that impinge on our personal freedom(s).

The facts are that more than 130,000 people have died from the coronavirus in the United States.

Contrary to a president caught in the throes of denial, the new cases being reported are not because of increased testing. It is because of new cases.

These new cases are not to be taken lightly or ignored. The pandemic is not over. It is not going to "just disappear."

COVID-19 is an equal opportunity danger to all of us. It does care if one is white or a person of color, wealthy or poor, Republican, Democrat or independent. It does not care about age, rank or title.

The coronavirus can be deadly, and we must get a handle on it quickly. Wearing a mask and social distancing are not political issues (Republican vs. Democrat). This is a human issue.

If you think wearing a mask is uncomfortable and constricts your freedom, what do you think a respirator will be like? Or a casket?

The virus is surging in Boone County. If the virus is not contained, it will continue to affect our local economy, our ability to return to work, whether school will reopen and much of our normal lives.

All Columbians can benefit economically, personally and socially by simply wearing a mask and following the parameters of social distancing.

I'm glad the Columbia City Council passed a mandatory mask ordinance for the common good of all Columbians. It just makes good, common sense.

But I have lived long enough to learn that common sense is not all that common. Despite what the City Council does, everyone please wear a mask in public and practice social distancing. It does just make good sense.

I asked 1,250 parents if they worried about kids returning to school. Almost all said yes

July 14, 2020

President Donald Trump and Secretary of Education Betsy DeVos are demanding that schools reopen this fall and have in-seat classes.

The reason for Trump's insistence has been cataloged over and over. DeVos, Trump's mouthpiece, is of course going to echo her boss.

Most school districts are trying to find a way to comply with Trump's mandate within the Centers for Disease Control and Prevention's guidelines. In places where the coronavirus is at record levels, the school districts are not going to reopen. To date, I know of two that are not going to comply with Trump's order — Los Angeles and San Diego.

Sending our children back to school this fall creates a dilemma of the following kind.

On one hand, all of us want our children to go back to school for multiple reasons. Returning to school provides socialization opportunities our children have missed since mid-March, when most of our schools went to remote/online learning models.

The effects of being quarantined are noticeable when considering the emotional and mental health of our children and I dare say their parents. Some argue that face-to-face classes are better in quality than remote learning.

I know that in my own case, I am good via Zoom, but I am an awesome teacher in a face-to-face setting. Not a brag; just fact.

But on the other hand, COVID–19 is growing at an incredible rate throughout Missouri and the U.S. The virus is real, and unlike the Trump administration, I believe the medical and scientific experts.

While I do not exalt the experts as gods with infallible knowledge, I think we ought to pay attention to what the research is saying and do the simple things like wear masks, social distance and wash our hands.

The data about how the virus affects children is still incomplete, but we know they can be carriers, and not only to their parents and grandparents. They can infect teachers, administrators, school staffs, custodians, bus drivers and cafeteria workers.

Sending our children back to school is a real dilemma.

The real issue is how parents and family members feel about the mandate to reopen. Unlike Trump and DeVos, I asked parents in Columbia and other places the following question: Are you concerned about sending your children and/or grandchildren back to school this fall?

In my simple survey placed on social media in two locations and with mask-to-mask interviews with 1,250 respondents, I received the following feedback:

• A total of 97% stated they were extremely concerned about sending their children back to school. About 93% of the 97% stated they were not sending their children to school but had elected to go with remote learning or homeschooling for their children. The other 4% of the 97% stated they were sending their children to school because of financial reasons but were afraid.

• Two percent stated that they trusted the school their children were attending and had little or no concern about the virus and that the mental health of their child, given the lack of socialization, was most important to them.

• One percent stated they had no concern at all regarding the virus because they believed that the virus was either a hoax or that they believe 99% of the people who are infected with COVID-19 recover.

Some of the comments and questions from responders were remarkably interesting:

• What do we do about buses full of children? Social distancing cannot be practiced, and we know that our children will be so excited to see their classmates that they will interact without supervision.

• If a teacher becomes infected, do all the students of that teacher need to quarantine for 14 days? Who will cover the teacher's classes? Who will pay for it?

• If one student becomes infected, how will we know in time, and what does that mean for all who came in contact with him/her?

• If schools are forced to shut down school again because of the virus, how are parents to reschedule work and child care?

These are just a few of the questions they asked. All of them are important. The fundamental existential question for me: Are we playing Russian roulette with our children, our teachers, our school workers or ourselves?

Thanks to everyone that responded to my question about sending our children back to school this fall. Indeed, we are caught in the horns of a dilemma.

To learn the lessons of John Lewis is to honor his legacy

July 21, 2020

"If you're not hopeful and optimistic, then you just give up. You have to take the long hard look and just believe that if you're consistent, you will succeed."- John Lewis

U.S. Rep. John Lewis died Friday. He was 80 years old, and he was known as one of the Big Six organizers of the 1963 March on Washington.

His participation in the march across the Selma, Alabama, Edmund Pettus Bridge brought national recognition of the brutality of the segregated South. Lewis was severely beaten and almost killed by Alabama State troopers.

Many people believe his (and others') sacrifice that day led powerfully to the adoption of the 1965 Voting Rights Act. He was a civil rights icon who voiced the plight of Black and poor people. He was known as "the conscience of the Congress" and had the respect of his colleagues on both sides of the aisle.

Remembering the history of a person like John Lewis is one thing. Learning the lessons of his legacy is quite another.

There are many lessons that Lewis' life left to us if we are willing to be good students.

• He has taught us the fight for racial justice is a marathon and not a sprint. Systemic/institutional racism is so deeply embedded in the structure of America that it will not be dismantled overnight. While Lewis had great accomplishments, he also experienced great disappointments. Through it all, he maintained hope and understood that the race toward justice is not given to the swift but to those who endure until the end.

• His life and legacy remind us that white supremacists will use whatever means at their disposal to attempt to maintain the status quo. Lewis was not beaten by the KKK but by people who were commissioned "to protect and serve." White supremacists will rewrite laws, enact ordinances that deny health care, maintain economic disparity, defend police brutality, produce false narratives, and physically beat and murder those who fight for justice. You cannot tell a white supremacist by the way they look. Only their actions reveal the depth of their racism. They are dangerous and will perform any act to maintain privilege and power.

• Lewis' life demonstrates that true allies are determined not by skin color but by their commitment to justice. During the height of the civil rights era, lots of Black people were opposed to the movement, and lots of white people stood shoulder to shoulder with Lewis. In this age of spin, we too must remember that they who are for us are not against us, and they who are against us are not for us. I learned from John Lewis that one must not only pick one's battles well, but one must also pick one's allies with wisdom.

• Lewis believed that the God of hope stands with those who fight the good fight. Lewis did not employ supernaturalism to correct the evils he saw in this society. Instead, he realized that since human beings constructed the systems of racism, economic disparity, brutality and the other social evils all around us, human effort can dismantle the evils we experience. The God of Lewis grounded his hope, enlivened his courage and confirmed that his work was not in vain.

Too often the hyper-spiritual want God to undo our messes instead of giving us the wisdom and courage to stand against the sociopolitical Goliaths in our lives. Lewis knew that the God of hope empowers the warrior for justice and has placed the power to overcome in our hands. Give me the God of hope that Lewis revered. That God is the God we need.

I honor Rep. John Lewis, and I give thanks to both God and history for his lessons. May he rest in peace, and may we live in a manner that honors his legacy.

We have a moral obligation to vote for Medicaid expansion

July 28, 2020

Now more than ever, Missourians need to be able to access care in their own communities and protect thousands of local frontline health care jobs.

Amendment 2 will help keep rural hospitals and urban clinics open by bringing $1 billion of our own tax dollars back from Washington, instead of going to the 37 other states that have expanded Medicaid. — Jack Cardetti

On Aug. 4, Missourians will have an opportunity to do the right thing. The right thing is to expand Medicaid.

We had an opportunity to expand Medicaid once before, but we chose to do the wrong thing. We were seduced into believing that Medicaid was only for urban centers like Kansas City and St. Louis.

That was conservative-coded language for "Medicaid is only for Black people and people of color." We now know that Medicaid expansion helps our white rural communities and all Missourians in general.

We were given a false narrative. Now, we know the truth. We must expand Medicaid.

Thirty-seven states plus the District of Columbia have expanded Medicaid. Missouri is one of 13 states that has not.

Other states have realized that it is the moral obligation of state governments to act in a manner that assists the citizenry to live better and healthier lives.

Good health care can no longer be a luxury for just the wealthy. Medicaid expansion will move us toward narrowing the health disparity that exists between the rich and poor in Missouri.

We have a moral obligation to address medical/health disparities in our state. We can no longer allow political rhetoric to prevent us from doing the right thing. We abrogated our collective moral responsibility once, let us not do it again.

The pandemic in Missouri has powerfully demonstrated that the need for Medicaid is without question. More and more of our citizens are becoming ill and or dying from COVID-19.

The virus is not going away soon, and now, with the foolishness of schools reopening amid the pandemic, the need for health care will increase.

We know that Gov. Mike Parson does not get it. We, who are parents and grandparents, understand that the well-being of our children, our family members and our neighbors is far greater than the economic issues Medicaid expansion raises. When the issues are life and health versus profit, we must always choose life.

Here is the no-brainer: If we help people acquire the medical care they need, they will be better able to work and improve the economy. An investment in people is an investment in the common good.

When rural hospitals are open and functioning well, it helps Missouri as a whole. When folks in urban centers have access to good medical care, all of Missouri prospers.

The time for excuses is over. The time to expand Medicaid is now.

So, fellow citizens, let us do the right thing this time. Vote "yes" on Amendment 2 on Aug. 4. A "yes" vote for Medicaid expansion is morally correct and will help Missouri be a better state for all of us.

Remembering Miss Stella Johnson's legacy in Columbia

August 11, 2020

"Education makes a child unfit for slavery." - Frederick Douglass

On Aug. 4, Columbia lost one of the great ladies of its community. Her name was Stella Johnson. She was born in 1934. She was a longtime resident of Columbia. She died at home at the age of 86.

Miss Stella, as most of us referred to her, was a lady of class and elegance. She had a powerful sense of self wherever she was. Whether sitting in a meeting among other Christian people, or lovingly chastising a young child, Miss Stella let you know that she believed you were somebody, and that she expected the best out of you.

Stella Johnson was dedicated to the education of Columbia's youth, particularly Black youth.

She was an educator who understood that obtaining an education was not merely about acquiring a degree. Education for Miss Stella was about obtaining a well-rounded understanding of the world we live in and incorporating a historical perspective from which an individual could construct a positive future.

She particularly wanted Black children to understand their history both as a Black person and as a Black person in Columbia. She taught that racism was real, but not insurmountable.

She taught those who encountered her that all have a gift in them and all they had to do was to nurture it to be successful in life.

Miss Stella was not a woman who sought out confrontation, but she did not shy away from it either. If it meant standing for the right, she would confront a student, a parent, a teacher or an administrator. She would fight tooth and nail for a student who needed defending. She loved Black children not just with words, but with deeds.

We shall all miss Miss Stella. She did so much for the Columbia community. I do not know what her conversation was with God when God called her home.

What I do know is that God said to her: "Well done thy good and faithful servant. Well done!"

A celebration of the Negro Baseball League

August 20, 2020

Major League Baseball and America celebrated the 100th anniversary of the Negro Leagues on Sunday. The league was the home of magnificent Black talent who were not allowed to participate in the white league because of segregation.

The Negro Leagues were the home of players such as Josh Gibson, Oscar Charleston, Cool Papa Bell and Buck Leonard. It also helped players like Jackie Robinson, Satchel Paige, Ernie Banks, Hank Aaron, Monte Irvin, Larry Doby and so many others get professional experience before joining the majors after Robinson broke the color barrier.

The narratives about the Negro Leagues circulated with pride, gusto and humor. I can remember as a youth hearing about a young Satchel Paige pitching against the New York Yankees in an exhibition game. The Yankees were led by Babe Ruth and the boys, with Paige on the mound for the St. Louis Browns. The story goes that Ruth got a single in the first inning. Afterward, Paige called a timeout, walked over to the coach of the Browns and said, "Not another one of them will get a hit the rest of the game!"

Ultimately, Paige pitched a one-hitter and the Browns won 2-0.

Whether the above story is true or not, it demonstrates how much Black people loved their sports heroes in the Negro Leagues. Lots of stories peppered the Black community about Cool Papa Bell, Josh Gibson and others. The stories were told to remind Black people that even though the white American baseball league hid behind the curtain of segregation, we knew that there were Black players as good as, or better, than their white counterparts. In a time of degradation, Black folks had something to hold onto with pride. Whites bragged about Jackie Robinson being the first Black man to enter the white league, but Black folks smiled and said, "He was good, but there were so many that were better that were either forgotten or overlooked."

`When one thinks about how Black players were underpaid and sometimes badly treated and yet played for the love of the game, it should warm the human heart. Lots of Black baseball players sacrificed so much. Indeed, they should be celebrated.

If you want to know more about these awesome ballplayers, visit the Negro Leagues Baseball Museum in Kansas City. It will be worth your time.

Happy 100th anniversary to the Negro Leagues. You were great, and we remember you.

Retaining lessons along life's way, and more to come

September 15, 2020

Sept. 11 is a very emotional day for me. On Sept. 11, 1977, I was ordained as a Christian minister. The power and sacredness of that event still resonate powerfully within me.

On Sept. 11, 2001, two of my Princeton classmates were tragically killed in the twin towers attack. To know that my friends and colleagues, as well as many other Americans, could die so horrifically still brings me to tears.

Both Sept. 11 events have taught me some lessons along life's way.

Life is a continuous journey full of highs and lows. It is a marathon and not a sprint. There are no promises in life. You may aspire and dream of what your life will be, but in the end, life gives us what it gives us.

Our task is to make the most out of every life experience, good and bad. The ancient philosopher Longinus allegedly stated that, "it is better to exist than not to exist and it is better to live at a higher level than a lesser."

Life gives both. Because this journey is full of ebbs and flows, one ought to live life with gusto. Now, having lived more than six decades, I invite you to live your life with passion.

Real success is measured not by wealth, power or privilege but by our ability to commit to something greater than ourselves. That is why fighting to overcome injustice, feeding the hungry, educating our youth and working for the common good is so important.

It forces us to break out of our comfort zones. It makes us care about others at least as much as ourselves. It is comfortable to live as a self-righteous navel grazer. It is magnanimous to work for the good of others. To live a life of magnanimity is to be tremendously successful.

Never allow your critics the power to make you ignore the meditations of your heart. If you have the courage to speak truth to power, you will have critics. Many of them will attempt to make you feel foolish and unimportant. They are often heartless and cruel. However, not listening to the meditations of your own heart will rob you of peace and joy.

Players are going to play, and haters are going to hate. To be true to one's own heart is more important than any possession or public acclaim. The Nazarene once said, "out the heart flow the issues of life." Be true to the meditations of your heart.

Cherish your family and friends. One never knows how long our family and friends will be with us. The coronavirus, natural disasters, violence and life's horrors make us aware that our family and friends can be here today and gone tomorrow. True friends are few. Family ties are fleeting. Cherish family and friends so that in the end we did not say, "if I could of, would of..."

Cling to the God you know. So many people live by what a tradition or doctrine says about who and what God is. Know the God that meets you at the altar of your heart. I no longer attempt to fit someone's religious ideas. I simply hold fast to the God I know: the God who brought me through the Middle Passage, who sustained me through slavery, Jim Crow segregation, systemic racism and oppression, sickness, poverty, anxiety and despair.

Whether that God fits someone else's conceptual framework is irrelevant to me. My conversation about God does not start with "God hates..." My God loves male, female, people of color, people of other faiths, folks who are LGBT, and on and on. I know that God is real because I believe love is real. Find the God who sustains you, and you will find a peace that the world did not give, and the world cannot take away.

I give just a few things I have learned along life's journey. I know as I live, I will learn so much more.

Getting ready with a Plan B

September 22, 2020

In the highly acclaimed movie "Roots," Chicken George stated, "when Plan A doesn't work, you have to have a Plan B." With the way things are going in America, I am wondering if we are prepared with a plan B.

I truly hope two things will happen. One, that progressives, moderates, people of color, laborers, farmers and folk of every kin and kind will vote out Mr. Trump, his corrupt administration and his political allies including Gov. Parson.

Two, I hope that the Senate will not confirm a Supreme Court Justice until after the November election. If four Republican senators realize the hypocrisy of placing a judge in an election year after denying President Obama that opportunity, I believe good things will happen.

But it is possible that America will make a wrong choice — again — and reelect Mr. Trump, and that the Senate will push through with seating Trump's choice to the Supreme Court. If that happens, what will we do? What is our plan B?

Sometimes the worst circumstances create the best opportunities. Four more Trump years will cause the worst socioeconomic and political situation we have seen in many years.

Let us be honest, under Trump's leadership, or lack of it, America is sicker; we are in the worst economic condition since the Great Depression; and we are experiencing horrible social division and unrest.

The results of a Trump appointee to the Supreme Court will affect America for 30 years or more. And I believe it will affect us for the worse.

What then is plan B? If Trump is reelected the situation may force America to come together as one. It will become painfully obvious that we will need one another more than ever before. Under a corrupt presidency we may finally realize that forming authentic community is the power in our own hands. We may have come together to educate our own children. We may have to police the police in our own neighborhoods. We may have to create financial opportunities for one another. We will have to make America better on our own.

The bottom line for me is this: How do we survive if we, once again, have a president who does not care about all Americans? We survive by caring for each other, "by whatever means necessary."

A cultural change is happening. Everyone knows it, which is why the conservatives are fighting so vigorously to maintain the status quo. The change is coming, and it cannot be stopped. Cultural shifts are always painful and frightening. Things will no longer be the same. The problem is that it may not come tomorrow. Racial injustice, economic disparity and the pandemic may not end soon. So, in the meantime we must be psychologically, physically and spiritually prepared to survive. We must be ready to go to plan B.

Everyone, please vote. Voting can implement the change we all want and need. But if worse becomes worse, have a plan B.

Being community means helping our neighbors in need

September 29, 2020

What constitutes the greatness of a community? Is it the ability to build great infrastructure or dazzling buildings?

Is it the creation of a bustling business district or fantastic churches, mosques and temples?

All of these and more are signs of prosperity, but none are the telltale signs of what it truly means to be a community.

What makes a community is the willingness of citizens to care for those who are in need.

Last week, the city announced that it will resume shutting off water and electricity services on Oct. 5 for households with unpaid accounts.

Best estimations suggest that over 5,800 families in our city will be without utilities.

Most of these families were in desperate economic situations before the pandemic hit. Now they will be in a worse situation if their utilities are shut off.

It seems to me that we should rally to help those who are facing shut-off. We can assist our neighbors.

I lay two suggestions before you.

One, ask the Columbia City Council to either extend the shut-off extension or give utility amnesty to those families that cannot pay their utility bills.

The weather is getting cooler, and most of these are families with children. No one, adult or child, should have to sit in a house or apartment without heat or water.

The economy is still reeling from the pandemic. The little money these families have barely pays for food and rent.

We need the City Council to act with compassion. We need the council to grant either an extension or debt forgiveness to these families.

Two, we need churches, organizations and people to create an emergency fund to pay utility debts.

There are some large and wealthy churches in Columbia that by working together could wipe out the debt for those most in need.

Civic organizations in Columbia, as well as our most prosperous citizens, can create a safety net for community members most in need. Columbians have the resources; we just need to act.

The wonderful thing about people helping people is that it is not political, it is social.

This call to be community is not about being Republican or Democrat, progressive or conservative, Anglo or a person of color.

Responding to need is about being human. It is time for Columbians to come together and be kinfolk, not just dwell on being skin folk.

All of us have been hurt by the pandemic. All of us have felt economic strain. But little becomes much when we pool our resources. Let us make sure that no family goes without electricity or water.

Why? Because helping the least among us demonstrates what it means to truly be a community.

It's time to seek knowledge over opinion in fight against COVID-19

October 6, 2020

Since the time of Socrates, we in the West have defined knowledge as a justified, true belief. Knowledge demands truth and reasonable evidence to justify the belief. On the opposite side, opinion is defined as a belief without truth or justification. Opinion can be motivated by feelings, prejudice, irrational hero worship and/or political agendas.

We are currently living in a time where knowledge is being replaced by opinion, and the result is a threat to our democracy and the common good.

For example, we know that the coronavirus is real and not a hoax. We know that 210,000 Americans have died from this deadly disease. We know that African Americans, Indigenous Americans and Latin and Hispanic Americans are disproportionately infected and dying at a greater rate than Anglo Americans. We know that wearing a mask, social distancing and hand washing reduces the spread of the virus. We know that testing, contract tracing and quarantine/isolation protects others. These things we know.

Yet so many Americans are of the opinion that the virus is no more than a mild case of the flu or that the "fake news media" has overstated the seriousness of the pandemic. Some have even equated mask wearing as an infringement of their civil rights and to quarantine and isolate is like slavery. Oh, how slaves would have loved to be privy to door delivery food, cable television and internet access. Such is the character of opinion: a false, unjustified belief.

The president of the United States still chooses opinion over truth. He is contagious but refuses to do what is rational and responsible. The saddest part is that many Americans are following his lead. Despite being hospitalized, he treats COVID-19 as no big deal, and in doing so, he is influencing people to act in the same manner.

Several of my students told me this week that the coronavirus has been blown out of proportion and that they do not believe the death toll nor that masks make any real difference. These are bright young people who have swallowed untruth and are operating by it. How sad and dangerous.

For years, as a child, I would hear my mother say, "Some folks don't believe fat meat is greasy." For those of you who do not know what "fat meat" is, fat meat is generally fat pork used for seasoning greens, beans, etc. in the boiling process. It adds flavor, but beyond a shadow of a doubt, it is a greasy item. Not to believe that "fat meat is greasy" is to demonstrate pure irrationality. Far too many Americans, from the White House down, are acting like they do not believe that fat meat is greasy.

The issue of COVID-19 is more than a political issue with me. It is a matter of public health and the common good. Our children are at risk in public schools. We were told that they cannot contract the virus. That information was false. Those who work in stores, custodial service, nursing, trucking, factories, meat processing, etc. are being endangered. How would you tell someone who has lost a family member to COVID-19 that the virus is not real or deadly?

It is time for us to get it together — here in Columbia and across the nation. We need to dismiss the political agenda — and the irrational behavior of the POTUS — and adopt a sense of responsible social action. We are all in this together.

If we merely would think about one another and move beyond our egos, we can save each other from sickness and death. Believe me, you will not receive the kind of A+ treatment in the hospital like the president experienced. There are a lot of issues we need to deal with in this country, and we cannot do it if we are sick or dead. We must take care of each other. Wear a mask.

Keeping chokeholds as Columbia Police policy maintains barbarism in our city

October 20, 2020

"Life is about choices. Some we regret, some were proud of. Some will haunt us forever." - Graham Brown

On Monday night, the Columbia City Council discussed a proposal, sponsored by Councilperson Ian Thomas, suggesting that the use of chokeholds by the Columbia Police Department be banned. No vote was taken.

Although no person in Columbia has died from police use of a chokehold, there are many reasons why the use of chokeholds by police officers — and similar kinds of restraint — should be banned in every city in America. Here are just a few.

There are too many other methods police have at their disposal to restrain a suspect other than a chokehold. How about de-escalating conversation for one option?

Moreover, police officers are trained in various forms of martial/combat art. To resort to a chokehold is to be led by fear or an insatiable feeling of power. In both cases it demonstrates that the police officer is not professional and well-trained.

We have witnessed police officers too often employ the hammer of chokeholds, and citizens are treated like nails. Remember Eric Garner and George Floyd, as well as others, were the victims of such methods. We do not need someone to die in Columbia to know that chokeholds are dangerous and oppose the common good.

Chokeholds are immoral and unethical. The use of them reduces the suspect from the level of human being to that of sub-human. In most cosmopolitan centers, if I use a chokehold on a pet, in most cases a dog, I would be arrested and either jailed or heavily fined. Public disdain would follow me at every turn. Yet a police officer can use the same method on another human being and not be charged or arrested, and receive acclaim for being "a good cop." Something here is fundamentally wrong. A human person should receive at least as much moral consideration and respect as a nonhuman being.

The authorization of the use of chokeholds moves our society closer and closer to barbarism. Think of this: A chokehold is a mini and partial lynching. It cuts off the flow of oxygen and, if maintained, leads to death. Lynching in America has been outlawed for being both cruel and unusual. Is not the same principle applicable to chokeholds? Of course, it is. Add to that the clear historical record of both chokeholds and lynching used against people of color, particularly Black people; chokeholds are indisputably brutal and immersed in racism. Our choice to continue to allow the employment of chokeholds moves our community and the society toward barbarism.

So that I may be clearly understood, I understand how police officers face threat daily. I realize that all police officers are not blood-thirsty racists looking to exercise domination and humiliation on people they swore to protect and serve.

The problem of policing in America is systemic, not personal. And yet abuse and brutality by chokehold has occurred far too often. It seems we should prevent another incident of death by chokehold from happening by simply eliminating chokeholds. We should choose to stop potential death by chokehold before it becomes an actuality.

We still have work to do to solve America's problems

November 4, 2020

We are witnessing a great historical moment. More than 100 million Americans have cast absentee or mail-in ballots in this presidential election. Most expected the record turnout at the polls. I am proud of the way Americans utilized their right to vote, whether Democrat or Republican.

Of course, I am hoping for a change after all the ballots have been counted. I hope for a change in the White House and a change in the U.S. Senate. I hope to see a change in leadership in Missouri. I am hoping for a change in the Missouri legislature. I did not merely passively hope but actively encouraged people across Missouri — and across the country — to vote.

I realize, however, that President Donald Trump and those who support him may be reelected once all the votes are counted. Trump's supporters are passionate. They are resolutely committed to four more years of the current administration. They will challenge the election in the courts, and they are hoping that conservative judges will aid their cause. Again, we will see.

However, now that the election has ended — and we may not know the final results for days to come — we must not assume that a Biden victory constitutes the end of the fight for justice and the common good in America and in Missouri.

There is much to be done, and no single party, person or plan can solve all the problems we must face. Here are a few things we must face:

The pandemic is continually growing out of control. The virus is not a hoax or a joke. It continues to kill people and people's livelihoods. We must get the virus under control immediately.

The issue of racial and economic disparity must be addressed immediately. We can no longer ignore the toll of these two phenomena. They are destroying our sense of the common good. Because of the division present in our society, we have Americans hating Americans. No nation divided against itself can survive. We must find a way to be united.

We must act more responsibly when it comes to the environment. Climate change threatens our existence on this Earth. If our planet becomes inhabitable, political ideology is irrelevant. We must invest in saving the Earth for our children and grandchildren. Clearly, time is running out.

The criminal justice system must be completely overhauled. The Black, brown and poor go to prison, and the rich go on vacation. Michelle Alexander, Angela Davis and others have tried to warn us about the problem. Now we must fix it.

Health care. Enough said.

I believe that we can solve the problems that plague this society. We must confront these issues with the same vigor and passion as we voted. We must not resort to violence but respond with intelligence and compassion. The fight continues.

Republicans must break with the Trump cult so democracy can survive

November 17, 2020

Americans have made their choice. We have elected Joe Biden to be the next president of the United States. Kamala Harris will be the first woman, and woman of color, to be vice president.

While Mr. Trump is tweeting fraud and how he won the election, the facts are that there is no evidence of widespread fraud, nor did he win the election. Such are the rantings and ravings of an immature narcissist.

Most Americans have been fed up with the divisive rhetoric and behavior of Mr. Trump for some time. It was time for a change, and a change has come. We can finally feel like we can breathe again. A celebration was and is in order.

Besides getting the pandemic under control, fixing a broken economic system and addressing racial injustice, there are in-house tasks that need to be addressed.

The question looms large as to whether the Republicans can break the Trump cult and restore the party to being the "party of Lincoln."

Currently, Donald Trump rules the Republicans with Jim Jones-like characteristics. They are afraid to question his actions and bathe in conspiracy theories.

They refuse to tell him that he lost the election, instead rallying around him as if he is their savior.

The Trump cult includes not only misguided individuals that believed he would protect their interest, but the cult also consists of white supremacist groups like the Proud Boys.

It is a dangerous situation that easily could result in armed conflict. The saddest thing to observe is how Mr. Trump does not care about those who follow him unquestionably. He only cares about himself. Such is the character of cult leaders.

Can the Republicans restore the basic principles of the party that made them a great party? Only time will tell.

If the Republican leadership had confronted Trump's antics when he became president, we would not have the trouble we have today. The past is the past and it cannot be changed.

The Republicans can, however, do something about the present and the future. We shall see if they have the courage and integrity to be the "Grand Ole' Party" or will they continue to succumb to the Trump cult.

In the "Second Treatise of Government," John Locke wrote: "As usurpation is the exercise of power, which another hath a right to; so, tyranny is the exercise of power beyond right, which nobody can have a right to. And this is making use of the power anyone has in his hands, not for the good of those who are under it, but for his own private separate advantage."

Locke reminds us that liberty is not doing whatever one wants to do. Liberty, for Locke, is the freedom to do what is right.

Liberty is to act with a commitment to the common good. When we divide into rigid ideological groups, we threaten democracy at its core.

We must reject fascism as ardently. Too many Americans died in World War II fighting against fascism. We cannot allow fascism to now rule under the authority of Mr. Trump and his cultic followers.

I believe that we can be the democracy we ought to be. We can overcome racial injustice. We can put an end to this global pandemic. We can revive and restore the economy. We can effectively and responsibly act regarding climate change.

The power is in our hands. But we must rid ourselves of cultic worship and xenophobic reaction. We must commit to building a more perfect union. Only if the Republicans and the Democrats work together do we have a chance to restore the common good.

It begins by the Republicans breaking ties with the Trump cult and being the statesmen and stateswomen they know they ought to be.

I call on every American to lay aside their ideological differences and commit to reimagining and creating the common good. Justice is at the core. There can be no love or unity without justice.

So, let us put on our hard hats and grab our lunch pails and diligently work for "a more perfect union." There is much to be done, so let us get on with it.

Take time this season to remember gratitude for little and big things

November 24, 2020

"I am grateful for what I am and have. My thanksgiving is perpetual." - Henry David Thoreau

Thursday we shall gather with family and friends to give thanks for all the good things we have experienced this year. While Thanksgiving has strong religious and cultural roots, Thanksgiving is celebrated more and more as a secular holiday.

Modern society confronts us with chaos daily. We live hustle-bustle lives, bombarded with demands of various kinds: vocational, personal, economic, social, political, etc. The opportunity to pause, give thanks for who we are and what we have, provides us with the occasion to center ourselves, be humble and bask in the light of love and joy. Even in the midst of a pandemic, we can still be thankful.

I am learning to delight in the little things. A smile from a stranger, an encouraging word from a colleague, the greeting wave of a child, or the embrace from a senior citizen raises my sense of gratitude. I am convinced that if one does not give thanks for the little things in life, one will never appreciate the "big" things.

We live in a materialistic world. We are judged by what we have. Sometimes this same materialism seduces us into an artificial sense of self: I am better if I have more things. The reality is that who we are cannot be measured by our acquisitions or our positions, but by our character. After all, none of us get to keep what we have when we die. We will have to leave it all behind.

I live in an area where I see many homeless people every day. I am surrounded by the working poor who must grind daily just to make ends meet. A cloud of despair hangs over many people, young and older. Circumstance can make one, in the words of Marvin Gaye, "want to holler and throw up both your hands." And yet there is much for which we must be thankful. Allow me to name just a few.

We can give thanks for family and friends who love us for the right reasons. All of us have haters, but the fact is that we also have people in our lives who truly love and cherish us, and they do so for the right reasons. They recognize that there is something in us and about us that is worthy to be loved.

We can be thankful that we are alive. Life sometimes is hard and frustrating. Yet if we live, we can change our lives. If we are in debt, get rid of it. If we are surrounded by negative people, change acquaintances. Our circumstances need not be our conclusion. You have the power to change your world. And for that be thankful.

We can be thankful for those who are praying for us. I still believe that prayer changes things. I know that I am here because someone prayed for me. I am not just talking about Christian prayer. Muslims, Jewish practitioners, Buddhists and Hindus all pray for the community of humanity. I am grateful for their prayers.

I am grateful for a deep sense of justice, faith and love. I realize that injustice seems to be winning and common sense is at an all time low. But there are justice warriors among us who are fighting the good fight. My grandmother once stated that she believed that "trouble won't last always." My faith affirms her belief, and my sense of love is that all systems and people can and will be transformed for the good. Hope that is seen is not hope. I am thankful that "weeping may endure for a night, but joy will come in the morning."

As we feast this Thanksgiving Day, let us commit ourselves a perpetual thanksgiving that works within us every day.

Behaviors will do more than 'miracle' vaccine to quell COVID-19

December 1, 2020

We are being told that a vaccine to fight COVID-19 is on the horizon. Medical experts are saying that vaccines could be available for frontline workers and high-risk citizens by the end of December, and then available to the rest of Americans by the spring.

The experts say the vaccines are 70% to 95% effective, which will make a dramatic change in the way the pandemic has impacted lives and livelihoods. All of this is good news, but I suggest we need to be cautiously optimistic.

According to the major polls, there is a hesitancy within the population to take the vaccines when they are available. Among people of color the hesitancy is grounded in history: too often "medicine" was used to experiment on African Americans. We remember the Tuskegee experiment and, because we do, we come to these vaccines with trepidation.

One of the things that causes anxiety within me and many people I know is the lack of information regarding the side effects of the vaccines. All of us who take medication(s) know that the side effects of many pharmaceuticals can be horrendous. They can be worse than the malady we are attempting to treat. Could the side effects of the vaccines be as bad or worse than the virus? I wonder. I would at least like to know what side effects the medical experts anticipate.

I hope that the emergence of the vaccines will not make us act foolishly. I fear that some Americans will see the vaccines as "miracle" drugs and return to reckless behaviors that will perpetuate the virus. We must still wear masks, practice social distancing and wash our hands. We must avoid large gatherings. As a person who has witnessed and is experiencing the effects of contracting COVID-19, I can emphatically attest that you do not want to get this virus.

I hope the vaccines work. The pandemic has crippled our society in various ways: economically, personally, psychologically and physically. Far too many Americans have been hospitalized. I am glad that President-elect Joe Biden is making the pandemic one of his highest priorities.

Please be safe as we welcome the vaccines. Remember that our behavior will do more than our hope for a miracle drug.

A future filled with hope

December 15, 2020

"Just as despair can come to one only from other human beings, hope, too, can be given to one only by other human beings." -Elie Wiesel

Preliminarily, I want to thank the many Columbians who demonstrated acts of love and compassion to my wife and I as we battled the coronavirus. Columbians of all kindred and kind prayed, sent words of support and fed us during this horrible experience with the disease. I am happy to report that we are much better. Recovery from the virus is slow, but we are alive and that is saying a lot.

Several of my friends and colleagues died during our time in quarantine, and yet, we are still here. The virus is not a hoax. Over 300,000 Americans has died from COVID-19. It is a serious debilitating virus that affects the body in strange ways. We must take it seriously and practice the safety methods suggested by the scientific/medical experts. If we are diligent now, we may be able to return to old-fashioned holiday celebrations next year. The choice is ours, but I believe in us because I have hope.

With the emergence of the new vaccines on the horizons we have a renewed sense of hope. Vaccination of frontline hospital workers and emergency personnel is scheduled to begin this week in Missouri. Now we have one vaccine. A second may be available next week with FDA approval. A third and fourth vaccine will be, hopefully, available in January. The experts say that we can have a significant number of Americans vaccinated by June or July. That is, of course, if we take the shot.

I am happy to see President-elect Biden and Vice President-elect Harris willing to both take the vaccine and encourage all of us to practice virus safety. How hopeful it is to have a real president again who cares about Americans. I hope Gov. Parson will follow suit and care about Missouri residents. The governor and his wife contracted the virus just like me and my wife. We both survived. We both know how deadly the virus can be to victims. Let us hope that he has freed himself from the Trump-cult and will do what is necessary to protect and safeguard Missouri residents.

The virus does not care if you are Republican or Democrat. The virus simply seeks out whomever it may destroy. While the governor and I are politically in opposition, I believe his experience with the virus will motivate him to do what is right. At least, I hope so.

I have hope that a meaningful stimulus bill will come out of Congress before Christmas. So many of our fellow citizens are in a desperate situation. Many are without food, face possible eviction and have run out of money. While I do not have to face these challenges today, I know what is like to be evicted before Christmas, or to worry if we will have anything to eat, or to have a pocket full of nothing but buttons and lint. I have been at the bottom, so my sense of compassion for my fellow Americans is "deep like the rivers." Thus, a word to Reps. Blaine Luetkemeyer, Jason Smith, Sam Graves, Vicky Hartzler, Ann Wagner and Missouri Attorney General Eric Schmitt: You have embarrassed Missouri residents by supporting the fallacious and counterintuitive Texas court case that attempted to overthrow the fair election of President-elect Joe Biden. You knew better, Republicans support states' rights. You violated your claim to be a Republican. Stop acting like prostitutes for Pimp Trump and get to work on helping the American people. We need you to pull together a stimulus package that will help not only Missouri residents, but all Americans. You pledged allegiance to the republic and the Constitution, not to a man who wants to be king. Live up to your pledge. Give us hope.

Hanukkah, Christmas and Kwanzaa are seasons of hope amid despair. They remind us of how we can be victorious despite the challenges and obstacles we face. Missouri residents hold fast to hope. Hope, love and faith will find a way.

Let's create, maintain a 'common good' for 2021

December 19, 2020

"We will open the book. Its pages are blank. We are going to put words on them ourselves. The book is called Opportunity, and its first chapter is New Year's Day."- Edith Lovejoy Pierce

2020 challenged us in ways we could have never imagined. It was a year of anxiety, despair, frustration, sickness and death. We have witnessed racial economic injustices in every sector of our society, unbelievable incompetency in the White House, the adherence to conspiracy theories absent of evidence, small business owners losing everything they had, families unable to put sufficient food on their tables, unemployment reminiscent of the Great Depression, children separated from their families and placed in cages and a pandemic that has cost the United States over 336,000 deaths. Truly 2020 has been a year that has tried the human soul.

Now we stand on the precipice of a new year, 2021. If Edith Lovejoy Pierce is correct that the new year is a book called opportunity, what shall our narrative be?

Perhaps we should begin by articulating our desire and total need for the common good. The question is how we shall envision making it a reality. In previous columns I have mentioned restoring and creating the common good. One woman suggested to me that we no longer know what the common good means for a society. I think we have an intuitive understanding of it expressed in the Constitution. The common good is a society where every person has a real opportunity for life, liberty and the pursuit of happiness. For too long only those with privilege and power could have meaningful life and liberty. Aristotle taught us thousands of years ago that happiness is the establishment of a moral state, not a feeling, which is essential for establishing the common good.

Now is the time to make the new year one of creating and maintaining the common good. It should be a reality for all. No one in America should be hungry. All Americans should have proper health care. No person of color should have to have "the talk" about the police with their child or grandchild. Injustice is unacceptable. Every worker needs to have a living wage. To garner an education should not be an albatross of debt but a social investment for our future. Clean water and air are not a luxury but a right. We must return to a sense of the common good.

Maybe in 2021 we can talk about democracy. This republic was to be "of the people" and "for the people." Instead, we have become so immersed in political ideologies that autocracy almost destroyed our democracy. We still have 50 million people who think the election of Joe Biden for president of the United States was rigged, yet the evidence states otherwise.

Our society needs different voices to be the best we can be. We need conservatives and progressives, Republicans, Democrats and Independents. What we do not need and cannot tolerate are cult worshippers who would be willing to sell our democracy to a man who was elected president but wanted to be king. We need a refresher on what democracy is and what it is not.

May our book of 2021 reflect our willingness to make compassion the bedrock of our narrative. May our pages articulate that whatever we do is not just because it is legal but because we love each other. The shootings and killings of one another in places like Columbus, Nashville, and Columbia is not only expressions of the material conditions of racism, economic disparity, patriarchy, etc. They are also the demonstration of the hole in our souls. Only compassion can overcome the hurt and pain so many of us feel. The bottom line is this: Do you care?

So, in the spirit of Hannukah, Christmastide and Kwanzaa, let the new pages in the book called "Opportunity 2021" reflect our recommitment to the common good, our belief in democracy and the power of compassion. Happy New Year.

2021

Here's a path toward real social change in Columbia

January 5, 2021

'The play's the thing

Wherein I'll catch the conscience of the King."- Hamlet, Act 2, Scene 2, 603–605, William Shakespeare

In last week's column, I suggested from the writing of Edith Lovejoy Pierce that the New Year is a book called "Opportunity" in which we have the power to write on the pages.

Keeping with that idea, I believe we have a golden chance to organize powerful coalitions for the purpose of recreating a just and noble democracy.

Despite Trump's attempt to destroy this democracy (aided by his "retrumplican" minions), we the people can move toward wholeness and become the republic envisioned by so many who have come before us.

The way to be a more perfect union rests in our commitment to working together.

Indeed, there is a lot of work to be done. Will the Republicans remain the party of Trump, or will they regroup and return to the party of Lincoln?

Will our personal desire for power and privilege once again impede movement forward? Will we continue to grasp at conspiracy theories or seek the truth, knowing that the truth shall set us free? The power of choice is in our hands.

Let me be clear. What if all the social action groups in Columbia would band together for systematic change? What a powerful witness that would be.

I am talking about Race Matters, Friends, The Minority Men's Network, Intersectionality, Columbia Faith Voices, NAACP (just to name a few) joining together to commit to just three items of social change in Columbia.

It could be affordable housing, or community/police relationships, or employment with livable wages, or justice system reform. Whatever the issue, if they spoke as one voice, it would be a play that captures the conscience of the king!

Of course, what I am purporting will take some personal and communal changes in attitude. Such an effort demands that attitudes and egos be left at the door.

No coalition can be successful when the work is reduced to egoism. The group must be comprised of people from various perspectives: radicals, moderates, conservatives, people of color, members from the white community, members from the LGBTQIA+ community and religious perspectives of various types.

If the goal is a perfect society in Columbia, we need various voices to contribute. Homophobia, sexism and elitism must not be allowed to rule the day and destroy the mission.

No one group or person can bring about the changes needed in Columbia. It must take an "aggregate" (borrowing from Traci Wilson-Kleekamp) of people willing to work for stated goals in order to be the community we look like.

I have always said that the problems Columbia has are solvable if we are willing to solve them.

This year, let us work together, for united we stand but divided we fall.

We've met the enemy. It's racism and white supremacy.

January 12, 2021

"We have met the enemy and he is us." - Pogo, a comic strip character by Walt Kelly

The above quote comes from "Pogo the Possum," popularized by Walt Kelly. It is preliminarily used to alert us to be environmentally vigilant. But its use in this column is a reflection on the insurrection we witnessed last Wednesday at the nation's Capital.

Rabid, violent Trump supporters stormed the "People's House," killed police officers and desecrated the center of this democratic experiment. All of it was incited by a mad man in the presidency and his imps. After what we witnessed last week, the quote, more succinctly stated, should read, "We have met the enemy, and they are us."

It is hard for some to think the mob that perpetrated these vile acts at the Capitol are us, but they are. They were Americans.

As a Black man in America, I was horrified but not surprised. Those of you who have taken the time to study indigenous, Latin or African American history know that there has always been a historical propensity for violence in white America. Wednesday was just another example of what white America can and will do. Trump merely fanned the flames for the last four years.

What did we expect a racist to do? Are we genuinely surprised the Proud Boys, Boogie Boys and other white supremacist groups under the Trump spell would act in such a manner?

Will there be more violence in the coming days? Of course, there will be more demonstrations of senseless violence. There is already a warning of possible violence on Jan. 17 and following. I believe Trump supporters who use violence to make their point will not stop. They are irrational and refuse to be moved by truth and moral persuasion. They want their way and are committed to use any means necessary to achieve their goal. They want to "Make America White Again."

We are hearing calls for unity and healing in the wake of the assault on the Capitol. The words sound good, but that is all they do — sound good.

There can be no unity until injustice is vanquished. Like so many others have said, there must be accountability for what happened at the Capitol and for what happens every day to people of color. We must acknowledge that racism, in its various forms, is the root of the problem. For example, law enforcement was slow to respond primarily because most of the Trump crowd was white. When Black Lives Matter peaceful protests occurred last summer in D.C., law enforcement was quick to dress in tactical gear, use tear gas and rubber bullets against the crowd. Could this be a coincidence? We know better.

The enemy is us. We hate to admit that we are they. The fact is the mob that showed up at the Capitol is the other side of America. The violence was not by the hands of the Russians, Iranians or the North Koreans. It was Americans against America. Listen to what they call themselves: patriots. I call them white supremacist thugs motivated by lies and years of white privilege.

If we are ever going to be a United States of America instead of a "Divided States of America," there must be a serious act of confession of how so many Anglo-Americans have benefitted from and supported white supremacy, sincere acknowledgement that racial and social justice must be a top priority and a willingness to create the common good. If these things do not happen, we will continue to meet the enemy — and it will be us.

Christians should stand on the side of justice, not riots

January 19, 2021

"For many will come in my name, claiming, 'I am the Messiah,' and will deceive many." - Matthew 24:5, NIV

One of the most disturbing videos I have watched of the insurrection by Trump supporters at the Capitol is the one where a man was hanging a noose on Capitol grounds while others in the mob were in the Capitol invoking the name of God and Jesus to bless their violent and illegal insurgency.

After killing five people and injuring many more all because of a lie, hanging the symbol of lynching on the peoples' property and then invoking that God bless their rebellion is more than anyone should be able to stomach.

All of us can recall how Christianity has been used to justify oppression, intolerance, racism, sexism, homophobia and the like. History is jam-packed with stories of people who, claiming to be agents of God and Jesus, have committed horrible crimes against humanity. One needs only to think of the Crusades, the enslavement of Africans in America, lynching, the attempted annihilation of indigenous people in the U.S. and around the world, and the repression levied against women and the LGBT community. All these historical events demonstrate how people who claimed to be Christians have been the biggest enemies of humanity. Facts are facts, truth is truth.

However, I want to suggest to you that all these acts are not what it means to be a Christian, and the episode we witnessed at the Capitol was a bastardization of Christianity.

Christianity is about building the beloved community, not about division and disunion. The fundamental prayer of Jesus was "that we might be one." The mob at the Capitol epitomized the very actions that are antithetical to the fundamental desire of Christianity. Dr. Martin Luther King Jr. knew it, and those of us who are trying to be a Christian (a la Maya Angelou) also know it. His Christian faith informed and empowered his social action and his call for civil rights. Christians stand on the side of justice because we know there can be no love where there is no justice.

Christianity is about the affirmation of the human community, not the subjugation by the few. The gangsters who perpetrated the violence at the Capitol were white supremacists. They see Trump as 'the Messiah" and participate in a lie that has fooled too many. Anyone who supports white supremacy is not a Christian. They are agents of evil.

How can you tell a true Christian from a false Christian? Time and space will not give an opportunity to elucidate the complete picture, but please accept the following: Judge them by the fruit they bear.

If they are agents of reconciliation, if they love those that evil despises, if they feed the hungry and clothe the naked, if they love the environment because it was created "good" and act with compassion and humble grace, they are Christians. If not, they are not.

This writing is not to convince someone to be a Christian. Frankly, I believe other faith practitioners who are not Christians share these characteristics as well. I simply want to inform you that there is a difference between being a Christian and claiming to be a Christian. Before you condemn all Christians for the behavior at the Capitol, please know, they are not us.

Black History Month and the white history of America

February 9, 2021

"It is impossible to understand politics, the Black community's relationship with the police, or why we even need to say 'Black lives matter' if we don't learn the history of this country. So, yes, let's have a White History Month! Let's have 12 of them!"- Amber Ruffin, comedian and TV host

Each February, we celebrate what is called Black History Month. It is a good thing, in principle, for Black and white people in America. It gives us an opportunity to celebrate the accomplishments and struggles of Black Americans in a society that has been hostile to Black existence. It can provide necessary information for white Americans who often are ignorant of the Black saga in America. For Black Americans who are "woke," every month is Black History Month.

I was intrigued by actress and comedian Amber Ruffin's commentary on "Why We Need a White History Month."

She makes some interesting points that need reflection. Ms. Ruffin asserts that white people know truly little about white American history. The history taught in most public and parochial schools has been so whitewashed with a false veneer that it is no wonder why many Americans do not know the historical truth.

For instance, we know the glorified stories of George Washington cutting down cherry trees and crossing the Delaware and that Lincoln freed the slaves. However, few Americans know that Washington had 18 slaves by the time he was 18 years old, and that Abraham Lincoln did not want to emancipate the slaves and certainly was not an advocate of racial equality.

For example, history taught in most schools does not articulate that the real motivation behind the Second Amendment was not to protect Americans from foreign enemies, but rather to ensure that white slaveowners had the weaponry to keep their slaves under control. How about the fact that police originated from the "slave catchers," which later became the Ku Klux Klan.

While I do not advocate a "White History Month," I do think that white America needs a historical reeducation. Dr. John H. McClendon, my friend and professor of philosophy at Michigan State University, always stresses that if one does not appreciate the material conditions that surround a historical event, one will never understand the actions that have taken place nor the motives of the actors.

Nate Turner, Frederick Douglass, Harriet Tubman, Marcus Garvey, Ida B. Wells, Malcolm X, and Martin Luther King Jr. did not rise in a bubble. The material conditions that vaulted them into action was the long bloody history of racial injustice perpetuated by white America.

I was curious why the top six Southern Baptist seminaries in the United States have removed critical race theory from their curriculums. It then dawned on me that if critical race theory is taught, it will make white denominations, and their churches acknowledge their complicity and cooperation in the barbarism of slavery, segregation, lynching and racial injustice. Clearly some white Christians refuse to embrace Jesus' statement, "You shall know the truth and the truth shall set you free."

When people believe a lie, we get the madness. The madness will take numerous forms, like the death of Breonna Taylor, George Floyd and others, as well as Jan. 6's mob and violence at the Capitol. If we are to move beyond the madness and become a more perfect union, then we need a proper historical reeducation. May Black History Month be the first step toward true education and unity.

Remembering Dorothy Irene Height: advocate and activist for civil rights

February 23, 2021

As we come to the end of Black History Month and move into Women's History Month, I thought it would be appropriate to highlight a Black woman. Many say she was one of the most influential women of the modern civil rights and women's rights movement.

I am talking about Dorothy Irene Height.

For almost half a century, Dorothy Height gave leadership to the struggle for a just society. She was passionately committed to the human rights of all people.

Dorothy Height was born March 24, 1912, in Richmond, Virginia. With the promise that living in the North would bring better opportunities, her family moved to Pennsylvania where she attended and graduated from Rankin High School in 1929. She then attended NYU where she received her undergraduate and master's degrees in four years. She later did postgraduate work at Columbia University and the New York School of Social Work.

In 1933, she became leader of the United Christian Youth Movement in the New Deal.

It was in this context that her gifts as an orator, organizer and civil rights advocate began to emerge. Perhaps the two most memorable events for many were her work with Dr. Mary McCleod Bethune, who had organized the National Council of Negro Women. At Dr. Bethune's invitation, Height joined the council and worked tirelessly for women's rights to equal employment, pay and education. She was an articulate voice against lynching and for criminal justice reform. She later became the fourth president of the council and served the organization for 40 years.

The second event that she was instrumental in organizing was the 1963 March on Washington. Working alongside Dr. Martin Luther King, the Rev. Ralph Abernathy, Wyatt Tee Walker and other men, she was the prominent woman in the organizing effort. One might note that she was the only woman seated on the stage with the noted civil rights "Big Six."

Dorothy Height accomplished much in her life. She was awarded the John F. Kennedy Memorial Award, the Citizen's Medal from President Ronald Reagan, the NAACP Spingarn Medal, the Presidential Medal of Freedom from President Bill Clinton, and on her 92nd birthday, she was awarded the Congressional Gold Medal by President George Bush, which is the highest and most distinguished civilian award presented by the United States Congress.

Truly, Dorothy Irene Height was a woman of greatness and a warrior for justice. Despite facing both racism and patriarchy, she refused to be discouraged or detoured in her quest for a just society. She refused to allow society to define her identity as a woman of color. Instead, she worked to define what a society based on equality and justice should look like.

As we conclude Black History Month and begin Women's History Month, may the life and work of Dorothy Irene Height inspire us all to be creators of a more perfect union.

GOP seems to be idolizing Trump and that isn't good for the future of America

March 2, 2021

"And the people said, 'Come, make us gods who will go before us.' And they fashioned a calf made of gold and said, 'These are your gods...'" -adaptation of Exodus 32:1-2

The CPAC meeting of the Republican Party in Orlando was both interesting and frightening. It featured several conservative speakers, including the CEO of Goya who introduced Trump as the "legitimate president of the United States."

The rhetoric stated at the meeting of the Conservative Political Action Conference by right and far-right wing Republicans was as expected: the lie that the November presidential election was stolen, Trump is still the president, the insurrection of Jan. 6 was perpetrated by Antifa, etc.

Most alarming were two things: Trump's pronouncement of his enemies list, and CPAC's unveiling of a golden statue of Donald Trump.

We all are aware of Trump's vindictive nature when it comes to people who disagree with him, but his enemies list is over the top.

We know who he listed: Sens. Ben Sasse, Nebraska; Adam Kinzinger of Illinois; Liz Chaney of Wyoming; Mitt Romney of Utah, along with other Republicans in both the Senate and the House of Representatives who voted to impeach him.

As a person who claims a broad and deep commitment to religious ideas, I am most troubled by the creation of the golden Trump statue. The story from the Tanakh, a Jewish sacred text, is pertinent. The golden statue of Trump symbolizes an absolute allegiance to him and his ideas, as if Trump is the ultimate reality for America. It is a call to worship him as if he is a god and that America should go as he leads us, without question and/or critical reflection. The "Trump cult" is poignantly presenting Trump as our deity.

Notice how the "Trump cult" acts as if his fallacious claims are inerrant. He says he won the election, and he is believed, despite evidence to the contrary. He incites a riot at the Capitol and the cult states: "Stop believing what you saw, believe that he is above reproach." The "cult" has bestowed upon Trump god-like characteristics, and that is a serious and real danger to American democracy and the common good.

I am surprised that conservative, evangelical Christians have not objected to the obvious deification of Trump. For a group of people who claim strict adherence to the biblical text, why do they not challenge the assertion that Trump is the truth, and he is above all moral and spiritual reproof?

Not all Republicans are part of the "Trump cult." Many Republicans want to return to talking about policy and ideals. Not all conservative evangelicals support the "Trump cult." Many know the edict from the law: "Hear ye, the Lord thy God is one, and you shall have no other gods before me." The problem is that their silence breeds complicity. We must remember that if we do not stand for the truth, we are bowing down to a lie. We must not bow down. Silence cannot be an option.

America will never be what it once was. We are a multicultural, diverse society. The "Trump cult" yearns for the good 'ol days when people of color stayed in their place, women were to be obedient, pregnant, and in the kitchen, and LGBT folks remained in the closet. Those days are gone — thank goodness — and it is time to recognize that the enemy to democratic values is within our midst and is lead by its "god" Donald Trump. The only question that remains is: Will we stand for this phenomenon or will we stand against it?

It's time to end voter suppression and restore the common good in Missouri and America

March 30, 2021

We are witnessing a move to deny Americans the constitutional right to vote. The state of Georgia has signed into law one of the most aggressive and atrocious voter suppression laws since before the Voting Rights Act of 1965.

Forty-three states, including Missouri, are attempting to suppress our voices at the polls. Many people who realize the horror of voter suppression are calling these moves "Jim Crow 2.0" and rightly so.

Unquestionably, voter suppression is the Republican and white supremacist backlash to the defeat of Donald Trump in 2020. It is also a direct attempt to retaliate against Black and brown voters who showed up in huge numbers to oust the former president. They call their efforts an attempt to provide election integrity. We know that it is election invalidation. In a time when we should be encouraging more Americans to vote, the Republicans are trying to discourage voters, particularly those who are Black, brown and indigenous people.

We who are older have seen this before. The new antics of voter suppression are reminiscent of the old "poll tests" that were pervasively used against Black Americans in the past. Questions like 'how many beans in the Mason jar' or the command to recite the Gettysburg Address backwards were all used to suppress the Black vote. While the new tactics are much more sophisticated in fashion, it nothing but the same old song, only with a new verse. The song is: "Suppress the vote of people of color so that we might stay in control."

As maniacal as voter suppression laws are, their architects have forgotten two major points, which in the end will cause their demise. First, people of color will find a way to overcome the barriers. We had to do it before, and we will do it again. Second, they have forgotten that America is Blacker and browner than it has ever been. The sheer numbers of voters of color will overturn their attempts.

As an added plus, there are too many white people who are disgusted and tired of these shenanigans. They want to create the common good of America, not destroy it. I believe they will join people of color who affirm their right to vote. Those who are for us are not against us, and we can and will stop this madness.

It is important that we vote out of office those who are trying to divide this country. The perpetrators of voter suppression must go.

We must put people in office who care about all Americans, not just white Americans. We have the power to stop the idiocy; after all we voted out the man who would be king. It is time to clean the house of democracy and place into positions of power those who believe in and affirm the common good of America.

Let us fight back against voter suppression, especially in Missouri. Let us make our will known and our voices heard. Tell our state legislature, and those in the U.S. Senate, that we will not return to Jim Crowism, but we demand a better and more united republic.

Anti-Asian hatred is another shade of racism

April 6, 2021

"Hatred is corrosive of a person's wisdom and conscience; the mentality of enmity can poison a nation's spirit, instigate brutal life-and-death struggles, destroy a society's tolerance and humanity, and block a nation's progress to freedom and democracy."- Liu Xiaobo, Nobel Peace Prize laureate, Chinese writer and activist

The recent episodes of anti-Asian hatred within American society have caused us to pause and reevaluate what it means to be "the many and the one".

Anti-Asian persecution is not new in America. One needs to only remember the internment of Japanese Americans during WWII or the largest single day lynching of Asians during the building of the Western railroads. Our history is one filled with stories of how we have oppressed the Asian community.

To some people, the recent events of violence against Asians seems odd. After all, Asians have always been vaulted as the "model minorities" in America. Many Asian communities fully embraced capitalism, and if they were light enough in complexion, they were more readily received. The fact of the matter is that the Euro-centric, Anglo-American, white supremacist mindset always considered them second-class people.

We know that the past presidential administration fanned the flame of anti-Asian hatred. The calling of COVID-19 as "Kung Flu" or "the China Virus" only exacerbated racist narratives and actions.

J.L.A. Garcia wrote a piece years ago called "The Heart of Racism." In it, he suggests that racism, at the core, is a heart issue. Our xenophobia, institutional and systemic racism begins in the heart and soul of human beings. If so, how do we combat anti-Asian, anti-Black, and anti-Latin racism?

If racism is of the heart, it exposes a lack of moral consciousness and spiritual decay. Only our willingness to recognize, confess and correct our heart problem will end the hatred we are experiencing in this culture.

That is why Critical Race Theory is so important for us to fix our heart problem. Critical Race Theory does not aim to call all white people racists. Instead, it attempts to acquaint us with the truth of our historical narrative and provide an avenue for reconciliation.

The more we know our collective history, the better prepared we are to construct a better union.

What I am suggesting takes intentionality. One must do the work of overcoming anti-Asian hatred. It does not fall out of heaven. We cannot wish it away, and gradualism is simply a mask for wishful thinking. We must be intentional in dismantling racism at every place and space.

Let us stop anti-Asian hatred. Let us defeat racism of every kind in this society. The power is in our hands and heart. The question is: Are we willing to be part of the solution and not part of the problem?

Chauvin verdict proves now is the time to change policing efforts

April 21, 2021

Many communities in the United States are breathing a little more easily now that the Derek Chauvin trial is now concluded.

The jury convicted Chauvin of all three counts: second-degree unintentional murder, third-degree murder and second-degree manslaughter. He could face up to 40 years in prison for second-degree murder, up to 25 years for third-degree murder, and up to 10 years for second-degree manslaughter.

The verdict matters. It not only matters in Minneapolis and Brooklyn Center, Minnesota, but it affects communities such as Chicago, New York, Portland and Columbia.

For so long people of color have watched bad law officers act without any sense of accountability to the Constitution, to the profession and to the communities they serve. Finally, a bad cop is being made to account for his killing of George Floyd.

We have all seen the 9:29 minute video of the murder of Floyd. We were first introduced to a video that was 8:46 minutes. When the trial began the prosecution introduced the longer video, which they believed demonstrated totality of wrongdoing by Chauvin. We observed Chauvin putting his knee on Floyd's neck. We heard Floyd say, "I can't breathe." We heard him call for his mother before he finally died.

The importance of the video is without question. The initial response of the Minneapolis Police Department was that George Floyd died of a heart condition. If teenager Darnella Frazier had not recorded the murder of Floyd, we may never have gotten to the truth.

Why should Columbians care about what happens in Minneapolis, Brooklyn Center or Chicago? It is because what happened in those places could happen here. People, particularly people of color, are sick and tired of experiencing police brutality and racial injustice. It can no longer be called "a Black thing." It affects Asians, Latinos and Indigenous folk alike.

If you are a person of color and see a police car in your rearview mirror terror floods your mind. The fundamental question you ask yourself is: Will I survive this encounter? You are aware that you may not. No person of color is immune from the terror because you know that how you will be treated has nothing to do with your age, gender, education, social rank or economic status. It simply is a matter that you have melanin in your skin, which makes you guilty before proven innocent. The terror is real for we who are different shades of black.

All of us have noticed that gun violence in Columbia has risen at an alarming rate. My fear is that some young Black or brown youth, or some police officer will be shot and killed. I do not want to die either. The chaos it will create in Columbia is more than any of us want to experience.

I listened to an interview with Police Chief Geoff Jones, Lt. Mike Hestir and Officer Toni Messina, conducted by KFRU's David Lile. I was encouraged to hear all three talk about how the job of CPD officers is to solve problems, gain more training and engage the community more. These are the right moves for Columbia. But follow through is a must. We cannot merely talk a good game; we must walk it.

Something must change. The deaths of Daunte Wright and Adam Toledo demonstrate that policing in America must change. Policing in Columbia must be community oriented if we are going to prevent tragedy here. We must support good policing and rid ourselves of bad policing. Once a death occurs it is too late to fix it.

Missouri governor shows lack of integrity by failing to fund Medicaid

May 18, 2021

On the Missouri Capitol in Jefferson City are the following Latin words: "Salus populi suprema lex esto." Translated into English, it means, "The welfare of the people shall be the supreme law" or "Let the good of the people be the supreme law."

It is a reminder to all of us that we live in a constitutional representative democracy where the will of the people is the supreme law. Unfortunately, Gov. Mike Parson has forgotten this fact.

When Gov. Parson came into office, he stated repeatedly that he would follow the will of the people. On Aug. 4, the people of Missouri approved the expansion of Medicaid in this state. It would provide much-needed health care for approximately 275,000 Missourians. While Gov. Parson has never been in favor of Medicaid expansion, it seemed he would fulfill his constitutional obligation to follow the will of the people. But, Thursday, Parson stated he will not expand Medicaid.

Parson's refusal to follow the will of the people is troubling indeed. I do not want to call Gov. Parson a liar, but his actions indicate that he does not understand what it means to lead with integrity.

We who were born and reared in Missouri grew up with a motto, "Your word is your bond." We were taught that is a motto to live by. Clearly Gov. Parson has forgotten this motto or has willfully ignored it.

One must ask, "Why has Parson reneged on his word to uphold the will of the people?" Several excuses come to mind, but here are two. Perhaps it is because he wants the support of conservative "Re-Trump-licans" so badly that he is willing to violate his constitutional and moral obligation to obtain it. If that is the problem, then he is unfit for office. Ideological compliance is not good leadership; it is merely political prostitution.

Perhaps he really does believe that Medicaid expansion is a bad idea for Missouri. I can respect his opinion, yet I must remind him that the sovereign state of Missouri is not an aristocracy, but a representative democracy. As such, the will of the people rules over his opinion.

Many Missourians would be helped by the expansion of Medicaid. Missourians know it. That is why Missourians approved it. The quality of life for more than 275,000 Missourians could be improved dramatically. That is why Missouri Faith Voices, Jobs with Justice, medical professionals and others all urged the governor to move forward in expanding Medicaid. Why? Because Medicaid expansion is not just a political issue; it is a moral issue as well. Supporting Medicaid expansion demonstrates what Aristotle calls "arete" or excellence of character. Not expanding Medicaid illustrates a lack of moral integrity.

Is it not interesting that Republicans are so concerned about the "integrity of elections" to the point of trying to institute voter suppression laws but are uninterested in expanding Medicaid to the citizenry, which will improve life? Which action displays authentic integrity?

We all know how this will — or, at least, should — end. The issue of Medicaid expansion will go to the courts. The courts will rule that Parson's decision is unconstitutional. Parson and his cronies will appeal until the courts give a final judgment in favor of expansion. It will cost Missourians millions of dollars in tax money.

All of this could be avoided if the governor would have acted with a sense of compassion and integrity. Spencer Johnson was correct when he wrote, "Integrity is telling myself the truth. And honesty is telling the truth to other people."

It's time for Columbia to stop gun violence

May 25, 2021

The violence we are witnessing in Columbia has taken a particularly personal effect on our family. The death of 24-year-old Junous O. Kelly shocked and horrified us, as we had known him since he was a baby. In fact, we called him our "godson."

I offer our deepest condolences to the Kelly family and all the families who mourn the death of their loved ones because of gun violence.

This article is not to garner sympathy for my family. Rather, the death of Kelly and others in this community ought to be a wake-up call to all Columbians that the acts of senseless violence committed in this city must stop. I have grown weary of eulogizing and burying young Black men.

Enough is enough.

I realize that Columbia is not the only place that Asian, Black and brown young people are experiencing violence. It is a nationwide phenomenon. The question is, "What must we do about it?"

One thing is certain. It is too easy to purchase a firearm in Columbia, the state of Missouri and the United States as a whole. I know that it is our Second Amendment right to bear arms and that Missouri is a "carry" state. I am also aware that guns alone do not kill people; people with guns kill people.

I am not anti-guns. I have owned weapons and been around weapons all my life. Most people I know are responsible gun owners. Yet, the irresponsible ones are killing us, and we must address the issues and stop playing petty politics.

Something is wrong in this society when it is harder to get married than to buy an automatic weapon. No hunter goes hunting with an automatic weapon. Those guns are made to kill people. Why are we not banning assault weapons? It makes no sense.

We must change the narrative of conflict in Columbia to change our behavior. Lately, we have become a people that if we disagree with someone the next step is to kill them.

We do not fistfight anymore. Now we resort to pulling out a weapon to settle the matter. One day, I asked my adult college students how many of them had a weapon in their purse or in their cars. Of a class of 20 adults, all of them said they had a weapon in their car. We are an armed citizenry.

We are destroying ourselves. We must stop the violence. The problem is not a Black problem or a Latino problem — it is a community problem. Only when we act like a community can we rid ourselves of this evil.

How? We need more older men and women to mentor younger people. We must teach our youth that violence is not and cannot be the solution to conflict. We must promote mental health programs and peer counseling to address the frustration many of our fellow citizens experience, which becomes the source of violent action. We need politicians to stop condoning violence and start promoting unity. We need stronger legislation regarding gun purchasing, like background checks, etc., and we need to ban automatic weapons.

While these acts will not eradicate gun violence in America and in Columbia, it is a positive first step. I do not want to see another young person die. Only we can do something about it.

Cry out with me, "Stop the Violence!"

Critical Race Theory tells the honest, inclusive history of America

June 1, 2021

The movement to eradicate critical race theory from American education systems is a terrible mistake.

Oklahoma Gov. Kevin Stitt signed a controversial bill into law Friday that will restrict how race- and gender-based content can be taught in public schools and universities. The target, of course, is CRT, which would also include the 1619 Project,

Black feminism/womanism, LGBT studies and Black critical theology.

The Missouri legislature is in a similar boat, as it wishes to eliminate CRT from public education in the state.

Why? The conservative argument is that CRT divides society instead of uniting us. They say it makes our children "feel bad" and scars their psyches by being exposed to the horrendous acts of violence and oppression people of color in this country have had to endure.

Opponents of CRT suggest that we do not need to remember events such as the Tulsa Massacre, the Trail of Tears or the lynching of Asian Americans in the days of building the railroads. They insist that we simply need to move on and let the past be the past.

As one who has taught critical race theory for 30-plus years, the portrayal that conservatives present is plainly false. CRT is about telling the whole historical truth.

For example, CRT (and particularly the 1619 Project) reminds all Americans that Memorial Day was started by former slaves in Charleston, South Carolina, on May 1, 1865.

A group of 257 African American soldiers who fought as Union soldiers were buried in a mass grave dug by the Confederate Army. For two weeks, African Americans in Charleston organized, dug up the bodies from that mass grave and reinterred them with proper burial rites. They called it Memorial Day, and so do we.

My point is that CRT is not about placing guilt on white America. It is about telling the truth and presenting a more honest and inclusive history of America. CRT addresses the root causes of oppression and asks, "What contemporary strategies are needed to ensure the mistakes of the past are not repeated?"

Frederick Douglass was correct when he said, "Education makes a child unfit for slavery." If we continue to whitewash history in America and in Missouri, our children will continue to be slaves to ignorance and mediocrity.

I believe most Americans and Missourians want to know the truth. They understand that only the truth can set us free from biases and prejudices. If state legislators refuse to allow CRT to be taught in our public K-12 schools, we will suffer dire consequences.

Not only should public schools include a CRT curriculum, but so should Moberly Area Community College, Stephens College, Columbia College and MU.

We must rid ourselves of false narratives and cosmetic lies. While the truth hurts, it also heals. Do not let small-minded people with too much power keep us from knowing the truth. Support the inclusion of critical race theory for the good of our community.

Juneteenth has shaped Black life in America. Let's celebrate it.

June 15, 2021

On Saturday, June 19, African Americans and their allies will celebrate what is called Juneteenth.

Juneteenth is a triumphant event worth remembering. It is the celebration of the day in 1865 when the people of Texas were finally informed — two and a half years after the fact — that all enslaved people in the Confederate states were no longer property of their masters.

Juneteenth, also called Emancipation Day, is the oldest known celebration commemorating the end of chattel slavery in the United States.

Forty-six of the 50 U.S. states and the District of Columbia have recognized Juneteenth as either a state holiday or ceremonial holiday, a day of observance. The four states that do not recognize Juneteenth are Hawaii, North Dakota, South Dakota and Montana. In most parts of Missouri, Juneteenth is celebrated, but in cities like Boonville and Joplin, Emancipation Day is celebrated Aug. 4.

While Juneteenth is a commemorative celebration, thinkers like Harvard historian Jarvis Givens believe that the celebration is also aspirational.

Givens states, "While this holiday is about commemorating the end of slavery and about past suffering, it has also shaped Black life in the contemporary moment — whether that be Jim Crow, aggressive neglect of Black segregated schools, the rise of mass incarceration or the ongoing traumatic experiences that Black people have with violent policing. Black people's ongoing pursuit of equality and justice has to do with challenging the idea that full citizenship in the American context can only be understood as another name for whiteness. The holiday of Juneteenth, like all black civic practices, has been a critique of the fact that whiteness continued to be a metonym for citizenship."

There will be several Juneteenth celebrations in Columbia this weekend. I encourage you to attend scheduled events to increase your knowledge and understanding. I also suggest to you some ways that you can celebrate Juneteenth.

Decorate your workplace with meaningful decor. Hang festive decorations throughout the hallways, office spaces and other open areas in your workspace.

Set aside time at work to debunk common racial stereotypes.

Review company initiatives that celebrate diversity.

Invite a keynote speaker to your workplace.

To all, happy Juneteenth.

Celebrate the Fourth of July by rediscovering democracy

June 29, 2021

"Until that year, day, hour, arrive, with head, and heart, and hand I'll strive, to break the rod, and rend the gyve, the spoiler of his prey deprive — So witness Heaven! And never from my chosen post, Whate'er the peril or the cost, be driven." - from Frederick Douglass's July 4, 1852, speech, "What to the Slave Is the Fourth of July?"

On Sunday, we celebrate the 243rd anniversary of independence. Two hundred and forty-three years ago, this democratic experiment shook off British rule and affirmed our right to life, liberty and the pursuit of happiness. Given our current state of discord and division, how shall we celebrate Independence Day?

Influenced by Frederick Douglass's Fourth of July speech, perhaps the best way to celebrate the Fourth of July is in the following manner.

1. We should commit to overcoming oppression. Douglass stated, "Oppression makes a wise person mad (insane)." Oppression anywhere is oppression everywhere. Voter suppression is a form of oppression, as is racial injustice of every kind and sexism. And homophobia is oppression. The economic disparity in Columbia is a true form of oppression. We celebrate Independence Day rightly if we recommit to overcoming oppression in all its forms.

2. Rediscover what democracy means. To be a democratic society is to believe that the power of

government is grounded in "we the people." Who are we? How do we think about what it means to be a democracy?

3. Sound the alarm for freedom. Freedom can no longer be the privilege of the rich and the powerful. Freedom must be accessible to all Americans. To be free is to have the freedom to create a life of meaning, apart from the systems that crush our hopes and dreams.

4. We must recommit to truth and justice. Truth emerges in rational discourse. Justice is the actualization of fairness. Ask yourself: is the narrative in America one of truth and fairness or is irrationality trying to rule the day and hold us in bondage. For example, what sense does it make to celebrate Juneteenth as a national holiday if we do not understand its significance? The answer is obvious, which is why critical race theory is a must. Truth and fairness must be our battle cry.

Douglass stated in his address, "I say it with a sad sense of the disparity between us. I am not included within the pale of this glorious anniversary! Your high independence only reveals the immeasurable distance between us. The blessings in which you, this day, rejoice, are not enjoyed in common.

"The rich inheritance of justice, liberty, prosperity and independence, bequeathed by your fathers, is shared by you, not by me. The sunlight that brought life and healing to you, has brought stripes and death to me. This Fourth [of] July is yours, not mine. You may rejoice, I must mourn."

This was true in 1852, but it must never be true again. I am part of this America. People of color have tears in the bricks and blood in the mortar of America. We must find a way to be one. Only then will we be able to sing, "O say, does that star spangled banner yet wave o'er the land of the free and the home of the brave."

Could Columbia be facing a policing crisis? If we don't hire more officers, it might

July 6, 2021

It is rumored on the street that the Columbia Police Department is facing a crisis in staffing. The word is that the police department is understaffed, which creates various problems: over-worked officers, low morale, higher possibilities of conflict between patrol officers and the community, etc.

If the rumors are true, then Columbia is in a dangerous situation.

Preliminarily, let me state that I am not anti-police; I am anti-police brutality. Too many people, and particularly people of color, have been the victims of police brutality. Yet, policing is needed. The absence of a professional, well-trained police department easily breeds vigilantism. And that is something none of us want.

I do want, however, a police department that is community oriented. It is impossible to "serve and protect" this community in a responsible manner if you do not know the people you are serving and protecting. Police officers without a community-oriented mindset too easily fall prey to operating by stereotypes and false narratives.

An understaffed police department means that officers will be working longer shifts, which leads to fatigue and heightened irritability. I, for one, do not want an irate exhausted person with a weapon on his/her hip trying to police in this community. If that is not a recipe for disaster, I do not know what is.

Some may ask why don't we just hire more cops? The problem, from my perspective, is that I do not want just any police officer engaging in policing in this community. We need and desire police officers that are well trained and of good moral character. I want to be able to believe that the officer will not succumb to bias and will interact with the citizens of Columbia like a professional. I do not want Barney Fife of Mayberry fame either.

The second reason we have a shortage is that we do not pay qualified police professionals enough money. Every rational person knows that to be a police officer means you put your life on the line every day. No amount of money is enough for that risk. Yet, we can do better. We can do much better.

So, if the rumors of understaffing within the police department are true, we need to fix the problem. I urge the mayor, City Council, city manager and human resources director to proactively engage in a nationwide recruiting program to bring in qualified police officers to join the ranks of the good police officers we currently have. And yes, I said it, there are some good police officers in the Columbia Police Department.

We need officers who reflect Columbia. We need more female officers and officers of color. We need more openly LGBTAA+ officers because we are a community of LGBT folk. We do not need a Derek Chauvin; we need more officers of integrity.

Let us fix the understaffing problem of the police department for the common good of the City of Columbia.

It's common sense that without vaccinations, coronavirus will spread

July 13, 2021

Years ago, while serving as the senior minister to the Grandale Church of the Master in Detroit, I was bemoaning the fact that people in the neighborhood were not acting like they had common sense.

Two of my senior citizens listened to me go on and on about how all people should operate with common sense.

At the end of my tirade one of the ladies said to me, "Well Pastor, you have to realize that 'common sense' ain't all that common." A point well taken.

We are witnessing a time when common sense ain't all that common. The Delta variant of the coronavirus is growing in leaps and bounds. It is particularly growing in the Springfield area.

The latest reports indicate new cases are rising in Kansas City, St. Louis and Columbia. Young adults 20-35 years old seem to be the main targets, but now we are worried about our children who are elementary school age.

One of the ways to combat the variant is to get vaccinated, and yet the resistance to a COVID vaccine is unbelievable. So many people I know still refuse to get a vaccine. For some it is fear; for others it is a political statement. In toto, it is a demonstration that common sense ain't all that common in America.

Isn't it interesting that millions of people in other parts of the world are begging for the vaccine and cannot get it, while in the U.S., the vaccine is readily available, and people will not take it? Amazing.

Common sense states if we do not become vaccinated the variant will spread. That means we will have to go back to mask mandates, quarantines and the lot.

The freedom we all so desperately want will be taken away simply because we refuse to do the sensible thing. We will have to go back to virtual learning, Zoom religious activities and the cancellation of concerts and sporting events. Do we really want this to happen?

The coronavirus is not a political issue. It is a health issue. Whether you are Republican or Democrat, COVID does not care. Anyone can become sick and die.

Regardless of political affiliation we have a moral obligation to do what is best for the society. I understand the hesitancy in the Black community regarding vaccinations.

Our history is one that is filled with examples of how the medical/scientific community has been unfaithful to us. However, this is one time we must trust the science. Too many people of color have already died from this virus. We must be vaccinated.

No one can make anyone do what they do not want to do. But common sense says that if we want to return to some semblance of normalcy, we must be vaccinated.

Don't let conspiracy theories and bad news media/social media prevent you from doing the right thing. I urge you to please get the vaccine if you have not done so already.

If a booster becomes available, get that too. Let us not rob ourselves of health and vitality due to being foolish. We owe it to ourselves to have healthy lives.

Critical race theory revisited after legislative hearing in Missouri

July 20, 2021

"Ye shall know the truth and the truth shall set you free."- Yeshua

According to KOMU/NBC, the Missouri legislature's Joint Committee on Education held a hearing Monday on critical race theory. The Missouri legislative committee's hearing was on how race and racism is taught in schools, but the hearing lacked testimony from any Black Missourians.

"No Black parents, teachers or scholars testified Monday to the Joint Committee on Education during the invite-only hearing on critical race theory," the station reported.

While I find this report amazing, it is not surprising that no Black Missourians were invited to testify before the Joint Committee on Education. The committee only wanted to hear one side of the issue.

It seems to me that for the Joint Committee to make the best decisions/recommendation for the good of all Missourians its members need to hear from people of color, particularly Black people. I realize I am employing common sense, but you will remember in my last column I reminded all of us that "common sense ain't all that common."

Succinctly, critical race theory is divided into two main components. The first is an analysis of race and how populations in America are racialized. Critical race theory maintains that race is not a biological characteristic but a social construct used to stereotype and dehumanize racialized groups.

Second, critical race theory is an analysis of how systems and institutions perpetuate racism in America. Thus, racism is systemic and institutional. The dismantling of racism is not about how Joe and Suzy like or do not like Juan and Malcolm but instead centers on how the systems and institutions continue to support socio-political and economic disparities in the U.S. context.

Given this simplified explanation, critical race theory demands an examination of the history of

America and touches every discipline in academia. This theory affects how we think about history, education, philosophy, religion, sociology, science and medicine.

Most white people who are afraid of critical race theory are for three main reasons.

1. They think that teaching critical race theory will enable people of color to enslave white people like they were enslaved. They think people of color want revenge and that critical race theory justifies such desire. They fact of the matter is that critical race theory is opposed to all forms of oppression and dehumanization. Critical race theory claims that if we know the truth of history, we will stand against all forms of enslavement. The theory affirms the words of Frederick Douglass who said, "Education makes a child unfit for slavery." If Yeshua is correct, only truth can set us free.

2. They think critical race theory will make white children feel bad. Critical race theory will enable our children to throw off the tyranny of racism and xenophobia and see people of color as allies, kindred and kind. Critical race theory will not further divide us but begin to unite us as one. That should make all our children feel better.

3. Critical race theory is Marxist and therefore un-American. Critical race theory analyzes all available theoretical notions: democracy, oligarchy, aristocratic systems and, yes, Marxism. However, it is false that critical race theory is a Marxist ideology. Again, the questions for critical race theory are how we racialize populations, and how do systems and institutions promote oppression or liberation.

I hope the Joint Commission on Education will seek the truth and not allow irrational fear to lead its decisions. There are several well-versed scholars who can articulate critical race theory in a manner that will be understandable. I hope they will invite them to speak. Critical race theory is good for Missouri.

Remembering tradition: Marking Aug. 4 as Emancipation Day

August 3, 2021

The most celebrated holiday of Emancipation in African American life is Juneteenth. It warmed my heart that Juneteenth is now a federal holiday. We should not forget, though, that many African American communities celebrate Aug. 4 as Emancipation Day.

In part the celebration is because for many decades, freedmen in Oklahoma celebrated Aug. 4 as Emancipation Day. This date relates to the ratification of the Reconstruction Treaties signed by the Five Tribes in 1866. It was these treaties that provided for emancipation in Indian Territory. Due to the close relationship of African Americans and Native Americans, African Americans incorporated Emancipation Day into Black culture.

As I child growing up in Joplin, the fourth of August Emancipation Celebration was the highlight of Black life. African Americans from near and far came to Joplin for the August celebration.

Black educators from the community taught why a celebration of emancipation was important to remember. Black preachers spoke with power and authority about how the fight for freedom should not be taken lightly and how none are free until all are free. It is interesting to me that they were engaging in critical race theory before the term became popular. The white schools ignored the narrative of struggle, but the Black church did not.

Ewert Park was the gathering place for picnics, food vendors and fellowship. The Ewert swimming pool would be filled with Black bodies, and at night the Ewert Park Community Center overflowed with R&B music, and Black folks doing the "Philly-Dog." We danced until the floor would sweat. We celebrated and remembered.

I do not know if Joplin has continued the fourth of August festivities. Some traditions of meaning have been lost. The older "pillars" have died and many of the younger generation are not interested.

I am encouraged that there is an emerging generation of people who realize that the lessons of the past are important for the formation of the future. Emancipation Day must be remembered and celebrated.

So on Wednesday, I will read some writings from Frederick Douglass, Sojourner Truth, Zora Neale Hurston and Langston Hughes. I will sing some long-meter hymns and end it with the line from "Oh Freedom:" "and before I be a slave, I'll be buried in my grave, and go home to my Lord, and be free."

I will tell the story of how my mother was born in Oklahoma before it became a state, and how my father was a proud member of the 9th Calvary in World War II during a time of segregation and Jim Crow laws. I will remember that the fight continues, and the story must be told. I will celebrate Aug. 4.

How will you celebrate?

Unitarian Universalist Church takes big steps in welcoming Black minister

August 10, 2021

From April 1 to Aug. 1, I had the privilege and honor of serving as sabbatical interim minister for the Unitarian Universalist Church of Columbia where the Rev. Molly Housch Gordon is the senior minister.

It was a wonderful and unique experience in so many ways. Although I have served various churches for over 40 years, I have never had the opportunity to serve a church like this one.

I am African American; they are 99% white. I am theist, though many of the members are non-theistic. I am Christian (in the non-European, Anglo-American broad sense of the term); most of the members are not. I was molded and shaped in the tradition of the Black church; they were not. It sounds like a recipe for disaster, doesn't it? Yet, it was a successful and meaningful experience for me and the congregation. Why?

First, it was wonderful and unique because they had the courage to accept Black leadership. While many churches of every kind talk the talk of diversity and inclusion, only one of them, Bethel Baptist Church, have hired a Black person to lead the congregation even on an interim basis. All the other churches that have had vacant positions have thought "white first" and then filled the position. There are many gifted African American clergy who would love an opportunity to serve a predominately white congregation. Far too many Black clergy are overlooked because of color, pure and simple.

Second, they did not allow our differences to interfere with what we hold in common. For both of us social justice is paramount to doctrinal confessions. Both of us believe in the ultimate worth of the human person, regardless of race, gender, sexual orientation, class. etc. We agreed to be who we are. I am a very enthusiastic preacher. Never did they rebel because of it. We learned to affirm each other's style of worship. I believe in ontological evil (after all, I am a philosopher shaped in the Black experience), most in this congregation do not. We learned to affirm each other's style of worship with intellectual integrity and historical background.

Third, we took the risk of loving each other. We decided to commit ourselves to building the beloved community. Loving one another in this society is a risk. "Can I trust you?" is the fundamental question. We trusted one another even when it was somewhat difficult. How many times have we looked for a place where one can trust the other?

The Unitarian Universalist Church of Columbia is not a perfect church, but it is a healthy church. There are so many toxic churches that claim "we love everybody" but are color struck and money hungry. Toxic churches are about status and class, healthy churches are committed to "koinonia," community. Healthy churches extend radical welcome and truth in love. Sometimes they fail, but they try.

I encourage you to visit the Unitarian Universalist Church of Columbia. They have a wonderfully gifted pastor, and they are about the work of building a beloved community. It will be worth your time.

Look for places to show and develop gratitude in life

August 24, 2021

"The most powerful weapon against your daily battles is finding the courage to be grateful anyway."- Unknown

The other day, I engaged in a conversation with an acquaintance about life. In this 10- to 15-minute exchange, my acquaintance did nothing but complain. He complained about the government — national, state and local; he complained about mask mandates and COVID-19 and accompanying variants; he complained about how rude people are; how there was nothing to do in Columbia; how irrelevant churches have become; how young people do not respect adults, and on and on. After walking away from this gentleman, I thought to myself: What ever happened to gratitude?

Life is full of struggle and disappointment. Regardless of your wealth, political power and education, all of us live life through our pain and proclivities. All of us have things that challenge us in ways that sometimes seem unbearable. If you are looking for a perfect life with no hurdles to leap over, you are delusional. Somehow, we must reclaim an attitude of gratitude if we are to live what Aristotle called "the good life."

Gratitude is not an automatic response to life. It must be developed within us. It is easy to complain, and indeed there is much about which we can complain: job or no job, the environment, the "isms" in American society, people we work with, school, etc. The task, however, is to find a way to be grateful despite the vicissitudes of life.

As a child, I was taught that one should count their blessings one by one. In counting what we have and not focusing on what we do not have, gratitude begins to spring forward. OK, so you do not have that new Mercedes you always wanted, but you have an automobile that works. You do not occupy your dream house, but you have a place to lay down your head. You may not have to eat what you want, but you have something to eat. You may not be in the best of health, but you are alive.

I think the ancient philosopher was correct when he stated: "It is better to exist than not to exist, and it is better to live at a higher level than a lesser." With so many people in the world and this country who have so little, to have what we have should motivate us to be grateful.

Most people do not get their first choices in life. Most of us do not marry our first choice, live in our first choice of homes, work at our first choice of jobs, etc. However, sometimes not having our first choice means we have our better choice in life. For that we must become thankful.

For what are you grateful? Try counting your blessings one by one and see an attitude of gratitude emerge within you. Meister Eckhart wrote: "If the only prayer you said in your whole life was, 'Thank you,' that would suffice."

I urge all of us to learn again how to say, "Thank you!"

Colorism claim in a world of whiteness raises big questions

Aug 31, 2021

If you're black, stay back;

If you're brown, stick around;

If you're yellow, you're mellow;

If you're white, you're all right."

- Children's rhyme

About a week ago, an African American man told me he believed he was discriminated against in a hiring process here in Columbia. The interesting thing to me in his claim was that he did not believe he did not get the job because he was a Black man per se, but because he was a dark-skinned Black man. He was, according to him, a victim of colorism.

In Oprah Winfrey's interview with Meghan Markle and Prince Harry, Harry conveyed a family member's concerns about the color of their then unborn son, Archie. Meghan's comment and the conversation with a Black Columbian reminded me of a prevailing form of discrimination known as "colorism."

What is colorism? Colorism is the practice of favoring lighter skin over darker skin. The preference for lighter skin can be seen as a tool of discrimination against members of racialized groups by the dominate white culture and among members within communities of color.

While many people say they are colorblind, it's hard to deny many people not only see color, but also use it to judge or determine someone's character. Far too often, dark-skinned people as seen to be prone to violence, lazy and dumb, while lighter-skinned people of color are seen as beautiful, of worth and smart.

The prejudice of colorism is not only experienced by Black Americans. Colorism has had a devastating and powerful effect on the Latin and Asian communities as well. I asked one of my dark-skinned Asian students if she believed she was treated differently and worse than her fellow lighter-skinned Asians, and her answer was an unequivocal "Yes."

Colorism has existed for a very long time. In thinking about the U.S. context, the slave owners used colorism to divide the slave community against itself. Light-skinned Blacks were given preferential treatment by being assigned to being house slaves, while dark-skinned Blacks were sent to fields.

During Reconstruction, the practice of colorism continued to further divide the Black community by shade and hue. Blue-Vein societies arose in various parts of the country, affecting Black sororities, fraternities, churches and businesses. The Brown Paper Bag test was frequently employed to determine not only beauty, but status.

The question is whether colorism is still a formidable phenomenon in American society and in Columbia. Do we still, consciously or unconsciously, make judgments about people of color based on the shade of their skin? Do light-skinned Blacks receive preferential treatment regarding employment and economic opportunity over dark-skinned people in Columbia? Are dark-skinned people more likely to be imprisoned and jailed over their lighter-skinned counterparts? Do white and Black churches practice colorism when it comes to diversity and inclusion of potential members?

These are questions I am very interested in receiving feedback about. If you have a comment or experience you would like to share concerning colorism, I would appreciate hearing from you.

On anniversary of 9/11, let us strive for unity

September 7, 2021

On Saturday, we will gather to remember the horror of 9/11. It is a day of infamy as we recollect the deadliest attack on U.S. soil by a foreign group in American history. That event 20 years ago changed all of our lives forever.

We were aware of terrorism. American history is a history of terrorism: the Tulsa Massacre, Rosewood, genocidal attacks against Indigenous nations, the lynching and killing of Asian Americans, just to name a few.

But never have we as a country been the target of terrorism from an outside force like what happened on 9/11. Some 2,750 people were killed in New York, 184 at the Pentagon and 40 in Pennsylvania, where one of the hijacked planes crashed after the passengers attempted to retake the plane.

The attack has personally affected me as two of my Princeton classmates were killed in the attack on the twin towers. While the pain of their loss has become manageable, still, there is a hole in my heart that I know will never heal.

Until that day, we as a country believed we were immune from a terrorist attack of this sort. Now, we realize that we are not immune and that the kinds of violence that are perpetrated in other parts of the world can also happen here.

We are a divided nation. The removal of Trump from office did not solve the problem of national division. Perhaps remembering 9/11 will reacquaint us with what it means to be one nation.

On 9/11 and subsequent days after the attack, I saw people who normally would not speak to one another work together to rescue victims in the twin towers. We watched Americans give their lives to stop a hijacked plane. We watched Americans embrace and encourage Americans. If we did it once, we can be united again. Hopefully, it will not take a tragedy to get us to that point.

To be a strong nation, we cannot allow our differences to tear us apart. There are still enemies of America that yearn for our demise. Only united can we defeat these enemies. Only our unity can maintain this great democratic experiment.

To mask or not mask, critical race theory or no critical race theory, becomes irrelevant if we do not survive as a nation. Sept. 11 reminds us that our continuation as a country is not automatic. We must diligently find a way to be one nation, one society, one people.

As you remember 9/11, think about ways you can foster unity in your own world. Seek ways to bring us together as a country. We must never allow the tie that binds us to be eradicated because of our lack of unity. It is our moral obligation to be united. We owe it to our children.

With Treece's impending departure, where will Columbia look for new leadership?

September 21, 2021

Last Friday, Mayor Brian Treece announced he will not seek reelection next April. To many of us, this was shocking news.

Personally, I like Mayor Treece. I find him to be compassionate, very intelligent, a powerful public speaker and a man who truly cares about Columbia. I do not and did not agree with everything he said and did, but I am not one that needs my colleagues and friends to agree with me about everything. I think he was a good mayor, and I shall miss his leadership.

But now the question on the table is: Who shall be our next mayor? The next mayor of Columbia has some huge issues to tackle. Whoever wins the position will realize that the burden of leading this "blue dot in a red state" is no easy task.

Here are just a few challenges that will need serious attention and wise decision-making:

• The pandemic is not over, and it is wreaking havoc on our community. Do we mask or not mask? Will there be a vaccine available for our children 5-11 years of age, and will parents in the community vaccinate their children? If we have a serious spike of the delta COVID-19 variant, will we be forced to endure another shutdown, which hurts the business community, churches, schools, etc.?

• How should we invest our money? Do we invest more in people or policy? Everyone talks about the shelterless population, which is growing in Columbia. But a huge segment of this city that is ignored is the "working poor" among us. The median income of Columbia is approximately $50,000 per year. Yet most of the people in my section of the First Ward don't make $20,000 yearly. There is a huge economic gap in Columbia that needs to be addressed. Economic disparity breeds crime.

• What will policing look like in Columbia for the next five years? Will policing be more community oriented? Will mental health professionals be included in policing? Will we be able to staff the police department with effective and compassionate officers who are not overworked and underpaid? What policing will look like in the next five years or more will affect all of us in a significant way.

• We need more Black businesses and programs that enhance the Black community in Columbia. It is embarrassing how few Black businesses and projects we have in this town. The few Black businesses we have need creative and meaningful support — money through grants, accounting partnerships, opportunities to learn from other successful entrepreneurs, etc. Food and hair care cannot be the totality of Black expansion in Columbia. The new administration will be called into question in regard to Black opportunities in Columbia.

There are many talented people in Columbia who can build on what Mayor Treece has done and take us to the next level. I hope some of the candidates for the next mayorship will be women and people of color.

Indeed, there is much to be done in Columbia, but I have always stated that whatever challenges this city faces, we have the expertise and resources to solve our problems. So come on Columbia's best and brightest — step forward and show us what you're working with.

Capital punishment should not be a justified act

October 5, 2021

At 6 p.m. Tuesday, the state of Missouri executed Ernest Lee Johnson.

Johnson was convicted of robbery and killing three people at a Casey's store in Columbia in February 1994. Now 61 years old, Mr. Johnson has served 27 years in the penitentiary.

Mr. Johnson has a verified cognitive disorder and, at the time, a significant addiction to crack cocaine.

I have written about this tragedy in a previous column: How Johnson came before the congregation at Second Baptist Church and begged us to help him, and in our naivete, we prayed for him but then let him go on his way.

If we were wise we would have taken him to a rehab center immediately after church. But we did not, and thus he murdered three people. I count it as one of the greatest mistakes I have made in 44 years of ministry.

Thousands of people have asked the governor to stop the execution. He did not.

Given the age, race and mental challenges of Mr. Johnson, is there no better alternative to execution? In the mind of Parson, the answer is no.

Let me be clear. The crimes Ernest committed deserve punishment, but too much of what passes for justice in Missouri is simply shadowed racism and good ole boy blood thirst.

We easily could allow Johnson to spend the rest of his life in prison. He would be permanently removed from society. Is that not enough?

Some people try to make the argument that we should execute people who commit murder on the justification of lex talionis, the law of retaliation: An eye for an eye, a tooth for a tooth.

The problem is that if a person has killed more than one person, and the law of retaliation is rooted in death for a death, the state would have to be able to kill Mr. Johnson three times for three murders.

To my knowledge, we cannot kill a person more than once. So, in the end what poses as justice ends up being sheer barbarism.

Of the 197 countries in the United Nations, 107 countries have abolished capital punishment for all crimes. Missouri leads the country in executions per capita. Something is seriously wrong when capital punishment is a justified act.

Once again, the execution of Ernest Johnson and others in Missouri is barbarism simple and plain.

Today, we mourn for Ernest Lee Johnson. We mourn for the families of those victimized by Mr. Johnson in 1994. We are saddened by Gov. Parson's lack of wisdom and compassion, and we mourn for our state, which seeks blood at every opportunity. History will hold us in shame for not ridding ourselves of the moral disgrace of capital punishment.

Gruden account shows beat of prejudice goes on in NFL

October 12, 2021

Jon Gruden has resigned as head coach of the Las Vegas Raiders NFL team. Gruden's resignation comes after reports in The Wall Street Journal and The New York Times that detail emails in which he repeatedly used racist and homophobic language.

For football fans, Gruden was a coach that many people looked up to for leadership and development. He is also a homophobe, misogynist and racist — though he said he is not racist.

He believed that because he worked with women, people of color and gay people that he was immune from appropriate behavior. Wrong.

In none of the reports about Gruden did he admit his behavior was wrong. He only stated that he did not want to be a distraction to the Raiders team and organization and that he was sorry if he hurt anyone. Really?

I am not surprised that a football coach acted this way. Football — and frankly sports in general — can be a breeding place for this kind of behavior. Not all football coaches, players, etc. are like Gruden. But the sad fact is that there are far too many who are just like Gruden, or worse.

When a football coach says that Frank "hits like a girl" or needs to "stop acting like a sissy" you get the point very quickly. What disappoints me is that many coaches, owners and players knew how Gruden was and did nothing about it until now. Hmm.

A white student once told me that racism in America ended with the Emancipation Proclamation. The problem, he stated, was that Black people — and I assume all people of color, and the LGBTQ+ community — were just too sensitive. He asserted, "Blacks just need to be good Americans and stop complaining." I thought to myself, I would love to stop complaining if you would not give me so much to complain about.

Stories like the Gruden account make me realize that we may have come a long way, but we have such a long, long way to go.

Yes, there are more openly gay players in the NFL, but not that many. Yes, people of color are playing a more prominent role in the NFL as coaches and players. But what about head office positions and owners? It is good to see some women as referees, judges and linespersons, but they are few and far apart. We have a long way to go.

So, until we get there ... the beat goes on.

A tribute to Colin Powell

October 19, 2021

On Monday, America lost a great leader and patriot, in the true sense of the word. His name was Colin Powell.

As The Associated Press writers Corey Williams and Aaron Morrison stated, "Colin Powell's credentials were impeccable: He was chairman of the Joint Chiefs and Secretary of State." He was also a great Black man.

Some people thought that Colin Powell should have used his voice and position in this society more loudly to promote the African American agenda for racial justice. But that was not his style.

Colin Powell was a person of action. He created the Colin Powell Center to develop student leadership and campus community engagement. The program was eventually renamed the Colin Powell School for Civic and Global Leadership.

In the wake of George Floyd's slaying and the Black Lives Matter protests, the school launched a racial justice fellows program as a joint initiative with City College New York's Black studies program. Powell wanted to be an instrument for developing African American leaders of the future.

In my eyes, Colin Powell was a man of integrity. He admitted that he made a mistake before the United Nations when he reported that Saddam Hussein had "weapons of mass destruction." He later said, "it was the one blot" on his professional record.

When the Republican Party moved away from being the party of Lincoln to becoming the party of Trump, Powell renounced his affiliation with Republicans and condemned Donald Trump as a disgrace. Such actions took courage and integrity, something I wish more Republicans would demonstrate.

Many of the things Colin Powell affirmed I do not agree with. The most central idea is that the best way to change the system is to participate in it and change it from the inside. He was committed to this thought.

My critique is simply that if the system is corrupt to the point where it refuses to be moved by moral persuasion, how can any system be profoundly changed? A new system is needed and not the perpetuation of the corrupt one. One does not need to agree on every point to be colleagues for change. My respect for Colin Powell is without reservation.

I extend my deepest and sincere condolences to the Powell family. He will truly be missed, and I hope he will be remembered and celebrated.

Fayette church is testament to perseverance

October 26, 2021

On Sunday, I had the honor and privilege of speaking for one of mid-Missouri's oldest historically Black churches: St. Paul United Methodist Church in Fayette.

Organized in 1856, St. Paul continues as a testimony to perseverance, service and faith. St. Paul Church began before the Emancipation Proclamation in the slave state of Missouri and within a slave holding county —Howard County. In defiance to slavery, segregation, oppressive Jim Crow laws, lynching and other forms of racism, St. Paul Church refused to give up the fight for justice.

Despite the attempts to dehumanize Black people in Fayette and Howard County, St. Paul affirmed that "we are somebody."

People who are familiar with Black theology understand how important a church like St. Paul is to a community like Fayette. Black theology takes seriously the "lived experiences" of people who experience oppression.

It is why the church is the central institution in the Black community. When Black people could not count on white institutions to be allies in liberation, they could trust the Black church to a sanctuary amid the storms of life. St. Paul is no exception.

On the morning of July 22, 1899, a white mob abducted a Black man, Frank Embree, from officers transporting him to stand trial in Fayette and lynched him in front of a crowd of over 1,000 onlookers.

The pain of that event was devastating to Black residents in Fayette. St. Paul ministered to the Black community. They reminded Black people that "trouble will not last always," as the Rev. Timothy Wright's song lyrics say.

The church boldly stated that the universe bends toward justice and one day, if we keep fighting the perpetrators of such cruelty will be vanquished. St. Paul retained hope in the midst of hopelessness.

People unfamiliar with historic Black churches and Black theology often ask if white people are welcome in Black churches. Churches like St. Paul have always had white members. Unlike the traditional white church, the motto of the Black church is "whosoever will, let them come." St. Paul continues that sentiment.

There are white members of St. Paul, their pastor, the Rev. Susan McCollegan, who is marvelously gifted, is a white woman. They are attempting to be a real church that's non-racist, non-sexist and non-homophobic.

St. Paul UMC is not a perfect church, but its members have a perfect vision shaped by the history and lived experiences of the Black community, their understanding of a God that stands on the side of the poor and oppressed, and their commitment to justice.

Indeed, I was honored to be their 165th Anniversary speaker. I encourage you to visit them sometime. They will make you feel welcome.

Remembering the Trail of Tears

November 2, 2021

In 1830, Congress passed the Indian Removal Act, which required the various American Indian tribes in today's southeastern United States to give up their lands in exchange for federal territory located west of the Mississippi River. Sixty thousand Indigenous people were forced to migrate.

The impact of the resulting Trail of Tears was devastating.

On Nov. 1, 1831, the Choctaw Nation was forced to move from Mississippi to what is now known as Oklahoma. One of every three people died in that move. Most Indigenous communities fiercely resisted this policy, but as the 1830s wore on, most of the major tribes — the Choctaws, Muskogee Creeks, Seminoles and Chickasaws — agreed to be relocated to Indian Territory.

The Cherokee were forced to move because a small faction of the tribe signed the Treaty of New Echota in late 1835, a treaty that the U.S. Senate ratified in May 1836. This action — the treaty signing and its subsequent Senate approval — tore the Cherokee into two implacable factions: a minority who were allied with the "treaty party," and the majority that bitterly opposed the treaty signing.

In May 1838, the Cherokee removal process began. U.S. Army troops, along with various state militia, moved into the tribe's homelands and forcibly evicted more than 16,000 Cherokee people from their homelands in Tennessee, Alabama, North Carolina and Georgia. "They were first sent to so-called 'round up camps,' and soon afterward to one of three emigration camps," according to the Trail of Tears National Historic Trail.

Once there, the U.S. Army gave orders to move the Cherokee west. In June 1838, three detachments left southeastern Tennessee and were sent to Indian Territory by water. Difficulties with those moves, however, led to negotiations between Principal Chief John Ross and U.S. Army General Winfield Scott.

Later that summer, Scott issued an order stating that Ross would oversee all future detachment movements. Ross, honoring that pledge, orchestrated the migration of 14 detachments, most of which traveled over existing roads, between August and December 1838.

More than a thousand Cherokee — particularly the old, young and infirm — died during their trip west. Hundreds more deserted from the detachments, and an unknown number, perhaps several thousand, perished from the consequences of the forced migration. One in three Choctaw died as well. The number of other members of the other tribes who died are not recorded but one can imagine that the numbers are like those of the Cherokee and Choctaw.

"The tragic relocation was completed by the end of March 1839, and resettlement of tribal members in Oklahoma began soon afterward," according the Trail of Tears website. The Cherokee, and the other Indigenous tribes, in the years that followed struggled to reassert themselves in the new, unfamiliar land. Yet, they are proud, independent tribes, and their members recognize that despite the adversity they have endured, they are resilient and invest in their future.

Why should we remember the Trail of Tears? Because it reminds us of how cruel we can be as well as how resilient we can be. Understanding our American history does not separate us but informs us and equips us for the future. We become more aware of how racial injustice is not just a "Black-White thing," it is the historical reality of all people of color who reside in America.

Serious critical race theory addresses these vital facts. To not support a rigorous critical race theory is to act foolishly and dangerously. To refuse to acknowledge the wrongs of the past will cause us to repeat them in the present and the future.

Observations on Mid-Missouri's political theater of the absurd

November 9, 2021

"Theater of the absurd: A form of drama that emphasizes the absurdity of human existence by employing disjointed, repetitious and meaningless dialogue, purposeless and confusing situations, and plots that lack realistic or logical development"- American Heritage Dictionary of the English Language, Fifth Edition.

At the Columbia School Board meeting Monday night, Rep. Chuck Basye said that he felt that critical race theory, often referred to as CRT, was being taught in Columbia Public Schools. Critical race theory asserts that racism is embedded in American institutions and acknowledges the impact of slavery and segregation in society.

The lawmaker said that he has proof critical race theory is being taught.

"I believe CRT has been taught in CPS schools. The evidence is in grade schools, middle schools and high schools," Basye said. "We want accurate history, good and bad, taught in our schools. I would just like to have a discussion in the public discussion where they would let people speak on the topic of what they claim is not happening and that's the teaching of critical race theory and the 1619 Project and other things," Basye said.

"They're doing it, and they want to deny it. That's fine, but I'm gonna call him (CPS Superintendent Brian Yearwood) out on it, and I have concrete facts that they are, in fact, teaching this hatred in our schools."

Ladies and gentlemen, what we are witnessing is political theater of the absurd produced and enacted by Rep. Basye.

There are so many points of disinformation in Basye's disjointed rhetoric that one does not need to be a logician to apprehend it without much trouble. However, since Basye is a Missouri state representative, his office and position demand that we analyze what he is saying.

1. What is critical race theory, or CRT, and the 1619 Project?

CRT is simply the exploration of the effects of racism on American history and society. Basically, it suggests that every social institution in this society has been infected by racism.

It therefore claims that understanding such things as institutional, systemic and individual racism will better prepare us to dismantle racism.

Is Mr. Basye suggesting that we ought not know our history? Or is he suggesting the absurd notion that racism has not played a devastating role in American culture? Or, perhaps, Mr. Basye wants to deny the existence of racism and thinks if we do not discuss it, it will go away. Such thinking is unrealistic.

2. Why do Basye, and people like him, think that teaching CRT is promoting hatred in schools?

Clearly, CRT and the 1619 Project present the hatred that has been propagated against people of color in the United States. This theory exposes how Indigenous peoples of America have been displaced, brutalized and robbed of land and nationhood. Critical race theory reveals that Africans were not brought to this country as "hired workers" but instead enslaved. It brings to bear the mistreatment of Asians and Latins throughout our history as a nation and that colorism is still a major problem in American life.

Critical race theory tells the truth about our history and what causes us to be the way we are in the present. What Basye and others have missed is that it also tells a narrative of courageous Anglo (white) people and white institutions that stood against racial injustice of this sort throughout our history. Critical race theory clearly states that we cannot judge people by color, but we must judge by character. Is the possibility of being judged by character, or the lack of it, what frightens Mr. Basye?

Maybe we could make better sense of what Basye's issue is with critical race theory if he would simply define in a coherent and logical manner what he thinks it is? Assertions like "it (CRT) teaches hatred" or "it deprives our children of a good education" is disjointed and meaningless monologue. It is dramatic but absurd.

Many of us are tired of the political theater of the absurd. Most parents and grandparents want our children to be immersed in the truth, not whitewash. It is time to stand up against proponents of falsehood like Rep. Basye because we all know that only the truth can unite us as a nation and set us free from biases and prejudices.

Reinstating a sense of community could help Columbia solve issues of violence

November 30, 2021

In response to my last column on violence in Columbia, I received the following comment that I believe is worthy of reflection. I have omitted the name of the person to maintain their confidentiality.

I read your op-ed, 'Gun violence in Columbia demands collaborative fix' in today's Missourian. I wonder if there aren't important additional considerations.

One of my children is (a member) of the Special Victims Unit at CPD, and he notes a disturbing trend. In his investigations, he runs across young children, sometimes as young as 3-4, who are already cursing out others, calling them M-Fs, etc., with no correction (or perhaps even encouraging or modeling) from parents and other adults. He is very pessimistic that these children, already learning to be thugs, will be salvageable in their teenage years. How can the community come together and fix this parenting problem? It needs to start very early.

It is true that "thug life" is being modeled by far too many youths and adults in Columbia and throughout our nation. The same phenomenon the commentator mentions above can be found in all parts of our society. It is a severe problem that threatens to destroy the fabric of American civil society.

However, one must look at the root causes of this occurrence. There are many factors that contribute to why a child or adult believes that being a "thug" is better than being a good citizen.

Clearly, "thug life" is glamorized in movies, videos, etc. But this fact is not new. Those my age grew up with gangster movies and actors playing "tough guy" roles, like with James Cagney. So, the entertainment industry cannot be the sole cause.

It is not purely racial either. While Black and brown people kill Black and brown people, white people kill white people, as well.

Nor can we simply blame the cause on parenting. Let us face it, most of the antisocial behavior we learn, we did not learn at home.

The root of the matter is a loss of hope. Too many people are living hopeless existences. The American dream for many in our country is a nightmare.

The population of the working poor is growing. Educational systems are being railroaded in teaching falsehoods or white-washings that make our children doubt the value of education.

Society has promoted wealth as the only factor that determines worth, so no wonder Pookie and Juan think the only way to express the frustration of living in a hopeless situation is to call everyone names. We have not listened to the underclass, and we are failing to listen to them now.

We know that the economic disparity in Columbia is formidable. And while we want to ignore it, racism, colorism, sexism and classism challenge our hope for a life where we can truly pursue liberty and happiness.

What can overcome hopelessness? I believe a recommitment to community in real sense is the answer. We must reinstitute fictive kinships. Fictive kinship is an earnest effort to act in a manner that purports the idea that all children are our children. It is a continuation of the belief that it takes a village to rear a child.

Yes, we need more role models of color. Yes, we need to dismantle racism and economic disparity. But the solution lies in our willingness to be vulnerable and responsible to one another.

Hopelessness is the problem. Hopelessness is a heart problem. Only an open-hearted effort on the part of Columbia's and America's citizenry can heal a heart broken by despair. The question really is: How much do we care?

Reclaiming the joy of the season

December 7, 2021

This is the time of the year when we should be filled with joy. Unfortunately, lots of people are not.

The new omicron variant sets us on edge. "Will our vaccines protect us against this new variant?" we wonder, hopefully. The recent violence in Michigan and in Columbia makes us wonder, "What is wrong with us?" Everyone I know is struggling financially. And when you have little money, the grocery and gas prices make us both pray and curse.

How do we reclaim the joy of the season? My suggestions are simple, but they work.

1. This year let us focus on relationships with family and friends instead of presents and gifts. I love gifts like everyone else, but it is the blessing of the giver that means more than the gift. A hug, a kiss, a belly laugh, all remind us that the season is about love, not the lust for things.

2. Speak and smile at a stranger. How many times have we walked into a store and all who we meet are frowning? We need to take the initiative and smile and say, "Good morning." I believe a smile can conquer more than rhetoric. I know smiling is contagious. Try it, you might love the results.

3. Perform a random act of kindness. Buy someone a cup of coffee next time you are in one of Columbia's great coffeehouses. Pay ahead for someone in the store. Be a secret "Santa Claus" for someone. Volunteer to feed the hungry at Loaves and Fishes. Random acts of kindness restore civility in our society.

4. Turn off the technology and have a real conversation with someone. We are so absorbed by our cell phones, computers, etc. that we have forgotten how to talk to one another. Let us talk. We may find out we have more in common than we think.

I am sure you have your own list.

The point is that we need to restore the joy of this season. Like you, I am tired of the division and hatred that infects quadrants of our society. I miss seeing each other as members of the same community instead of enemies. Restoring a sense of joy can help us in more ways than we can imagine.

Be joyous and be blessed.

Preparing for a new year emotionally, spiritually, politically, financially

December 21, 2021

As we come to the close of 2021, the question each of us faces is whether we are ready to enter a new year.

We can simply function as if engaging 2022 will be like all the other years of the past, or we can prepare ourselves emotionally, intellectually, socio-politically and spiritually for what may in fact be the "fundamentally new."

I do not believe 2022 will be the same as it has always been. The signs are that radical changes are on the horizon.

We have a new COVID-19 variant to deal with. And while many act as if it is no big deal, people are getting sick and dying every day.

Everyone I know is struggling financially. The ranks of the working poor are growing day by day. Food challenges are all around us.

And quite frankly, there is a constant cloud of "the blues" that hangs over the heads of our society.

Will violence increase in our cities and schools? Will health and physical well-being be a reality in our lives? All these things and more make us think about how we shall prepare for 2022.

A tradition in my family is that the 2nd of January is "throwaway day." We inventory and then throw out those things that we do not need.

We all need to throw away some old things that thwart our progress. We need to throw away old biases and prejudices that have hampered our growth.

Old attitudes of division and superiority need to go to the trash pile. Our self-centeredness and anger must go if we are to experience the new possibilities 2022 will present.

While I am not trying to meddle, I posit that all of us have some habits that need to go. I leave your list with you.

There are some things we also need to acquire. As a society we need a fresh spirit of unity and concern for the common good. I believe in the power of spiritual renewal.

I am tired of religious communities that focus on the worst in us instead of uplifting what is good and of excellence in the human experience.

I suggest adding a spiritual component that reaffirms our humanity and our connectedness. We need a faith that reminds us that "I am because we are."

My father used to proclaim on a regular basis that "preparation is the first step toward success."

When I was young, I thought that was a silly motto to live by. But now that I am older, I am a witness that some of the worst mistakes of my life happened because I was unprepared to claim the moment.

Like you, I want my latter days to be better than my former days.

If we prepare our minds, hearts, bodies and souls for the wonderful things that await us in the new year, we shall be part of something fantastic, something fundamentally new.

I wish you all a Merry Christmas, a wonderful holiday season and a Happy New Year.

2022

2022 is a time for vigilance

January 4, 2022

Vigilant

1. keeping careful watch for possible danger or difficulties.

In my last column I spoke about how 2022 will demand a need to be physically, emotionally, politically and spiritually prepared. I believe that this year will present us with tremendous opportunities to reignite a sense of the common good, progress and change. It will also confront us with danger and difficulties. Given the possibility of both, it is time for us to be vigilant.

Several areas demand a vigilant posture. I will simply name a few.

1. The COVID phenomenon is not over. The omicron variant is real. Our hospitals are overrun with people who are sick and who are dying.

Yet many of our fellow citizens refuse to be tested and vaccinated. The science is clear: we need to be vaccinated, and we need to be vigilant in masking ourselves and our children.

To not do the things the medical/scientific community has urged us to do is playing Russian roulette with our public health.

2. Our country is deeply divided.

In every gathering place where people of color meet, someone will utter the fear that we are on the verge of civil war. We remember Jan. 6, 2021. There are those who try to change the facts with political cosmetics, but the truth of the matter is that our democracy is being threatened. The fundamental question is: Do we want to be one nation, or are we so arrested by cultural tribalism that unity is impossible?

America is no longer white. It is Black, Asian, Latin and indigenous. If we are not vigilant in creating arenas of oneness, we shall surely self-destruct.

3. The violence in Columbia and other parts of the country needs serious addressing. Poverty, lack of education, hopelessness and self-hatred breed violence. Civility is about gone. Kindness is perceived by too many as a form of weakness.

In a book from the past called "All I Ever Need to Know I Learned in Kindergarten," by Robert Fulghum, two things stand out. In kindergarten we are taught, don't hit other people, and to say you are sorry when you hurt someone else. We have forgotten our kindergarten lessons.

4. We must vigilantly reclaim truth. Black Lives Matter because we have acted as if they do not. Sexism is not cute. It is boorish and destructive to our society. Homophobia is the practice of simple-minded people, and critical race theory is not the enemy of proper education, it is a process of getting the narrative right.

When we allow QAnon, White supremacists, Margorie Taylor Greene, Josh Hawley and the lot to pollute truth, we are headed in the wrong direction. It will be interesting to see if the Missouri legislature decides to stand with truth, or if political interests rule the day.

All of us must be vigilant in these areas and more. It is exhausting. But nothing worthwhile has ever been easy.

The power to make 2022 great or horrible is in our hands. I challenge you to be vigilant.

Lessons learned from MLK still ring true today

January 18, 2022

"What I'm saying to you this morning is communism forgets that life is individual. Capitalism forgets that life is social. And the kingdom of brotherhood is found neither in the thesis of communism nor the antithesis of capitalism, but in a higher synthesis.

Life's most persistent and urgent question is, 'What are you doing for others?'"- Rev. Dr. Martin Luther King, Jr.

After a week of celebrating Dr. King's birthday, the perennial question is, what have we learned?

If our celebrations and reflections on King's social philosophy only made us feel good, we have missed the point. In 2022 we must want to do more than feel good, we must be committed to doing what is right.

We have the challenge of voter suppression. The "lie" still haunts us. Republicans and their cronies still claim that the 2020 presidential election was stolen. Their response has been to suppress the vote. The fact that we cannot get the Republican Senate to pass the "For the People" voting rights act epitomizes their desire to send the country backward.

Every American should be able to vote, simple and plain. Our failure to recognize this fact threatens the democracy we hold dear.

Racial equity is fundamentally tied to economic equity. We must change our thinking about wealth in America. The gap between the rich and the poor is widening. King was right, neither capitalism nor communism is the answer. We need a new synthesis of economic action.

We need to find a way to overcome the division in this country. While people point at Trump, the Oath Keepers and the Proud Boys as the problem — and indeed they perpetuate the division — the real problem is us. We can dismantle the division if we decide that collaborating with one another is more important than being divided. I am talking about even here in Columbia. All of us must come to the table and participate in making Columbia, Boone County, the state of Missouri and America better. I remind you that a house divided against itself cannot and will not stand.

So, the lessons I hope we have learned this MLK Day is that dreams demand action. We must be intentional in our efforts to create and maintain the common good. I say this not as a Democrat or Republican, but as an African American who believes that we can be better than we have been.

Building bridges could unite talents, spread wealth in the community

January 25, 2022

"These are the times that try men's (humans') souls." - Thomas Paine

These are contentious times. Violence and warfare are on every front. Globally, we are witnessing a Russian military buildup on the Ukrainian border, and North Korea's continuous missile firing.

Locally, a celebration of life for high school student Roberto Lauer was held at Battle High School. Lauer died after his friend, thinking the pistol was empty, fired a loaded gun at him and ended his life.

Everywhere we look there is trouble. What shall we do in these troubled times?

Last Sunday I had the privilege to speak at the Unitarian Universalist Church of Columbia. There

I suggested that these are times when we need to not only tear down walls of separation but also build bridges of unity. I believe we must engage in bridge-building on the local level as well.

If we are ever going to overcome the racial and economic disparities in Columbia, we must have a serious discussion about wealth. A bridge between Columbia's wealthiest communities and its poorer ones needs to be constructed.

Too many people have too little to survive in our city. We can no longer entertain ridiculous notions like "people are just lazy and refuse to work hard."

We not only need good jobs with good pay, but we must also re-imagine the systems of wealth and the distribution of goods. I am not talking about Marxism or capitalism per se; I am speaking about creating a new synthesis of economics.

Violence is tied to economic conditions. If we want to address the growing problems of violence in Columbia, we must develop economic strategies that confront the problem head-on. Let me state that it is not the new city manager's problem alone — it is Columbia's problem. For example, churches in Columbia generate a significant amount of capital. It seems reasonable that churches lay aside their theological differences and come together and organize an economic program that serves the needs of people.

I am aware of Love, Inc., Turning Point and others. But they are not enough. We need Black and Brown folks to be integral in the discussions. We need their perspectives born in lived experiences. But we need wealthy white Columbians to teach, train, open doors and support those who need economic renewal.

Alas, to do any of what I present demands a bridge between the wealthy and the economically disenfranchised of Columbia.

Building bridges demands courage. There will be rejection from people of both sides. It demands patience and openness. No bridge builder can be faint of heart. But I believe that it can be done.

As Columbians, we are some of the brightest, most talented and creative people in this state and country. How about building a bridge for the good and uniting our talents? Does that not sound fascinating?

Tips for people who want to celebrate Black History Month

February 8, 2022

It is the time of year that Americans celebrate the history of Black Americans.

According to History.com, the celebration of the achievements and contributions of African Americans began with historian Carter G. Woodson and the Rev. Jesse E. Mooreland in 1915. Together they founded the Association for the Study of Negro Life and History (ASNLH). "The group declared its dedication to researching and promoting achievements by Black Americans and other peoples of African descent."

It is ironic that the celebration of blackness began in the same year that the movie "Birth of A Nation," which gloried the Ku Klux Klan and slaveholding, was introduced in American theaters.

While a monthlong celebration is an honorable endeavor, Black History should be celebrated every day since Black history is American history. The more we know about each other, the better the possibility of us becoming one nation.

Many white people seem perplexed when they are encouraged to join the celebration. Some say that since it is about Black people and I am not Black, why should I celebrate? One woman said to me that she did not know where to start. Who and what should I read? How do I begin?

There is a plethora of material available. Sometimes it can be overwhelming. Rather than being critical of fellow Americans, I suggest some ways to become better acquainted with the saga of Black people.

1. Remember ignorance is not bliss. The history of Black Americans is not presented to make white people feel bad or demean whiteness. It is simply the narrative of Black life in America. When we fail to know our history, we become susceptible to repeating past failures.

2. Engage credible sources. Do not allow social media to become your only teacher. Talk to other Black people about what they recognize as reliable sources of knowledge. Do not be afraid to ask. My mother used to say, "A closed mouth doesn't get fed." Ask and you shall receive.

3. Find a genre of interest to you. Do you like poetry, music, education, fiction, aviation, religion/spirituality, medicine? Knowledge comes best when you research in an area that captures your thinking and imagination. Black history offers all the above, so pick a genre and start there.

4. Studying Black history does not mean you are attempting to be Black. Sometimes other people will try to discourage us from learning about other people because of their implicit biases and prejudice. Again, the goal is to learn about your fellow Americans. Do not carry other people's prejudices. Learn to better yourself.

5. Realize learning about Black history is a marathon and not a sprint. No one gets it all by reading one book, attending one seminar or having one Black friend. Understanding other cultures in America is a lifelong process. Remember, the joy is in the journey.

I hope these suggestions help you participate in the celebration and learn more about Black history. I believe the more we learn about each other, the better the hope of unity can be achieved.

Freedom requires sacrifice and accountability

February 22, 2022

"May we never forget all those who suffered and died because they asserted their basic human right to be free." - Unknown

As we come to the close of February and the official celebration of Black History Month, the above quote takes on a profound meaning. All of us stand on the shoulders of those Black women and men who sacrificed everything for the basic human right to be free.

Freedom is a curious phenomenon. In the most elementary form, it is freedom from something and freedom to do something. In the case of Black America, it is freedom from oppressive forces that prevent full actualization of personhood. For our ancestors it was primarily freedom from slavery. Today it is freedom from classism, colorism, economic disparity, institutional brutality and other forms of dehumanization.

Freedom is also freedom to do something. In contemporary America it has come down to having the freedom to study American history without whitewashing, the right to vote and the freedom to fulfill our dreams for family, community and ourselves. Real freedom allows all of us to pursue our aspirations and goals with hope and meaningful substance.

Freedom, however, comes with responsibility. True freedom demands that we are accountable for our actions. For far too long we have blamed someone or something for our conditions and circumstances. Racism, in all forms, has plagued the Black community since we arrived in America in 1619.

Yet we built Black Wall Street, invented the traffic light, created some of the most amazing art, philosophy and religiosity ever recorded in human history. We did these things because we realized that united, we are unstoppable; divided, we remain slaves. Freedom demands a sense of responsibility to one another. Radical individualism is the sorcery of the oppressor. To be free we must be one.

Freedom costs. Each of us must decide what we are willing to give up and contribute to the quest for freedom. Since all of us are in this together we must confront our biases and prejudices. We can no longer speak the language of freedom and continue to be sexist and homophobic.

If freedom is truly the goal, we can no longer hide behind a first-century theology and simultaneously claim that we want to be free. Meaningful theology is liberating theology. It is contextual and collaborative. It understands that none are free until all are free. Our preferences can no longer outweigh our progress. Not to recognize this fact is death and destruction.

When I was a boy, we used to sing, "Oh freedom, oh freedom for me. And before I'd be a slave, I'd be buried in my grave, and go home to my Lord and be free." Freedom is obtainable in the here and now if we are willing to sacrifice as our ancestors did.

Let us be free.

An opportunity exists to 'build bridges' in Columbia

March 1, 2022

The Columbia City Council will consider a resolution that will affect city residents March 7. The resolution is constructed and being presented by City Council members Pat Fowler and Ian Thomas and other community members.

The resolution reads: "That the City of Columbia will commit 100% of the City's American Rescue Plan Funds to providing direct assistance to those disproportionally impacted by the pandemic, relieving the conditions of systemic poverty, racial inequality and building robust pathways toward economic security and public health."

This resolution moves us forward in addressing the most pertinent problems that plague our community.

In my column on Jan. 25, I wrote that for Columbia to combat homelessness, racial and economic disparity and violence we need two important dynamics: the building of bridges between communities of color that are most affected by the above conditions; and, to build bridges between the wealthiest and economically oppressed people of Columbia.

This resolution, in my estimation, is an attempt to build the necessary bridges that will make us a better a stronger community.

If the resolution is passed it will take an extraordinary effort to turn this idea into reality. Who will orchestrate the distribution of funds? How many paid staff and volunteers will be needed to accomplish the goal? How will we make sure that the voices of those who have been silent will be incorporated into the discussions and implementation of the plan? These questions and others will have to be addressed. And yet, I believe that as a community, we can do what is necessary for success.

There will be naysayers in our community who will object to this plan. But no attempt to assist those who need help goes without critics.

This plan will take courage and vision, both of which we have in our community. We have an excellent opportunity to create something magnanimous in Columbia. Let us not let this opportunity pass us by.

The gift within us

March 15, 2022

Last Sunday, I had the privilege to preach for the Unitarian Universalist Church of Columbia. I like being in its company. I find it to be an awesome group of thinking people committed to social justice and building a just society.

The power of that fellowship is that its commitment is not just in words, but in demonstrable deeds as well. It is not the only faith fellowship in Columbia that puts its actions where its mouths are, but Rev. Molly H. Gordon and the congregation deserve to be acknowledged.

I tried to suggest that all of us possess a unique gift within us. It is a message not just for the Unitarians, but for all of us. I believe if one finds their individual gift and feeds it, the gift within will make room for the person in life. Fame is fleeting and status is temporary, but the gift within is eternal.

Why this reminder? Because I meet so many people who are despondent and feel purposeless. Because of socioeconomics, health, age and a myriad of other reasons they are on the precipice of despair.

I am watching talented young people choose violence over being victorious. I am seeing gifted aged people giving up on creating a beloved community because of the divisiveness in the nation. I suggest that the gift within us can provide the solution to being whole as a person and a community.

The interesting phenomenon of the gift is that it is given to us to be given away.

The more we use our gifts to encourage and lift others, the more they will multiply. The old Black song rings true today perhaps more than ever before, "If I can help somebody along the way, then my living will not be in vain."

The gifts are many in kind — intellect, faith, vision, hope, kindness, perseverance and compassion, just to name a few. Like Aristotle's moral virtues, they are the mean between extremes. They have the capacity to keep us grounded and build an excellence in character. Knowing one's gift prevents us from being jealous of others and being trapped in self-righteousness.

One of the things I love about living in Columbia is that we are a community of very gifted people. We are poets and musicians, builders and thinkers, chefs and stewards of compassion. If we ever decide to combine our gifts and work toward the common good, the problems of Columbia will be overcome.

I write this to encourage us to use the gifts within us that we might build the dream we all share — a more perfect union.

Americans need more help with economic hardships

March 22, 2022

In the winter of 1776, Thomas Paine wrote, "These are the times that try men's (humans') souls." Of course, Paine was speaking about the struggle America was facing in its quest for independence from British rule. In 2022, once again we are facing times that try the human spirit in America.

All of us are facing economic hardship. The soaring prices for food and gas are crushing many of us. People talk about how the economy is difficult for the shelterless, but it is the working poor who are suffering incredible hardships.

I was joking with a fellow patron at one of our local grocery stores about how all of us enter the store praying and leave the store cursing. The same is true at the gas pumps. With gas near $4 per gallon, those of us who have minimal paying jobs wonder how we are going to get to work each day and buy enough food to sustain our families. These times make us quote Marvin Gaye as he sang, "makes you want to holler and throw up both your hands."

President Joe Biden and the White House Administration is reported to be thinking about ways the government can help all Americans in this crisis. Once they thought about giving citizens "gas cards" as a means of relieving the economic pressure. That idea was quickly discarded given the possibilities of fraud, abuse or other potential issues. No one wants to think about giving more Americans food stamps or other food assistance because of the troubles that emerge in the current situation regarding food stamps.

While the average annual income in Columbia is around $50,000, most of the working poor in Columbia do not come near that amount. Many people who used to donate to places like the Food Bank are finding themselves needing the Food Bank to survive. Churches and other benevolent organizations are at their limit. How are we to survive?

Unfortunately, I do not see an answer coming soon. If the wealthiest among us would help, that would be wonderful in the short term, but that cannot be the final solution. It is obvious America needs an economic overhaul. We need a redistribution of wealth so that all may live. But to even mention such a change causes people to think it's socialism or communism. While such thinking is absurd, many Americans think any conversation about redistributing wealth in America is communist rhetoric.

The bottom line is that something must change. We are already a divided nation on edge. If the economic situation gets much worse, civil rebellion will be next. We must figure out a united effort by government, corporate industry and the private sector that addresses meaningfully our economic problems. I am open to reasonable suggestions. Does anyone have one?

What will Columbia look like after the election?

April 5, 2022

Columbians voted Tuesday on the complexion and tenor of the future of city government.

The mayoral and City Council races are intriguing since whoever will be elected will determine whether we move in a progressive manner toward the future, or whether we will allow conservatism to rule the day.

Will the new administration be more committed to people and the issues that effect everyday life for Columbians, or will business interests determine the agenda?

There are some major concerns that the new administration will have to face, and how these issues are managed will rest in the hands of whoever is elected.

How will Columbia manage the increased violence in the city? Will policing and mitigation strategies be community-oriented or will "might makes right" become the modus operandi? There are no simple solutions to this problem.

However, a good starting point will be whether the new administration will include more voices in the discussions about violence in Columbia. We can no longer rely on Columbia's favorite folks to reflect upon the issues — that strategy has clearly not worked.

It is time to hear from the underrepresented of Columbia to address violence in our community.

Will the new administration tackle the problem of economic disparity in Columbia? Clearly a huge gap exists in our town. The wealthier citizens of Columbia are getting wealthier, and the working poor are getting poorer.

For people to say that all that is needed is for the least among us to "just work harder" is the epitome of foolishness. A conscientious reflection about wealth in Columbia needs to take place, or the economic gap will never be properly addressed.

Along with addressing the problem of wealth is the issue of homelessness and those without shelter or decent, affordable housing. For this writer, the question is not merely how can we find places for the homeless to live. The question is how do we respond to the mental health and substance addiction needs as well. Homelessness is complex, as we all know. And, yet, it is an issue that cannot be avoided.

I believe in Columbia. I have always said that whatever our problems are, we, as a community, can fix them. We have a wealth of talented people who have the expertise to make meaningful change in this community. I hope that the results of the election will move us in the right direction.

Easter season brings hope for a new day

April 19, 2022

One of the things I am committed to doing is trying to bring people together for the common good. Together, we can do such marvelous things. Divided, we compound the things that keep us in oppression.

What can we look to that can uplift our spirits and strengthen our resolve? It is Easter season.

We all are aware that Easter is a Christian holiday. Christians affirm that a human being by the name of Yeshua was uniquely connected to the Ultimate Reality in such a way that his life and sacrifice can transform human experience in unbelievable ways. Such is the claim. I suggest that Easter can be meaningful for non-Christians as well. Here is how.

Easter represents that despite the vicissitudes of life that hold us in bondage, no circumstance is final. Christians talk about resurrection from death. Death seems final. Yet, Christians claim that what seems final can be overcome.

Many Columbians find themselves in death-like situations. They lack money, food, shelter and a sense of belonging. Some fight depression and/or anxiety; they worry about their children or other family members. Hopelessness rages as we see racism, sexism and homophobia increasing.

The old Black spiritual asks, "Is there a balm in Gilead?" And Easter unashamedly asserts "Yes!"

There is a way to house those without shelter, to provide the necessary resources that people need to not just survive, but live well. The solution is not supernatural, but human.

The solution is us.

Easter is a sign of hope and a reminder that the power of resurrection from the oppressive realities that far too many endure is in our hands.

The fact that Easter is celebrated in the spring states that it is the symbol of vitality, creativity and new beginnings. Easter urges all of us to be about the business of planting new dreams and visions.

The pandemic tried to crush us, but we survived. Now we can create the fundamentally new. I am speaking about new relationships between people and communities. New positive discussions and strategies about what is proper education for our children instead of fostering the racist rhetoric we hear in too many corners of our society.

This not a call to action for Christians only, but for atheists, agnostics, pagans and all human beings. The time of division must end. Since Easter is a time of new beginnings, let it start now.

The power of stories

April 26, 2022

Last Thursday, I was honored to participate as a panelist with Valerie Berta and the WE Project with the UMC Bridge Program, titled "Liberating Stories." The other panelists were Marekka Nickens, the Rev. Sarah Klaassen, Ezra Komo, Bini Sebastian and Evonnia Woods. Each of us talked about our life journeys and the moments of finding liberation to become who we are. We were a collective of Columbia's narrative — people of color, white, male, female, transgender, gay and straight. It was a powerful experience for each of us.

There is something very authoritative and potent about having a safe environment to tell our individual stories and hearing the stories of others. It allows us to briefly step into the world of others, and upon hearing liberating stories, it both affirms and empowers our own journeys.

As human creatures we love stories. All the great spiritual leaders were exceptional story tellers — Gautama, Jesus, Lao Tzu, Shakira, Muhammad and the prophets. They have the power to arrest our imagination and transform the mundane into a vision of something greater.

We live in a society that is attempting to destroy the story of America and its people. We hear calls to resist critical race theory, ignore the struggles of women and to demean the plight of the LGBT community. We now even want to punish Mickey Mouse and friends. And it does not stop there. Farmers are in a dire situation. The average family can barely make ends meet. Dogma and doctrine are touted as more important than deep spirituality, and profit as more important than people.

We are getting divisive, angry stories filled with hatred and pseudo-patriotism, but not stories that set the spirit free. More than ever, we need to tell and hear stories of liberation and victory so hope may rise within us.

There is a saying that emerges out of the Black church that goes, "You may see my glory, but you don't know my story." Until we know each other's story, we can never be one.

It is time to tell our story. We need to express our hopes and desires, our pain and struggles. I believe we will find out that despite our differences we have more in common than we can imagine.

Your story is important and powerful. Tell your story, share the depths of your heart. It will allow you to help somebody along life's way.

Exploring an ugly little secret

May 3, 2022

Kenya Barnes wrote: "Colorism is a divisive tool used by the powerful to separate the powerful."

"If you're Black, stay back;

If you're brown, stick around;

If you're yellow, you're mellow;

If you're white, you're all right."

— A childhood saying

America has a dirty little secret. The secret is called colorism.

What is colorism? Merriam-Webster Dictionary defines colorism as "prejudice or discrimination especially within a racial or ethnic group favoring people with lighter skin over those with darker skin." The term, colorism, is attributed to Alice Walker in "In Search of My Mother's Garden." Related to internalized racism is colorism, which is discrimination based on skin color. Therefore, colorism is a phenomenon that confronts racialized groups and challenges the relationship between different racialized groups, particularly in the interaction of white Americans and Americans of color.

Colorism is both an implicit and explicit bias. The Kirwan Institute for the Study of Race and Ethnicity posted, "(Colorism is an) implicit bias (that) refers to the attitudes or stereotypes that affect our understanding, actions, and decisions in an unconscious manner." These biases, which encompass both favorable and unfavorable assessments, are activated involuntarily and without an individual's awareness or intentional control. Residing deep in the subconscious, these biases are different from known biases that individuals may choose to conceal for the purposes of social and/or political correctness.

Colorism is an implicit bias. Implicit bias refers to the attitudes or stereotypes that affect our understanding, actions and decisions in an unconscious manner. These biases, which encompass both favorable and unfavorable assessments, are activated involuntarily and without an individual's awareness or intentional control. Residing deep in the subconscious, these biases are different from known biases that individuals may choose to conceal for the purposes of social and/or political correctness.

However, colorism is also an explicit bias. Sociologist Robert L. Reece in his article "The Future of American Blackness: On Colorism and Racial Reorganization" stated, "Researchers have done excellent work detailing the far-reaching impact of colorism. A broad cross-section of research shows that skin color stratification is almost ubiquitous, affecting mental and physical health, the criminal justice system, school punishments, sports, and income. But much less research focuses on understanding how colorism works and how it may shape the future of the American racial landscape, two questions that are inextricably linked."

If it is true that colorism has affected every socially constructed institution in America, then what about Protestant Christianity? Since Protestant Christianity's institutional presence is the Protestant church, has the church also been affected?

I am engaged in a research project examining this question. I am looking for people who have narratives of their (or their family's) experience with colorism. I need your help. If you are interested in this question and you would like to help me, please contact me and let us examine America's dirty little secret.

Colorism and Christianity deserve thought and consideration

May 10, 2022

In last week's column I presented one of America's dirty little secrets. It is called colorism.

I suggested the following about colorism: Colorism is a preference of white and light skin over dark skin. It is a derivative of racism that is both an implicit bias and an explicit bias. It is ubiquitous in nature as every population of color experiences its effects.

The white community is not exempt from its effects. As such, colorism has impacted every quadrant of American society: employment, housing, health care, education, beauty, the justice system and more. The perennial question is: Has colorism affected the Protestant Christian Church?

Why research such a topic? While it is reported that Americans are less likely to be affiliated with a church in recent years than in the past, the church, as an institution, still influences American culture in a major way.

For many people, the church is an integral part of their everyday lives. Equally, for many people that have been hurt by the church, Christianity is a constant internal battle that must be reckoned with daily. So, to ignore colorism and Christianity is to ignore a significant part of American history and culture.

The psychological impact of colorism on people of color cannot be denied. Colorism has, more often than we might want to admit, negatively impacted individual and communal self-worth. It is reported that a young Black girl had just returned from Sunday school at one of the white megachurches in America. Her mother saw her standing in front of the mirror in her room staring at herself and crying profusely. The mother quickly asked what was wrong. The little girl asked, "Momma, why does God hate me?" Her mother inquired, "Honey, why do you think God hates you?" She stated, "because in Sunday school the teacher told us that God loves everything that is pure, white, and holy; and, that God hates all things that are Black and evil. God made me Black, so that must mean God hates me too!"

How many women of color have been taught that all things evil are Black and that God must hate them because they are Black?

The issue of colorism and Christianity must be investigated thoroughly. Many Black and white Christian churches in Columbia have engaged in discussions and book studies about race. Such efforts are commendable. But talking about race but failing to tackle the issue of colorism provides only a partial narrative. If we are serious about building a more just society, we cannot avoid seriously discussing colorism.

I invited you to join me in the research project on colorism and Christianity. The research will make us ask questions about ourselves: How many times have we acted based on colorism, or behaved in a manner to demonstrate we are "color-struck?" How can we combat colorism and move beyond the foolishness of white-skin, light-skin discrimination?

Finally, I believe that we can overcome any "ism" that stands in the way of uniting us as one people. My interest in investigating colorism is not to attack Christianity, but to better it.

I believe that Christianity at the core is an attempt to make us one. We must face the obstacles that separate us if we are to fulfill the vision of becoming a beloved community.

Remembering those who have given the ultimate sacrifice

May 24, 2022

I'm going to lay down my sword and shield,
Down by the riverside,
And study war no more."
- An African American Spiritual

On Monday, May 30, we remember those who gave their love for this democratic experiment. I am thinking about the men and women who died defending the ideals of America. They died believing that America was worth it. Their hope was that by giving their lives, America would live out the promise to be one nation with liberty and justice for all.

I particularly remember soldiers of color: Black, Asian, Latin, and Indigenous who fought in hopes that America would one day see them as equal citizens worthy of honor and respect. They knew that America had a color problem. But they decided that the hope of the future was worth the sacrifice in the present. They believed that one day America would be the nation they envisioned.

My father was a WWII soldier in Ninth Calvary. The Army was segregated at that time. And yet he and his fellow Black soldiers knew that fighting for the American ideals was better than submitting to fascism. He used to say to me, "One day, boy, America will wake up and get it right. We just have to keep on fighting until she does."

The country the soldiers of color fought for has not gotten it right yet. We are still divided by racism, sexism, homophobia and pure meanness. The political foolishness that is going on at every level must make those who died for America want to turn over in their grave. The way we are acting does not honor those who died. Placing wreaths on graves, while noble, is not alone the answer. The answer lies in our commitment to form a just society free of discrimination.

I am not a pro-war person. Too often war is about quests for power, cloaked in a false sense of patriotism, grounded in a lust for wealth. However, I realize that sometimes war is necessary until humans realize that we are all in this human journey together. Until then we will have devastating conflicts like we are witnessing in Ukraine. The horrors we are watching take place there should remind us that there are no victors in war.

My hope is that one day we will cease our warring ways. But alas, as war continues, I am thankful for those who pay the ultimate price for the hope of freedom. I am pro-soldier, but I am anti-war. May we one day lay down our swords and shields and study war no more.

Healing the hole in our hearts

June 1, 2022

After preaching for the Unitarian Universalist Church of Columbia last Sunday, a woman of the congregation came to me and asked, "What should we say to our children given the recent shootings in Texas?" I have pondered this question and similar ones for a while now. What is wrong with us? Why is human life so trivial to so many? After the series of shootings we have experienced in this country, clearly there is a hole in our hearts.

Our children have many questions. The following is an effective way to discuss the events to our young ones.

We must be willing to listen to the questions they have before we bombard them with our answers. The age of our children will determine the questions they ask. They may ask the same questions over and over, so patience is key.

We must be truthful but not overdo it. The truth is that the world is a good place, but there are some violent people in it. School is a safe place, but sometimes it is not. Therefore, we must be aware of potential danger. The key is awareness, not crippling fear.

Give permission to be sad. Feeling the pain of the events is not a sign of weakness, it is instead an expression of our mutual humanity. It is OK to be angry. After all, all of us are angry, too. Do not be afraid to exhibit your own pain.

Never lose our optimism and faith in a better future. I am convinced that our circumstance is not our conclusion. I refuse to give up hope and suggest the same to you.

It seems to me that the same methodology we use to help our children is needed for us as adults. I suggest that we find others who are feeling the pain and openly share. If we need to visit a professional, we should see one. Again, it is not weak to seek help.

We need additional mental health care. I wish the government would put more money toward mental health care for the citizenry. When we think about Texas, Orange County, California, and Buffalo, New York, the demand for mental health assistance is painfully obvious.

I add that we must meditate and pray. Some of the answers to the vicissitudes of life are found not externally, but within. How can we be peacemakers and not merely peace seekers? Through meditation and prayer, we may find healings for our hearts and power to stop the madness that resides in this society.

May our warring ways cease. But until then, may we find a balm for the hole in our heart.

On Juneteenth, tell our story of survival and perseverance

June 14, 2022

"Hold those things that tell your history and protect them. During slavery, who was able to read or write or keep anything? The ability to have somebody to tell your story is so important. It says: 'I was here. I may be sold tomorrow. But you know I was here. "- Maya Angelou

On Sunday, African Americans across this democratic experiment will celebrate Juneteenth. Last year I wrote:

"Juneteenth is a triumphant event worth remembering. It is the celebration of the day in 1865 when the people of Texas were finally informed (2½ years after the fact) that all enslaved people in the Confederate states were no longer property of their masters. Juneteenth, also called Emancipation Day, is the oldest known celebration commemorating the end of chattel slavery in the United States."

I still affirm that Juneteenth ought to be celebrated. Juneteenth was the hope of enslaved Africans. It was the hope that they would not only be liberated from chattel slavery, but that they would also experience equity in this strange land.

Juneteenth is also a promise. It is the promise of white America that we shall all be free.

This year I am more focused on reflection about what Juneteenth is demanding of the future for Black people and America as a whole.

First, the challenge of Juneteenth is to remember our story and who we are. Despite attempts to erase our story by the whitewashing of American history, it is incumbent upon us to tell our story to ourselves and our children.

Our story is a story of survival and perseverance. If we do not remember our story, we will forget who we are.

Second, we must decide our direction. The goal of Black America cannot be one of materialism. We, indeed, must understand wealth in America, but we cannot aspire to be like the oppressor.

Wealth is not for individual agendas but to improve the community. We return to a motto that states, "I am because we are."

Third, we must reclaim the God of our weary years and the God of our silent tears. Have we become so fooled to think liberation is about merely changing rules and laws?

Dr. Martin Luther King, Jr. insisted that the law can keep people from killing us, but it cannot make people love one another. The God of hope set us free, not the government. To forget this is to follow after false gods with the end result being destruction.

Fourth, Juneteenth points us to the need to align with our allies. These days we need to build coalitions with the progressive white, indigenous, Asian, Latin and LGBTQ community.

The adage is still true: "They who are for us are not against us." Oppression for some is oppression for all.

This year I am celebrating our past, but my eyes are on the future. Will you join me?

Battle for freedom after Roe v. Wade must continue

June 28, 2022

"You may have to fight a battle more than once to win it." - Margaret Thatcher

The Supreme Court decision last Friday that overturned Roe v. Wade demonstrated once again that we who believe in human freedom and justice are in a battle.

The issue of a woman's reproductive rights has been a major one for more than 50 years. In fact, whether a woman has the final say over her body has been in conflict since the beginning of time.

So what women are experiencing right now is not new. With Trump's appointments to the Supreme Court, we knew this was coming.

All who believe in justice are disappointed but not surprised. Overturning Roe v. Wade w another chapter in the fight for freedom and liberty.

What I will say in this column comes with an acknowledgement. I am a male, and I am a Christian. I have no internal knowledge about what it means to be a woman.

Although I have reared six girls and live with a woman as my wife and partner, I realize the world I live in is grounded in white patriarchy and pseudo-Christianity.

All I have to say is centered in my own experience of being a second-class citizen, my history of loving the women who have been part of my life and my experience fighting battles in America.

One thing that must be remembered in fighting battles is that you must be able to recognize who is your enemy and who is your ally.

Since the SCOTUS decision, I have heard a lot of rhetoric that expresses anger but does not recognize that "they who are for you are not against you."

Many have said that all humans who have a penis are the enemy. Some utter that all Christians are the enemy. Some say all politicians are the enemy.

There are many men who have been educated and nurtured by great womanist thinkers and actors. Men who have demonstrated ally-ship should not be castrated because we are angry with small-minded men who have too much power.

Many of us (me included) have lost all standing for women's rights. Remember, I was fired from a major teaching post because I dared to stand against the status quo and with women. There are men who are willing to sacrifice all to stand with their sisters.

Many speakers are blaming religion, Christianity, for the SCOTUS decision. They assert that the principle of separation of church and state means the religious views should take no part in political decision-making.

First, all Christians are not against a woman's right to choose. Progressive Christians have been and are allies of choice and believe that choice is sacred.

Second, there is an enormous difference between Black Christianity and white, Western, European, Anglo-American Christianity. As a Black Liberation theologian, I understand what it is like to have others try to control the body and rob me of choice.

My people have been enslaved, tortured, raped, mutilated, lynched, bleached, used as experiments and forced to endure indignities that baffle the imagination.

So please do not tell me I do not understand. I have painfully understood since 1619.

Third, there is a difference between religious ideas that make society better and those that worsen it. I assert that religious people like Sojourner Truth, Fannie Lou Hamer, Dr. Martin Luther King, Jr., John Lewis, and countless other religious thinkers have been us better, or at least attempted to do so. Remember that Ruth Ginsberg was religious.

The bottom line is that the battle is not over. We are now at a point where we must fight even harder than before.

The real enemy are the Trump Republicans and sympathizers who say they care about babies, but they do not care about children after they are born.

The real enemies are those who like to use women but do not honor them. We must stand against the real enemies and not be fooled by falsehood or fear.

The battle is not given to the swift, but to those that endure until the end.

Freedom may just be another word for privilege

July 5, 2022

Freedom: the power or right to act, speak, or think as one wants without hindrance or restraint: The power of self-determination attributed to the will; the quality of being independent of fate or necessity.

On Monday July 4, most of America celebrated Independence Day. I say most because many women and people of color wonder if Independence Day is for all Americans or for only white men. Independence Day ought to be a day in which we celebrate our American freedom.

However, given the recent decision by the Supreme Court regarding Roe v. Wade, women no longer have the freedom to make decisions regarding their own bodies. Frederick Douglass, in his Fourth of July Speech of 1852, reminded Black Americans that Independence Day was not a celebration of freedom for African Americans. Some pose that his words still ring true today.

So, what does it mean to be free? Ideally freedom is, as posted above, the freedom to act, speak and think without hindrance. And freedom is the power of self-determination. The current Supreme Court has caused us to question how many of us are free?

The simple-minded suggest that because women can vote, be employed, or attend the educational institutions of their choice, they are free. The same group argues that Black America is free because slavery and segregation is no longer the law of the law. They conclude that people of color in this country can do and be whatever they want to do or be, so subsequently, all Americans are free.

The recent decision of the Supreme Court in the case of Oklahoma v. Castro-Huerta makes one ponder if the freedom of self-determination is being eroded. Should Tribal Nations be considered sovereign when dealing with tribal issues? The Supreme Court said no.

Thus, their freedom is, once again, determined by the Great White Father. How many more communities of color will suffer the same fate?

Indeed, I am not advocating anarchy. The results of anarchy are more devastating than we can or want to imagine. But the question of freedom remains before us. How free is free in contemporary America?

Too many people think fascism is on the social-political horizon. I think we should be on guard, but I am not convinced that America will become fascist. I do, however, recall the words of Carlos Castaneda's main character, Don Juan, when he stated that the greatest enemies of freedom are fear and false clarity.

I agree wholeheartedly. As Americans, we must not be overcome with fear. Yes, for those of us who believe in and fight for justice, the quest toward freedom will be an uphill journey plagued with assassins on all sides. Yet we must not be afraid.

Nor can we think we know more than we do, or think we can see the result of this situation. To do so is to be seduced by false clarity.

I am believing that the possibility of freedom for all Americans is within our reach. We must be diligent. We must be steadfast. In the end we all shall sing, "Free at last, free at last, thank God Almighty, we are free at last."

Three principles to help you hold on during troubling times

July 19, 2022

"Hold on (hold on), change is coming (change is comin')

Hold on (hold on), everything's gonna be alright (don't worry 'bout a thang)

Hold on (hold on), said you can make it (you can make it)

Hold on (hold on), everything (everything will be alright)

Everything's gonna be alright!"

- From "Hold On (Change is Comin')" by Sounds of Blackness

All around us we encounter people filled with anxiety, dread, despair and hopelessness.

The social, political and economic circumstances that confront the average Columbian make the human spirit grieve.

Prices for everything are high. The recent episodes of gun violence make us wonder if we have forgotten how to be human.

Match the lunacy of state and national legislatures, the betrayal of the Supreme Court and the plain meanness we experience daily, and the myriad things in life that, in the words of Marvin Gaye, "makes you wanna holla and throw up both your hands."

Yet this column is not about the troubles of the human experience, but an attempt to encourage you, my fellow citizen, to hold on.

I realize that someone reading these words is saying, "Right, hold on? How?"

The power to hold on comes from incorporating three main principles. These principles have helped human beings endure incredible obstacles and continue to stand when it looked as if disaster and trouble would overwhelm them.

These principles I share with you.

The first demands that during trouble we must exercise our memories. Our memories point to the fact that this situation is not the first time we have encountered troubling events.

We have been in tight economic circumstances before. We have been ill before. Our society has chosen stupidity over wisdom before, and yet we are still here.

We survived those threats to health and wholeness, and memory proclaims we will survive this hell again.

The second principle suggests that we must fill our existence with the things that strengthen our spirit and not weaken it.

Sometimes we need to take a break from the negativity on social media. I am a great believer in the healing effects of music, prayer and meditation.

Listen to music that inspires whatever the genre may be. Spend time in prayer and meditation.

Do not ask your ultimate reality to fix the problem but instead ask for the wisdom and power to overcome.

Use meditation to refocus and re-center. Most struggles we encounter are caused by our egos. Meditation keeps the ego in check.

And more than anything else, avoid negative people. Their poison will pollute your mind and spirit.

The third and final principle states that we must always cling to hope. Just because things are bad today does not mean that things will be horrible tomorrow.

All kingdoms rise and fall. People change, and so do the material conditions of life.

Cling to hope. Like Dr. Bernard Rieux in Albert Camus' "The Plague," refuse to give up, despite how things look. A dogged, absurd hope is needed to hold on.

We all go through challenges in life, but we must hold on to see what the end will be.

Associate circuit judge race is one to watch

July 26, 2022

Columbians will have the opportunity to cast their ballots on Tuesday in what is shaping up as an interesting election. One race has captured my attention.

The race for Boone County associate circuit judge for District 10 between Kayla Jackson-Williams and Angela Peterson is truly one to watch.

Both women are Democratic candidates and African American. To my recollection it will be the first time an African American will be elected to that position.

Both women are experienced barristers and stand on a platform of compassion and justice for all who will enter their courtroom.

The reputation of both women is one that demonstrates that they care about people, particularly those who have historically come to see the judicial process as one geared to protect the rich, white and powerful.

How wonderful it would be to have more judges that truly understand the plight of the poor and people of color.

What all of us are hoping is that the politics of the position will not cause either woman to forget what they have promised once elected.

All candidates promise to be fair and just. The problem is that once elected, many get caught up in the good ole politics of the position.

We need the victor in this race to remain true to who they claim to be. Without a doubt, we need justice in the judiciary and not "just us."

The race for U.S. Senate is interesting only in the sense of whether voters will elect Vicky Hartzler or Trump-supported Eric Greitens.

Neither candidate will add a fresh sense of responsible leadership. Both are only concerned about maintaining the mindless conservatism already fostered by Josh Hawley.

The only thing worth watching is whether Trump's endorsement will have any real effect on Missouri voters. This race could be a foretaste of what we all can expect in November.

The main thing is for us to go to the polls and vote. So many people around me believe that voting doesn't matter.

I maintain that voting is not only a civic duty, but also our way of making our voices heard.

When we do not vote we get what we get, and that is not good. I encourage all Columbians to go the polls and vote.

We must address the issue of economic disparity full force

August 16, 2022

"We reaffirm that on days like this, there are no Republicans or Democrats. We are Americans, united in concern for our fellow citizens." - Barack Obama

"Where there is unity, there is strength." - Yeshua

I realize that most of what I write in these columns is a form of "preaching to the choir."

The people who consistently read what I think already affirm similar notions and concepts. The people I most want to engage in dialogue will not.

I hope that those who support Mr. Trump's agenda, white supremacists, anti-LGBTQIA+ folks, crass materialists, environmental naysayers and the lot all consider me a bleeding-heart liberal, or at least something like that. Such a cross I gladly bear.

Yet I am seriously concerned about the fact that the America that I love is becoming more divided every day. Since the people we most need to engage in conversation about national unity will not converse, the question is what should be our course of action?

We must become a multicultural force for justice. The time for unified action is past due.

Indigenous people, Black people, progressive Anglos, conscious Asians, awake Latins and the LGBTQIA+ community must form a solid political and social block.

Too often we are divided by what has happened in the past. How about we all admit we have come short of the ideals of America and reconcile in love?

Love I do not mean pithy sentimentality. I mean, as bell hooks asserts, "an ethic of love" that fights vigorously for the right of every individual in this society to have the opportunity to activate their self-determination.

An ethic of love demands more than gathering to read a book about racial justice. It means being just.

We must envision what it means to be a beloved community and then act on it.

For example, why are we having colloquiums on diversity when all of our educational institutions are epitomes of racial segregation?

We hire people of color to do custodial work and provide food service, but why are there not more people of color in administration and teaching?

Why are we not generating businesses of color downtown? Why are our prominent white churches talking Black, but hiring white?

And when we do employ, why is no one questioning our common practices of colorism and tokenism? Please spare me the "we-cannot-find-qualified-people" excuse. There may have been a time when that was true, but not now.

We must address full force the issue of economic disparity. For instance, we say we are concerned about crime and violence, but we have known for a long time that lack of education and economic opportunity breeds crime and violence. We need to put some money where our mouths are.

I realize that I have listed issues that seem insurmountable. And some of you will say I have only scratched the surface. However, I do not believe that they are. To overcome and to be unified demands action.

We must pool our resources, knowledge, and creativity to withstand the onslaught before us. I believe that we will win.

Banning books robs children of wisdom and ideas

August 23, 2022

"Where ignorance is bliss, 'tis folly to be wise." - Thomas Gray

The recent ban on books by public school districts is alarming, to say the least.

The case in Texas would be humorous if it were not so sad. While the Texas case caught the public eye, it is not the only case of book banning in school districts across the country.

Alfred North Whitehead is correct when he stated, "Not ignorance, but ignorance of ignorance, is the death of knowledge."

Book banning is the ignorance of ignorance par excellence.

Unequivocally, the banning of books is a dangerous practice. It is reminiscent of Nazi Germany and the great book burnings that happened under the reign of Adolf Hitler.

Book banning, like book burning, is an attempt to control information that leads to knowledge. Books present a particular idea or concept that can be debated, questioned, agreed with or rejected.

When people start banning books, they rob students of the opportunity to be serious critical thinkers. And is not the goal of public education to create an atmosphere where ideas can flow, and critical reflection can take place?

I sympathize with school board officials. They are caught in the middle. On the one hand, they try to provide for students the best possible environment for learning.

However, they are elected officials who must answer to parents who sometimes are not very well informed or rational (note the ridiculous debate around critical race theory!).

Teachers are being robbed of the ability to provide credible pedagogy when the resources are controlled by others.

Personally, I want my grandchildren to read everything. I not only want them to read a Bible, but I also want them to read a Quran, a Bhagavad Gita and writings by atheists.

I want my children to question all sorts of ideas so they can decide for themselves what path they should follow. I am not afraid of literature that promotes homosexuality. We need to discuss what it means to be gay in a homophobic world.

I hope Columbia School Board officials continue to resist the book banning phenomenon that is plaguing other parts of the country.

I hope parents who believe in wisdom and the free flow of ideas will maintain a stance to support knowledge for the next generation of American citizens — all of our children.

Only with the free flow of ideas that books contain will we be able to withstand the onslaught of fascism and tyranny.

Frederick Douglass is correct that "education makes a child unfit for slavery."

Research project aims to develop ways that we may all be welcome

September 6, 2022

As many of you are aware, I have begun an exhaustive research project titled "Colorism and the Protestant Christian Church in North America." Colorism, the preference of white and light skin over dark skin, has affected every socially constructed institution in the United States. As a form of racism, colorism has negatively influenced concepts of beauty, employment, housing, the justice system and education, just to name a few institutions.

What is alarming is that extraordinarily little research has been conducted around how colorism has affected the Christian Church in America, particularly the white and Black church in America.

The history of colorism in the Black church reveals how Black congregations too often have been "color struck" — emphasizing the alleged superiority of light-skinned Blacks over dark-skinned African Americans.

The roots of the colorism bias can be found in the history of American slavery. It continued to dominate the thinking of the Black community after the Emancipation Proclamation and continues to promote racism even today.

The white church perpetuated colorism by making symbols of goodness, holiness and purity cast in white, and insisting that all that is evil, sinful and demonic is black.

It is not by accident that for generations white Christians — and subsequently many Black Christians — envision God, Jesus Christ, the Apostles and saints as white.

It is undeniable that colorism has influenced Christian thought in America since the inception of this democratic experiment. The research will examine how much colorism continues to influence and impact American Protestant Christianity.

I am extremely grateful for the citizens of Columbia, Christian and non-Christian, who have financially supported this work.

I also am deeply appreciative of the pastors, board members and lay people of churches in Columbia who, too, have financially supported the research project.

Those churches are The Unitarian Universalist Church of Columbia, The Crossing Church and Calvary Episcopal Church. Rock Bridge Christian Church has consented to be a co-sponsor of the project.

The only way we can ever overcome racism in this society is to dismantle all its forms.

Liberation from racism cannot be simply reading a book or celebrating a holiday. It must consist of engaging the phenomenon and challenging racism in every segment of our society. This project is a major step in that direction. None of us are free until all of us are free. To uncover colorism is to forcibly fight against racism.

In the '60s a motto was uttered that captures the essence of this fight, it goes, "If you are not part of the solution, you are part of the problem." Please join me in attempting to be part of the solution in Columbia, in Missouri and in America.

After 45 years on the job, these are the things I've learned

September 13, 2022

On Sunday, I celebrated 45 years of ordained ministry.

I say celebrate but it was more of a day of reflection, personal inventory and goal setting. Doing anything for 45 years ought to make one contemplate the journey.

I can say that I have experienced the greatest of joys, the most horrible defeats, some major victories and some absolute failures. In other words, I have experienced life.

Many of you sent truly kind words of encouragement. Thank you. Some of you even shared that I have positively influenced your life. Again, thank you.

What is most important to me is to ask the question, "Dawson, what have you learned in 45 years of ministry?" Here are a few thoughts.

To be clear, by ministry I mean the activity of sharing your gift with others. The minister is one who gives of his/her whole self to others.

Ministers are clergy, but they can also be musicians, artists, teachers, physicians, community leaders, therapists, etc. All who live to give are ministers.

True ministry is not about religious or denominational proselytizing. Ministry is best when it is centered in empowering and equipping people.

I began this journey thinking that ministry was about how many people I could convert to Christianity, how many denominational awards and positions I could claim, how I could be the brightest, most articulate and popular Baptist preacher in the 20th century. I realize that all of that was about me and not about the essence of ministry.

The only important activity any committed minister can ever ask is, "Have I helped someone along life's way?" Popularity is fleeting. Brilliance is relative, and there is always someone who can preach or speak better than you.

What remains forever are the ways you comforted the broken, how you encouraged the despairing soul of others and how you created the occasion in someone's life for enlightenment.

Therefore, authentic ministry is never about one's ego, it is always about "the other." All the others — Christian and non-Christian alike.

The best minister is the one who realizes he/she does not have all the answers. We have been called to wrestle with the big questions in humility and faith.

Why is there evil in the world? How did divorce occur after 25 years of marriage? What happens to me after I die? Am I still important and of worth when I become older? If I demonstrate who I really am, will you still love me?

Why did my child, spouse, brother, sister, or friend commit suicide? These questions and others demand that the minister not be the answer person but the wounded healer who walks through the valley of death with the other.

Ministry makes one aware of the fact that you will fail sometimes. Every idea will not produce success.

Sometimes you will be dead wrong. Such is the reality of every spiritual leader. For years no one listened to Muhammad except his family. Gautama Buddha's teachings were rejected by his own home country.

Only the faithful women gathered when Yeshua was crucified. Rejection is part of the journey, and no one escapes it. If everyone likes you, no one respects you.

Make sure you make meaningful relationships with people who are not in ministry. Ministry is lonely. It is not by accident that ministers comprise one of the largest populations that becomes addicted to alcohol, drugs and sex.

Connect with others who will love you and support you, and not only your title or position.

Finally, I have learned to laugh. Life in ministry can drain every ounce of power from your being. Laughter refreshes and recreates. Take time to laugh and your ministry will be fruitful.

I am grateful to have served for 45 years. I hope I have helped you along the way.

Lack of wealth just might be intertwined with violence in Columbia

September 27, 2022

I had an interesting conversation the other day with a fellow Columbian about the continued violence and shootings in the city.

Her position was that the violence we are experiencing is a matter of a lack of respect that people have. She was convinced that parents have failed to teach their children to be respectful and that the root of the problem lies in a lack of home-training that plagues certain areas of our city.

While she did not openly say it, we know that she is talking about the Black and brown communities in Columbia. I hear these kinds of comments often.

The position that she and many others in Columbia hold is basically that if Black and brown parents would be better parents the violence in Columbia will cease. Interesting, no?

Blaming the victims is a common error in our society. "If those people would just act rightly..." I, however, suggest that the root cause of violence in Columbia has more to do with economic conditions than poor parenting.

There is no question that economic disparity is the elephant in the room. We may want to blame other factors, but the lack of wealth and meaningful work fosters the frustration that manifests itself in violence.

The gulf between the wealthy and those that are not wealthy is widening in Columbia. For example, the average income in my neighborhood is approximately $18,000 per year.

What then is the solution? Frankly, I do not know. I am not advocating some sort of giveaway program.

Actually, I think that ultimately we are going to have to think seriously about a total redistribution of wealth in this country, but I realize that people immediately think communism and all rational conversation ceases.

More immediately I believe that we must provide more meaningful work opportunities. One cannot pay utilities, rent and buy food working in fast food or janitorial service jobs. Yet, for many people in Columbia that is all that is available.

Of course, race and colorism are a factor. When I talk about the Douglass Park area, most people think Black. The truth is that many White people live in this area, but the stereotype is Black. And of course, if it is Black, then it is violent.

The focus in Columbia must not continue to be distracted by racial stereotyping. Meaningful work must be the short-term solution. If we fail to address the issue of economic disparity, the violence in Columbia will increase dramatically. I for one, do not want that to happen.

In the midst of tragedy, we can still give thanks

October 4, 2022

Hurricane Ian has wreaked havoc in the Caribbean, Florida and along the East Coast. The devastation of life and property continues to mount. We may never know the full effect of this natural disaster.

Many of us who have family and friends in the Caribbean and Florida worried and prayed, hoping that they would be safe. I am glad and fortunate to say all the people I know survived the storm. I realize that far too many people cannot say the same, for all who have experienced loss, my prayers are with you.

However, in the midst of this horrific event there are some things for which we may give thanks.

We should give thanks for the way people of different classes and colors responded to neighbors in need.

It was awe-inspiring to watch neighbors rally to help one another. No one was concerned about politics, race, class, or any of the things that are dividing this society currently. The focus was simply, “How may I help my fellow human being?”

It is one thing for someone in the center of chaos to help another in chaos, but it is quite another thing to watch how people across this country volunteered to go to Florida and be of assistance.

Case in point is that people from Missouri left their families and friend to be an agent of mercy to those in need. Such acts of selflessness and true concern warmed my heart.

With all that is happening politically and socially it is easy to be jaded and negative about our fellow human beings.

One can be tempted to think that everyone is only about themselves, and that no one cares about the other. And, yet, in the wake of Ian we watched people help people. It rekindled a sense of shared humanity and the possibility that compassion is not dead.

It is amazing how tragedy can bring out the best or the worst in us. Repeatedly, we have seen examples of how it can demonstrate the worst in us. With Hurricane Ian we observed some of the best in us.

Oh, how I wish that the best in us would surface more frequently. But that is human life: sometimes we are magnanimous, sometimes we are base.

For all of those who have sacrificed their life and comfort to help those in need, we salute you and thank you. Thank you for reminding us that all of us have the capacity to demonstrate the divinity in us. All of us can be an angel of mercy and compassion. And for these things, we give thanks.

Goal of creating more diverse communities sometimes gets stymied by lack of interaction

October 11, 2022

"Diversity is about what makes each of us unique and includes our backgrounds, personality, life experiences and beliefs, all of the things that make us who we are. It is a combination of our differences that shape our view of the world, our perspective and our approach. Diversity is also about recognizing, respecting and valuing differences based on ethnicity, gender, age, race, religion, disability and sexual orientation. It also includes an infinite range of individual unique characteristics and experiences, such as communication style, career path, life experience, educational background, geographic location, income level, marital status, parental status and other variables that influence personal perspectives." - From the Victorian Government website

There is a lot of conversation these days about the need for diversity in every sector of our society. We hear the call for diversity in business, schools, civic organizations, churches, government and on and on. What many speakers are calling diversity is mere aggregation. If the goal of diversity is simply to put different people together, then the local laundromat is the best example of diversity going. Clearly, the hope is more than bunching people together.

What most people are desiring in the call for diversity is inclusion: the creation of space and place where different people can feel that they belong and can contribute their gifts and talents.

There are, however, two factors that hinder diversity and inclusion. One is tribalism. Tribalism is the insatiable need to only be with and around one's own kind. It usually is coupled with an unreasonable fear of the "other." Tribalism is hindering our quest to be a just society. It stymies progress and halts all attempts to create an environment that produces collective advancement.

The second enemy of diversity and inclusion is tokenism. We are all aware of the practice of tokenism in business. But tokenism in other areas of our society gives a false sense of being bias free. How often have we heard an organization brag about how diverse they are because they have one or two people of color within their ranks? Or, churches that claim they are a model of diversity with one African family and Latin members. Tokenism is the game played to look on the surface as "open and inclusive," but underneath they are still prejudiced and racist.

Creating a diverse and inclusive community enriches all of us. Innovative ideas can flow freely. Such a community gives us the opportunity to hear different narratives about life. We need more efforts to construct diverse arenas of interaction. Without them, we may not survive as the world's greatest democratic experiment.

How do we start? Start where you are.

Get to know the Latin neighbor, or Afghan co-worker, or your African American mail carrier. You might find that you have more in common than you think. At least you will move beyond stereotypes and prejudices and toward building a beloved community. Sometimes we get caught up in trying to do the massive things when simple acts of compassion can accomplish more. Do not let tribalism and tokenism prevent us from being great.

What will we learn from the midterm election

November 8, 2022

The results of the midterm election will be very interesting indeed.

Most political analysts suggest Americans are more concerned about the economy than any other issue. One can see why the economy is taking center stage, particularly after visiting your local grocery store or neighborhood gas station.

But, there are some other factors that will be revealed with the midterm election:

Will people turn out and vote as the did in the last presidential election? This factor is particularly important in the Senate race between Raphael Warnock and Herschel Walker in Georgia.

Will women and their allies determine the direction of this country regarding reproductive rights? Will Black and brown voters be enough to stem and stop the Trump tide?

Will Trump be a serious challenge in 2024? If the candidates Trump has endorsed are elected to office, the MAGA-mania will comfort us again. Despite Trump being the worst president in American history, his base will become more formidable if his candidates are elected.

Will money make the difference in the midterm elections? Many note that the Republicans have spent vastly more money for their candidates than the Democrats. We all know that money has always had a huge impact on contemporary elections. The question is will it have the effect that the Republicans hope for? In other words, will they be able to buy the House and the Senate? I believe after a while people become numb to the TV ads, etc. The spending craze may have the opposite effect in this election.

Some people are predicting a "red wave" this election with the Republicans winning both the House and Senate.

Perhaps. It could end up with the same situation we have currently.

What difference will it make for the regular person out here? Will food become cheaper? Will we be safer in our communities? I wonder what impact this election will have on us. We shall soon see.

Commit to Thanksgiving with the coming holiday

November 22, 2022

"I am grateful for what I am and have. My thanksgiving is perpetual." - Henry David Thoreau

Thursday we shall gather with family and friends to give thanks for all the good things we have experienced this year.

While Thanksgiving has strong religious and cultural roots, the day is celebrated more as a secular holiday now.

Modern society confronts us daily with chaos. We live hustle-bustle lives, bombarded with demands of various kinds: vocational, personal, economic, social, political, etc. The opportunity to pause, give thanks for who we are and what we have, provides us with the occasion to center ourselves, be humble and bask in the light of love and joy.

Even in the midst of a continuing pandemic, we can still be thankful.

I am learning to delight in the little things. A smile from a stranger, an encouraging word from a colleague, the greeting wave of a child, or the embrace from a senior citizen raises my sense of gratitude. I am convinced that if one does not give thanks for the little things in life, one will never appreciate the "big" things.

We live in a materialistic world. We are judged by what we have. Sometimes this same materialism seduces us into an artificial sense of self: I am better if I have more things. The reality is that who we are cannot be measured by our acquisitions or our possessions, but by our character. After all, none of us get to keep what we have when we die. We have to leave it all behind.

I live in an area where I see many homeless people every day. I am surrounded by the working poor who must grind daily just to make ends meet. A cloud of despair hangs over many people, young and older. Circumstance can make one, in the words of Marvin Gaye, "want to holler and throw up both your hands." And yet there is much we must be thankful about. Allow me to name just a few.

We can give thanks for family and friends who love us for the right reasons. All of us have haters, but the fact is that we also have people in our lives that truly love and cherish us, and they do so for the right reasons. They recognize that there is something in us and about us that is worthy to be loved.

We can be thankful that we are alive. Life sometimes is hard and frustrating. Yet if we live, we can change our lives. If we are in debt, we can get rid of it. If we are surrounded by negative people, we can change acquaintances.

Our circumstances need not be our conclusion. You have the power to change your world. And for that, be thankful.

We can be thankful for those that are praying for us. I still believe that prayer changes things. I know that I am here because someone prayed for me. I am not just talking about Christian prayer. Muslims, Jewish practitioners, Buddhists and Hindus all pray for the community of humanity. I am grateful for their prayers.

I am grateful for a deep sense of justice, faith, and love. I realize that injustice seems to be winning and common sense is at an all time low, but there are justice warriors among us who are fighting the good fight.

My grandmother once stated that she believed that "trouble won't last always." My faith affirms her belief, and my sense of love is that all systems and people can and will be transformed for the good. Hope that is seen is not hope. I am thankful that "weeping may endure for a night, but joy will come in the morning."

As we feast this Thanksgiving Day, let us commit ourselves a perpetual thanksgiving that works within us every day.

Colorism pervades even during holiday season

December 6, 2022

"While colorism is decisively extinct in the modern Black church, its remnants remain. Part of the idea of whiteness as purity, holiness and innocence also has implications of sexuality. Whiteness or, in the

case of Black folks, lightness is piety, demure and subdued behavior. Blackness beyond that of a paper bag is associated with promiscuity, Sapphire-stereotype and evil. Essentially, whiteness is sanctified while Blackness is demonized." -From the website Colorism at the Cross.

Most of you are aware that I am engaged in a research project on colorism and Protestant Christianity in the United States. The project is an examination of the effects of colorism on both the Black and White Protestant Christian Church within the U.S. context. It has been an interesting process to say the least.

Colorism is the implicit and explicit bias toward white and light skin. It is well documented that colorism has affected every socially constructed institution in the U.S. It has affected who gets the bank loan, who goes to prison, who is employed, who is married and who isn't. The question that has been unexamined is: How has colorism affected the Protestant Christian churches in the U.S.?

Christmas is an example of the effects of colorism on Christianity. For a long time, I have agreed with my Jamaican friends that Santa Claus was a Black man. However, what about within the context of Christian religiosity? In both the Black and white church, we are too often greeted by a white Jesus, white shepherds, white angels and on and on. We all know that Yeshua (Jesus), Mary and Joseph were people of color — not blond haired, blue-eyed Europeans. The fact that we are still plagued with this white, Western, European, Anglo-American lie is proof positive that colorism is still with us within Christendom.

One might ask, what difference does it make? The difference it makes is this and other forms of colorism within Christianity perpetuate white supremacy. If all things good and holy are white and all things evil and perverse are black, it doesn't take a genius to figure out what that says about people of color. It purports a false and damaging concept that whiter and lighter is better.

One Christian lady said to me that my research project was just airing "dirty laundry and causing trouble." Reflecting on that notion, my response is simply this: You cannot clean up what is dirty if you don't air it. All of us, in the sentiment of John Lewis, need to cause "good trouble" sometimes. If investigating colorism and Christianity is airing our dirty laundry and causing trouble, then I am convinced that I have embarked upon an important mission.

I want to thank the many people and churches that have financially supported my research project. Progressive and conservative churches and individuals realize that if we are going to be serious about dismantling racism in this society, we must tackle colorism as well. If you are Christian, think about what you are presenting with your Christmas decorations. Are you suggesting that all of us are part of the universal love of the season, or only those who are "white and bright"?

Recapturing the joy of the holiday season

December 13, 2022

Numerous people have said to me that they are not feeling the joy of the season. One reason, I have been told, is the high price of things: food, clothes, toys and more . When one's money is funny, it is hard to feel in the spirit of the holidays.

Of course, if the lack of holiday joy is because of economic conditions, that is a sad commentary on our materialistic attitude regarding the holidays. The season is not about things. The holidays should be about something far greater than money.

I was reared in a Black preacher's household. My father did not make lots of money. In fact, by contemporary standards, I grew up in poverty. Yet, the holiday season was one of my greatest joys growing up. My parents made sure that Christmas, my religious tradition, was a time of fellowship and love. It was a time to decorate the house with things my mother and her friends made from a creative imagination, rather than brought from the store. The house filled with food smells of various kinds: wild turkey shot by my father, baked yams, greens that had been canned in Mason jars by my mother, and of course, chitterlings. The holiday was a time of reflection, prayer and giving thanks for surviving another year in a cruel and racist America.

My point? Maybe we need to think more about what we have, and can have, rather than what we can buy. Economists talk about how we incur so much credit card debt during this time that the New Year is a time of depression and anxiety. Maybe we need to return to old fashion values about the holidays and stop entering the madness.

Here are some simple activities that may help you recapture the joy of the holidays.

Reconnect with an old friend you haven't communicated with in a long time. All of us enjoy knowing that someone is thinking about us. Reconnecting with a friend will not only give joy to someone else, it will bring joy to you.

Make a gift from the heart and not your pocketbook. Most of us are a lot more creative than we give ourselves credit. Bake some cookies, create a handmade holiday card, sing a song from your past. Be creative.

Participate in corporate worship. Go to church or the synagogue. Participate in community celebrations of Kwanza. Joy is contagious. Go to places where people are infected with joy.

Give social media a break. There is so much negative stuff on social media that it will depress you and make you think the world we live in is horrible. Give your devices a break and interact with people instead.

Volunteer. Join volunteers at Loaves and Fishes or some other serving organization. Give yourself to others brings joy.

Tell your family narrative to the young ones in your family. Our children are lost because they don't know the history of the family. While some parts of our narratives are negative, the fact that we have survived the struggles brings a sense of purpose and joy. Tell your truth.

While it is hard to have joy in these difficult times, it is not impossible. May the joy of the holidays fill your heart and mind.

Kwanzaa is a holiday everyone can celebrate and practice

December 27, 2022

Since 1966, Dec. 26 through Jan. 1 has been a time when African Americans in the United States and people of the African diaspora celebrate Kwanzaa.

Kwanzaa was instituted by Dr. Maulana Korenga, and the name comes from a Swahili phrase that means "first fruits of the harvest."

Initially the holiday was meant as an alternative to Christmas, but later it was said to be in addition to other religious holidays.

Kwanzaa is the celebration of seven principles. They are:

Umoja —unity: To remain united in the community.

Kujichagulia —self-determination: To be responsible for yourself and your community.

Ujima —collective work and responsibility: To work together.

Ujamaa —cooperative economics: To create African American-owned businesses.

Nia —purpose: To build and develop the community.

Kuumba —creativity: To improve our community and make it more beautiful.

Imani —faith: To believe that the world can become a better place.

When we consider the seven principles of Kwanzaa, it is evident that it is not just for people of African descent. These are principles all people can celebrate and practice.

For example, all people need to recommit to a deeper sense of community. A committed community will liberate us from the violence and division we are experiencing across America and in Columbia.

Individuals committed to community are aware that it takes all of us to create the kind of society we desire.

One of the strengths of Kwanzaa is that religious and nonreligious people can affirm the seven principles.

One needs not be Christian, Jewish or Muslim to believe in collective responsibility or cooperative economics. An atheist, like a theist, understands that creative efforts to beautify our community benefits all of us.

One need not be part of a faith community to exercise imani. One can ascribe to "faith in community" and practice imani.

Too often the things that can help our country be a united society are compartmentalized. Kwanzaa is not just a "Black thing." It is "a people thing."

We must find a way to be one as Americans and as Columbians. Perhaps Kwanzaa can assist us in finding the oneness we all seek.

I urge you to find a family and/or a community group and join in the celebration.

Find a family that is creating the feast of karamu on the last day of Kwanzaa. We become united when we learn more about each other.

Take time to learn and you may discover that the principles of Kwanzaa may empower you and generations to come.

2023

A list of wishes, dreams for 2023

January 3, 2023

"You are never too old to set another goal or to dream a new dream."- C.S. Lewis

The celebrations have now ended. The Christmas, Hanukkah and Kwanzaa decorations have been removed and life returns to the routines of everyday life. We go back to work, kids go back to school, and we settle in to face the challenges of a new year. Will 2023 be different than 2022, and if so, how so?

The holidays were for me a time of reflection and dream-making. When one gets to the age where you realize you will not live as long as you have already lived, dreaming becomes immensely important to one's well-being. I think Lupita Nyong'o is correct that no matter where you're from, your dreams are valid. Allow me to share some dreams for 2023 with you.

I am dreaming that Columbia seriously engages in a plan to confront the huge economic gap that exists in our community. The gap between wealthy Columbians and poorer citizens in our city is increasing in leaps and bounds. It is particularly evident in Black and brown populations in our city. Economic disparity contributes greatly to the increase in drug trafficking, sex trafficking and violence. We must do things to put more dollars in the hands of Black and brown Columbians and create more opportunities for people of color to become entrepreneurs and not merely consumers.

Of course, people of color must do our part. We must encourage our children to reject crass materialism and find ways to economically connect with other people of color. With modern technology, we can build global economic communities that move us to self-sufficiency and cooperate responsibility.

I am dreaming that Black, brown and Indigenous communities will build sustainable coalitions in Columbia and mid-Missouri. There is much we can learn from one another. We allowed racism to divide us and fool us into seeing each other as the enemy. It is time to move beyond the false narrative we were taught and realize that as a coalition we are a significant economic, social and political force in Missouri. If we stood as a united coalition the Republicans can no longer perpetuate the lie that critical race theory is the enemy of democracy.

I am dreaming that white America as a whole and white Columbia meaningfully confront its racism, systemic and personal. Too many speak the right language but do not act in a responsible manner. Once again, isn't it interesting that on every college and university campus in this city, you find more people of color in janitorial service, food service and security than on the faculty or in administrative positions?

It is not accidental. It is intentional and reflects the depth of the systemic and personal racism that is in play in our academic institutions. I haven't even mentioned the business community. It is time to get serious about confronting our racism.

Ultimately my dreaming is one dream: it is a dream that the city I live in becomes truly multicultural and inclusive and not just look like it. I am dreaming that in 2023 we make giant steps toward becoming one. Are you dreaming with me?

How shall we think of Martin Luther King's dream?

January 10, 2023

Next Monday, we shall celebrate Martin Luther King Day. Each year, people gather in churches, schools and other places to reflect on the Rev. Dr. King's message to and for America. King was not simply a speaker for the Black community but a prophetic voice to all Americans and the world.

Most celebrants concentrate on the "I Have a Dream" speech. Indeed, it was a powerful utterance given by a gifted orator. People like the hopeful prospect of King's "Dream" speech. It makes us feel good. And we all know that in this society many people would rather feel good than be good.

I suggest, however, that too often the "Dream" becomes a sedative for American society. If one dreams of unity, then one does not have to participate in constructing the reality of the dream. We can merely dream about justice and unity, and then say to ourselves, "See I am a good person because I have a dream!"

For many people in America the "Dream" has become a nightmare. Yes, we have made some progress in race relations since MLK and the civil rights movement. We can all sit and eat in the same restaurants. We no longer have "colored" water fountains or legally segregated schools. But the racial and economic disparity that exists in American society cannot be overlooked. The threat to democracy exists. The laws restricting voting, the control of women's bodies, and the prevention of critical race theory in schools demonstrate that the "Dream" is threatened by a nightmare. In many ways we are more divided than in the days of the 1960s.

Dr. King gave the "Dream" speech Aug. 28, 1963. Now 60 years later we are still singing "We Shall Overcome." The question all serious thinking people of color and justice ask is when will someday get here? I had someone say to me recently that America just needs more time. In time, the person said confidently, the dismantling of systemic racism, institutionalized colorism and personal prejudice will happen. It just takes time.

My response was and is, how much more time do you need? You had my grandparents' time, my parents' time, and 68 years of my time. How much more time does America need?

I am no longer impressed with MLK celebrations filled with pithy sentimentality. Kumbaya doesn't do it for me. No more eloquent speeches about what the "Dream" means. No more candlelight marches that make us feel good. We have done that for 60 years. Now it is time to make the "Dream" a reality if we believe in it. We cannot overcome unless we start by confessing our sins to one another. People of color need to confess their sins to other populations of color about how we have objected to white racism but have practiced the very ideology of the oppressor. Black fights brown, Indigenous fighting Asian, on an on. Anglo America needs to confess before reconciliation can take place. Stop asking me to move on when you will not say I am sorry and mean it.

We must start somewhere, and starting with confessing our corporate and individual sins makes sense to me. It worked in South Africa; it can work here in America.

Making the "Dream" a reality is the challenge for this present age. When we are about the business of creating a just society, celebrating MLK Day takes on meaning and worth. If we are not involved in transforming the "Dream" into reality, we are nothing more than sounding brass and tinkling symbols: sound and fury signifying nothing.

Kings' chaos or community still exist in America today

January 17, 2023

"For in a real sense, America is essentially a dream, a dream yet unfulfilled." - Martin Luther King, Jr.

In Dr. Martin Luther King, Jr.'s famous book, "Where Do We Go from Here: Chaos or Community" we were challenged to address the evils that will either lead to utter chaos both in America and in the world, or the fruition of building community on both the national level and the world stage. The book was published in 1966 and yet holds relevance for us today.

In an article published in The Atlantic in February 2016, the writer suggests that the three evils King saw that threaten the building of community are racism, poverty and war. Indeed, these three persist as enemies of community. Systemic racism still prevails in this society and the global community as well. Economic disparity is not a U.S. problem only, but a worldwide phenomenon. Who can doubt the tragedy of war when we look at Russia and Ukraine.

Yet King's analysis is not one drowning in despair. On the contrary, King's thinking was one holding fast to hope. In 2012, I wrote that Dr. King's hope rested on a three-tiered foundation as seen in "The Liberatory Thought of Martin Luther King, Jr." by Robert Birt, Jr. Dr. King's hope was grounded in the belief in a God who stood on the side of the poor and oppressed. This God was one who "hears the cries of (her) people" and intervenes in human history. King understood that Abraham Lincoln didn't free the slaves, God did.

Secondly, King's hope believed that one day America would live up to its democratic values and become a society where liberty and justice for all was not merely discussed but practiced. On Jan. 6, 2021, that hope is threatened by the radical right. But hope in this democratic experiment does not fade because of the insurrection, it digs in and fights the good fight.

Third for King was the hope of the beloved community realized. In King's mind all of humanity is tied together in an interdependence that cannot be denied. What affects one in Brazil affects us here. King thought the more we realize our need for each other around the world, the greater the opportunity for the beloved community to be realized.

The question remains is the hope King envisioned possible in the 21st century? The three evils mentioned at the beginning still plague us. Yet I believe that we can become a beloved community and transform this divided society into a united one. It will not be easy. But nothing great and wonderful ever is easy. I believe that God will see us through.

After Tyre Nichols' death, Black communities remain cautious about police

January 31, 2023

The tragic death of Tyre Nichols has once again stunned America's consciousness. The death of another Black man at the hands of the police has become far too common in this society. If one thought that murder by police was a thing of the past, the tragedy in Memphis reminds us that the violence against people of color in America continues to rage on. According to the website Statista, 313 Black people were killed by the police in 2022.

What seems different about the Tyre Nichols case is that the killing of Mr. Nichols was at the hands of five Black police officers. The body cam video shows that Nichols was beaten and kicked savagely. It was a horrendous display of a lack of compassion. One would think that Black officers would not treat another Black person in such a vicious manner. How wrong we were in our thinking.

In conversations about policing in America, people suggest that if we constitute a police unit that reflects the complexion of the community it serves, police violence would disappear. The event in Memphis, however, reminds us that in the end color is not the final point. My father used to say, "You may be my color, but maybe not my kind." The five police officers who beat Nichols to death were his color, but not his kind.

A serious investigation into police training is needed. Is the training police officers are receiving robbing them of their humanity? Why are we still experiencing instances of police brutality to people of color across this country? Something is missing in police education.

Obviously, the bottom-line regarding policing is the character of the individual and not the skin color. Give me a person of good character and compassionate community policing will take place. An officer of good character will respect the dignity of another human being. Police departments need to quit hiring suspicious persons who respect neither themselves nor citizens in the community. We need officers who will truly protect and serve.

I live in a section of Columbia that is heavily policed. As a Black man, I am cautious. While most of my encounters with the Columbia Police Department have been positive and professional, not all of them have been so. The Memphis tragedy reminds every Black person that what happened to Tyre Nichols can happen to any of us.

One white woman once asked me: "Why do Black people act so afraid of the police?" It is because all of us realize that regardless of age, education, social influence, religious commitment and the lot, any of us at any time can become Michael Brown, Eric Gardner, George Floyd, Breana Taylor or Tyre Nichols.

My heart goes out to Nichols' family. My hope is that we will never have to witness a tragedy like this again, but my mind says remain vigilant, watch and pray.

Has American fallen in love with violence? Compassion could save us from demise.

February 14, 2023

The Rev. Dr. Martin Luther King said: "The ultimate weakness of violence is that it is a descending spiral, begetting the very thing it seeks to destroy. Instead of diminishing evil, it multiplies it. Through violence you may murder the liar, but you cannot murder the lie, nor establish the truth. Through violence you may murder the hater, but you do not murder hate. In fact, violence merely increases hate. So, it goes. Returning violence for violence multiplies violence, adding deeper darkness to a night already devoid of stars. Darkness cannot drive out darkness: Only light can do that. Hate cannot drive out hate: Only love can do that."

On Valentine's Day 2023 we awakened to another incident of senseless violence. This time it happened on the campus of Michigan State University. The result is three dead, five injured. On a day that ought to celebrate love, we are confronted with death.

The perpetuation of violence rears its ugly face in every sector of American society. No place feels safe. No place is exempt. Parents are afraid to send their children to school. Churches no longer offer sanctuary. When entering a restaurant or movie theater we now automatically scan the environment for the nearest exits. We cannot trust those who pledge "to protect and serve" to protect us, nor can we seek succor from our neighbors. We are a society that has fallen in love with violence.

Listing the symptoms does not help us. We are aware of the symptoms. We know that we need mental health treatment. Depression crosses all socio-economic, age and racial lines. We know we have a devastating drug problem. We know the pandemic took a toll on us at every level of our being. What we do not know is the root cause of our malady.

How do we get to the place where we love our neighbors as ourselves? Have we fallen so deeply into a pit of hopelessness and despair that our rage rules our rationality? Has hatred won the day?

Despite the violence all around us, I am persuaded that in the end compassion will save us from our demise. Like Stephanie Mills' "I Have Learned to Respect the Power of Love." Whether it comes in the form of a smile, a meal served at Loaves and Fishes, or writing a newspaper column yelling, "Hold on beloved, you are important and I love you," compassion will win the day.

Practice love and love will come back to you. Hug somebody today. Call someone and tell them they are important. Look in the mirror and tell yourself, "I love you!"

We can break the cycle of violence if we are willing to reach out to one another and practice compassion in every corner of the world in which we live.

A Black History Month reflection

February 28, 2023

"In our work and in our living, we must recognize that difference is a reason for celebration and growth, rather than a reason for destruction."— Audre Lorde

As we come to the close of Black History Month, it is imperative to ask ourselves what have we learned? Has the month simply about cosmetics and clothing, portraits of the grand Black queens and patriarchs of the past that endured great suffering which have hollow meaning to a contemporary, microwave, Tik-Tok generation? What have we learned?

One thing we have learned is that the problem of policing is not just about "white" policing, it is about policing in general. Policing has been a problem for the Black community since slavery. Memphis reminds us that just because law enforcement officers are your color they may not be your kind. Black communities across America need to demand accountability from its police officers not only after a tragedy but before.

Hopefully, we have learned that we need to have a serious conversation about wealth in America and Black wealth in particular. While corporate America makes a huge profit from Black spending, the economic gap between Black and white America continues to widen.

Recently, a poll suggested 41% of Americans did not feel financially better off under this current government administration. I wonder what a poll among Black Americans would reveal. As a parenthetical aside, given the widening economic gap, doesn't a serious conversation about reparations make more and more sense given the current situation.

Undoubtedly, we have learned that there are some internal issues Black Americans must address. One is the issue of mental health in the Black community, particularly among Black men. We can no longer simply blame white racism and patriarchy for the creation of the problem. We must address how we have perpetuated the problem by saying, "just pray about it" instead of encouraging mental health treatment. The pandemic took a toll on all of us, and the most in communities of color. We need to encourage fellow Black men to seek out help and stop thinking that needing someone to talk to is a sign of weakness. Real men know when to ask for help.

The issue of colorism is still prevalent in communities of color. The Black community is not exempt from it. We see skin tone discrimination in every sector of American society. And I realize this will shock my fellow citizens, but Columbia, Missouri, is no exception. Too often an "if you are light, you are right" mindset is practiced in our beloved city. It is mostly evidenced by how tokenism is carried out. The business community, for example, will hire a person of color if they are the right color. We as Black people cannot continue to either exercise the colorism bias among ourselves or refuse to point it out in the white community.

Audre Lorde suggests that difference is a reason for celebration and growth. It is being threatened by the Marjorie Taylor Greene and Candice Owens types who wish not only to remain "un-woke," but comatose. What Black history teaches is that we must constantly remain vigilant. The struggle for a just society is a constant battle. It is not won by one election, legislation or proclamation. Justice is an issue of the heart. To fight this battle is to fight with everything we have for the heart of America. For out of the heart flow the issues of life.

The power of the evangelical Christian church just might be in saving democracy

March 14, 2023

Let me begin by stating two facts. The first is that I am not an evangelical Christian. While I do practice Christianity, it is a progressive, African American Christianity of the authentic Black Church and not the conservative kind of the white Anglo-American evangelical Church. Second, I am not a Republican. I think the only Republican I have ever supported is Judge Josh Devine. I did not support him because he is a Republican. I support him because he is a good man.

Given what I have just stated there is a dangerous threat to American democracy upon us. It is instantiated by two political figures: Donald Trump and Ron DeSantis. Both individuals are the frontrunners of the Republican Party, and both are a danger to this republic.

All of us know that Trump exasperated the division that exists in this country. Now we are watching DeSantis fan the flames of division with his anti-woke rhetoric, banning of books, and racist anti-critical race theory methodologies. I believe both Trump and DeSantis are dangerous figures who have the support of the radical right.

The first question is: Who can stop these individuals from further damaging this democratic experiment known as the United States of America? Enter the Evangelical Church.

The evangelical church in America has what is necessary to stop both Trump and DeSantis. In the first instance they are large enough in population to prevent the MAGA people and DeSantis supporters at the polls. Second, evangelicals possess the economic resources to outspend Trump and DeSantis. And, we all know that money talks.

Some think the conservative evangelicals and the radical right are the same, but they are not. While both are conservative politically, evangelicals tend to support rational dialogue and projects that bring people together. They were embarrassed by Trump and are leery of DeSantis. I believe that the majority of evangelicals in this country know that both Trump and DeSantis will lead to a rift in this country that we may not be able to overcome.

Again, let me reiterate that I am neither a Republican nor an evangelical. I am, however, politically astute and I recognize that the Trump/DeSantis contingency is large and needs to be stopped. I also understand that evangelicals can stop Trump and DeSantis because they have the numbers and money to do so. My spiritual master says, "They who are for us are not against us."

The final question is will the American evangelical church stand up and be counted? Evangelicals insist that they are for unity. They will have a grand opportunity to show that they are willing to walk the walk and not just talk the talk.

If they do stand up and be counted, what unlikely saviors of democracy they would be.

Upcoming Columbia School Board election an important one for community

March 21, 2023

"Education makes a child unfit for slavery." - Frederick Douglass

Fast approaching is the election of candidates to the Columbia Public School Board. Seven candidates are running for three seats. In some ways this may be the most important public school board election for quite some time.

The fundamental question when electing school board officials is what kind of education will they support for our children? Will they propagate fear and prejudice, or will they promote an educational program that prepares our children for the challenges of the future? There is a clear choice. And who we elect will influence education in Columbia for a long time.

The issue is not Republican vs. Democrat, "woke" vs. traditional. The issue rests upon truth versus fallacy. The fallacy is this: if our children learn the truth about their history, they will hate one another. Some argue that if we allow our children to know what indigenous tribes occupied the Columbia area; or, if we teach what a gifted horseman Tom Bass was, such knowledge will somehow damage the psyche of our kids. I do not believe that. The more we learn the truth about our history, the better prepared we are to deal with the present and future challenges we will all face.

We have a problem with violence in Columbia. It is not evident only in certain sections of town, it is also affecting our schools. In some cases it is the result of mental health problems. Some of it is birthed by poverty and lack of resources. All of it affects our children and our community. The problem moves toward correction when education fosters unity, diversion and inclusion. It is imperative that those persons elected to the CPS board understand this fact.

It is hard for me to believe that parents want ignorance to take the place of knowledge in our educational system. I do not need courses on patriotism. When I learn the truth about America, I will be a patriot, but not a blind one. I will love the country that is and the country that America can be. Ignorance produces slavery to biases, ideologies, tribalism and falsity. Education of the right sort sets the captive free. I want my children to embrace freedom.

Each of us will have an opportunity to cast a vote soon. I know one of the candidates that will get my vote is James Gordon. If you listen to him he speaks with clarity and compassion. He believes in equipping our children for the future. We need a person of vision for the school board. He will get my vote and I encourage you to vote for him also.

Violence, again, keeps erupting in America

April 11, 2023

Once again violence has erupted in our society. Last week we witnessed a shooting in Nashville, Tennessee. This week a mass shooting happened in Louisville, Kentucky. All of us wonder what can be done to end this madness in our society. No place is immune from violence ... not even Columbia.

Many people suggest that the banning of assault rifles and stiffer background checks will stop mass shootings. Everyone knows that the only thing assault rifles are good for is killing people. No one rabbit hunts with an assault rifle. Yet, ideologues argue that banning assault rifles is a violation of the constitutional right to bear arms. Common sense states that access to assault weapons is the bane of our society, but of course, common sense is not all that common.

While I favor banning assault weapons and strict background checks, the problem will persist. If a person truly wants a weapon, one can buy one anywhere in this country. It will just be a little more expensive, but black-market weapons are available in generally every city in America. Plus, weapons need people to use them. The weapons do not kill Americans on their own. People are killing Americans.

So, what then is the cause of this disease of violence in America? Some people, like the thinker Thomas Hobbes, believe that there is a propensity in humans to commit violence to gain a sense of power. These individuals believe it is our thirst for power that drives us to be violent.

Some believe that the overall division in our society has driven us to anger and that anger has demonstrated itself in these mass shootings. Proponents of this idea suggest that most of us do not know how to deal with this deep-seated anger, and quite frankly any one of us could explode in rage at any time. These analysts state the hip-hop group NWA was correct about the general psychological state of too many Americans in singing: "Don't push me cause I'm close to the edge, I'm trying not to lose my head!"

Clearly many of us feel our lives are out of control. Most of us have dreamed of things and states of affairs that we will not experience. Most of us do not and have not gotten our first choice in jobs, homes, relationships, etc. Too many people feel trapped. Such situations produce despair and destructive behavior.

It is obvious that we need greater mental health resources in all our communities. Laws may be helpful in curbing the instances of death and violence, but laws alone will never be the answer. The violence we are witnessing is a result of a hole in our corporate souls. It cannot be filled with wealth, power, fame and/or pleasure. Something else is needed to fill the hole. I leave you to ponder what it can be.

My condolences to the families who have experienced the recent violence in Nashville, Louisville and other places in America ... and around the world. Perhaps one day we will learn to study war no more.

Intentional unity could bridge divides in today's society

April 25, 2023

"We are each other's harvest; we are each other's business; we are each other's magnitude and bond."- Gwendolyn Brooks

Woodrow Wilson once stated that as Americans we cannot be separated in interest or divided in purpose. To overcome the challenges that face us in society today, we must find a way to be united as a nation.

Wishful hoping for a unified society will not make this desire become a reality. Only intentional action will accomplish the goal. Several recent events have caused me to become more aware of the need for intentional unifying action. On Monday, I asked the students in one of my college courses if they knew of Uncle Tom and why was it offensive to call a person of color an Uncle Tom (Tio Taco for Latinos, Bananas for Asians, etc.). To my amazement none of them could answer the question.

None of them had ever read the book, "Uncle Tom's Cabin." And they lacked a knowledge of other racialized groups in America. No one in elementary school ever introduced them to Uncle Tom? Why has interracial knowledge become so absent in our society? If we do not know one another, how can we ever become one nation?

I do not lay all the blame on public or private education. Some of the blame is ours to acknowledge. As parents we have not prepared our children to live in a world that is multiracial and multicultural. Our other institutions are not doing the job either. I asked a devout Catholic did she know Father Tolton was Black and her answer was no. And all of us are aware that too many of our churches still place in our sanctuaries and in our literature images of a white Jesus.

Intentional unification must be our goal. Some things we must do immediately.

1. We must stop whitewashing our history. While understanding the impact of racism, sexism and homophobia may make Sally and Johnny uncomfortable, the fact is that if we do not teach the historical truth of this nation, we will continue to rear soft, ignorant children who become soft, ignorant adults. Truth sets the person free; falsehood makes us vulnerable to annihilation.

2. We must recultivate a sense of mutual responsibility. Crass individualism is perpetuating the mindset that it is all right to engage in shooting children who ring our doorbell by mistake or killing young adults at a Sweet 16 party. When we value one another as human beings of worth, regardless of race, color, gender, religion or political affiliation, we will become a society of one interest and purpose. The more we value one another, the less violence will happen in our community.

3. Collectively, we must be willing to move out of our comfort zones. For example, I love the fact that many white Christians are reading books about dismantling racism. Clearly that is a worthwhile endeavor. But until you break bread with me, be willing to sit and communicate with me in my environment, you will never know who I am. One of my African students told me that when she came to this country she was constantly encouraged to go to church with her white sponsor(s). Yet in all the time she has been in Columbia, she has never visited a Black church. She looks like me, but has never visited me? And we know her white sponsor has never visited the Black church. My point is that unless all of us are willing to break out of our comfortable

environments, unity will be nothing more than a dream.

No people divided can stand. The cost of our division will affect every level of our lives and the lives of our children. The time for action, intentional action, is now.

Cultivating relationships should be life's highest goal

May 16, 2023

"In all the world, there is no heart for me like yours. In all the world, there is no love for you like mine."- Maya Angelou

"What you going to do when death comes creepin' in the room?" - lyrics from an African American Spiritual

In the past two months death has taken from me two important people: my 48-year-old daughter, and my 68-year-old nephew who was more like a brother to me. To all of you who expressed to me your condolences and prayers, thank you.

Death has a way of reminding us of what is profoundly important in life. We spend so much time chasing the brass ring: fame, pleasure, success and wealth as if these elusive entities are what make life worth living. They are not.

It is alleged that the German philosopher Edmund Husserl stated that death has a way of setting our priorities in proper order. My experience is that he is right. What then should be our highest priority? I suggest it is cultivating and maintaining relationships.

Too often our egos cause us to forget two vital facts. One thing is certain: Life is short. All of us will have to leave here one day. And so, the relationships we have and can have will only be experienced in this brief lifetime. Therefore, we must make the most of the time we have.

The second fact is that relationships demand work. I wish I had a nickel for every time I heard someone boast, "I'm not letting a relationship change me!" If I did have those nickels, I would be a rich man. The truth of the matter is that relationships demand change and if one is not willing to change, that person does not want a relationship. Relationships progress by change.

What relationships should we cherish? Here are some hints.

Family. It is so easy to take family relationships for granted. We expect them to always continue in the form of unconditional love. The truth of the matter is that family relationships demand forgiveness, patience and acceptance of the person even if you do not like what they do.

Friendship. Aristotle suggested that three things make a healthy friendship: we enjoy their company, we affirm and admire some quality or qualities in the other, and the friend is dependable. Talk about a lot of work. Maybe if we paid attention to Aristotle, we would quit deceiving ourselves by thinking our 1,000 "friends" on Facebook are really our friends. To have a friend is to be friendly. I have learned that I have lots of acquaintances, but faithful friends are few. Cherish your friends.

Ourselves. Like far too many men, I have just started trying to be good to myself. I did not go to the doctor unless I had to go, I thought mental health care was overrated, etc. Now I realize that I must love myself to love others. Gentlemen take care of yourself. Go to the doctor. Be in touch with your whole self. You deserve it.

Your ultimate reality. I simply say this without explanation or interpretation.

Relationships make life complete. When we love our family, friends, and self rightly even death cannot break the bond of love.

Remembering Black soldiers ahead of Memorial Day

May 23, 2023

This weekend we honor those individuals who have given their lives for this democratic experiment known as the United States of America. This Memorial Day, I will focus on the Black men and women who fought and died for us.

It is a strange phenomenon in some ways. Beginning with Crispus Attucks, a former slave who was the first person to give his life to end British rule, and continuing with Black military personnel today, it is odd to ponder that Black people would die for a country where racism and sexism still rule the day. To be a Black soldier is to fight two battles simultaneously: the enemy on the battlefield, and the war against racism at home.

And yet, Black soldiers fought and died for the America they knew had the power to live up to its democratic ideals: "the many and the one."

I think about my father and his fellow soldiers in the 9th Cavalry during World War II. They were part of the segregated Army and also proud men who called themselves Americans. They could not eat in most restaurants or travel with their white counterparts yet had to face the possibility of being lynched. They put their lives on the line for an America that called them "niggas."

It is an integrated military today. And so, the evils of the past have been overcome — maybe. While more people of color have obtained high ranks, still racism looms large. Black soldiers still must suffer the indignities inflected in places like Southeast Missouri and Florida. As some things have changed, some things remain the same.

Those who were Black and died for America deserve special honor. They died for a country they loved that many times treated them as the unloved ones. They have taught all of us that sometimes you have to fight for something greater than yourself. They believed in the conceptual reality of a united society. They believed in an America that can be and did not allow the America that was and is now to prevent them from fulfilling their duty. These Black Americans deserve our highest praise.

So, as you celebrate and remember those who fought and died for the American Dream, please include a special prayer of thanks for soldiers of color, particularly Black soldiers who gave the ultimate sacrifice. May their lives not be in vain.

Colorism project continues with aim of understanding racism's roots

June 6, 2023

"Dark skin is not a crime.
Light skin is not a prize."
— Anan$i

"By virtue of living in a racist world non-Black people are raised to be anti-Black. We are all taught that lighter is better." -Poet Rupi Kaur, "Home Body"

Many of you are aware that I am conducting a research project titled "Colorism and Christianity." In a column from May 2022, I discussed that colorism is a form of racism that preferences light skin over dark skin. This bias permeates every social construct in America, and around the world.

Colorism is not just an American problem; it is a phenomenon that affects all people of color in all societies. It is, however, particularly devastating in the U.S. context.

Colorism influences who gets imprisoned, who gets the loan for a house, who is employed, where people live and their access to resources, who is chosen for marriage and who is not. Colorism affects us all in substantial ways. These facts are well documented. What has not been investigated in a serious manner is how Christianity has perpetuated or confronted colorism in the past and whether it continues to do so in the present. Such is my research.

Phase two of my project is now underway. For the summer I will be interviewing local area church members, historically Black and white, regarding the issue of colorism. In the next two weeks I will be interviewing the leadership and laity of Fifth Street Christian Church and Second Christian Church of Fulton. Both congregations are historically Black. I hope that in the coming weeks to interview historically white First Christian Church of Columbia, and First Christian Church of Fulton. I also want to interview these churches in Columbia: First Presbyterian Church, Calvary Episcopal Church, Columbia, Missouri United Methodist Church, St. Luke United Methodist, First Baptist Church and Second Baptist Church.

Each of these churches are the "pillar" Protestant Christian churches of Columbia. They are historically white and Black, and it will be interesting to see how they perceive the influence of colorism here in "little Dixie." At some point I would also love to engage the Crossing Church in this conversation.

Please note that the focus of this project is Protestant Christianity and not Christianity as a whole. I will engage in a research project on colorism and Roman Catholicism next, but for now the research focuses on Protestant Christianity. Protestant Christianity is the No. 1 religious expression of Black people in America and mid-Missouri. It was the Baptists, Episcopalians, Methodists, Presbyterians and Disciples of Christ who were the most active is "converting" enslaved Africans in America. This point is true in Columbia and Mid-Missouri.

I suggest that most African Americans in Columbia that practice the Christian religion are of one of the above groups. So, it makes logical sense to initially interview these church congregations to hear the story of colorism both past and present. I hope the forementioned churches will agree to be interviewed.

Why is this work important? It is another way of addressing the evils of racism. Unless we dismantle racism in all its forms, including colorism, we will be continually plagued by its power.

Juneteenth observations tell us to keep striving for freedom, equality

June 13, 2023

On Monday, Americans will celebrate Juneteenth, or "Freedom Day." The holiday commemorates the official end of the enslavement of African Americans in this country. It was 1865 when federal troops arrived in Galveston, Texas, to announce that all slaves were to be freed. While the Emancipation Proclamation was signed two years earlier, the symbol of freedom is celebrated across this nation.

Earlier, I suggested that the African American community ought to celebrate Juneteenth whether it was federal holiday or not. Now it is a federal holiday, and I am happy about it. But the power of Juneteenth is not in the creation of a national holiday. Juneteenth represents something much deeper.

Juneteenth reminds us that while freedom is a desire of every human being, freedom cannot be merely wished for. Freedom comes with struggle and pain. Our ancestors realized that freedom was not something that would come without great sacrifice. In contemporary society the question is: What are we willing to sacrifice to be truly free?

True freedom is a communal experience. We may not see chattel slavery in this country anymore, but many Americans, especially those that are Black and brown, are enslaved. Institutional racism still plagues Black and brown communities across the nation.

Economic disparity, the prison system, drugs, lack of mental health resources hold many brothers and sisters in captivity. Coupled with far-right wing lies and half-truths, freedom seems like a dream hoped for but never realized. Common sense suggests that no one is free until all are free. It is a shame that common sense is not all that common.

Juneteenth is the communal expression of the quest for freedom for all. I asked a local pastor if he felt free in the U.S. context, and would he be celebrating Juneteenth this year. His response was no. It was clear to him that Black people in America are not free. He said, "Blacks in America will never be free until the kingdom comes."

While it seems that freedom for Black people is an illusion, I believe that freedom is possible. I cannot expect God to do what we as human beings can do, and that is to create a just society where all are free. It is our charge to create such a society. Juneteenth says to keep on striving, keep fighting, keep pushing toward the goal before us — freedom.

"And before I'd be a slave, I 'd be buried in my grave and go home to be with God."

A few tips in your search for happiness

June 27, 2023

"Happiness is a state of mind."- Author unknown

I am noticing more posts on social media about being happy. We are urged to follow advice from the sages, or to incorporate habits into our daily lives, or spiritual practices all promising to make us happy.

One young person said to me, "I deserve to be happy!" I thought to myself: "hmmm, who promised that to her?" Clearly, many people are trying to find the secret of being happy.

Here are a few thoughts on happiness from an older man:

Happiness is an internal state and not the result of externalities. External things can give one a moment of joy, but not true happiness. Externalities will fade away and the continuous quest of trying to latch on to things to be happy ends in futility. More money, more problems. The more items, the greater the need for security. Fame is fleeting and pleasures easily can become perversions. Lao Tzu stated that all one needs is inside of us already. Happiness is internal.

Expecting someone to "make us happy" is a recipe for disaster. If we allow our happiness to depend on someone else, that is giving another person too much power. If the other can make us happy, that same person has the power to make us sad. Rather, the goal should be learning to be happy with the other person. If more marriages understood this concept, there would be less divorce.

Doing the right thing results in happiness. The Greeks called happiness eudaimonia. Aristotle suggested that happiness involves living a virtuous life. In other words, doing the good will create happiness. What is the good? Some may argue the good is debatable, but one thing is certain: When we treat others like we would want to be treated, happiness flourishes. People who lie, cheat, steal, scam, etc. live well. But people who treat others with respect and dignity sleep well.

Avoiding negative people contributes greatly to one's happiness. Hanging out with negative folks will cause you to be negative. Too much of their negativity will blind you to the beauty that is in the world and other people. Dismiss negative people and seek out those who still live in the world with a sense of childlike wonder.

Remember that your circumstance is not your conclusion. Everyone has trouble in their life sometimes. Some of us feel as if we have more than our fair share. Yet, we must remember that our troubles are only part of our life narrative. The old Negro spiritual states, "I'm so glad that trouble don't last always!" It doesn't and it will pass in due time. This too shall pass.

Find a spiritual practice. I am not advocating religiosity. I am talking about a spiritual practice that strengthens your resolve, connects you to the world in which you live and brings peace to your inner self. It can be deep breathing, meditation, prayer, reading sacred texts or spending time in nature. Whatever the practice, I have noticed that those who have a spiritual practice are happier in life. Don't be fooled. Spirituality is not opium; it is a way to have clarity.

Commit to something greater than yourself. I have talked about this in previous articles, but it is worth repeating. When you commit to something larger than you, you realize that life is worth living. When I was diagnosed last November with idiopathic pulmonary fibrosis, I almost gave up. Then it dawned on me that I have students that need my philosophical teaching, people that need to hear me preach, homeless folks who appreciate my words of encouragement. I have a research project on colorism and Christianity that will contribute to the dismantling of racism. I realized that "a charge to keep I have and a God to glorify," so no time for self-pity. When you commit to something greater than you, joy and happiness flood the soul. I hope these words bring you a greater sense of happiness.

Some African Americans question celebration of Independence Day

July 4, 2023

"We hold these truths to be self-evident, that all men are created equal, that they are endowed by their Creator with certain unalienable Rights, that among these are Life, Liberty, and the pursuit of Happiness."- From the Declaration of Independence

On July 4, members of this social experiment gather to celebration the separation from British rule declared in the Declaration of Independence. It is America's birthday.

There is a growing conversation in the Black community as to whether African Americans should celebrate the Fourth of July. Clearly the writers of the Declaration and its subsequent document, the Constitution of the United States omitted three groups of people from their thought and writings: women, Native Americans and enslaved African Americans. It is true that some of the architects of these documents were slaveholders, and because of these two facts many African Americans (as well as women and Indigenous people) are questioning whether we should celebrate the Fourth of July as Independence Day, since all of us were excluded in the mind of the framers.

It is a legitimate question to raise. When one considers the recent activity of the Supreme Court regarding women and their bodies, the movement to eradicate critical race theory and true history, the assault on voter rights, affirmative action, community policing and more, it makes you wonder if we who were left out of consideration in the beginning are still being ignored in the present. Why should I celebrate when I am seen as both "invisible and the problem"?

I suggest that African Americans should celebrate Independence Day despite the current realities we face daily. Why?

We should celebrate because the ideals expressed in the document are true. All humans are created equal and do have a right to life, liberty and the pursuit of happiness. While the writers only had a certain group of people in mind when they constructed the document — white male landowners — the truths of the document are bigger than the men who wrote it. All humans in this republic are important and worthy of dignity and respect. When government refuses to acknowledge or enforce our rights, we have the right to cry out "Black Lives Matter," "Our bodies, our choice."

We should celebrate Independence Day because we are Americans, too. We have tears in the bricks of this country and blood in the mortar of this democratic house. And while the words of James Baldwin remind us that this house is on fire, in the words of Harry Belafonte, we as African Americans are called to be firefighters in this house. This is our house. Yes, we are free of British rule, but the work of liberation goes on. As Black people, we are the soul of this nation. Therefore, we celebrate Independence Day as the "is but not yet!"

Since 1619, our struggle has been continuous. But we are Americans and despite what the Proud Boys, Oath Keepers, Donald Trump, Ron DeSantis, Marjorie Taylor Greene, Josh Hawley and the rest may say, America is our country. Lester Maddox, the KKK, Strom Thurman, Bull Connor did not stop us, and neither will the contemporary haters of democracy. Go celebrate Independence Day with hope because freedom for all will come.

Reading between the lines: a challenge for the Black church

July 11, 2023

"Education makes a child unfit for slavery. Education means emancipation. It means light and liberty. It means the uplifting of the soul of (humans) mans into the glorious light of truth, the light by which (humans) can only be made free."- Frederick Douglass

'The most common way people give up their power is by thinking they don't have any." - Alice Walker

Given the Supreme Courts reversal of affirmative action regarding college admissions, the banning of books by various school districts, the vicious attacks on critical race theory and the opposition to diversity and inclusion in education, it is painfully clear that conservative white America is no longer interested in educating Black youth.

The handwriting has been on the wall for some time, but we ignored the signs and failed to read between the lines.

As a Black community we have one of two choices: we can sit and gripe, or we can become proactive and address the reality of the situation.

We must take on the challenge of educating our children. There is no better institution in our community to tackle the issue than the Black church. It is one of a few institutions owned and operated by Black people. Since the Emancipation Proclamation, the Black church has been the center of Black communal life. It is time for the Black church to be the leader in education given the onslaught of racist, conservative politics in education.

While the situation we now face is alarming, it is not new. This is not the first time conservative white America has wanted to avoid educating Black people. Our response in the past has culminated in the creation of great educational institutions such as Fisk, Howard, Morehouse, Hampton, and other Black colleges and universities. Only during the fictitious promise of first-generation integration and the subsequent seduction of public and private white institutions did we abdicate our responsibility to educate ourselves. Now we are being forced to be educators, and rightfully so.

How do we accomplish such a task? Here are some preliminary actions that can empower us in the education of our community:

Stop copying white churches and recognize that we have a powerful and unique character as the Black church. Our theology is not grounded in white western European concepts, but instead in a theology from below which understands the significance of lived experience. Black biblical interpretation is matched with our experience of struggle in America. Instead of being something we are not, we must assert our uniqueness and reject racism, homophobia and sexism. Those are the characteristics of the oppressor and should not be incorporated in our actions.

Make Christian education - education. Why can't we incorporate math and science in our teaching about Abraham, Isaac and Jacob. Develop youth and senior adult gatherings for "storytelling." I began this column by quoting Frederick Douglass and Alice Walker. I would bet that most of the Black youth in our community do not know who Alice Walker is, nor why Frederick Douglass is an important figure. For example, if a school wants to ban Toni Morrison, we should make Morrison available to our youth. They should know that Father Tolton, Augustine and Origen were great Black thinkers. While the conservative love the fact that we are great entertainers, athletes and musicians particularly, we must demonstrate that we are also a great people worthy of dignity and respect.

Start encouraging our youth to attend HBCUs. If white institutions do not want us, support our historically Black higher education institutions. We must free ourselves of thinking that white is always better than Black. We must liberate our minds.

There is more to be said, but my limit is upon me. We have the power to become the educational force in the Black community. Next week I will discuss the creation of Black think tanks for the education of the Black community. The time of action is upon us.

Missouri prisoners are suffering in summer heat wave. We should fix that.

July 18, 2023

I guess I just do not get it. Regardless of our differences in race, gender, complexion, class, and politics I believe that most of the humans that I share this society with are basically good people.

I think most white people want to be good people but have allowed their access to privilege and power to get in the way of their common sense. Most Black Americans aspire to a life of liberty and happiness, but too many of us sabotage our own success by either taking on the characteristics of the oppressor, or, in the words of Professor John McWhorter, become comfortable with being the victim instead of the victor.

Overall, most Missourians are good people. So, when I found out the following, I was shocked: Of the 18 prisons in Missouri only seven are fully air conditioned, six are partially air conditioned.

This means that five prisons — Algoa, Moberly, Cameron, Bowling Green and Fordland — have no air conditioning at all.

Missouri is not alone in not providing universal air conditioning to its prisons. Alabama, Arizona, Georgia, Florida, Mississippi, Louisiana, North and South Carolina are states that are some of the hottest in America and do not provide universal air conditioning.

So, is the mindset that we should not only punish criminals but also cook them?

Across America we are experiencing heat temperatures that are record breaking. While Donald Trump tried to convince us that climate change is a farce, the proof is in the pudding. There are places in the U.S. that have recorded temperatures that are the hottest on earth as we know. Can you imagine being in buildings that have little or no air conditioning at simply 85 degrees? In such a situation with a heat index of 100 degrees or more, locking people in concrete buildings constitutes cruel and unusual punishment for the prisoners and the prison staff.

Surely there must be a better way than not providing universal air conditioning in our Missouri prisons. I cannot speak for other citizens of other states, but we who live in Missouri are better people than this, Democrats and Republicans, progressives and conservatives, white and people of color, we need to come together and rectify this situation.

If the temperatures continue to heat up as it has recently, we are going to see more prison violence. Why create such a situation when we can prevent tragedy from happening?

If you believe that universal air conditioning is best for Missouri prisons, I strongly encourage you to make your voice known. Write to your representatives and tell them to stop the cruelty by making prisons safe for prisoners and prison staff by universally air conditioning the prison facilities.

'The benefits of slavery' lessons in Florida leave out important details

July 25, 2023

The Florida Board of Education wants its students to have "a full picture of slavery." Thus, the Board is requiring teachers to instruct students on the benefits of slavery for the enslaved in America. Their argument is that enslaved Africans gained important skills while enslaved that would benefit them later. Therefore, slavery was a benefit for African Americans, right? Wrong.

This attempt to rewrite American history boggles the mind. Succinctly, there were no benefits to the phenomenon of slavery. If an African survived the Middle Passage, being a slave was a horrendous experience. People of African descent were tortured and murdered by their slaveowners. The raping of Black women was a frequent occurrence. Families were destroyed and Africans were robbed of their language and culture. Only by strength of heart and pure determination did Black people survive.

There are some consequences of slavery that the Florida Board of Education refuses to acknowledge. The psychological impact of slavery still haunts the Black community. Slavery created a sense of Black self-hatred that still must be confronted today. Everyday Black people must encourage themselves to overcome the residual effects of slavery.

Slavery reminds us of how cruel humans can be to each other. To deny another human being basic rights and dignity all in the name of wealth and prosperity is nothing short of cruelty.

Slavery also reminds us of how religion can be used to perpetuate the institution of slavery. False Christians used Christianity to fortify their right to control the enslaved. They preached and taught that "slaves should be obedient to their masters for slavery was the will of God." Such misinterpretation of the biblical texts was an instrument of white superiority with results being the concept of a white, male god, white Jesus and whiteness as the condition for holiness and purity. For example, all of us grew up with a picture of a white, blond haired, blue-eyed Jesus. All thinking people realize that Yeshua was not white. The picture was intentional. It was a way of implanting in the mind that whiteness was salvation.

The Florida Board of Education further demonstrates the need for critical race theory in the classroom. Only then will our children learn the truth about who we are as a society. Only the truth can set us free.

Looking ahead to possible candidates in the November election

August 2, 2023

In last week's column I suggested that the most interesting electoral race to watch is the one for Boone County associate circuit judge for District 10 between Kayla Jackson-Williams and Angela Peterson.

It will be interesting to see how voters cast their ballots Tuesday. Both women have impeccable credentials, and both women are Black.

I still think it will be an important race to watch, but now I must confess that I forgot to mention another important race. It is for the 47th Missouri House District featuring Chimene Schwach.

My understanding that if elected to the Missouri House, she would be the first Black woman to represent the 47th District. While that fact is extremely important, it is not the only reason she should be elected if she wins the Tuesday primary.

I have gotten the privilege to observe Ms. Schwach's work in this community, and she truly is an advocate for women and families in mid-Missouri. She has served on many committees and boards in our area and has proved that she is committed to justice for all people.

Chimene is both intelligent and kind. She would bring theoretical and practical knowledge, grounded in compassion to the Missouri House — something that is obviously needed in that body.

I do not believe that she will be corrupted by the status quo but continue to fearlessly fight for those who cannot fight for themselves.

I support Chimene Schwach, and I hope you will, too, if she goes on to face Republican John Martin in November. We need her voice in the Missouri House.

Was Alabama riverfront brawl racially motivated? It might be hard for some people to say so.

August 8, 2023

By now you have likely seen the viral video of a group of white men attacking a 65-year-old Black security guard at the Montgomery, Alabama, riverfront. Allegedly the incident occurred when the security guard asked a group of white boaters to move their rivercraft. In the video two white men began to fight the security guard, which led to two more white men attacking the guard.

Subsequently, Black men came to the rescue of the security guard, and that escalated to a full brawl between Black and white people on the riverfront. The police arrived and arrested several people, and the mayor of Montgomery has called for a full investigation as to whether the incident was "racially motivated." One thing is without question: The security guard was simply trying to do his job.

While I appreciate that the mayor of Montgomery has called for a full investigation, and promised that "justice will be done," what evidence can be presented that will prove to a divided America that the incident was racially motivated? One thing I have learned about living in America is that people do not see racist actions until they see it. For the most part, many white people just do not see it.

The one redeeming quality about the melee is that no guns were involved. It was an old-fashioned fist fight. I am not advocating violence or condoning fighting, but in a society where people are so quick to pull a gun and shoot someone, I am glad no guns were involved.

There is a group of people in our society that believe that they are entitled and that their historic access to privilege and power gives them the right to do what they want. Clearly those who attacked the security guard were not going to let that old Black man tell them what to do. Could the same event have happened by Black men and a white security guard? Of course. The problem is that such acts of assumed entitlement happen with white people against people of color more often than vice versa. But you cannot see it until you see it.

In a previous column I suggested there is a hole in the soul of America. The increased incidents of hatred and schism point to the hole in our soul. If we do not find a way to overcome racial hatred, we may find ourselves in a situation where we cannot recover. History teaches that great societies are destroyed not by external factors but by the enemy within. We have seen the enemy and it is us.

Nevertheless, I still have hope. We are a great society. We can overcome any obstacle that divides us, if we make up our mind to do so. A person asked me recently how I can be hopeful in times like these. My simple response is "Hope that is seen is not hope. Faith is the substance of things hoped for and the evidence of things not seen."

What is the vision for America? We have to be willing to create it.

August 15, 2023

"Write the vision and make it plain..." -From the Tanak, Habakkuk 2:2

"Vision is the art of seeing what is invisible to others."- Jonathan Swift

Recently on one of our local radio stations the question was asked that if you had three wishes for the next 10 years, what would they be? One respondent said that his first wish would be that we as people in this society would remove the division that exists between us and come together. What a marvelous wish.

The problem with wishes is that wishes without action and passion is simply daydreaming. For wishes to become reality the wish must be comprised of vision, work and commitment.

What is the vision for America? If it is unity, how do we accomplish the goal? We have learned (I hope) that political maneuvering is not bringing us together. Unity cannot be accomplished by one political party, regardless of the rhetoric we are hearing. It is not about a conservative agenda or a progressive agenda. The vision of a united

America must be grounded in a human agenda, one that recognizes the dignity and worth of every American.

We will disagree about aspects of the vision, but it need not make us disagreeable or willing to engage in senseless violence. Aristotle once stated that the evidence of an educated mind is the ability to entertain a thought without accepting it.

Without a clear and constructive vision of America we are headed toward chaos. Dr. Martin Luther King Jr. reminded us of the possibility of chaos in his book, "Where Do We Go from Here: Chaos or Community?" It is worth reading again. King reminds us that we have a choice about how the future will be shaped.

As a process thinker, I am convinced that the future is radically free. I suggest that even God does not know the future, but rather God knows every combination of every possibility. Which action we will take is totally left to us. Such is the awesome and dreadful gift of free will.

Our power to imagine a new and better society lies within us. The vision needed is not with politicians but with us. Are we willing to commit to a beloved community where all are treated justly? We can imagine it; we just must be willing to create it. Our children desire and deserve better than what we are experiencing now.

What are you envisioning for America, for Columbia, for your neighborhood? Are we going to continue to be divided by racial injustice, classism, economic disparity, sexism and homophobia? Or instead, will we commit to the fundamentally new? The power is in our hands. What is your vision?

The March on Washington, Black church activism and the challenge for today

August 29, 2023

Monday commemorated the 60th anniversary of the March on Washington. The March, on Aug. 28, 1963, is also referred to as the March for Jobs and Civil Rights.

It was a landmark event organized by over 50 different groups, particularly Black church organizations. The March's chief organizer was the Rev. Dr. Martin Luther King, Jr. It is estimated that over 200,000 people participated in the March, and it is recognized as the pivotal event that led to the Civil Rights Act of 1964.

To simply see the March on Washington as a commemoration alone is a huge mistake. With the recent acts of violence against people of color as in Jacksonville, Florida and Montgomery, Alabama, the attempts to whiten Black History, and the banning of books in many school districts across the nation, the March on Washington is a call to the Black church for social activism.

The Black church in recent years has been far too complacent. Too many Black church leaders have remained silent in the current environment of racial division and racial injustice. Now is the time for the Black church to address the economic disparity that exists in this country. We can no longer be satisfied with demonstrations of religious exuberance; we must be part of the vanguard that confronts the racial injustice that is evident all around us.

Too often I think we, as Black people, assumed that the Civil Rights movement of the 1960s was the end of the struggle. It is true that some things have changed. Colored water fountains no longer exist. Overt discrimination is now unlawful. Yet, racism remains a threat to the health and well-being of Black people, and all people of color, in America.

So, what must we do? First, we must hold people responsible for their actions. When injustices occur, we must open our mouths and stand together. We must recognize the political, social and economic power that is in our hands.

This action also demands that we overcome the pettiness and egoism that thwarts our movement toward justice. The time of the big "I" little "you" syndrome must come to an end.

Second, we must build coalitions with our fellow members of color. A great opportunity to unite with the Latin, Indigenous and Asian communities is before us. The same tools of oppression that are used against the Black community are used against other people of color.

Third, we must be willing to remember that they who are for us are not against us. If the goal is justice, religious doctrine cannot stand in the way of progress. There are non-Christian folks who are committed to justice among us. We must adopt a more inclusive approach if we truly want the beloved community to become a reality.

I believe that though the battle will be tough, victory is before us. We must be willing to seize the opportunity. The March on Washington of 1963 is asking all of us, "Are you willing to be a solution, or are you going to be the problem?" There is not an in-between position.

Rediscovering joy in your life

September 5, 2023

"Joy, joy

Down in my soul

Sweet, sweet soul saving joy Oh, joy down in my soul!"

— Lyrics from a contemporary Black Gospel song

Far too many people I know are miserable. Situations in life can cause one to think "what's the use of trying when nothing good comes my way?" Such melancholy and despair can be caused by several things: illness, lack of financial resources, domestic issues with children and/or partners, unsatisfying employment or unemployment, loneliness, and on and on.

I challenge us to think about the possibility that life can be wonderful and filled with joy. I suggest that the rediscovery of joy demands intentional action on every person's part. It does not simply come out of the sky. It demands work.

In attempting to rediscovery joy in life I posit the following actions.

• Joy as happiness is a moral state and not a feeling state, as Aristotle stated. In other words, to be happy and receive joy one must learn to live in the right relationship with oneself and other people.

We cannot participate in destructive behaviors if we are to rediscover joy. Self-destructive behaviors sabotage our quest for joy. Gossip, pettiness, overindulgence and obsession with things/wealth, pleasures and fame all are joy killers and lead to depression and self-loathing.

When we live rightly with other people the relationship becomes a catalyst for joy. Racism, jealousy, sexism, irrational political indoctrination and homophobia treat other people as "the other" that leads to immortality and pain. Even when we acknowledge that we haven't treated ourselves or others rightly, intentionally acting to correct the problem brings joy.

Then one can say, "I may not be what I ought to be, but I affirm that I am not what I use to be … and that brings me joy," as Dr. Martin Luther King said.

• Take a break from social media. Our constant use (obsession maybe?) with electronics interferes with finding joy.

Being constantly tethered to social media prevents interaction with self and others, causing us to be lost in a virtual world. Joy is found in the actual world. Thus, spend some time with yourself living mindfully in the present.

Hear the birds, observe the wind rustling in the trees. Living mindfully in the present will save us from guilt and shame about the past and worry about tomorrow as the Chinese philosopher Lao Tzu advised.

Separation from electronics will help you to discover that people are interesting. All people are not jerks, some of them have amazing narratives and personalities worth knowing. Watch how much joy you experience in the discovery.

• Commit to something bigger than you. I have stated this before, but it is worth stating again. Committing to something greater than myself gives me purpose in life. I have a terminal disease.

It would be easy for me to say, "I give up" and wallow in self-pity. But I realized that in engaging in the "Colorism and Christianity" research project, I have an opportunity to contribute something meaningful to the human project.

Whether people support it or not, whether people accept it or not, if I am ill or not, I have joy knowing that I am giving my all to something bigger than myself — and that brings me joy.

You may not want to engage in a research project but find something to commit to that is bigger than yourself and I guarantee it will bring you joy.

• Hold on to your faith, however you interpret that faith. It may be the type of faith that believes justice will become a reality.

It may consist of formal, traditional religiosity, or not. But your faith will remind you that "it ain't over til its over!" Hold fast, be of good faith, and high step into tomorrow.

May something written cause you to rediscover your joy in life. The world we live in is rife with problems. But life is still good. Find joy.

Reflections on Sept. 11 linger after 22 years

September 12, 2023

Sept. 11 holds a very special meaning for me.

On Sept. 11, 1977, I was ordained into the Christian ministry. For 46 years I have tried to give a word of encouragement to those who feel disenfranchised, disinherited and disillusioned. I have been striving to bring "good news" despite so much bad news around us.

On Sept. 11, 22 years ago, two of my classmates died in the World Trade Center attack in New York City. It was one thing to see the devastation. It is quite another to personally know someone who died in that horror. Sept. 11 holds a profound place in the museum of my memories.

These two events shaped my life and thinking in very critical ways. My ordination reminds me that even though you are called to a task, it does not mean you will always be accepted and understood. Because you have a gift does not mean that sometimes you will not fall flat on your face. I have experienced some of the best and worst in Christianity. I have observed great acts of compassion and sacrifice for others by Christians; and, I have observed some of the most hateful and cruel things enacted and stated by so-called Christian people. I am reminded that in all of us, and our socially constructed institutions, there is some good in us, and there is some evil in us.

The same is true about the 9/11 attacks of 2001. I watched Americans come together as one people even if it was for a moment. In New York, people of every kindred and clan searched for survivors, tended to people's physical and emotional wounds, and spoke of life and hope in the midst of darkness. But I also watched us divide by religious and ethnic communities. A real anti-Muslim sentiment was fostered in America that continues to this day.

Sept. 11 causes me to ponder what I believe and what is important to me. I think about what I mean by God, faith, love, trust and community. There is no one answer to these concepts. Theologians and philosophers agree and disagree. If you think that there is only one true faith or way we can become a community, or one definition of love, you are fooling yourselves.

Tragedy has a way of forcing us to prioritize our lives. When I was traveling around the country preaching revivals 20-25 weeks per year, I thought I was making a difference. But was I making a difference or simply giving nice talks? The attack of 9/11 reminds us that life can change in a moment without warning. Given that fact, what is truly important to you and what have we claimed to be important because of social pressure and cultural nuance and tradition?

9/11 holds special meaning for me.

Remembering our daughters

September 26, 2023

Last Sunday was National Daughters Day. Celebrated the last Sunday of September, it is a time to tell our daughters how happy we are to have them as part of our lives. Having a daughter is truly a blessing.

I have five daughters. They are each beautiful, unique and wonderfully gifted.

One of the first things I had to learn was that a good parent must recognize the similarity and individuality of daughters.

Every time I forgot to accept my daughters as unique individuals, chaos erupted. They would forcibly remind me that they were their own person and that I should respect their uniqueness.

I am a slow learner, but once I get it, I get it.

More than the obvious, daughters are not sons. Rearing them in a nontoxic environment takes work.

There are different patterns of thinking, different priorities and different visions that daughters hold.

I am not talking about the sexist rhetoric of making girls one way and boys another. I am talking about how girls conceptualize the world they live in. Woman are different creatures than us men.

Watching my daughters figure out their own strategies of how to survive in the world was miraculous. I say miraculous because like too many men, many times I wanted to "jump in and fix it" instead of letting them tell me what they needed. Finally, I learned to listen more than talk.

Recently, one of my daughters died. She was 48 years old. She had some lung issues, but she had been released from the hospital and seemed to be doing well at home. Suddenly she contracted COVID-19 and subsequently died.

The other thing I learned is that nothing can separate us from the love we shared, not even death.

Let me be clear: There are times you may not like certain things your daughters do. There are times they do not like some things we do as parents.

After all, being a parent does not make one a perfect human being. But, at no point should we ever stop loving one another.

At a Baptist church where I once was pastor, there was a mother who refused to invite her daughter to the family reunion. The daughter had married a Muslim man.

The mother fumed and fussed about how the daughter had turned her back on the Christian faith and had shamed the family, was going to hell and was a disgrace, etc. I suggested that she was still the daughter she gave birth to and the love between them should overcome everything else.

So, while she can't have the pork ribs because of her new faith, give her some barbecue chicken, and hug her tightly, because you never know when one of you will die, and you don't want to go to the grave saying, "If I could have done differently ... I should have!"

One of the coolest things that is happening in my life is that now I am watching my granddaughters mature into young women. Every time I look at them, listen to them talk, or watch them in action I realize that God has blessed me tremendously. I am watching these girls become their own person and I am grateful.

If you haven't told your daughters or granddaughters that you love them, do so today. You will be glad you did and tomorrow may be too late.

Who sits at the decision-making table? City needs to hear from people living with violence

October 3, 2023

The news of the tragic death of a Columbia toddler rocked the soul of our community. Once again gun violence has caused us to mourn and ask why?

The mayor has stated that she wants a special Office of Violence Prevention to address violence in Columbia. She has stated that her hope is to bring members of the community together to raise the critical issues and form productive strategies to make Columbia safer. Good idea.

Too many citizens in Columbia have thought of the city as immune to the kind of gun violence seen in places such as Chicago, New York and other metropolitan cities in America. Of course, those of us who live in central Columbia have known for a long time the difference of violence in Chicago and Columbia is a difference of degree and not kind. We live with the threat every day.

I am certainly supportive of the mayor's initiative. Anything we can do will help if we address the root causes of the violence we see in Columbia and not avoid the issues. Allow me to state some obvious ones, though not all.

Economic disparity in Columbia is a real problem that breeds violence. While it is estimated that the average income in Columbia is approximately $50,000 a year, that is very misleading. The fact is that people in the south and west of Columbia have incomes exceeding $100,000 a year, while communities I live in and citizens I speak with have incomes less than $25,000 a year. Such a huge disparity causes anger and violence.

Our educational system needs a serious overhaul. Too many of our children cannot read or do simple math. Too often students are passed from one grade to another while schools know that they are functionally illiterate. To add insult to injury, our teachers are underpaid and overworked and end up being juvenile officers instead of educators.

We have a racial problem in Columbia. While we look like we all get along, the fact is that the systems people of color must encounter daily are extremely racist. Thinking we are being diverse and inclusive, most times we are perpetuating tokenism and thinking we are post-racial agents of change. Until we invite members from the underclass to sit at the table where decisions are made, our efforts to address the root causes of violence are nothing more than exercises in folly. I know what the elite think the problem is. I want to hear from those who live with the problem every day.

I believe Mayor Buffaloe is moving in the right direction. I just hope that we really do include the voices of the underclass and not just the privileged.

Some tips for finding peace amid the storms of life

October 17, 2023

"Peace begins with a smile."- Mother Teresa

"Peace is its own reward."- Mahatma Gandhi

In every corner of human life, storms are raging. The war in Israel with Hamas, as well as the conflict between Ukraine and Russia, reminds us poignantly of how destructive storms can be. The continued labor strike by United Auto Workers and Screen Actors Guild-American Federation of Television and Radio Artists point to the fact the storms are not just "over there somewhere," but are indeed right here at home. The ridiculous situation in the House of Representatives is proof that we are living in a time where common sense is at an all-time low.

If these occurrences do not cause our hearts to bleed, the propensity for community violence, the situation at the Mexican-U.S. border and acts of racial and religious hatred in every sector of society certainly should do so. It is truly the winter of our discontent.

Yet our human spirits yearn for peace. With so much discord and conflict surrounding us, the question is how do we maintain a sense of equilibrium in a world of chaos? Is it even possible to find peace during these turbulent times?

Times of discord, division and disharmony are also opportunities to create conditions for peace. Here are a few suggestions.

We must stop being merely "peace-seekers" and be peacemakers.

The quote "Peace is its own reward," from Mother Teresa is so simple yet powerful. To smile at ourselves, others and our situations reminds us that we can create peace in our own spheres of influence: the grocery shop, the open market, the gas station, etc. Peacemaking is a verb, not a noun. It is something we do and not just desire. The time is upon us to be the solution we want to see.

Breathe.

We are constantly bombarded via the media in all its forms with images of violence and destruction. We are humans and basically good. When we see so much devastation it causes us to be tense and sometimes despondent, which saps us of our sense of peace. But if we turn off our electronics and just breathe deeply, we will realize that goodness, justice and compassion still exist in the world. A Hindu friend of mine once stated that it is impossible to remain angry when you take the time to breathe deeply. I agree. Take time to breathe and you will come to the realization that trouble will not last forever.

Trust the God that dwells at the altar of your own heart.

I am not talking about being religious. Being religious has contributed to the destruction of peace we are experiencing in the contemporary moment. I am talking about the faith you have in whatever you hold as ultimate in your life, trust it to carry you through the storms of life. There is peace when one communes with one' s ultimate reality.

All of us go through storms. Some of the storms are personal. Others are storms that affect the whole human community. If we become peacemakers, take time to breathe and trust the God of our own hearts, I believe that we will experience a peace that is its own reward.

Build your character with persistence and courage

November 7, 2023

"Courage is the most important of all the virtues because without courage, you can't practice any other virtue consistently."- Maya Angelou

If you are like me, life is a continuous stream of hectic activity. Given the constant demands we face each day, it is difficult to practice persistence.

Persistence is the firm or obstinate continuance in a course of action despite difficulty or opposition. Notice that to be persistent is to acknowledge that life is full of difficulty and opposition. Perhaps that is why Maya Angelou states persistence requires courage.

I think most people want to be persistent regarding their dreams and ideals. No one wants to be wishy-washy in living. We want to be the type of person who is steadfast and unmovable, with our actions matching our words. But the question is how do we remain persistent in achieving our highest goals?

There are a few suggestions I became acquainted with that I believe will help us be persistent actors in a world of chaos, fickleness and inconsistency.

1. To be persistent one must set small, achievable goals in life. Each accomplishment encourages and empowers one to continue to stick to the task. As a child, an older Black man once asked me, "Boy, how do you eat an elephant?" I responded, "I don't know, sir." He concluded, "One bite at a time." Achieving small goals is like eating an elephant one bite at a time.

2. Remain in the moment. The busyness of life can make our actions inconsistent, bouncing from one thing to another, robbing us of persistence. To remain in the moment frees us from agonizing about the past and worrying about the future.

3. Remember the "why" of the task before us. Why did you commit to environmental responsibility? Why did you believe that social justice is of paramount importance? Remembering the "why" keeps our commitment strong and rejuvenates our passion.

4. Focus on the journey and not the end. Being engaged in the journey is far more important than the anticipated result. I wish I had learned this fact early in my ministry. I was so focused on the end vision that many times I lost sight of the joy of working with others, experiencing creativity and the wonder of serendipity in the

journey. The journey is the real impetus for persistence.

5. Avoid negative people. The negativity of others can sap your energy. Surround yourself with positive people. The collective positive energy will help you to remain persistent.

6. Express gratitude. If we are not careful, we can be so absorbed and seduced by the spirits of wealth, success and fame that we forget to be grateful for all the universe has sent our way. I used to hear the community of my nurture say, "If you can't be grateful for what you have, you never will be grateful for what you get." Be grateful for all things: the mountaintop experiences and the valleys, the victories and the defeats, for they both teach us something.

I wish you the power of persistence. Persistence builds character.

Criticism can help us move forward in life, work

November 14, 2023

Isn't it interesting that you can receive one hundred compliments about your abilities or talent and receive one criticism and you focus on the criticism more than the compliments.

Unless you have committed your life to isolation and non-productivity, you will face criticism. It is one of the eternal truths of human existence.

Given the fact that all of us experience criticism at some point in our life, the question is not how to avoid it, but rather how do we best deal with criticism. Here are a few suggestions.

Criticism comes in two basic forms: constructive and destructive. We must accept constructive criticism with a sense of gratitude, if it is truly constructive, it will help us become better at our craft. Destructive criticism should be allowed to go into one ear and out the other ear. If the criticism cannot help you, ignore it and keep moving forward.

Most people who are constantly critical of others are usually unhappy with themselves. Since they are unhappy, they gleefully attempt to make others unhappy as well. Don't carry other peoples' crosses. Realize that you have worth and don't let negative people rule your life.

Know and believe in yourself. Socrates taught us that the greatest task in life is to 'know thyself.' If you know who you are then believe in your worth. Know that the value of your worth is not dependent on other people's opinion. I truly believe that everyone has a gift inside of them. If you care for and nurture your gift, your gift will make room for you. And none of this based on other people's opinions.

Stop being soft-skinned. We have become too fragile thus, subsequently, we are rearing fragile children. Never in my lifetime has the suicide rate been so high among adults and our youth, especially Black adults and Black youth. We must remember that we come from hearty stock. There have always been bullies. But our fore parents taught us that the best way to beat a bully is to be successful. Negative criticism will come, but your resolution to stir up the gift within you will bring you the kind of success that vanquishes bullies.

Be grateful for your haters. Your haters — and everyone has haters — make you stronger. The comedian Katt Williams once said, "If you don't have more haters now than you did this time last year, you are not on your job, baby!" I am trying to increase my haters every day. The more naysayers and negative criticism you experience, the more you are on your job.

I am not minimizing the fact that negative criticism is painful, however enduring the pain is a necessary condition of growth. There are four kinds of people in our lives:

1. Those who like and love us for the right reasons;
2. Those who like and love us for the wrong reasons;
3. Those who dislike us for the right reasons; and
4. Those who dislike us for the for the wrong reasons.

Only those who like and dislike us for the right reasons are the ones who truly matter. So be strong, suck it up and face negative criticism with faith and courage. For this, too, shall pass.

Being thankful after Thanksgiving

November 28, 2023

Last week we gathered with family and friends to celebrate Thanksgiving. I hope that for all of you it was a joyous and digestible time. But now that the turkey and fixings are gone, how do we continue to express a spirit of thankfulness once the holiday has passed?

It is notable that many people experience sadness after holiday festivities. Gone are the guests and Thanksgiving decorations and we return to the ho hum of everyday life.

For many people post-holiday depression is a reality.

Perhaps a refocusing is needed to avoid the doldrums; perhaps we need to find a way to practice thanksgiving every day. How you may ask? How about the following:

I think we should give thanks for life.

A year ago this month, the first medical team informed me that I have idiopathic pulmonary fibrosis. The youngest member of the medical team walked into the room, told me that I had the disease and he estimated that I would be dead in six months or so. As you can see, I am still here.

What the young fellow did, however, was to poignantly remind me that life, no matter the state, is precious. More than ever, I am thankful to be alive. I may not have everything I want but I am alive. The fact that we are alive is something to give thanks for every day. Afterall, the alternative is far worst.

• We should give thanks for true friends.

I have learned that most people have lots of acquaintances but very few true friends. Aristotle stated that friendship consists of three characteristics: 1. If one has a friend, that person has some characteristic that you admire. It could be their sense of purpose and drive, or their compassionate spirit. But whatever it is, that quality in them is admirable. 2. A true friend is dependable. You can count on them in the ups and downs of life. 3. If the other is truly a friend, you enjoy their company. It is alleged that Aristotle concluded that if one has a true friend that person has been blessed. I give thanks for my true friends, for through and by them I have been blessed. Isn't the same true for you?

We can be thankful for becoming the person that we are.

No, we are not perfect and yes, we have proclivities and issues, But we are not what we use to be. We are growing and evolving. We must realize that each of us are the most unique persons on the planet. No other human being has your swagger, your thoughts, your style. We can stop seeking affirmation from others and start celebrating and giving thanks for who we are.

• Of course, as a theist, I am continuously thankful for the God who resides at the altar of my heart.

Once a fellow philosopher told me that I would be a pretty good philosopher if I got rid of that God stuff, my reply to him was that he would probably be a pretty good person if perhaps he had a little God stuff. I do not try to make people believe in God. Instead, I try to let people see the God in me. The God of the altar of my heart is not contained in a doctrine or dogma. I no longer need others to affirm our relationship nor set the context of who and what God is. God and I are cool. And the God I know is teaching me how to love others without making them in my image and likeness, even when they are racist, sexist and homophobic. For this, I give thanks.

I hope your sense of thankfulness extends beyond the holiday, and that someway, somehow, we together may learn to be thankful every day.

When words become more than just words

December 12, 2023

Let me begin by saying I am an avid proponent of free speech. I believe that for a society to live up to its true democratic ideals, freedom of speech is a necessary component.

Yet with the rise of antisemitism and other forms of hate speech, we must ponder what is the line between free speech and the abuse of free speech.

The testimony of the three elite university presidents last week only complicated the matter. Clearly antisemitic speech cannot be condoned. Yet, these highly educated women seemed befuddled about when an institution should prohibit hate speech. To them it seems that it boils down to an issue of freedom of speech.

This question seemed simpler in the past. Most of my generation operated by a notion that, "sticks and stones may break my bones, but words will never hurt me." Indeed, that notion is false.

The rise of hate speech has greatly contributed to the rise of suicide in youth and adults, racial conflict, discrimination against women, attacks on the LGBTQ+ community, and overall discord within this democratic experiment. We no longer merely "agree to disagree." Now, we disagree and seek to destroy the other.

What is the root cause of the amount of hate speech we are observing today? Part of it lies in xenophobia. The fear of the other creates the necessary and sufficient conditions for what we are experiencing. Social media did not create hate speech. It is simply a tool used by xenophobes. Trump didn't create it, he merely fanned — and is still fanning — the flame.

I posit that xenophobia is a sickness of the soul and that if we do not find a balm for it, xenophobia will cause our demise as a nation.

Somehow, we must discover new ways to reconnect with each other. We must insist that difference is not bad, but destroying others is.

Every institution must commit to stopping hate speech and affirm the beloved community. I am not advocating sentimentality. I am suggesting that we must become intentional in both speech and action to create the common good. We can no longer just wish for change; we must be the change we desire.

We can create laws to prohibit hate speech. But a long time ago I learned that laws cannot make us love and respect one another. Respect and love come from the heart. Both are the result of good character. So, ultimately it is about character. Good character always says," I won't harm you with words from my mouth; I love you, and I need you to survive."

A meditation for the season

December 19, 2023

In this time of polarization and conflict, it is difficult to find depth and meaning in the traditional affirmation "Peace on Earth and Good Will to All Humanity."

While the statement is found in the narrative of Christianity, it is not confined to Christianity.

This declaration expresses a universal hope that is beyond religiosity. I believe that we deeply desire peace, but we live in a constant state of war. Antinomy makes us question whether peace and good will are possible.

Part of the problem is that too many humans are peace-seekers rather than peacemakers. Being a peacemaker means that we must step out of our comfort zones and allow ourselves to be vulnerable.

Peace seeking is admirable, but peacemaking is painful. We cannot allow political agendas, cultural falsehoods and/or our egos reign over our actions if we are to be peacemakers on earth.

Accepting the challenge of peacemaking promotes goodwill to all. Indeed, there are numerous examples of willing the good for our kindred and kind. But that kind of 'willing' only promotes tribalism. Willing the good for all humanity demands willing the good for those who do not look like us or live like us. It is a kind of 'willing' that insists that all human beings are worthy of dignity, honor and respect.

I realize that many people will find this meditation a flight of fantasy. I agree that its roots are within the human imagination. But I maintain that what can be imagined can be realized.

If we practice peace, we can construct an arena of goodwill to all. I am committed to the idea in both word and deed. I hope you are too.

And so, I wish you peace and will the good for your life. Happy holidays.

2024

Make resolutions for 2024 that will make you feel and be better

January 2, 2024

This is the time of the year that we make resolutions for a new year. Whether the resolution is to lose weight or fall in love, resolution-making is a favorite American activity.

The goal of human life is to find eudaimonia (happiness) and so our resolutions ought to bring us closer to a happier life. Here are a few resolutions suggestions that hopefully will make 2024 better than 2023.

Resolve to be kinder in 2024 than I was last year.

All of us are aware that humans can be both hard and cold or warm and compassionate. I am resolved to be a kinder person this year. I want to not only be kind to others but to myself. We must remind ourselves that we are special and deserving of kindness. When we are kind to ourselves, being kind to others becomes much easier.

- Demand truth over opinion.

We are bombarded with misinformation on every front. Only truth can set us free. Just because the information you receive is tantalizing or purported to come from your favorite personality or politician does not make it true. Truth demands rational justification. Ask yourself "what is the evidence for the proposition?" If it lacks solid justification, reject it. One can never be happy if we live a lie. Resolve to know the truth.

- Dismiss negative people.

Life is short. If you are constantly surrounded by negativity, it will hurt both your body and soul. Hang with positivity. Associate with people who believe in the possibility of a new day, a better society, the building of a beloved community. I guarantee you will feel and be better.

- Make gratitude a daily practice.

Start every day being grateful for life and opportunity. We may not live in our dream home or have our dream job, but we can still practice gratitude for what we do possess. We may not have the best health, but we have a portion of health and strength and for that we can be grateful. Ungrateful people are mean and bitter. The practice of gratitude will elevate your life.

- Forgive those who have wronged you and forgive yourself for the wrongs you have committed.

Forgiveness allows you to heal and grow. Without forgiveness we end up sleeping with ghosts from the past. When we forgive, we will experience forgiveness. I posit that all of us need to be forgiven for some error we have committed in the past. Forgive and be forgiven.

- Expect a miracle in your life.

Every day I expect something miraculously wonderful to happen. Why not? Isn't it better to expect a miracle than to pessimistically anticipate something bad? Go and expect something wonderful and might be pleasantly surprised.

Happy New Year and may your days bring you happiness and joy.

Let's work harder at finding the good all around us

January 23, 2024

"Find the Good. Seek Unity. Ignore the divisions among us." - Aristotle

For the next three weeks I will concentrate on the above Aristotelian thought. Why? It is clear to me that this simple utterance compels us to act in a manner that is most needed in Columbia and the country.

We are urged to find the good, but what is that? Far too many people I talk with function as if the good is neither knowable nor obtainable. We have operated in the realm of individual, subjective relativism for so long that our sense of an objective good has almost vanished. Finding the good demands moving beyond our self-centeredness. If what we find is good, it will constitute an environment that produces goodness for all of us.

I do not pretend that I have all the answers in our quest for the good, but I believe that if something is to stand as the good it must benefit all members of society.

For instance, when senior citizens are forced to make decisions monthly on whether to buy food or medication, something is drastically wrong. If free health care is impossible, can we at least have affordable health care and take the foot of Big Pharma off people's necks?

There is goodness all around us. How about the marvelous sense of wonder that small children possess? Or think about how a musical piece or work of art captured your passion and imagination? Remember how spectacular it was to have a conversation about ideas and possibilities and not divisive party politics? The good exists, we just must seriously look for it.

We know that the good for this society will never be found if we do not learn to harness our egos, move beyond our greed and commit to the well-being of those around us. We, too often, are our own worst enemy. Much of the hatefulness and viciousness we see daily can be eliminated if we would simply love the other person as we love ourselves. But, of course, what is simple is often the hardest thing to do.

Find the good and manifest it everywhere we go. It will make us better people and a better society. Next week: Seek unity.

Black History Month is a good time to start work of redeeming 'blackness'

February 6, 2024

"The challenge of the Black church and Black culture is to counter the pervasive stigmatization of blackness, to counter the hyper sexualization of the black body, to redeem the black body, and to redeem blackness." - Ronald E. Hopson

Black History Month in 2024 feels different than previous years. Of course, there is the proud reflection upon the past accomplishments, contributions and struggle of Africans in America that creates the atmosphere of the heart to "lift every voice and sing." And yet there is an urgency in the air that demands more than singing.

In years past there existed an understanding about blackness that is no longer present. Prior to today, blackness was a symbol of liberation and progress. To hear James Brown shout, "Say it loud, I'm Black and I'm proud..." caused a resolute to spring up in the Black person. It was more than a color; it was a truth rising from the ashes of hopelessness and despair. Blackness epitomized greatness and beauty, after all blackness meant eternal hope because God is Black. Right?

A while ago I was speaking to a Caucasian woman about the current trend of white school officials to re-write and even eradicate Black history from school curriculums. She stated to me that she does not investigate nor read literature about Black history because it makes her so sad. Hmm.

The call to redeem blackness is upon all of us. With the rise of anti-Black tropes in education, business and society it is incumbent to act now. We all must be engaged in the redemption of blackness. Black history is not just about Black people. Black history is America's history.

Once I stated that the time for the Black church to take its rightful place in society was now. It is past time. For the Black church to be an instrument of redemption some serious things must happen. For the Black church to be at the center it must give up its colorism, sexism and homophobia.

America has enough forces that are trying to divide the democratic experiment. The Black church need not be another divisive force. Religion that is only about personal piety is not the faith of our ancestors and mothers. The songs of the authentic Black church were about justice for all: the anthem of the Black church was and is "if I can help somebody along the way, then my living will not be in vain.'

This Black History Month is a call to action. The action is redeeming blackness. We shall see who is for us and who is against us.

Setting the agenda for Black America in 2024

February 27, 2024

As we conclude Black History Month, it is essential for Black Americas to engage in agenda setting for 2024. It is good to celebrate the accomplishments of Black Americans who have lived in this democratic experiment since 1619. But coupled with our celebration we must ask ourselves where do we go from here? Celebration without confronting the challenges before us is nothing but sound and fury signifying nothing. There is work to be done.

We must mobilize the Black vote. We cannot and must not let Donald Trump become president of the United States again. We must not be seduced by the narrative being purported by the MAGA people nor the Black conservatives who insist the Donald Trump is good for America and that Joe Biden is too old. We must never forget how Donald Trump orchestrated the division that we experience in this country. He does not want to be president, he wants to be king. If Trump is allowed to become president, I fear that it will constitute the first stage of failure of democracy. This is our country. America was built on the backs of people of color, particularly Black people. It is our calling to save America again.

We must confront the economic disparity that the majority of Black Americans are facing every day. Most of us are in the category of the working poor when compared with White wealth in this country. So, the excessive cost of food and medicine (to cite two things) affects us more than the rest of America. We must think seriously about spending Black dollars with Black business. Now is the time to reject the fallacious assumption that if a product is produced by White people, it is better than items produced by Black people. Black dollars need to circulate among Black hands at least five times before it leaves the Black community. We must build wealth within our community.

We must take hold of the education of our youth and community. I understand why we encourage our children to be great entertainers, but it cannot be at the expense of intellectual development. We are being called to teach our true history to Black youth and stop being intimidated by White supremacists who label Critical Race Theory as antithetical to society. We must teach our youth that being successful in

America is not just throwing a football, or dunking a basketball; it is also being an educator, a banker, a doctor or a nurse, a writer, etc. True success is grounded in self-discovery of the gift within us and perfecting that gift to the best of our ability.

Much confronts the Black community in 2024. I have not even mentioned the plight of Black LGBTQAA+ folks, the right of Black women to make decisions regarding their bodies, violence in the Black community, or the critical state physical and mental health in Black America. It all points to the fact that we have much to do. I am a believer that Black America can overcome the Goliaths before us if we are willing to join hands and hearts. We have experienced hardship before and have been victors and not victims. We can do it again, for we have been called for such a time as this.

It's time to help women combat colorism and redefine beauty

March 12, 2024

As we celebrate Women's History Month in March, we must reflect on how colorism has influenced our concepts of beauty as it applies to women. Colorism, grounded in racism, is a discrimination based on skin tone. It is the implicit and explicit bias against dark skin. Since beauty is a social currency, colorism heavily affects women of color. Our society prefers light skin over dark skin, thus the standard of beauty in America is whiteness coupled with European features, such as long hair, thin noses and light skin.

While more women of color are being seen as models of beauty, the tendency is still toward favoring lighter-skinned women over darker-skinned women. This is particularly true when we are considering women of African American and Latin descent. In her book, "Race, Gender, and the Politics of Skin Tone," Margeret L. Hunter writes:

"These images (light skin, European features as standards of beauty) are not just a thing of the past, however. Controlling images such as these influence our perceptions of beauty and our ability to acquire social capital, European domination of both Africans and Mexicans has left a legacy of seeing beauty only in whiteness...." (p. 7)

Beauty as whiteness has had a devastating effect on women of color, not only in the United States but also in other parts of the world. There is a history of dark-skinned women (and men) attempting to alter their appearance using skin-bleaching products. There are documented reports of mercury poisoning in Saudi Arabia, Pakistan, Tanzania and southwest parts of the United States using skin-bleaching products.

The devastating effect of colorism on women of color has not only been physical, it has also been psychological. Whiteness has been portrayed as the symbol of rationality, civility, intellectual excellence, purity and holiness. Subsequently, Black is conceptualized as irrational, uncivilized, stupid, dirty and demonic. Therefore, the darker the skin the more negative the characterization. Darker-skinned women are seen too often as hostile, uncivilized, of low intellectual and moral character and ugly. This characterization of dark skin women impacts their options for marital relationships, employment and overall well-being in the U.S. context and throughout the world.

What can be done to combat the negative effects of colorism regarding women? First, we must recognize that colorism exists. Too many people assume that the depth and scope of discrimination against women is only manifested in gender discrimination. Colorism is present as well, but we must recognize its existence. The pastor of Fifth Street Christian Church stated that, "too often we don't see it until we see it." I would add that once you see it, you cannot overlook it. But we must recognize it before we can combat the negative effects colorism has on women.

Second, we must be intentional about placing darker-skinned women in places of prominence so they can be models of beauty and excellence for girls of color in our community. There are many women of color who are darker-skinned who are gifted and accomplished. We must place them in positions of influence so that our implicit and explicit stereotypes can be challenged, and girls of color do not have to accept or believe that to be darker-skinned means that they are inferior.

As you celebrate Women's History Month ask yourself if you are a colorist and whether your assumptions regarding excellence and beauty of women is trapped in the net of colorism? If so, it is time to combat them.

Trump's hate speech could incite violence in 2024 election cycle

March 19, 2024

"There is a fine line between free speech and hate speech. Free encourages debate, whereas hate speech incites violence." - Newton Lee, author

It is apparent that hate speech will be at the center of this year's political season. We have heard Donald Trump state that a blood bath will result if he is not elected. While some Republicans have argued that we must take his comment in the context of foreign automobiles and the American auto industry, blood bath talk is dangerous talk. We have heard the former president say that if any American Jew votes Democratic, they are being unfaithful to Judaism and disloyal to Israel.

This kind of rhetoric is not uncommon for Mr. Trump. As president of the United States, he contributed more to the disunity and division of American society than any other president in the modern era. Yet, his MAGA minions continue to support him. We shall see if other Republican candidates will follow his lead or follow the urging for civility and rational debate. Speech incites violence. I am hoping for the later and not the former, but time will tell.

Newton Lee is correct that hate speech incites violence. We saw the epitome of this on Jan. 6, 2021. It is not difficult to imagine that a blood bath could occur if Mr. Trump does not win the election. Too many people of the far right are more than able and capable of engaging in violence if their choice is not the final verdict.

A wise Scottish gentleman reminded me once that "it is easier to take back a rock once it is thrown, than a word once it is spoken." The rhetoric of hate and division lingers for a long time. It eats at the very core of who we ought to be as Americans. Hate speech sows the seeds of mistrust and bitterness. While we may wish for a crop failure, many times that does not occur, and we are left with a poison harvest.

One of the saddest results of hate speech is that many people believe it. I am particularly concerned about how the minds of our youth are corrupted by hate speech. Look at the reports of how hate speech floods social media. Who is listening? The majority are young Americans seduced by the deluge of hateful speech.

What can we do about it?

No one can stop Mr. Trump's hateful speech. That is who he is. But we can demand something better from those who wish to represent us. We can loudly object to speech that divides us and not unites us. We have the power to change things. We need not be victims. We can be victors over hatred in all its forms. It is a time for action.

The amazing power of the solar eclipse

April 9, 2024

For the past few years, I have been committed to trying to find ways to unite our divided American society. Thousands of words have been published, a myriad of sermons and lectures have been uttered and still we remain divided and fractured. It has been a very real source of frustration. But then a miracle happened on Monday.

For approximately four minutes America was united in observing the solar eclipse. No one asked what political agenda anyone was advancing. For a moment, we were united in amazement created by a cosmic event. For a few minutes we were one: one in vision, and one in purpose.

As the sun and moon engaged in a cosmic dance, the majesty of the created order caused us to look beyond our economic, political, racial and religious differences. Pagans observed the cosmic marvel with Christians, white people and people of color sat together with their individual "special" glasses on, sharing in the excitement of the moment. We shared a common astonishment and awe of nature. The moon and the sun did in four minutes what no politician, philosopher or prophet did. The celestial bodies made us act like the United States of America.

Two things captured me while I was observing the solar eclipse. The first is that despite all the negative rhetoric we hear daily, it is possible to create a beloved community in America. For four minutes we did it, we came together without operating on ideology. We were simply humans observing a magnificent event. It was a taste of what it means to be one people united.

The second thing that arrested my awareness is that the eclipse reminded all of us that the universe is greater than our petty differences. We are merely travelers on a ball of dust. What we sometimes think is so important in the light and darkness of the eclipse pales in comparison. We have spent so much energy and time fighting one another over gaining power and privilege that it took a cosmic event to remind us how fragile and insignificant our issues are when compared to the majesty of the universe.

Of course, the phenomenon was a natural event explainable by science. But I suggest to was more that. The eclipse was an opportunity to realize that we can look beyond ourselves and to be one in purpose and action. It was four minutes of unity.

My hope is that we can recapture that moment of unification again. At least we were there for four minutes. Can we be again?

Religious chaos wouldn't be present if we show compassion and respect to others

April 23, 2024

Most of you are aware that I am a religious practitioner. I am a theist and a member of the Abrahamic traditions of Judaism, Christianity and Islam. My personal choice is African American Christianity, which is, at its best, qualitatively different from white, Western, European, Anglo-American Christianity. However, it seems to me that we are witnessing record chaos within the religious community in America and around the world.

We are all aware the religion can be either a help or hinderance to the human experience. When religion is grounded in and practiced with compassion, respect for the other, benevolence, justice and mercy, religion can be a benefit to humanity. Too often, however, religion has been the "opium of the people."

History demonstrates that religion has been instrumental in inflicting cruelty, supporting xenophobia and creating systems of oppression and slavery. Religion has a bloody past that cannot be denied. But what about the present?

So many instances are before us that illustrate the lack of rationality among the religious community. The war in Middle East is ruled by religious — Jewish and Muslim — radicalism. Antisemitism is at an all-time high in the U.S. Islamophobia is raging in our society. Evangelical Christianity has led the way in denying women's rights to their bodies, refusing to show dignity to the LGBTQ+ community, especially Black trans women, and supporting a racist, womanizing and divisive presidential candidate in the likes of Donald Trump. We are hearing increasingly about the division within the United Methodist Church every day. Is this what Jesus would do?

Some people will read this and think, "That is why I am not religious. There just too much chaos associated with religion." It is true that a lot of chaos has and is being committed by those who claim to be religious. But every ideological concept can be manipulated for evil. Atheists and agnostics are no less capable of perpetuating evil than Christians, Muslims or Jews. Observe the history of Chairman Mao Zedong of China if you think that I have erred.

Of course, I am most concerned about the house I live in: Christianity. It is time for Christians to stop hiding behind racist, sexist and homophobic creeds and doctrine claiming that they reveal the will of God, and follow the "God in Christ" we proclaim we believe in.

So, the first order of business is to confess our sins. The sins and evils we have committed against Indigenous peoples on every continent, women everywhere, people of color that are Black, brown and Asian. We claimed it was to bring salvation to the world when it was a guise to acquire power and wealth. We need to confess our sins.

We next need to be about the business re-education. The world of the first century is not the world we live in today. We need to watch our language and become more astute in how we speak to people. I consider myself aware and yet I make mistakes. Two Sundays ago, in a sermon at the Universal Unitiarian Church of Columbia, I made a joking reference to myself as "retarded." I did not realize that that term is used repeatedly as a negative slur against people with developmental disabilities. The pastor, board and members of the congregation made me aware. I was not aware, but I am now and will never repeat that error. We must be willing to be re-educated.

Finally, we must put action with words. Christians can no longer sit around and sing, "We are one in the Spirit, we are one in the Lord." We must be about showing real compassion and respect to the entire world. After all, WWJD?

The problem of white Christian nationalism in America

April 30, 2024

Samuel L. Perry, a sociologist at the University of Oklahoma, has said: "(White Christian Nationalists) believe in the idea that America was founded by Christians who modeled its laws and institutions after Protestant ideals with a mission to spread the religion and those ideals in the face of threats from non-whites, non-Christians, and immigrants ... the phenomenon bubbles up during periods when white Christians feel threatened by outside forces — amplified by war, heightened immigration, or periods of economic instability."

There has been a lot of talk about white Christian nationalism lately. While many scholars in sociology and American history date white Christian nationalism as a phenomenon that arose in the 1600s, white Christian nationalism captured the attention of the public during the insurrection of Jan. 6, 2021. Since that date, the white Christian nationalism movement has grown significantly.

There is nothing wrong with love for America. I am excited to root for American athletes during the Olympic Games in Paris this summer. I am proud to be an American when I think of James Baldwin, Harriet Tubman and George Washington Carver. When I hear Miles Davis, Leontyne Price or Charley Pride my nationalism soars. But when nationalism is fostered on misinformation and hatred, nationalism is a curse. White Christian nationalism is a curse.

The desire to make America white and Christian is wrongheaded. While clearly Christian ideas and concepts have shaped the culture of America, our nation was not founded by Christians nor formed to be a Christian nation. The historical record will prove that most of the Founding Fathers (I do mean "fathers" since "no women allowed" was their attitude). were deists and not Christians. Many of them were slaveholders or supporters of slavery and women did not have equal rights with white men. White Christian nationalism presents a false understanding of what this democratic experiment was meant to be.

The "ideals" of this democratic experiment are greater than what white Christian Nationalism purports, and if left unchecked, white Christian nationalism could destroy this society. For America to be genuinely great it must be multicultural and pluralistic. Anything other than that spells demise for our nation.

Lots of people blame Donald Trump for the growth of white Christian nationalism. I do not blame him; he merely fanned the flames of a fire that was already present. After all, the Ku Klux Klan existed before Donald Trump, and they were a white Christian nationalistic organization.

Our calling as true members of this society is to put out the fire of white nationalism in all its forms. When the Americans who honestly believe in an America that offers freedom and justice for all, the evil of white Christian nationalism will be overcome. If not, we shall die a tragic death.

Courage amid the chaos

May 15, 2024

"These are the times that try men's (humans') souls ... yet we have this consolation with us, that the harder the conflict, the more glorious the triumph. What we obtain too cheap, we esteem too lightly; it is dearness only that gives everything value. Heaven knows how to put a proper price upon its goods." - Thomas Paine

Courage is the mental or moral strength to venture, persevere and withstand. Indeed, all of us realize that we are amid chaotic times. College protests, which have raged across the country regarding the war in Gaza, remind us that chaos is present both at home and abroad. The recent tornadoes and storms that have ravaged many parts of our country, the Trump court proceedings, the violence in Haiti or in our communities, the economic woes we are experiencing and the war in Ukraine prompt us to wonder how long will chaos continue to raise its ugly head?

Two options stand before us: we can cower and give up, or we can decide to live courageously. In 1952, Paul Tillich wrote in his book, "Courage to Be" that "courage to be," specifically, is "the ethical act in which (humans) affirms his/her own being despite those elements of existence which conflict with (one's) essential self-affirmation."

Thus, to live courageously requires that we be in tune with our self-affirmations despite the presence of things that attempt to negate us. It is a matter of exercising our choices. I choose to suggest that there is a way to affirm free speech and, simultaneously, stand against hate speech. One can affirm that it is important to have a president of good moral character that unites the populace and not divides it.

How does one maintain a courageous stance amid chaos? Here are a few suggestions.

Avoid negative self-talk. Believe in yourself. You have all the gifts you need to be victorious in life. Be your authentic self and go on and live your best life.

Avoid negative people. Negative people bring negative vibes, they can encourage despair and fear. I conclude that it is better to be alone than to surround oneself with negative people.

Practice random acts of kindness. People will question the why of being altruistic, but the benefits outweigh the negatives. Random acts of kindness remind us that the best in us is demonstrated when we care for others as much as we care for ourselves.

Realize that "fair" is for 4-year-olds. Life is not fair. It is full of difficulties. To be courageous is to stop looking for life to be fair. Instead, we must ask ourselves, "How do I deal with disappointment and what can I do to demonstrate character in the midst of this storm?

Hold fast to your faith. Faith is the substance of things hoped for and the evidence of things not seen. Faith comes in many forms: faith in community, faith in the human spirit, faith in the power of justice, etc. For me, I have faith in an ultimate reality and the power of love. Whatever the construct of your faith, hold on to it with all your might. Faith is victory.

I encourage you to be courageous in these chaotic and troubling times. I am convinced that the old Negro spiritual is correct, "I'm so glad that trouble won't last always..."

Remembering those who have given the ultimate sacrifice

May 21, 2024

"And they will beat their swords into plowshares, and their spears into pruning knives. Nation will not lift up a sword against nation, and they shall study war no more." -Isaiah 2:4 (New American Standard Bible/King James version)

This weekend we remember those soldiers who gave their lives in war to defend a dream. Young men and women who believed that this American democratic experiment was worth dying for in combat. While the narrative recalls white soldiers as the "freedom fighters," the truth is that the Americans who gave their lives were also Black, brown, Asian and Indigenous. People of color fought not because the America they experienced was the "land of the free and the home of the brave," instead they fought in hopes that America would become a place where all would be free.

The war of my youth was Vietnam. I watched so many young men, particularly Black young men, drafted in what at that time was called the "southeast Asian conflict." It was not a conflict; it was war. Since then, we have seen the ugly face of war repeatedly, which makes us wonder will the vision of Isaiah ever be truly realized?

We know what fundamentally perpetuates war: wealth and the desire for power. When human beings overcome these two seductive entities we will cease to be in a constant state of war and practice what it means to be the beloved community. I am aware that this is easier said than done (and so does everyone who is truly "woke" and not asleep), yet it is still possible.

My father, as well as my father-in-law, was a World War II veteran. He enlisted because was moved by the ideology of W. E. B. Du Bois that if Black Americans would serve their country in military service, white America would treat Black people as fellow Americans. Thus, my father enlisted with the hope of being recognized as being an American. He was wounded in battle in the China-Burma campaign. I tell all who will listen that my father left America as a proud soldier, only to return to America as a "nigga." Second-class citizenship was what he received.

My point is that war never elevates people in a society, it only brings out the worst in us.

So, as I honor those who gave the ultimate and penultimate sacrifices for this country, I am opposed to war. My hope is that we remember the dead and never study war again, as in the words of "Lift Every Voice and Sing," by James Weldon Johnson:

"God of our weary years,

God of our silent tears,

Thou who hast brought us thus far on the way;

Thou who hast by Thy might,

Led us into the light,

Keep us forever in the path, we pray.

Lest our feet stray from the places, our God, where we met Thee,

Lest our hearts, drunk with the wine of the world, we forget Thee;

Shadowed beneath Thy hand,

May we forever stand,

True to our God,

True to our native land."

Juneteenth is another day to celebrate independence

June 18, 2024

On Wednesday, America is called to come together and celebrate Juneteenth. While Juneteenth became a federal holiday in 2021, the holiday has been celebrated in the Black community since 1865.

Juneteenth was birthed by the fact that enslaved Black people in former Confederate states were not released from institutional slavery when President Abraham Lincoln had signed the Emancipation Proclamation in 1863. Texas was the last state to sustain slavery. More than 250,000 enslaved people were freed when Union troops arrived in Galveston Bay, Texas, on June 19, 1865, and thus, Juneteenth was born.

Juneteenth is a time to remember the strength and resilience of African Americans over the centuries. The historical narrative is one fraught with tears and prayers, hope and dreams deferred, defeat and victory. Juneteenth reminds those who are willing to learn the narrative that the journey toward freedom is continuous and not an accomplished reality.

However, Juneteenth must be more than celebration. Juneteenth must also be a call to action. There are several areas that we must address if Juneteenth is to have lasting meaning.

We must address the wealth gap between white families and Black families in America. In a new book titled "Fifteen Cents on the Dollar: How Americans Made the Black-White Wealth Gap," co-authors Louise Story and Ebony Reed demonstrate that for every dollar a white family has in wealth, the average Black family has 15 cents. This gap between white and Black families has persisted since the 1950s. The economic gap between white and Black families in Columbia is proof positive that the issue of wealth, and not just income, needs to be analyzed and addressed.

The "whitening" of history within public education must be confronted. While white racists, and their Black allies, want to teach our children that "slavery was a benefit to African Americans..." and that "Black families were better during the Jim Crow Era," it is incumbent that the truth of the Black experience be articulated and taught to our children. Frederick Douglass is correct that "education makes a child unfit for slavery."

We must register to vote. We know what is before us. We must stop listening to people tell us that our vote does not count. Obama was elected president of the United States twice because Black folk went to the polls. The Black vote in this election may be more important than ever. After all, it is important enough to make Trump go to Detroit. Think about it. Register and vote.

The stresses of life, in the words of Marvin Gaye, can "make you want to holla, and throw up both your hands." But remember you are not alone, and taking care of your mental health does not mean you are weak; it means you are strong.

I have been celebrating Juneteenth for many years. I long ago realized that it is America's Second Independence Day. While you join in joyful fellowship, please remember that we still have a long way to go. But also know that the race is not given to the strong nor swift, but to the ones that endure until the end.

Black men are facing a mental health crisis. We must act now.

July 2, 2024

Men's Health Month is observed during June, but it would be negligent to focus on men's physical health without considering mental health.

Millions of Americans experience mental illness, which affects how people cope with life. Although mental health issues don't discriminate based on gender, it's often overlooked as an integral part of men's overall health.

As we come to the close of celebrating Juneteenth, we need to remind ourselves of the state of Black male mental health. Too often in the Black community we discuss physical health without conversing about mental health.

Historically, Black men are taught that mental health issues are "white people's problems" and that Black men do not need to concern themselves with mental health. Simultaneously, many Black faith communities have taught that mental health issues are the result of a lack of faith, and if one just "trusts in God" all mental health problems will disappear. Thus, a dangerous silence exists in the Black community that is devastating Black men.

It is time to break the silence.

It is estimated by some mental health professionals that 12.9% of Black men per 100,000 commit suicide. For Black construction workers the percentage is higher than 12.9%. We are all aware of how men in general and Black men in particular attempt to use other means to treat their depression, anxiety, etc. As men, we too often self-medicate with drugs, alcohol, sex and/or gambling just to find a moment of relief.

The bottom line is that we as Black men must overcome the stigma of caring for our mental health. Seeking the help of a mental health professional is not a sign of weakness but an act of strength. I recognize that there is a need for more mental health professionals of color in Columbia. However, that cannot be an excuse for not seeking treatment. Life will not permit us to overlook mental illness any longer.

And so, I am asking you to care for your mental health. It is important.

Which America do you choose?

July 24, 2024

"Dominator culture has tried to keep us all afraid, to make us choose safety instead of risk, sameness instead of diversity. Moving through that fear, finding out what connects us, reveling in our differences; this is the process that brings us closer — that gives us a world of shared values, of meaningful community." - bell hooks

The election for President of the United States of America has become more exciting as the days roll on. No longer is it the battle between two senior citizens.

Now it is the battle between a man who wants to be king and a woman who promises a more inclusive and diverse future. It is now truly a choice between two visions of what American society should be.

With the choice of president of the United States between Donald Trump and Kamala Harris we shall see whether America can do two things: overcome its racism and overcome its sexism. We did not do a respectable job confronting our ageism.

For those who want to claim that we have proven that we are a "color blind" by the election of Barack Obama, let me simply say voting for a light-skin man of color is far less threatening to our collective colorist and chauvinist psyche than making a woman of color president.

We have all heard the pseudo-rational arguments about why a woman should not be president. None of them are credible, but we live in a society that can be fooled by the absurd, though standing in the light of reason. Will women, particularly white women, rally around Harris?

As a man well-schooled by both feminist and womanist role models, I know that sometimes women are their own worst enemy. Clearly women and people of color can determine the outcome of the presidential race.

The question remains as to whether women will support Harris for president. The answer is not obvious. The same question I pose to Black and brown Americans: Will we stand with Kamala? As a parenthetical aside I must say that every time I see a Black person supporting Donald Trump, I ask myself how did this brother or sister become so fooled?

I should not be surprised as the history of Black people in America is one that has many narratives of Black people who loved the oppressor more that life itself.

Will Black people turn out and support Kamala Harris? Early indicators suggest that Black women are giving significant massive support to Harris.

The amount of money the Harris campaign has raised in 48 hours is beyond impressive. If Black and brown Americans support Harris, she will win the election. But will Black unity be demonstrated, or will we be seduced into inactivity?

For me, this presidential race truly is about what kind of America do we want. We know Trump is divisive and self-centered. He demonstrated it when he was president before, and he has not changed.

I do not expect Harris to be super-woman, I expect her not to act like she just fell out of a coconut tree. The power to create the kind of society where our children and grandchildren can grow and thrive lies in our hands. Our vote has never been more important.

The problem with teaching religion in public schools

August 13, 2024

"Education either functions as an instrument which is used to facilitate integration of the younger generation into the logic of the present system and bring about conformity or it becomes the practice of freedom, the means by which men and women deal critically and creatively with reality and discover how to participate in the transformation of their world." - Paulo Freire

An interesting phenomenon is occurring in our society that should not be ignored. The phenomenon is the insistence by some state boards of education that religion and religious concepts should be taught in public schools. While, as Americans, we have always insisted on the separation of church and state as the primary modus operandi of American public-school education, the recent push of evangelical Christians has made us consider whether religion should be taught in our public schools.

Three states are preparing to make religion part of the public-school curriculum:

Louisiana will require schools to display the Ten Commandments.

Oklahoma has mandated that schools teach the Bible highlighting its cultural/historical significance.

Texas school curriculum now includes Bible lessons.

While I am a theist and a practicing member of the Abrahamic tradition (African American Christianity), I am not in favor of religion being taught in public school for the following reasons. First, there is a history of harm that exists in the United States when religion — particularly but not exclusively Judeo-Christianity — is not correctly taught. As a Black child, I was told by white Christians that the curse of Ham was God making Noah's son Black, thus making Blackness a curse, or, that Jesus was white because whiteness means purity and is holy. Both ideas are false.

But, will the people who put together the curriculums or teach the classes know that these ideas are false given the fact that in many churches we still have pictures of blond, blue-eyed Jesus and think Blackness is a sign of inferiority? Since many of our politicians are theologically incompetent, who will monitor what is taught? And I have not even mentioned the harm that has been inflicted on women and the LGBT+ community because of bad religious teaching. The history of harm by teaching religion in public school is too great to ignore.

Second, what do we do about the children of parents who do not want religious ideas taught to their children? Will parents lose their right to make religion decisions for their children? Such a move is a dangerous one and ought to be avoided.

I understand the move for religious training in public schools. Many people believe that our children need a strong moral foundation and that teaching religion in schools will give our children just that: moral excellence. The problem with this thinking is that its proponents fail to realize that one can be moral without being religious. We all know that there are religious people who are not moral; there exist people who are moral but not religious. One does not necessarily constitute the other.

Society does not determine my religiosity, nor that of my children. That is too much power to be given to small, minded people.

We're living in a state of uncertainty

September 3, 2024

"I spent a lot of years trying to outrun or outsmart vulnerability by making things certain and definite, black and white, good and bad. My inability to lean into the discomfort of vulnerability limited the fullness of those important experiences that are wrought with uncertainty: Love, belonging, trust, joy, and creativity to name a few." - Brene Brown

These are truly uncertain days. Most people I talk to express various levels of uncertainty regardless of gender, race, economic status or education. From agnostics to evangelicals there is an air of dubiety that surrounds us. We mouth the words of confidence, but at the very ground of our being we feel the gnawing presence of incertitude.

What is the source of our anxiety? Different minions plague our consciousness. Will we be able to buy medicine and pay the bills? How long must I put up with my child being bullied at school? Will America sell its democratic soul to a madman who does not want to be president of the United States but rather king? What does it mean to be Black, male, Afro-Christian and progressive in a state that bans books and denies a woman to make decisions about her own body? Am I really helping anyone along life's way or am I just entertaining with my proclamation and prose?

Like Brene Brown, I have spent a lot of time trying to outrun vulnerability. I am sure some of you reading this have too. But I am learning how to lean into my seasons of exposure. While discomfort is a companion of vulnerability, there is a way to arise and remain "steadfast, unmovable, and abounding."

• Remember who you are. Socrates is correct that the greatest task in life is to "know thyself." When we are willing to be more than a title, position, stereotype or troupe we have an opportunity to know ourselves in ourselves (Satre). One quick note about knowing oneself, you will recognize that you have been through challenging situations before, and you survived. You will survive again because your real name is victory.

• Know that you belong. You are not out here alone. There are people out here who love you. They may not be "blood-relations," but they are fictive kin. There is a beloved community out here that will nourish and sustain you. They may not be your color, but they are your kind and that matters most. There is a reason our elders tried to teach us to not judge a book by its cover. To pre-judge is to be caught in the oppression of prejudice. Don't be a slave. Make yourself available to it.

• Realize you are here for a reason. As many of you know I am a theist. I believe God has placed in every person a gift that is unique to the person. I believe that if we nurture our gift, our gift will make room for us. The fact that you are gifted means, subsequently, that your purpose in life is to help someone along life's way. Too often we look at what we do not have instead of acknowledging what we possess. Use what you possess and help someone in this shared experience of uncertainty. After all, we are all in this together.

As Alice would say "curiouser and curiouser, I begin to think I'm in Wonderland." Though we may often feel that we are in Wonderland, know yourself, cling to your community and engage in your purpose and everything will be all right.

Truth and a democratic society are at odds this election cycle

September 17, 2024

"You shall know the truth, and the truth shall set you free." - Yeshua

This political season we are observing not only an attack on democracy, but an assault on truth. While every political race I have witnessed in my short 70 years on earth has had snippets of half-truths and disinformation (remember the Willie Horton foolishness?), it has never risen to the level it is to date. Succinctly, the lie about Haitian immigrants in Springfield, Ohio, perpetuated by former President Donald Trump and his running mate J.D. Vance is a dangerous threat to that community, to our sense of being a democratic society and to the very idea of truth.

n case you have forgotten, during the last presidential debate between Kamala Harris and Donald Trump, Trump stated that Haitian immigrants in Springfield, Ohio, were eating the pets of their neighbors. While city officials stated that the claim was false, the Trump campaign continues to promote and spread the lie. The result has been serious civil unrest (bomb threats) and communal tension in that community.

The governor of Ohio is a Republican. While he has reiterated that the claim of Haitians eating pets is unfounded, the Trump campaign has been undeterred in perpetuating the lie. If I understand Vance, he stated that they know it is untrue, but the false narrative demonstrates the problem(s) of immigration in the U.S., therefore it is a good lie to push. Hmmm.

We are all aware of the racist history of people saying immigrants eat animals in America. Asians have been the victims of such falsehoods for generations. So, the lie about Haitians is saddening but not surprising. The eating of pets story is an attempt to justify our prejudices regarding people of color. Of course they will eat our pets: They are savages, aren't they? It is another proof that the Trump campaign is racist.

I am most troubled about the effect this incident is having on young voters. Many of my students are voting for the first time this November. All of them are convinced that lying is the modus operandi of politicians. One student said, "All politicians lie. It is in their DNA, so they cannot help it. The only question is which politician lies the least." Is that what we would want the next generation of this democratic experiment to believe?

A second assassination attempt came against Trump last weekend. Vance and Elon Musk asked why is nobody attempting to assassinate Harris? I have no answer. What I do know is that only Trump has stated he will punish his political opposition and end the need for voting in the future. Only Trump has tweeted, "I hate Taylor Swift!" Only Trump has purposely continued spreading a lie when he knows it is a lie and sees that it is causing dangerous division in an American community.

Trump supporters (if they read anything I write) will dismiss my column and claim that what Trump will do for our economy is worth enduring his idiosyncrasies. One Trump supporter said to me, "When I go to the gas station and grocery store, I am more convinced that Donald Trump is the answer." Following this logic, Trump allegedly will lower prices of gas and groceries. Is it worth it to sell our souls and the soul of this democracy to him? Ladies and gentlemen, no political candidate is worth that kind of prostitution.

Kamala Harris faces a skin tone bias in American politics

October 1, 2024

"Although race and color are indeed related concepts, they are not synonymous. While racism may affect an individual regardless of the person's color, two individuals belonging to the same ethno-racial category may face differential treatment due to their varying skin tones," Trina Jones notes in The Case for Legal Recognition of Colorism Claims, Shades of Difference: Why Skin Color Matters.

As the presidential election heats up, the concepts of race and skin-tone concerning Vice President Kamala Harris are coming increasingly to the front of the conflict. America has always had a problem with race and skin tone.

History, not banned or hidden, reveals that racial categories and colorism (skin-tone discrimination) have had a primary and significant effect on our socially-constructed institutions and socially influenced behaviors. We are too often the victims of the racial/colorist ideologies we constructed.

This presidential contest between former president Donal Trump and Harris is not an exception to the rule.

When Trump exclaimed at the NABJ Conference that he did not know what "race" Kamala Harris was, many Americans seemed shocked. As the American body politic, we have been down this road before: Remember the birthers and Barack Obama? Black entertainers such as Janet Jackson seem confused as well.

I understand that Ms. Jackson is extremely talented but has never been thought of as the sharpest pencil in the box.

For her not to know that Harris is Black is astonishing. The pictures in Vogue magazine did not help.

How can photographers be so adept at tint, contrast, etc. and never get the hue of light-skinned people of color right?

Does the fact that Kamala Harris refers to herself as a biracial "woman of color" help the situation? Not really.

Again, because as Americans we do not understand what race is, adding terms such as biracial and woman of color transforms the opaque into impenetrable. I remember being in a conversation with a white Christian man at one of Columbia's large predominately white churches who honestly said to me during a fellowship communion service referencing racial identity, "I just don't know what to call you people: Black, Afro-Americans, colored, what?" I thought his comment was very revealing of the racial situation.

We need to take a quick look at the history of race relations in the U.S. and put this phrase into context.

The term "people of color" goes back to the 16th century when European explorers used it to describe native Americans in contrast to their own imagined "whiteness." By the 18th century, the term "people of color" was not only used in the English-speaking world but was also a French term, gens de couleur and an Italian one, gente de color.

With the start of the U.S. Civil Right movements in the 1960s, which called for racial justice, gender equality and an end to all forms of discrimination and oppression, many historians note that Black womanists and Black feminists coined, or reclaimed, the term "women of color."

In the 21st century, as America becomes less white and the multiracial community — formed by interracial unions and immigration — continues to expand, color will be even more significant than race in both public and private interactions.

Why? Because a person's skin color is an irrefutable visual fact that is impossible to hide, whereas race is a constructed, quasi-scientific classification that is often only visible on a government form. (See Lori Tharps' book "Same Family, Different Colors.")

Skin tone, savagery intelligence at play in politics today

October 8, 2024

One of the things that is so disheartening in the current presidential race between former President Donald Trump and Vice President Kamala Harris is the resurfacing of stereotypes that have been in American society since 1619. One gentleman said to me that he was "surprised" at Trump's perpetual negative comments regarding Harris' intellect. I smiled and told him that I was not surprised, and that Trump's statement about Harris being stupid is "par for the course."

Clearly my colleague was not aware of the history and willful perpetuation of concepts of savagery and unintelligence cast by white Americans against Black Americans.

These are usually matched with reference to dark skin, as well. Thus, we know that Black people are not fit to for this democratic experiment because they are Black, apelike creatures with low intellect.

It is not by accident that Black people have been called "monkeys" and "apes." I remember how former first lady Michelle Obama was called "an ape in heels."

When Trump refers negatively to Harris' intellect he is treading in old stereotypes. He knows that his supporters will either consciously or unconsciously engender the racial trinity of "colorism, savagery and low intellect" in thinking about Harris, which in turn will cause them to not vote for Harris.

I am sure that some readers will find the notion of skin tone, savagery and intellect, preposterous, claiming that America is too advanced and sophisticated to allow racist concepts to influence our social behavior. Some will vehemently assert that we are in a "post-racial" society now and the election will be solely determined by policy and not polluted by images of race.

I, too, would like to believe that as a society we have moved beyond racial stereotypes. I really want to believe that as Americans we now see each other as fellow humans who happen to be people of color with unique historical/cultural nuances worthy of reflection and affirmation.

Instead, however, we are confronted with the uncomfortable reality that society is still racist. We did not pick on the Haitians in Springfield, Ohio, by accident.

What was said about them points to savagery. Of course they would eat our pets: They are dark skin, Black, savages with low intellect, right?

The coming election is about more than two candidates for me. It is about whether I can still hope and believe that Americans will hold fast the precious gift of democracy. Or, will we sell our souls for pennies on the dollar? Should I still believe that one day we will get past racism, sexism and homophobia? Time will tell.

Where do we go from here? The future of our nation depends on Election Day votes

October 22, 2024

In two weeks, this democratic experiment will elect its 47th president of the United States of America. The choice between the two candidates is clear: either an intelligent, competent, biracial woman; or a white male that seeks to be king.

Most Americans have made up their minds about who they want to lead this country. I do not believe the hype about undecided voters. If there are people still undecided about who they want and what they want in a president, I find it most curious. We know who we want.

While the character of the person is the most important trait for a leader, the most critical issue we face is what kind of government will we have after the election? Will we still be able to call ourselves a democracy, or will we be an aristocracy led by a person who lusts for power? Call me paranoid if you want, but Maya Angelou is correct when she said, "When a person shows you who they really are, believe them." Mr. Trump has shown us who he is, and it causes me to worry about our democracy.

America has lots of problems. I have never believed that we are a perfect nation. Time after time we have demonstrated the worst human characteristics. We can be racist, sexist, homophobic and self-righteous. We can be greedy and unyielding. But we can also demonstrate the best of what it means to be an American.

For example, the way we have responded to neighbors in need in the wake of the last two hurricanes says something good about who we are. We have shown kindness both here in the U.S. and other places in the world. Our constitution gives us motivation to be better people. We understand that we can form "a more perfect union" despite our shortcomings. When we put our commitment to the heart and soul of our democratic ideals above party and personalities then I believe all the problems we face can be resolved. My hope is that we do not cast away what is best in us for what is worst in us all for the hope of crass materialism.

What will make the difference in this election? It will not be determined by Black males, white males, Latino men or the MAGA minions. This time the fate of our country lies in the hands of women. Will women stand with Harris, or will they sell out for a piece of the promised MAGA pie? I hope they stand, and quite frankly it is time for this country to have a capable woman of color in the White House. Come on ladies, do your thing.

In thinking about what lies before us, Dr. Martin Luther King's book comes to mind. "Where Do We Go from Here: Chaos or Community." Clearly the vote we make in two weeks will lead us into a state of aristocratic chaos or democratic community. As always, the choice is ours.

Until then, I hope this column finds you well.

Clanton C. W. Dawson, Jr., PhD

Area of Specialization: Ethics, Social Philosophy, African American Philosophy, African American Religion (Black Christian Theology), Philosophy of Race

Area of Competence: Epistemology, Metaphysics, Moral Psychology, Applied Ethics (Business), History of Philosophy, Existentialism, Philosophy of Religion

Education

Ph. D, Philosophy, University of Missouri-Columbia (MU), Columbia, MO, May 2006, posted August 2006 (the first African-American to receive a doctoral degree in philosophy from MU).

Master of Arts, Philosophy, University of Missouri-Columbia, Columbia, Missouri, 1991

Master of Divinity, *Concentration*: Systematic and Philosophical Theology, Princeton Theological Seminary, Princeton, New Jersey, 1979

Bachelor of Special Studies, Cornell College, Mt. Vernon, Iowa, 1976

Triple Major: Philosophy, Religion, and Political Science

Dissertation: *A Philosophical Analysis of Four Concepts of Race*

Dissertation Director: Dr. Joseph Bien, Department of Philosophy, University of Missouri-Columbia.

Dissertation Abstract: This project is a philosophical analysis of the dominant concepts of race that prevail within contemporary American society. It is the claim of this dissertation that four main concepts attempt to answer the question: what is race? The four concepts are: racial essentialism, race as a social construct with objective status, racial nihilism, and race as an existential/phenomenological process. Each concept fails, however, in providing the necessary and sufficient conditions for a satisfactory concept of race, and thus, the dissertation calls for a new conceptual framework for answering the question: what is race?

Publications:

Books

An Introduction to Ethics, Clanton C.W. Dawson, Jr., Louis Colombo, and William Rodriguez, editors, Kendall-Hunt Publishing, Dubuque, 2011.

La Conversation Fracturee: Concepts of Race in American, Clanton C.W. Dawson, Jr. Xlibris, 2018.

Contributing Author in a Book

"The Concept of Hope in the Thinking of Martin Luther King, Jr.," in *The Liberatory Philosophy of Martin Luther King, Jr.: Critical Essays on the Philosopher, King,* Robert Birt, editor, Lexington Press, 2012.

Published Articles

"God, Hope, and Suffering: An African American Perspective, Coping with the Anxiety

of Death through the Assurance of Future Hope," Testimentum Imperium Online

Journal, Spring, 2013.

"The Rediscovery of Joy" in *Open Mic Jacksonville, Vol. II,* Diane B. Barton, Marv Conn, Caryn Day-Suarez, editors, Usher Press, January 2, 2013.

"Race as an Existential Phenomenological Choice," *Bethune –Cookman University Research Journal, Spring* 2012.

"A Thing Called Race," The American Philosophical Association, Eastern Division, Philosophy and the Black Experience, Fall-Winter 2011.

"A Philosophical Examination of Race as A Social Construct with Objective Status," *Bethune-Cookman University Research Journal*. 2010.

"When the House is on Fire: Finding Hope in the Midst of Democratic Despair," in **Democracy, Racism and Prisons,** *Radical Philosophy Today*, Volume 5, December 2007.

Books Reviewed at Publisher's Request

Philosophy, Eighth Edition, Stump and Fieser, McGraw-Hill Publishing CO, 2009.

The New Testament: A Student's Introduction, Harris, McGraw-Hill Publishing, CO, 2010.

The Right Thing to Do, James Rachels, McGraw-Hill Publishing CO., 2011.

A Caste in Class: Racial-Class Distinctions in Black Communities in the United States and the United Kingdom, Paul Macomb, Routledge, Publishing CO. 2012

Invited Presentations:

Commentator, Philosophy Born of Struggle, American Philosophical Association, Central Division, New Orleans, LA, May 20-23, 2013

Guest Speaker, "This Thing Called Love," Bethune Cookman University Legacy Forum, Daytona Beach. FL, Spring, 2012.

Guest Speaker, "What's in a Name," Bethune Cookman University Convocation, Dayton Beach, FL, September 2012.

Guest Speaker, "Is a Post Racial Society Possible?" Jacksonville University Humanities Lecture Series, January 19, 2012.

Guest Speaker, Colorado Springs, CO Martin Luther King, Jr., City Wide Celebration, Shove Chapel, Colorado College, January 15, 2012.

Presenter, The Philosophy Born of Struggle Conference, Michigan State University, October 2011.

Guest Speaker, "This Man Called Thurman: A Discussion on the Theo-Philosophical Thought of Dr. Howard Thurman," The Howard Thurman Lecture Series, Bethune Cookman University, Fall, 2010.

Guest Speaker, "Colored Windows: A Discussion on Race and World Framing," Jacksonville University Humanities Seminar, Jacksonville University, Jacksonville, FL, January 2010.

Presenter, "An Examination of Race as a Social Construct with Objective Status," Florida Philosophical Association Conference, Emery-Riddle University, Daytona Beach, FL. November 14-16, 2008.

Presenter, "Must Be Music: An Eclectic Reflection of the Place and Power of Black Music as a Vehicle of Social Transformation," the Eighth Biennial Radical Philosophy Conference, San Francisco State University, San Francisco, CA, November 5-9, 2008.

Guest Speaker, Richard V. Moore Lecture Series, Bethune-Cookman University, Daytona Beach, FL, March 2008.

Guest Speaker, "Holla If Ya Heard Me: A Reflection on Difference and Otherness in the 21st Century," The Colorado College, Black History Month, Colorado Springs, CO, February 2008.

Guest Speaker, "The Concept of Hope in the Thinking of Dr. Martin Luther King, Jr.," and "When the House is on Fire: Finding Hope in the Midst of Democratic Despair," The Martin Luther King, Jr. Lectures, University of Detroit-Mercy, Detroit, MI, January 2008.

Presenter, "When the House is on Fire: Finding Hope in the Midst of Democratic Despair," and panel chair, Seventh Biennial National and International Conference of the Radical Philosophy Association, Creighton University, Omaha, NE, November 2-5, 2006.

Presenter, "Ontological Blackness Revisited: A Philosophical Examination of Victor Anderson's Beyond Ontological Blackness," Rocky Mountain-Great Plains American Academy of Religion Regional Meeting, Colorado Springs, CO, March 24-25, 2006.

Conference Co-Presenter, Four Concepts of Race and Black Nihilism, Roots of Racism III, Missouri School of Religion, Jefferson City, MO, August 2005.

Guest Presenter, Foundations of the Black Church, African American Institute, Jefferson City, MO, 2003, "Philosophical Reflections on Race," and "The Metaphysics of Liberation Theology," Roots of Racism Conference II, Missouri School of Religion, Jefferson City, MO, August 2004,

Guest Speaker, "Standing at the Portal: Malcolm X and Martin Luther King," and "Second Generational Black Liberation Theology," Department of Theology, University of Colorado, Boulder, CO, February 2002.

Presenter, "Hush, Somebody Is Calling My Name: An Analysis of African American Philosophical Theology," Regional Meeting, Society of Christian Philosophers, Boulder, CO, October 2001 (accepted by blind review).

Guest Speaker, Reformed Epistemology Revisited, Cornell College, Mt. Vernon, IA, March 1989

Service to the University, School of Arts and Humanities, and Department of Religion, Philosophy, and Humanities:

Parliamentarian, Bethune-Cookman University Faculty Association (2009-2011)

Convener, Bethune-Cookman University Faculty Association Nominations Committee (2008-2009)

Chair, Bethune-Cookman University Faculty Association Elections Committee (2007-2008)

Member, Bethune-Cookman University Faculty Association Parking Committee (2007-2008)

Member, Bethune-Cookman University Summer Grant Committee (2007-2008)

Secretary, School of Arts and Humanities Retention Committee (2007-2008)

Chair, Department of Religion, Philosophy, and Humanities Richard V. Moore Lecture Series.

Awards:

Jesse DuPont/ National Endowment for the Humanities Summer Session Recipient, Triangle Park- Chapel Hill, NC, June 2010.

Excellence in Teaching Award, Sigma Alpha Pi Chapter, The National Society of Leadership and Success, April 28, 2012.

Riley Scholar in Residence, The Colorado College, Colorado Springs, CO, September 2005-Ma, 2007.

Gus T. Ridgel Fellowship, University of Missouri-Columbia, Columbia, MO, September 1989- May 1991.

Benjamin E. Mays Fellowship, Princeton Theological Seminary, Princeton, NJ, September 1976-May 1979.

Employment History- Academic:

August 2020-2024. Adjunct Professor of Religion and Philosophy, Westminster College, Fulton, MO.

August 2016-2024. Adjunct Professor of Religion and Philosophy, Moberly Area Community College, Moberly/Columbia, MO.

August 2007-2012. **Associate Professor of Philosophy,** Department of Religion, Philosophy, and Humanities, Bethune-Cookman University, Daytona Beach, FL. **Courses Taught:** Introduction to Religion and Philosophy, Ethics, Ancient and Medieval Philosophy, Modern Philosophy, Contemporary Philosophy, Human Nature and Knowledge (Epistemology), Moral Psychology, Philosophy of Religion, Africana Philosophy. Promoted to Associate Professor, Spring 2012

September 1, 2006- May 30, 2007. ***Post-Doctoral Riley Scholar in Residence in Philosophy and Religion,*** The Colorado College, Colorado Springs, CO. ***Course Taught***: Ethics, Race and Philosophy, Black Religion in America.

September 1, 2005-May 30, 2006. ***Pre-Doctoral Riley Scholar in Residence in Religion and Philosophy***, The Colorado College, Colorado Springs, CO. ***Courses Taught***: Race and Philosophy, Black Religion in America, Philosophy of Religion.

January 2005-May 2005 Adjunct, Philosophy, Lincoln University, Jefferson City, MO, ***Courses Taught***: Social and Political Philosophy, Introduction to Philosophy, Business Ethics.

November and December 2004. Visiting Professor of Religion, Department of Religion, Blocks 3 and 4 November and December 2004), The Colorado College, Colorado Springs, CO, ***Courses Taught:*** Philosophy of Religion and Black Religion in America

September 2001-May 2004. Adjunct, Philosophy and Religion, William Woods University, Fulton, MO, ***Courses Taught***: Introduction to the Bible, World Religions, Basic Christian Beliefs, Introduction to Philosophy, Ancient and Medieval Philosophy, Critical Thinking, Business Ethics, Bio-Medical Ethics, Modern Philosophy, Graduate Seminar Business Ethics (Master's Level), Co-taught History of Psychology, Metaphysics, Epistemology.

1988-1994-Instructor, Missouri School of Religion, Jefferson City, MO ***Courses Taught***: New Testament Theology, Black Liberation Theology, Philosophical Theology of Paul, Social Political Thought of Garvey, Malcolm, and Martin King, Africana Philosophy, Preaching in the Black Tradition.

Graduate Teaching Assistant, University of Missouri-Columbia, Columbia, MO, 1989-91 ***Courses Solo Taught***: Introduction to Philosophy, Introduction to Ethics, and Introduction to Modern Philosophy.

Instructor, Philosophy and Religion, Moberly Area Community College, Moberly, MO, 1986-89, ***Courses Taught***: African-American Political Thought, Existentialism, Introduction to Logic, Introduction to Philosophy, Introduction to African American Literature, Introduction to Religion.

Professional Organizations:

Life Member, Miltonian Literary Society

Honorary Member, The National Society of Leadership and Success

American Philosophical Association, Eastern Division

American Academy of Religion, Rocky Mountain-Great Plains Region

Florida Philosophical Association

Hobbies:

Karate, Chess, Cooking, Jazz (play percussion, specialty congas)

www.ingramcontent.com/pod-product-compliance
Lightning Source LLC
LaVergne TN
LVHW061238100826
845148LV00008B/979

* 9 7 9 8 2 3 4 0 4 7 9 0 8 *